Preventing Family Violence

KEVIN BROWNE
University of Birmingham

and

MARTIN HERBERT
University of Exeter

JOHN WILEY & SONS
Chichester • New York • Weinheim • Brisbane • Singapore • Toronto

Copyright © 1997 by John Wiley & Sons Ltd,
Baffins Lane, Chichester,
West Sussex PO19 1UD, England

National   01243 779777
International   (+44) 1243 779777
e-mail (for orders and customer service enquiries): cs-books@wiley.co.uk
Visit our Home Page on http://www.wiley.co.uk
or http://www.wiley.com

Reprinted August 1997, December 1999

Other Wiley Editorial Offices

John Wiley & Sons, Inc., 605 Third Avenue,
New York, NY 10158-0012, USA

VCH Verlagsgesellschaft mbH
Pappelallee 3, 0–69469 Weinheim, Germany

Jacaranda Wiley Ltd, 33 Park Road, Milton,
Queensland 4064, Australia

John Wiley & Sons (Canada) Ltd, 22 Worcester Road,
Rexdale, Ontario M9W 1L1, Canada

John Wiley & Sons (Asia) Pte Ltd, 2 Clementi Loop #02-01,
Jin Xing Distripark, Singapore 129809

Library of Congress Cataloging-in-Publication Data

Browne, Kevin
     Preventing family violence / Kevin Browne and Martin Herbert.
         p.   cm.—(Wiley series in family psychology)
     Includes bibliographical references and index.
     ISBN 0-471-92771-6 (cased : alk. paper).—ISBN 0-471-94140-9
(pbk. : alk. paper)
         1. Family violence—Great Britain—Prevention.   2. Family
violence—Great Britain—Research.   I. Herbert, Martin.   II. Title.
III. Series.
HV6626.23.G7B76   1996
362.82′927′0941—dc20   96-28875
                                                                                CIP

British Library Cataloguing in Publication Data

A catalogue record for this book is available from the British Library

ISBN 0-471-92771-6 (cased)
       0-471-94140-9 (paper)

Typeset in 11/13pt Palatino by Saxon Graphics Ltd, Derby
Printed and bound in Great Britain by Biddles Ltd, www.Biddles.co.uk
This book is printed on acid-free paper responsibly manufactured from sustainable forestation,
for which at least two trees are planted for each one used for paper production.

This book is dedicated to all those individuals
who are entrapped in a cycle of family violence
and are looking for a way out

Special dedication by Kevin Browne
'For Clare'

Special dedication by Martin Herbert
'For Jenny'

CONTENTS

LIST OF FIGURES

LIST OF TABLES

ABOUT THE AUTHORS

Dr Kevin Browne, BSc(Hons), MSc, PhD, MEd, CBiol, CPsychol

School of Psychology, University of Birmingham and Glenthorne Youth Treatment Centre, Birmingham

Kevin Browne has been researching family violence and child abuse for 18 years and has published extensively on the subject. He is Chair of the Research Committee of the International Society for the Prevention of Child Abuse and Neglect (ISPCAN) and Co-Editor (with Dr Margaret Lynch) of both a Wiley book series on *Child Care and Protection* and *Child Abuse Review*, the Journal of the British Association for the Study and Prevention of Child Abuse and Neglect (BASPCAN) published by Wiley since 1992.

As a Chartered Psychologist and a Chartered Biologist, he is currently employed by the School of Psychology at the University of Birmingham, being a Senior Lecturer in Clinical Criminology and Research Co-ordinator for the Glenthorne Youth Treatment Centre, Birmingham.

Other publications include *Early Prediction and Prevention of Child Abuse* co-edited with Drs Cliff Davies and Peter Stratton (Wiley, 1988).

Professor Martin Herbert, BA(Hons), MA, PhD, Dip. Psych.

Department of Clinical Psychology, University of Exeter

Martin Herbert is Professor of Clinical and Community Psychology at the University of Exeter, a Consultant Psychologist at the Royal Devon and Exeter Health Care Trust, and a Fellow of the British Psychological Society. He is the author of many books and articles on child, adolescent and adult mental health problems and the therapies. Two recent books with Wiley are *Clinical Child Psychology: Behaviour, Social Learning and Development* and *Trouble Families: Problem Children* (with Carolyn Webster-Stratton).

FOREWORD

The opening up of the problem of family violence can count as one of the major accomplishments of social science in the last generation. When it first appeared on the scientific radar screen, the topic posed many challenges. Its nature, scope and variety were generally unknown. A great many ideological passions and preconceptions swirled around it, and many doubted the ability of social scientific research methodology to penetrate to its reality.

Yet today few would question that an enormous amount has been learned that has provided provocative grist for our understanding about the family and for public policy to aid in prevention and intervention on behalf of victims. The scientific literature on this topic now spans twenty years, hundreds of books, and thousands of articles, and includes specialist journals devoted to this subject and some of the most conscientious and ingeniously designed studies of the era.

Our knowledge about the topic has come in spurts and phases. Much of the early research was motivated by advocacy, as part of an effort to raise public awareness about the problem and stir the interest of professionals and policy makers. But as public and professional attention has become more secure, a second phase of research has got underway, on more difficult questions, and some of this research has cast doubt on or added complexity to earlier findings or assumptions of the advocacy phase.

There are still big gaps in our understanding. Among other things, we have yet to explore well the interrelationships among the various kinds of family violence. We have relatively less knowledge about its more minor and routine forms that tend not to come to the attention of social agencies. We have not begun to evaluate the effectiveness of most of our conventional strategies for trying to intervene and stop the problem. But given the interest family violence has provoked and the growing number of people working in this field, the answers to such questions do seem to be primarily a matter of time.

This volume by Kevin Browne and Martin Herbert provides a broad, synthesizing and critical overview of this accumulated knowledge. It brings together pieces of the puzzle that have not always been combined. And it organizes it in a way to make it useful to thinking about the urgent public policy issue of preventing family violence and its ravages. It is a most welcome addition.

DAVID FINKELHOR

PREFACE

The idea for this book on 'Preventing Family Violence' grew out of stimulating discussions on the topic, while the authors were working together in the Department of Psychology at the University of Leicester (UK). These discussions revolved around how theory and research could inform professional practice for the prediction, prevention and treatment of family violence. Specifically:

- How can sociological and psychological explanations of violent behaviour be applied to family situations?
- What has research shown about violent interactions among family members: their extent, causes and consequences?
- How best can knowledge on the topic of family violence be used to prevent spouse abuse, child abuse, sibling abuse, parent abuse, elder abuse and the neglect of dependents in the family?
- What evidence exists for the notion that informed professional practice is effective in stopping, or at least decreasing, violent incidents and the associated behaviours of offenders and victims in the family?

There is no doubt that the views of the authors, and the comprehensive interdisciplinary perspective taken to the topics presented in this book, were influenced by Leicester's Family Violence Research Group. This Group composed of esteemed colleagues in Medicine, Nursing, Psychology, Sociology, Social Work, Law and Social Policy, who promoted research and collaboration into all matters concerning the prevention of violence in the family. Indeed, it is students, professionals and practice workers from these disciplines who will probably benefit most from reading this book.

There is an extensive literature on spouse abuse and child abuse but other areas of family violence—sibling abuse, parent abuse and elder abuse—are less well known, and rarely considered together in one volume.

In reviewing these topics the authors have attempted to inter-relate the different types of family violence and present theory and practice that tackle more than one type at a time. Thus, the Introduction gives a general overview of the material to be covered in this volume and the concluding chapter offers practical suggestions for social policy and practice in the future to prevent all aspects of the pervasive problem of family violence.

KEVIN BROWNE

MARTIN HERBERT

ACKNOWLEDGEMENTS

The authors would like to acknowledge the help and collaboration of Ms Joanne Swaby, Leicester Social Services, on earlier drafts of Chapter 10 'Predicting and Preventing Elder Maltreatment'. This chapter was first written in association with Joanne Swaby.

They would also like to thank Sue Hanson and Vivien Doughty for their help in preparing the manuscript. The authors are especially grateful for the cooperation and patience of Wendy Hudlass of John Wiley & Sons Ltd.

INTRODUCTION: What is family violence?

Until recently, the subject of 'domestic violence' was poorly documented. Extreme violence was commonly thought to be rare and only to occur in 'problem families', whereas aggression between members of the family was considered to be a part of the rich pattern of family life. Thus family violence is not a 'new' problem. Historically, violence has been regarded as an acceptable way for adults to exert power and control over the behaviour of their relatives and dependents. Rather than condemn violent acts, law and social policy attempts to discriminate between socially acceptable 'normal' violence and unacceptable 'abusive' violence in the family. This has confounded most attempts to deal with the pervasive problem.

The widespread nature of extreme forms of aggression within the family was recognized in the 1970s (e.g. Pizzey, 1974; Steinmetz and Straus, 1974; Renvoize, 1978) and many books on the topic have substantiated this fact ever since (e.g. Straus, Gelles and Steinmetz, 1980; Finkelhor et al., 1983; Van Hasselt et al., 1987; Gelles and Straus, 1988; Sigler, 1989; Ammerman and Hersen, 1990, 1992; Frude, 1991; Viano, 1992; Dallos and McLaughlin, 1993; Hampton et al., 1993; Gelles and Loseke, 1994; Archer, 1994; Kingston and Penhale, 1995).

Clinical observations, empirical research, daily newspapers and news bulletins have painfully described acts of violence between spouses, by adults towards their own children and their dependent elderly relatives, and vice versa. These accounts have increased public awareness and forced us to recognize that violence within the family is a common phenomenon of modern society, and occurs across most cultures (Levinson, 1989). In turn, this has dispelled the myth that the family home is a peaceful, non-violent environment. In fact, 'people are more likely to be killed, physically assaulted, hit, beaten up, slapped or spanked in their own homes by other family members than anywhere else, or by anyone else in our society' (Gelles and Cornell, 1990: 11).

Indeed, newspaper reports, based on court and police records in Britain, show that 42% of murder or manslaughter cases involve a domestic dispute and one-third of the domestic victims are children. During 1991, 99 children under 16 years of age died of non-accidental injury in England, Scotland and Wales (*Independent on Sunday*, 12.1.92). However, this may be an underestimate as the National Society for the Prevention of Cruelty to Children (UK) claims that three or four children die each week at the hands of their parents (NSPCC, 1985). The homicide rate in Britain is 1.3 for every 100 000 citizens, with 58% of male victims and 81% of female victims killed by someone known to them. This compares to rates of 1.1 in Japan, 2.3 in Australia and 10 individuals per 100 000 in the USA (FBI, 1991). In the USA approximately 40% of homicides are a result of violence within the family (Gelles and Cornell, 1990: 67). Thus the homicide rate in the USA is eight times higher than in Britain, but the percentage caused by violence in the family for the USA (40%) is very similar to that for the UK (42%) and for Australia (44%) as recorded in official statistics (Strang, 1992). This suggests similar patterns of domestic violence.

DEFINITIONS

Browne and Howells (1996) identify three terms which are often used, sometimes interchangeably, in relation to acts of a violent nature: 'Aggression', 'Violence' and 'Criminal violence'. Previously, a number of writers (e.g. Megargee, 1982; Siann, 1985; Berkowitz, 1993) have offered helpful distinctions: 'Aggression' refers to a behaviour with the intention to hurt or gain advantage over others, without necessarily involving physical attack; 'Violence' sometimes motivated by anger and intent, involves the use of physical force against another individual; 'Criminal violence' is injurious behaviour specifically forbidden by law. Despite the usefulness of such definitions, Blackburn (1993) illustrates the value laden nature of such concepts and warns of the 'dependence of the identification of aggression or violence on the attributions and values of the observer' (p. 211).

Few individuals would disagree with the fact that murder is an act of violence as it is usually characterized by anger, intent and injurious behaviour. However, if one or more of these components is absent, or present to a lesser degree, there may be disagreement about whether the label of an 'act of violence' applies (Archer and Browne, 1989). Thus, these three components are best regarded as related but separate characteristics of violent behaviour; when all are present a typical case of aggression or violence can be described (Figure I.1).

Gelles and Cornell (1990) argue that an injurious behaviour is always present in an act of violence. They define violence as 'an act carried out with the intention or perceived intention of causing physical pain or injury to another person' (p. 22). They go on to distinguish acts of 'Normal violence' from acts of 'Abusive violence' based on a potential for injuring the victim. Normal violence involves slaps, pushes, shoves and spankings which are commonplace and are an acceptable part of family arguments and raising children. Hence many people object to these acts

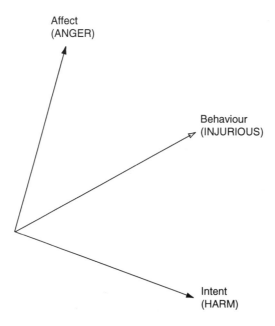

Figure I.1   Three components characterizing violent behaviour (from Archer and Browne, 1989)

being called aggressive or violent. Abusive violence refers to punches, kicks, bites, chokings, scaldings, beatings, stabbings and shootings—acts that have a high potential for injuring the victim.

There are two main limitations to this definition. Firstly, the consequences of the acts are not taken into account; for example, kicking may not cause any serious harm to the victim, whereas the consequence of pushing and shoving might on occasion cause very serious injuries. Secondly, the definition is restricted to physical aggression, it does not address the broader issues of mental or psychological violence, for example, through the damage of personal property and the restriction of personal freedom. Indeed, all forms of aggression and violence have the potential to be used by a person in an instrumental way to achieve specific goals such as an increase in wealth, power and control.

A broader definition of violence has been proposed by Archer and Browne (1989) and described as 'the exercise of physical force so as to injure or damage persons or property; otherwise to treat or use persons or property in a way that causes bodily injury and forcibly interferes with personal freedom' (pp. 10–11). This definition highlights the current usage of the term *violence*, which typically reflects physical aggression in a social context.

Psychological violence is less apparent and more difficult to dichotomize into what is generally considered to be acceptable and unacceptable. Edleson (1984) defined psychological violence as 'Verbal or non-verbal threats of violence against another person or against that person's belongings'. This may be of an emotional or environmental nature, for instance, threatening suicide, destroying pets, punching walls and throwing objects (Purdy and Nickle, 1981). It is important to consider psychological violence as 'abusive' because it carries with it the continual threat of actual physical violence and so creates an atmosphere of tension and uncertainty in the home which produces degradation and humiliation in the victimized partner.

The Latin *violentia* means vehemence or impetuosity (*Oxford English Dictionary*, 1933) but perhaps a more important aspect is the negative social judgement entailed by the word 'violence'. Therefore, the labels of 'conjugal violence' (Gelles, 1987a) or 'marital violence' (Borkowski, Murch and Walker, 1983) and 'intimate violence' (Gelles and Straus, 1988; Gelles and Cornell, 1990; Viano, 1992) refer to physical harm or psychologically damaging assaults which are not socially legitimized in any way. Hence, there is a tendency for some accounts to generalize from actual to metaphorical violence in describing forms of mental injury, emotional and material (or economic) abuse and neglect. This is particularly characteristic of approaches which seek to understand violence in terms of a wider social context. Gil (1978), for example, sees aggression in families as rooted in wider societal violence, and he uses a very broad definition which describes violence as 'acts and conditions which obstruct the spontaneous unfolding of innate human potential, the inherent human drive toward the development of self-actualization'. Such a definition is so wide as to include virtually any thwarting of wishes and activities, and is so vague as to be incapable of being useful.

A compromise between such wide definitions as proposed by Gil (1978) and those that take a more narrow perspective as described earlier, is the definition put forward by the Council of Europe (1986). They describe 'physical violence in the family' as:

> Any act or omission committed within the framework of the family by one of its members that undermines the life, the bodily or psychological integrity or the liberty of another member of the same family or that seriously harms the development of his or her personality.

The work of the European Committee on Crime Problems, in its terms of reference to study the problems posed by physical violence in the family, also interpreted the word 'Family' as:

> A married or unmarried couple, their descendants, the ancestors, descendants or collateral relatives of either and any child as soon as they live together or continue to have relations resulting from prior cohabitation.

The authors of this book have chosen to take these broad perspectives on 'physical violence' within the 'family' and will discuss acts of omission or commission that are judged by a mixture of community values and professional expertise to be inappropriate or damaging. Such an approach has previously been specifically applied to child maltreatment (Garbarino and Gilliam, 1980: 7). This broad approach gives a general perspective of 'maltreatment' within the social context of the family, involving both concepts of 'abuse' and 'neglect'. More specific definitions that describe the various forms of maltreatment are outlined in Chapter 1, together with the types of relationship in which they occur.

TYPES OF FAMILY VIOLENCE

When applied to the family situation, a broad perspective embraces two types of violence by adults: (spouse abuse and child abuse), two types of violence by children (parent abuse and sibling abuse) and one type of violence by children and adults (elder abuse) (Figure I.2). Chapters 4 to 10 present a review of each type of abuse in turn. This reflects the fact that research has examined them separately, one possible reason for this being that each type evolved as a recognized social problem at a different time. The sequence of chapters in this book also outlines the developmental cycle of violence, which shows the continuity of aggressive behaviour from one generation to the next (Figure I.2).

The importance of child maltreatment to the 'cycle of violence' and its links to spouse maltreatment is reflected by the amount of literature on these subjects (see Gelles and Loseke, 1994). In view of this, the authors dedicate two chapters (4 and 5) to the prediction and prevention of spouse maltreatment and two (6 and 7) to the prevention and treatment of child abuse and neglect. Nevertheless, the prevention of family violence must be based on a firm understanding of the causes of angry feelings and aggressive behaviour between all family members. Therefore, in the first chapter we shall attempt to identify common forms of maltreatment and classifications of prevention that apply to all types of violence in the family. In Chapter 2 the various models put forward to explain the causes of family violence in general are reviewed and in Chapter 3 the coercive relationships that are the foundation for aggressive interactions in the family are described. This provides the reader with a theoretical understanding of family violence, before considering the practical issues of predicting and preventing each particular type.

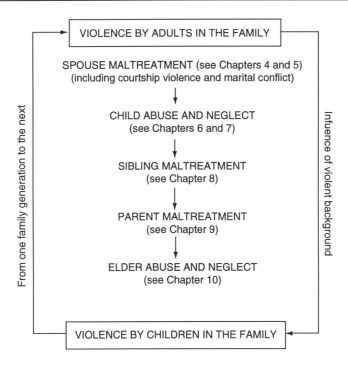

Figure I.2   Types of family violence and their developmental cycle

The developmental sequence presented—spouse, child, sibling, parent and elder maltreatment—is followed by a review of the processes that maintain the intergenerational cycle of violence from victim to offender and their implications for early intervention within families (Chapter 11). Finally, in Chapter 12 some practical ideas are given for working with violent families, and home-based methods of treating the family as a whole are offered.

The book concludes on a cautionary note, commenting on the consequences to individuals and the costs to society if recommendations regarding the prediction and prevention of family violence are ignored. The authors believe that the book will be useful to researchers and practitioners; indeed, it is hoped that by turning research into practice the book will have a significant impact on political and professional policy aimed at preventing all forms of family violence.

CHAPTER 1   Forms of family violence and levels of prevention

While different types of family violence are discussed in isolation from each other, it is important to realize that all forms of violence in the family are interrelated and have an impact on the family as a whole. This is reflected in a number of publications that take a holistic approach to the causation and maintenance of family violence (e.g. Browne, 1989a, 1993; Gelles, 1987b), and to intervention and treatment when working with violent families (e.g. Bolton and Bolton, 1987; Ammerman and Hersen, 1990, 1992; Hampton et al., 1993). There are close links, for example, between wife abuse and child physical abuse (e.g. Gayford, 1975; Merrick and Michelsen, 1985; Milner and Gold, 1986; Browne and Saqi, 1988a; Browne, 1993) and between wife abuse and child sexual abuse (e.g. Dietz and Craft, 1980; Truesdell, McNeil and Deschner, 1986; Goddard and Hiller, 1993). However, the implications of these contingencies for the recognition and prevention of family violence have yet to be determined.

COMMON FORMS OF FAMILY VIOLENCE

Every aspect of family violence can be characterized in the same way, and dichotomized into 'active' and 'passive' forms (Table 1.1). Active violence involves abusive acts in a physical, psychological or sexual context, where anger is directed at the victim. Passive violence refers to neglect within the same contexts, where anger is shown by a lack of concern for the victim and avoiding anger-provoking interactions with the victim. Neglect can only be considered violent in the metaphorical sense as it does not involve physical force. Nevertheless, it can cause both physical and psychological injury.

Table 1.1 Two-way classification of family violence with example of major forms (adapted from Browne, Davies and Stratton, 1988; Browne, 1993)

	Physical violence	Psychological violence	Sexual violence
Active abuse	Non-accidental injury. Forced coercion and restraint.	Intimidation Emotional abuse. Material abuse.	Incest. Assault and rape.
Passive neglect	Poor health care. Physical neglect.	Lack of affection. Emotional neglect. Material neglect.	Failure to protect. Prostitution.

Psychological injury refers to harm inflicted on the intellectual or mental capacity of an individual, which results in observable impairments in a person's ability to function within a culturally determined range of performance and behaviour (Landau et al., 1980). Psychological or emotional abuse and neglect are also the most difficult to quantify in terms of severity, but that is not to say it is easy to quantify the other forms of maltreatment. Hence, the paucity of literature on the subject of severity.

Nevertheless, it is important to give some indication of what are generally considered to be minor, moderate and severe incidents of maltreatment. Such a classification is, of course, influenced by the duration and frequency of incidents. A tentative attempt by the authors to classify incidents and their frequency in terms of severity is presented in Table 1.2.

The problem with a severity approach is that victims of family violence are unlikely to be subjected to only one form of maltreatment: for example, sexual abuse and physical abuse are preceded and accompanied by psychological, emotional and material abuse. Principally, this may consist of: degrading verbal assaults, including threats of sexual or physical abuse (terrorizing); isolation and close confinement, such as locking a person in a room; and other aversive treatment, such as withholding food and social interaction, or corrupting and exploiting the individual (Hart, Germain and Brassard, 1987).

It is important to understand the coexistence of different forms of maltreatment if preventative strategies are to be developed. The authors propose that, over time, violent or coercive interac-

Table 1.2   Severity of maltreatment

LESS SEVERE

Minor incidents of an infrequent nature with little or no long-term damage—either physical, sexual or psychological.

- *Physical*: e.g. injuries confined in area and limited to superficial tissue, including cases of light scratch marks, small slight bruising, minute burns and small welts.
- *Sexual*: e.g. inappropriate sexual touching, invitations and/or exhibitionism.
- *Emotional*: e.g. occasional verbal assaults, denigration, humiliation, scapegoating, confusing atmosphere.
- *Neglect*: e.g. occasional withholding of love and affection, weight parallel to or slightly below third centile with no organic cause.

MODERATELY SEVERE

More frequent incidents and/or of a more serious nature, but unlikely to be life-threatening or have potentially severe long-term effects.

- *Physical*: e.g. surface injuries of an extensive or more serious nature and small subcutaneous injuries, including cases of extensive bruising, large welts, lacerations, small haematomas and minor burns.
- *Sexual*: e.g. Non-penetrative sexual interaction of an indecent or inappropriate nature; such as fondling, masturbation and digital penetration.
- *Emotional*: e.g. frequent verbal assaults, denigration and humiliation, occasional rejection.
- *Neglect*: e.g. frequent withholding of love and affection, non-organic failure to gain weight.

VERY SEVERE

Ongoing or very frequent maltreatment *and/or* less frequent incidents with potentially very severe physical or psychological harm.

- *Physical*: e.g. all long and deep tissue injuries and broken bones (including fractures, dislocations, subdural haematomas, serious burns and damage to internal organs).
- *Sexual*: e.g. sexual interaction involving attempted or actual oral, anal or vaginal penetration.
- *Emotional*: e.g. frequent rejection, occasional withholding of food and drink, enforced isolation and restriction of movement.
- *Neglect*: e.g. frequent unavailability of parent, guardian or spouse, non-organic failure to thrive.

LIFE THREATENING

Long-term or severe psychological and physical harm that results in life-threatening situations (including perpetrators failing to seek help in time or victims harming themselves).

[Continued

Table 1.2 – *continued*

- *Physical*: e.g. deliberate or persistent injuries which have the potential of victim death or near death.
- *Sexual*: e.g. incest, coerced or forced penetration (oral, anal or vaginal) over a prolonged period.
- *Emotional*: e.g. persistent rejection, failure to nurture, frequent withholding of food and drink, enforced isolation and restriction of movement.
- *Neglect*: e.g. persistent unavailability of parent, guardian or spouse, non-organic failure to maintain weight.

tions in the family may shift along one 'dimension of harm' from psychological to physical injury and another 'relationship dimension' from intra- to extrafamilial maltreatment. At the same time, maltreatment may occur in an active or passive way within a 'dimension of activity'. It has been claimed that less than 5% of the various forms of maltreatment occur in isolation, and that emotional and physical neglect often appear to be precursors to emotional, physical and sexual abuse (Ney, Fung and Wickett, 1994). The interrelationships between the different forms of violence which occur within these dimensions are presented in Figure 1.1.

The model presents violent and coercive interactions within three major influences or dimensions, such that any one incident will have a level of harm, a level of activity and a level of relationship closeness. It can be seen in Figure 1.1 that psychological violence precedes physical injury and that intrafamilial maltreatment precedes extrafamilial abuse. The maltreatment may then oscillate along both dimensions of harm and incest. In a similar way, violent and coercive interactions between family members may change over time from active abuse to passive neglect and back along a dimension of activity. For example, in 23% of reported cases of child maltreatment, the parents both abuse and neglect their child (Crittenden, 1988). Furthermore, approximately 33% of sexually abused children have also been physically abused by their parents (Finkelhor and Baron, 1986) Hence, the model asserts that physical and/or sexual abuse and neglect carried out by a parent or relative, places the victimized individual at greater risk of further maltreatment by the same people in the family and/or others in the victim's environment, inside or outside the home, such as a friend or stranger. An understanding of this 'relationship dimension' is especially important for the prevention of re-victimization, as it has been shown that child sex offenders target vulnerable children and adults who are already victims of a broken and/or disruptive family (Elliott, Browne and Kilcoyne, 1995). Thus, over time, it is suggested that there is a link between intrafamilial and extrafamilial maltreatment along the 'relationship dimension'. This dimension is applied here in the broadest sense to cover physical, emotional and sexual abuse and neglect within the family, as recent studies have shown that the concept of 're-victimization' is related to all forms of maltreatment (Lloyd, Farrell and Pease, 1994; Hamilton and Browne, 1997).

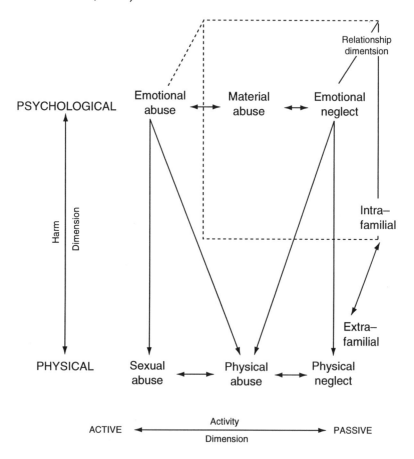

Figure 1.1   Coexistence of different forms of maltreatment

The overlapping nature of various forms of maltreatment results in a lack of consensus concerning their descriptive definition. This accounts for the wide variations in reports on the incidence and prevalence of violence in the family. For example, estimates of incidence for child abuse in the USA—that is, the number of new cases occurring within a given time period—range from 60 000 to 4 500 000 each year, depending upon the definition of abuse adopted (Besharov, 1982). Wide variations are also evident for estimates of prevalence—that is, the proportion of abused victims in a given population over a defined period of time. In the USA, severe child physical abuse for males and females

Table 1.3   Forms of maltreatment

ABUSE

Physical abuse   The infliction or threat of physical pain and/or injury, e.g. pushing, slapping, hitting, hair-pulling, biting, arm-twisting, kicking, punching, hitting with objects, burning, stabbing, shooting, poisoning, etc. Forced coercion and physical restraint.

Sexual abuse   Sexual contact without consent; any exploitive or coercive sexual contact including fondling, intercourse, oral or anal sodomy, attacks on the sexual parts of the body. Involuntary viewing of sexual imagery or activity and treating someone in a sexually derogatory manner.

Psychological (mental) abuse   The infliction of mental anguish by: controlling and limiting access to friends, school and work; forced isolation and imprisonment; involuntary witness to violent imagery or activity; intimidation, using fear of physical harm or harm to others; use of menacing, blackmail, suicide threats and harassment; destruction of pets and property.

Emotional abuse   Regular criticism, humiliation, denigration, insults, put-downs, name calling and other attempts to undermine self-image and sense of worth.

Material (economic) abuse   Illegal or financial exploitation and/or control of funds and other resources needed for economic and personal survival. Forcing a person to be materially dependent.

NEGLECT

Wilful neglect   Refusal or failure to fulfil a caretaking obligation, including a conscious and intentional attempt to inflict physical or emotional stress; e.g. deliberate abandonment or deliberate denial of food, money or health-related services.

Unwitting neglect   Failure to fulfil a caretaking obligation, excluding a conscious and intentional attempt to inflict physical or emotional distress, e.g. abandonment, non-provision of food, money or health-related services because of anxiety, inadequate knowledge, laziness or infirmity.

ranges from 9% (Brutz and Ingoldsby, 1984) to 68% (Dembo et al., 1987) and sexual abuse ranges from 6% to 62% for females and 3% to 22% for males (Pilkington and Kremer, 1995a, 1995b). These extreme differences between the various studies depend on the sample, the method of data collection and, most importantly, the definitions used (Browne and Lynch, 1995). Therefore, it is essential for this book to begin with operational definitions that describe the major forms of maltreatment. Table 1.3 presents descriptions for five forms of abuse (physical, sexual, psychological, emotional, material (or economic)) and two forms of neglect (wilful and unwitting). These descriptions apply to all types of family violence and form a basis for the discussions in the chapters that follow.

It should be pointed out, however, that the incidence and prevalence figures quoted in this chapter and elsewhere in the book may not necessarily be based on the classifications, definitions and descriptions provided by the authors (Table 1.3). Despite these discrepancies the following summary of the available statistics attempts to illustrate the wide extent of family violence within modern society.

THE EXTENT OF FAMILY VIOLENCE

Violence by Adults

The exercise of physical force by adults in the family results in child abuse, spouse abuse and elder abuse. These forms of abuse are considered by some theorists to represent the exertion of power and control by one family member over another (Dobash and Dobash, 1979, 1987). Adults may also neglect other family members as a way of coping with negative feelings of violence towards them. This may be an intentional and conscious action (wilful neglect) or an unconscious action without intention (unwitting neglect) as defined in Table 1.3.

Case conferences involving physical, psychological and sexual forms of child abuse and neglect, when added together, involve about 1% of English children (Browne, 1989b) only half of whom will be on a child protection register at any one time (Department of Health, 1995a). However, the reported incidence of child abuse is probably the tip of the iceberg in terms of prevalence. For example, it is estimated that 8% of men and between 12 and 16% of women in the UK claim to have experienced sexual abuse as children (Baker and Duncan, 1985; Hall, 1985). Similarly, between 5 and 15% of young adults in the UK claim that they were phys- ically abused in the family as a child (Davenport, Browne and Palmer, 1994; Browne and Hamilton, 1997).

In both the USA and UK, spouse abuse occurs in 25 to 28% of married couples at some time in their marriage (Straus and Gelles, 1986; Dobash and Dobash, 1987; Andrews and Brown, 1988), and similar percentages have been reported for severe vio- lence between dating couples (Gelles and Cornell, 1990; Browne and Slater, 1997). This abuse is interactive, so that women have been observed to abuse men and men to abuse women (Gelles and Straus, 1988). Nevertheless, it is well known to health pro- fessionals in Europe and North America that wife abuse is far more common than husband abuse, in fact in England it is about five times as common (Smith et al., 1992). This fact is also sup- ported by victim surveys. The most recent British Crime Survey (Mayhew, Maung and Mirrless-Black, 1993) estimated that 530 000 domestic assaults occurred in 1991, more than half of which were to women from their partners, ex-partners and other relatives living at home. The survey also confirmed that in Britain domestic violence between partners and relatives was the

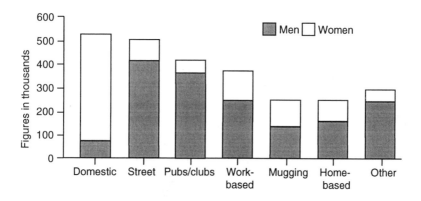

Figure 1.2 Types of violence, 1991 (from the 1992 British Crime Survey, repro- duced with HMSO permission from Mayhew, Maung and Mirrless-Black, 1993)

most common form of 'assault against the person'. As Figure 1.2 shows, street assaults and violence in pubs and clubs were nearly as common as domestic violence. However, unlike domestic violence, most of the victims were men. Muggings and violent assault in the home by an outsider had a similar number of male and female victims.

According to police records, wife abuse is more commonly reported than child abuse. Previous studies have shown that wife abuse is reported to the police seven times more often than child abuse (Dobash and Dobash, 1979, 1987). Despite the fact that the two types of abuse are linked, resources go directly to deal with treating and preventing child abuse. Even fewer resources are allocated to the 10% of elderly people who, living with their family, are subject to abuse and neglect (Browne, 1989c). Elderly dependants are people most vulnerable to material abuse by other family members, such as their children stealing from forgetful elderly relatives.

Violence by Children

It is generally thought that children are not physically capable of seriously injuring others. However, research has demonstrated that violence towards siblings and parents are common forms of family problems. Indeed, it has been estimated that approximately half the children in the USA violently abuse their brothers and sisters every year. Research suggests that four out of five children with one or more siblings suffer at least one physical attack from their brother or sister each year, with at least two being the victim of extreme and persistent intimidation and bullying (Straus, Gelles and Steinmetz, 1980, 1988).

Parents and caregivers may also have to bear the brunt of (and have the bruises to give witness to) punching, pinching and kicking received from their offspring. Such attacks by younger children may be an irritant, but when delivered by older children or adolescents can have serious consequences (Bolton and Bolton, 1987; Straus, Gelles and Steinmetz, 1980, 1988). Indeed, in the UK 6% of helpline calls by parents report that their adolescent children are physically abusing them (Parentline, 1990).

Furthermore, a recent study of 467 English university students found that 3% of young adults self report using serious 'abusive' violence to their father and 2% to their mother (Browne and Hamilton, 1997). Researchers in the USA find that the rates at which teenagers show aggression to their parents range from 5 to 12% with severe 'abusive' violence also occurring to 3% of parents (Gelles and Cornell, 1990).

Clinical Evidence of Family Violence

In the USA, it is estimated that 5% of female trauma patients presenting in a hospital emergency department receive injuries as a result of violence in the home. However, only two-thirds of cases disclose this fact without direct questions from the hospital staff (McLeer and Anwar, 1989).

In the UK, Smith et al. (1992) at the Leicester Royal Infirmary carried out an investigation of all individuals attending the Accident and Emergency Department. They found that 3 in 1000 cases treated for trauma presented with injuries were a direct result of domestic violence and assault in the home. Fifty-four per cent of their cases were victims aged 14–29 years. Of the offenders who caused the injury, 8% were wives and 4% were girlfriends (hence, 12% of their cases of domestic violence were as a result of women abusing men). Of course, assaults against women were much more common; 35% of offenders were husbands and 19% were boyfriends. Six per cent of cases involved adolescent children injuring their parent or adult guardian and a further 6% involved offenders from outside the immediate family. In the remaining 22% of cases, the offender was not reported. As far as this population was concerned there was little difference between male and female victims in the seriousness (or intensity) and the site of the injuries (Smith et al., 1992).

Even individuals who are not directly assaulted can also be seriously affected by family violence. Witnessing violence in the home is considered to be psychologically damaging as it teaches aggressive styles of conduct and distorts views about conflict resolution. This is especially the case for children, as 80% of children who live in violent families will witness an assault at some time or other (Sinclair, 1985).

The most important fact for prediction and prevention, is that the various forms of family violence do not occur in isolation. If spouse abuse occurs then there is a very high probability that child abuse is also occurring, and vice versa. Walker (1984) in the USA found that 53% of individuals who show violence towards their partner also abuse their children. Looking at this association from the other direction, research in the UK by Browne and Saqi (1988a) found that 52% of child-abusing families show other forms of family violence. Indeed, Straus, Gelles and Steinmetz (1980) claimed there was a 40% overlap between wife assault and child maltreatment. Therefore, it is necessary to address all forms of family violence in order to prevent the tendency for violence repeating itself from one generation to the next (Browne, 1993).

PREVENTION STRATEGIES FOR FAMILY VIOLENCE

Research has shown similarities between those who physically and sexually abuse their children, those who abuse their wives, and those who abuse their aged relatives. These include: a misperception of the victim, low self-esteem, sense of incompetence, social isolation, a lack of support and help, lack of empathy, marital difficulties, depression, poor self-control and a history of abuse and neglect as a child (Browne, 1989a).

Several characteristics found within the victims of abuse are common to all types of maltreatment. These include: a poor relationship with the abuser, dependency, emotional and social isolation, and ill health (Browne, 1989a).

Nevertheless, effective intervention strategies to control and prevent family violence in general are few and far between. The majority of current intervention techniques usually concentrate on just one type of violence in the family and many operate only at the last level of prevention; that is, 'treatment' after violence has occurred (Kingston and Penhale, 1995); this is despite the fact that there are three levels of prevention. As so many authors confuse the terms prevention and treatment (see Ammerman and

Hersen, 1990; Hampton et al., 1993) and there is disagreement in the literature about the precise location of the boundaries between the three levels (Butler, 1989), the three descriptions of levels of prevention used in this book, in relation to family violence, are presented below.

Primary Preventions of Fundamental Change

Primary preventions aim to reduce the 'incidence' of maltreatment in the family and attempt to prevent the problem before it starts. Usually these interventions operate at the societal level through public awareness campaigns and advocacy groups, and then by social, legal and educational processes of change to promote good family health and interactions.

Gelles (1993) suggests the following actions for the primary prevention of family violence.

1. Eliminate the norms that legitimate and glorify violence in the society and the family, such as the use of violence as a form of media entertainment.
2. Reduce violence-provoking stress created by society, such as poverty and inequality.
3. Incorporate families into a network of kin and community and reduce social isolation.
4. Change the sexist character of society by educational development.
5. Break the cycle of violence in the family by teaching alternatives to violence as a way of controlling children.

The above proposals call for fundamental changes in family life and society as a whole. Hence, some may claim they are not realistic. Certainly, they are long-term solutions that require major shifts in resource allocation and the organization of western societies.

Secondary Preventions of Prediction, Identification and Amelioration (the Risk Approach)

It is difficult to predict the chances of family violence as some people in the family resort to violence inconsistently while others may do so consistently but only under extreme stress. However, studies on the causes of family violence have identified factors that are usually present when aggressive incidents and violent interactions occur.

In the short term, techniques aimed at the early identification of factors associated with violence and the amelioration of potential violence are more realistic. Health and Social Service professionals can be instructed to routinely screen all families who come into contact with the service they are providing (see Chapter 6). This surveillance is the basis for secondary prevention which aims to reduce the 'prevalence' of family violence by shortening the duration of and frequency of coercive and negative family interactions and diminish the impact of risk factors through early detection and immediate effective intervention.

This risk approach to family violence can be seen as a managerial tool for the flexible and rational distribution of scarce resources and their maximal utilization. It is based on the assessment of families as high or low risk for violence, abuse and neglect. The aim of the risk strategy is to give special attention to those in the greatest need of help before severe violence occurs.

Health and social service agencies using this approach identify families in need of help from those characteristics (risk factors) that are associated with increased risk of undesirable outcomes such as violence. However, even this process requires extra resources for each local community to:

- develop methods for detecting risk factors;
- train health care and social workers in these screening methods; and
- provide intervention strategies to ameliorate undesired outcomes.

There are ethical and economic reservations about this process; especially when resources are unavailable to help ameliorate risk factors in a family, once they have been identified. Where resources for reducing the potential for violence are non-existent, then screening and assessment should not be carried out. The costs of labelling a family needs to be balanced with the

benefits of help, otherwise health and social service professionals will promote violence rather than prevent it.

Men and women are often reluctant to admit and talk about
relationship problems and may feel ashamed of their violent
interactions. Predictive characteristics are helpful, therefore, in
identifying the possibility of violence for both the family and the
care-worker. Where there is concern about the possibility of violence, the problem should be referred to the most appropriate
professional who may fully assess the coercive relationships and
adverse factors affecting the family.

Tertiary Prevention: Management, Treatment and Control of the Problem

At the tertiary level of prevention, techniques are employed
when family violence has actually been determined and is
already happening. This may be after many repeated episodes of
maltreatment have occurred and violence has become established in the family system. Thus, tertiary prevention is aimed at
reducing the risk of repeated physical injury and psychological
damage, in order to lower the chances of impairment, disability
or death of the victim. Establishing that 'significant harm' has
occurred in the past to a dependant, can justify a recommendation that the family members be separated or alternatively 'reha-
bilitated' through treatment.

Hence tertiary prevention is concerned with the treatment of
violent families and the management and control of aggressive
behaviour shown by family members. Of course, this may be less
helpful for those who are crippled, psychologically and physically, by violence prior to intervention and treatment. For some,
the tertiary approach to prevention is too late, as the abuse may
have had fatal consequences already. This is difficult to accept
when many methods of intervention and treatment are applicable to both secondary and tertiary prevention and lives may
have been saved. Therefore, this book puts forward ideas for
working with families identified as high risk for violence in the
family, the aim being to help families with serious problems
before the violence occurs. Even for individuals who were mal-

treated as children, prognosis may be good with effective intervention (see Chapter 11). Unfortunately, most of the intervention strategies outlined (see Chapters 7, 9 and 12) are more often included in tertiary prevention programmes to help manage and control maltreatment in the family rather than prevent it.

CHAPTER 2   Causes of family violence

From the previous discussion of the various forms of maltreatment within the family, it is evident that physical violence does not encompass the whole range of harmful acts observed within family interactions. Hence, some researchers distinguish between acts of physical violence and other forms of abuse, because the causes (of sexual violence, for example) and their potential solutions are different (see Frude, 1991). While all harmful acts have some causes in common, other factors are unique to physical violence. Therefore, we consider the following outline of causal factors in relation to family violence to be more relevant to physical abuse and neglect than to other forms of maltreatment.

In seeking to understand the many causal factors involved in violence in the home, several theoretical models have been proposed, which can be broadly classified into *sociological* explanations and *psychological* explanations.

SOCIOLOGICAL EXPLANATIONS OF FAMILY VIOLENCE

In general, most authors (e.g. Gelles, 1987a, 1987b, 1994a) who present a sociological perspective on family violence traditionally relate the causes to social stress factors in the family. Some authors go further (e.g. Gil, 1978) and describe the social stress factors as manifestations of the cultural values and practices that shape the structure of the family. They claim it's the society we live in that is ultimately responsible for violence in the family.

Social Stress Models

Factors such as low wages, unemployment, poor housing, over-crowding, isolation and alienating work conditions are seen by Gelles (1987a, 1987b) and Gelles and Cornell (1990) as causing frustration and stress at the individual level, which in turn may lead to violence. Gelles concluded from his research that 'violence is an adaptation or response to structural stress'. However, since family violence is not confined to families in the lower socio-economic groups but is spread across the class spectrum, this is a limited view. Other attempts to explain family violence in wider social terms include the resource theory of Goode (1971) and the general systems approach of Straus (1980), Giles-Sims (1983) and the social exchange/control theory of Gelles (1983).

Social exchange/control theory in relation to family life, is based on the notion of mutual rewards and punishments. Family members exchange or withhold personal sentiments, services and resources. When the balance of exchange matches the expectations of the individuals concerned then peace and order prevails. However, where there are imbalances in expectations, such as an unemployed adult offering full-time care to their increasingly dependent elderly mother or father, then the potential for violent control of the situation is realized (Phillips, 1986).

Goode (1971) argues that the family, like all social institutions, rests to some degree on force or threat to maintain order. He postulated that the more alternatives (or 'resources') an individual can command, or perceive to command, the less he or she will use force in an overt manner. Most people do not willingly use overt force when they command other 'resources' because the costs of doing so are high. Goode (op. cit.) assumed that middle-class families have more 'resources', arising, for example, from their greater prestige and better economic position, and consequently will be less likely to resort to violence or threat. O'Brien (1971) showed a similar line of thought in his 'status inconsistency' hypothesis. He focused on the economic problems of the husband and the different educational achievements of the husband and wife that may result in the husband's lower status in the family. Violence is seen as an option used to remedy a low-status position, and hence increase self-esteem.

Straus (1980) and Giles-Sims (1983) explains the occurrence of domestic violence in the context of a general systems approach, in terms of 'deviant family structures'. He referred to deviant authority structures and claimed that the level of violence is likely to be greatest when the wife is dominant in decision-making. This is especially the case when the male partner suffers from low self-esteem and a poor perception of self (Goldstein and Rosenbaum, 1985).

Cultural Models

An alternative approach, but also couched in terms of the social position of the people involved, can be referred to as the micropolitical view. This holds that individual violence reflects a microcosm of the power relations in the wider society. For example, a common feminist explanation of violence towards women and children views it as a function of women's generally oppressed position in society (see Yllo and Bograd, 1988; Yllo, 1994). Within this framework, the purpose of male violence is seen as that of controlling other family members. Hanmer (1978) has expanded this idea into a complete theory incorporating the whole state apparatus (which represents men), and in her view the policies of the Welfare State induce dependency in women. However, Dobash and Dobash (1979, 1987) are probably the most well-known theorists taking this general position in their writings on spouse abuse (see Chapters 4 and 5).

The most broad sociological perspective (Gil, 1978; Straus, 1980; Levine, 1986; Goldstein, 1986) holds that cultural values, the availability of weapons and the exposure to unpunished models of aggression affect personal attitudes towards violent behaviour. These, in turn, influence an individual's acceptance of aggression as a form of emotional expression and as a method of control over others. Some theorists claim that social groups and communities may develop an acceptance of aggressive interactions, leading to a 'Subculture of Violence' (Wolfgang and Ferracuti, 1982).

Gil (1978) goes on to distinguish between 'structural' violence (violence at the institutional and societal levels), which is embedded in sanctioned social practices, and personal violence, which usually involves acts which transcend social sanctions. As we noted earlier, Gil's definition of violence is a particularly wide one, which reflects his theoretical view that violence should be viewed in terms of the wider power relations in society. Therefore, he says that structural violence and personal violence should not be viewed as discrete phenomena: they are both symptoms of the same social context, the same values and institutions which interact and reinforce each other. He sees personal violence as being reactive, as being rooted in structural violence, since experiences which inhibit a person's development will often result in stress and frustration, and the urge to retaliate by inflicting violence on others. He considers domestic violence as reactive violence which originates outside the family but which cannot be discharged there. It can be discharged within the family because the family is more informal, most time is spent there, and less punitive sanctions will result from violence in the home than from violence in other social situations. This is seen as the 'function' of family violence which gives 'pay-offs' to the aggressor (Powers, 1986). Table 2.1 gives some examples of the function of aggressive behaviour in the family in terms of 'pay-offs' for the perpetrator of violence.

Table 2.1 Sociological explanations for family violence: functions and pay-offs for the aggressor (adapted from Powers, 1986)

- Gets attention and signals that needs are not being met.
- Coerces and manipulates others to meet own needs.
- Gains control of decisions and rule-setting in the family.
- Experiences increased power and self-esteem through inducing helplessness in others.
- Increases intensity and directness of intimacy.
- Avoids risks and vulnerability in intimacy.
- Dominates rivals for family members' love and approval.
- Protects self from attack and harm.
- Seeks revenge for being harmed by others both now and in the past.
- Re-enacts victimized experiences, but this time as the perpetrator in control.
- Harms others for inherent excitement, pleasure and feelings of power and control.
- Disrupts or changes unrewarding balances in family relationships.
- Manages impressions one makes on others.
- Conforms to cultural norms and expectations.

Indeed, Gelles (1983) has analysed the causes for family violence in terms of cost and benefit. His 'exchange social control theory' considers that the private nature of the home environment reduces the cost of overt aggression in terms of official reprimand. This, in turn, leads to a higher probability of aggression in the home, where there are fewer social constraints on behaviour. Thus privacy makes family violence less detectable and easier to commit. Indeed, it has recently been estimated by Dutton (1987) that the probability of 'wife assault' being detected by the criminal justice system in Canada is about 6.5%. If detected, the probability of arrest is 21.2%. Overall, the offender has a 0.38% chance of being punished by the court.

Generally, the sociological perspective has moved away from simple social stress explanations of family violence, such as poverty, to one involving the transactions that occur between the abuser and the abused within the structure of the family and society.

PSYCHOLOGICAL EXPLANATIONS OF FAMILY VIOLENCE

Psychological perspectives have traditionally focused on personal characteristics that can cause violent behaviour. More recently, however, psychological models have been proposed that are interactive in nature (O'Leary, 1994).

Individually Focused Models

The *psychobiological perspective* concentrates on inherent personality characteristics, often of a psychopathological nature. This research tradition is characterized by the use of rating scales to measure hostility, aggressiveness, temperament and anger expression (Buss and Durkee, 1957; Edmunds and Kendrick, 1980; Spielberger et al., 1983) and the study of biological variables which underlie a tendency to be violent (Archer, 1988; Coccaro, 1995). Perhaps the most extreme version of this perspective was the work of Mark and Ervin (1970), who advocated widespread psychosurgery as a solution to violent behaviour.

Other psychobiologically orientated authors have attempted to establish a causal connection between testosterone hormone levels and male violence (Persky, Smith and Basu, 1971; Rada, Laws and Kellner, 1976) and the identification of specific pathological conditions, such as alcoholism, which are likely to be predisposing or determining factors in violent behaviour (Byles, 1978; Gerson, 1978; Potter-Efron and Potter-Efron, 1990; Pernanen, 1991).

The *psychodynamic perspective* also focuses on the abnormal characteristics of the individual abuser, emphasizing the internal psychological conflicts and dysfunctions characteristic of certain abusing adults. Based on the theories of Freud (1940, 1949) and Lorenz (1966) to explain aggression shown by most individuals, the emphasis of a psychodynamic approach is the abuser's 'abnormal death instinct' or 'excessive drive' for aggressive behaviour in comparison to others. This is seen as the result of genetic make up and/or adverse socialization experiences that produce a 'psychopathic' character, with a predisposition to behave violently.

One form of this predisposition is referred to as 'transference psychosis' (Galston, 1965), involving transference from parent to child—for example, the parent often interprets the child as if he or she were an adult and perceives the child as hostile and persecuting, projecting that part of the parent's own personality he or she wishes to destroy (Steele and Pollock, 1968). Thus, the child is seen as the cause of the parent's troubles and becomes a scapegoat to which all anger is directed (Wasserman, Green and Allen, 1983). However, Kempe and Kempe (1978) suggested that only 10% of child abusers can accurately be labelled as mentally ill. Nevertheless, this model has been useful in recognizing certain predispositions of abusive individuals. These include a tendency to have distorted perceptions of their dependents (Rosenberg and Repucci, 1983); difficulty dealing with aggressive impulses as a result of being impulsively immature, often depressed, and self-centred; and a history of having been abused, neglected or witnessing violence as children.

The emotion of anger may be 'expressed' or 'repressed' showing 'rage' or 'irritation' respectively (Averill, 1983). However, Sears, Maccoby and Levin (1957) observed aggressive behaviour in the absence of any emotion and made a distinction between 'hostile' and 'instrumental' aggression. This has been later referred to as 'angry' aggression and manipulative aggression (Feshbach, 1964). Dollard et al. (1939), in their famous book *Frustration and Aggression*, were among the first to introduce the behavioural concept of 'Intent', believing that every aggressive action could ultimately be traced back to a previous frustration. The goal or 'intent' is that of removing the offending object or person.

The social learning perspective

This provides an alternative explanation for an individual's biological or psychodynamic determinism. Based on behavioural theories, this approach provides a less rigid understanding of human aggression and emphasizes observable changes seen in a person's behaviour as a result of learning. More than 30 years ago Schultz (1960) claimed that the source of violence in a marital context is unhappy childhood experiences and deviant marital relationships. Gayford (1975) later carried out research, in conjunction with Chiswick Women's Aid, attempting to show the learned character of domestic violence within the family of origin.

The process of learning is based on the notion that aggressive responses to environmental cues that are followed by a desired outcome (i.e. positively reinforced) are more likely to be repeated in future. Conversely, aggressive responses that are followed by an undesired outcome (i.e. punished) are less likely to be repeated.

It was from this perspective that Albert Bandura (1973, 1977) developed the concept of 'Social Learning Theory'. This theoretical approach began to bridge the gap between the behaviourist and psychodynamic ideas. Without denying the power of the environment, Bandura (op. cit.) recognized the importance of internal processes, such as thoughts and feelings. Greater weight was given to cognitive processes as individuals in childhood and adulthood were seen to learn by observing and imitating others. Bandura (op. cit.) also introduced the concept of 'social reinforcers' where a behavioural response is followed by another person's positive or negative reaction, which in turn enhances or inhibits the chances of the same behavioural response happening again (see Chapter 3).

Therefore, according to social learning theory, people learn violent behaviour from observing aggressive role models. In support of this argument, Roy (1982b) has stated that four out of five abusive men ($n=4000$) were reported by their partners as observing their fathers abusing their mothers and/or being a victim of child abuse themselves. This was in comparison to only one-third of the abused women. Findings from many other studies have supported this observation (Buchanan, 1996).

There is evidence that violence between parents affects the children in a family. The behaviour and psychiatric problems discovered in children of violent marriages include truancy, aggressive behaviour at home and school, and anxiety disorders (Hughes and Barad, 1983; Jaffe, Wolfe, Wilson and Zak, 1986b; Levine, 1986; Davis and Carlson, 1987). It is suggested that such children learn aversive behaviour as a general style for controlling their social and physical environments, and that this style continues into adulthood (Gully and Dengerink, 1983; Browne and Saqi, 1987).

The special victim perspective

In direct contrast with the viewpoints considered so far are suggestions that the victims may be instrumental in some way in eliciting attachment or neglect. Friedrich and Boroskin (1976) review the complex reasons why a child may not fulfil the parent's expectations or demands. The dependant may in some way be regarded as 'special': for example, studies have found prematurity, low birth weight, illness and handicap to be associated with child abuse (Elmer and Gregg, 1967; Lynch and Roberts, 1977; Starr, 1988). Indeed, it has been pointed out that the physical unattractiveness of these children may be an important factor for child abuse (Berkowitz, 1989, 1993).

With respect to wife abuse, Gayford (1976) distinguished various types of victim of domestic violence, offering names and descriptions which imply that the cause of the behaviour lies with the victim. Others (for example, Walker and Browne, 1985) have argued that such consistent response patterns are situationally determined.

A link between the social learning and special victim perspectives has been suggested by Lewis (1987), who claims that some women learn to accept violent behaviour towards themselves as a result of childhood experiences.

Interaction Focused Models

Owing to past experiences, some abusing couples tend to establish aggressive relationships because they are familiar, and therefore comfortable, with violence as an expression of intimate concern and attachment. Indeed, Hanks and Rosenbaum (1978) have commented on the striking similarity between the abused woman's current marital relationship and that of her parents.

Therefore, some researchers have advocated a more interactive approach that includes the social relationships of the participants and their environmental setting, rather than seeking to isolate the person or situation. This entails a move from the individual psychological level to a study of social interactions between members of the family.

The interpersonal interactive perspective

Toch (1969), for example, in his study entitled *Violent Men*, looked not only at the characteristics of men but also at the context of their violence and the characteristics of their victims. He concluded that aggressive behaviour was associated with 'machismo' and the maintenance of a particular personal identity in relation to others. Such a situational approach may be seen in apparent conflict with studies showing developmental consistency in aggressive reactions (Olweus, 1979, 1984). Indeed, there is evidence for developmental consistency in an overall trait which can be labelled 'aggressiveness'. However, even in 'aggressive' individuals, inconsistency is found across situations for measures of aggression taken at one particular time (Kaplan, 1984).

The person–environment interactive perspective:

There are three basic criteria for understanding violent behaviour in terms of person–environment interaction (Hollin, 1993): (a) the *situation* in which the violence occurs; (b) the *person* in relation to individual thoughts, feelings and actions; and (c) the *impact* of the violent behaviour on the environment (see Figure 2.1). This perspective facilitates a 'situational analysis' of the context in which the violence occurs and a 'functional analysis' of the sequence of events that preceded the violent incident. Classically, this cognitive-behavioural ABC approach considers the **A**ntecedents, the **B**ehaviour and the **C**onsequences of the violence. Frude (1980, 1989) puts forward the notion of a causal chain leading to 'Critical incidence' of child abuse. This is a function of complex interactions between individuals and their social and physical environments. A model of 'Critical incidence' for family violence is presented in Figure 2.1, and can be described as follows:

1. Environmental stress situations which are usually long term—such as poverty—influence domestic abusers to assess their personal situations differently from non-abusing family members (i.e. as threatening).
2. They perceive a discrepancy between their expectations for life and social interactions and what is really happening. This often results in feelings of frustration.
3. Their response to such situations is more likely to be anger and emotional distress rather than a problem-solving strategy for change.
4. Lack of inhibitions with regard to violent expression, together with a lower threshold of tolerance, increases the possibility of violence. This is, of course, enhanced by disinhibitors such as alcohol or drugs.
5. When the above conditions prevail, even a facial expression, perceived as a 'dirty look', can lead to, or trigger, an incidence of violence.

These causal links result in the individual being more easily provoked to take violent action. Frude (1989) challenged the assumption that 'abusers' differ from 'non-abusers' and suggested that they might more usefully be considered as occupying different points on a continuum. For this reason he argued that

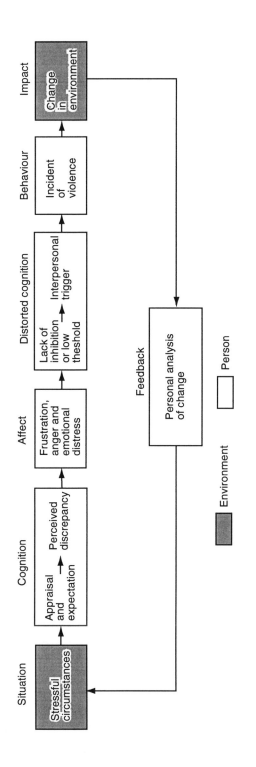

Figure 2.1 The cognitive-behavioural model of critical incidence (adapted and modified from Frude, 1980 1989; Hollin, 1993)

studies of interactions in the family may have much to contribute to our understanding of domestic violence and child abuse. Frude's causal chain model demonstrates the need to assess a violent person's own understanding of his or her environment as perceptions, attitudes and attributions will all influence the possibility of overt aggressive behaviour. In relation to this, Howells (1989) has developed the work of Novaco (1976, 1978) on anger arousal and its management and treatment. This work emphasizes the role played by cognitive processes, such as appraisal and expectations of external events in evoking aggressive responses (see Chapters 5 and 7).

Cognitive-behavioural approaches

These approaches to the study of aggression go quite a long way back. Dollard et al. (1939) were the early proponents of the frustration–aggression hypothesis. They focused attention on the role of frustration in its various forms as an intervening variable (along with perception, appraisal and other cognitive processes) in the manifestation, inhibition, and displacement of aggression. Research at this time did not continue along cognitive lines, perhaps because of the enthusiasm for more behavioural theories. Since the 1970s, however, clinicians and social workers have shown great interest in the study of anger and its cognitive determinants (e.g. Koneoni, 1975; Novaco, 1978).

Koneoni (1975) describes anger in terms of physiological arousal and cognitive labelling of that arousal which is a function of internal and external cues and of the person's overt and covert behaviour in the situation. For example, certain events function as 'provocations', particularly if a person is prone to provocation because of his or her dispositional state (e.g. being hungry, tired or tense). Anger is aroused because of the appraisal of that event as an aversive event. This, in turn, has a reciprocal relationship with these mediating cognitions; thus the experience of anger determines subsequent cognitions about the situation (see Chapter 5, Figure 5.3).

Berkowitz (1984) and Huesmann and Eron (1986) have developed a 'social cognitive' theory of aggression in which they describe violence witnessed in the home or in the media as being learned as a cognitive script to be used in later social situations. The aggressive script is learned as a way to behave, and its use will depend on the situation at the time of recall and the situation at the time the script is encoded in memory. Certain situations in the home environment may cue and trigger aggressive responses that relate to violence witnessed as a child. Aggression is elicited especially if the person is already frustrated or angry.

Overall, psychological explanations have moved away from accounting for family violence purely in terms of individual psychopathology towards models that attempt to integrate the characteristics of abusing parents, their children and the situation in which they live. Indeed, the authors of this book make the point that family violence cannot be explained by a single factor and that it is a consequence of complex interactions between individual, social and environmental influences (see Belsky, 1980, 1988; Browne, 1989a).

INTEGRATED EXPLANATIONS OF FAMILY VIOLENCE

The different explanations for the causes of violence between family members have been useful in that together they have served to emphasize the diverse nature of the variables involved in family violence. It must, therefore, be concluded that family violence cannot be explained by a single factor and that it is a multifactorial phenomenon (Gilbert, 1994).

Simple explanations make the solution of this pervasive problem appear too easy. For example, the 'Demon Rum' exploration of family violence is an old and popular one (Gelles and Cornell, 1990). It is true that alcohol appears to exacerbate pre-existing impulse control and emotional problems, increasing the likelihood of serious injuries (Coleman, 1980). This seems to be especially the case in the evening, at weekends and on holiday, when children and couples are alone with their problems and relaxing with drink (Frude, 1991).

However, the majority of alcohol-abusing individuals who are violent to members of their family when drinking heavily, also admit they have been violent while not under the influence of alcohol (Sonkin, Martin and Walker, 1985). Indeed, Rosenbaum and Maiuro (1990) state that: 'Alcohol abuse is neither a necessary nor sufficient condition for violent behaviour.'

Therefore, heavy drinking and drunkenness are not the causes of family violence but rather conditions that coexist with it, like many other factors. Nevertheless, they are often used as excuses for violent behaviour; personally, socially and legally (Pahl, 1985; Gelles, 1994b).

Psychosocial Model

The inadequacies of single factor explanations has led to a 'Psychosocial model' which integrates sociological and psychological explanations for family violence. Originally proposed by American researchers (e.g., Gelles, 1973), this model suggests that certain stress factors and adverse background influences may serve to predispose individuals to violence. As Frude (1980, 1989) suggested, the violence will occur in the presence of precipitating factors, such as a child misbehaving.

It has been claimed that the 'predisposing' factors may form a basis for identification of families 'at risk' of violence (e.g. Browne and Saqi, 1988a; Browne, 1989b). However, a more pertinent question is why the majority of such families under stress do not resort to violence. It may be that additional stress will only lead to family violence when adverse family interactions take place. Belsky (1980) and Browne (1989a) have taken this approach to child abuse. They conceptualize child maltreatment as a social-psychological phenomenon that is 'multiply determined by forces at work in the individual, the family, as well as in the community and the culture in which both the individual and the family are embedded' (Belsky 1980: 320). Given a particular combination of factors, an interactional style develops within the family and it is in the context of this interaction that abuse occurs. This approach may be equally adopted to explain other forms of family violence.

Multifactor Model of Family Violence

The study of social interactions and relationships can be seen as occupying a central and potentially integrating place in explaining the causes of aggression. In relation to violence between members of a family, Browne (1988, 1989a) presents a multifactor model of family violence which suggested that stress factors and background influences are mediated through the interpersonal relationships within the family (see Figure 2.2).

The model assumes that the 'situational stressors' comprise the following four components:

1. Relations between caregivers: inter-marriage, marital disputes, step-parent/cohabitee or separated/single parent.
2. Relations to children and elderly dependants: e.g. spacing between births, size of family, caregivers' attachments to expectations of their dependants.
3. Structural stress: poor housing, unemployment, social isolation, threats to the caregiver's authority, values and self-esteem.
4. Stress generated by the dependant(s): for example, an unwanted dependant—one who is incontinent, difficult to discipline, often ill, physically or mentally disabled, temperamental, frequently emotional or very demanding.

The chances of these situational stressors resulting in family violence are mediated by and depend on the interactive relationships within the family. A secure relationship between family members will 'buffer' any effects of stress and facilitate coping strategies on behalf of the family. By contrast, insecure or anxious relationships will not 'buffer' the family under stress and 'episodic overload', such as an argument or a child misbehaving, may result in a physical or emotional attack. Browne (1989a) suggests that overall this will have a negative effect on the existing interpersonal relationships and reduce any 'buffering' effects still further, making it easier for stressors to overload the system once again. Hence, a positive feedback ('vicious cycle') is set up which eventually leads to 'systematic overload', where constant stress results in repeated physical and emotional assaults. This situation becomes progressively worse without intervention and

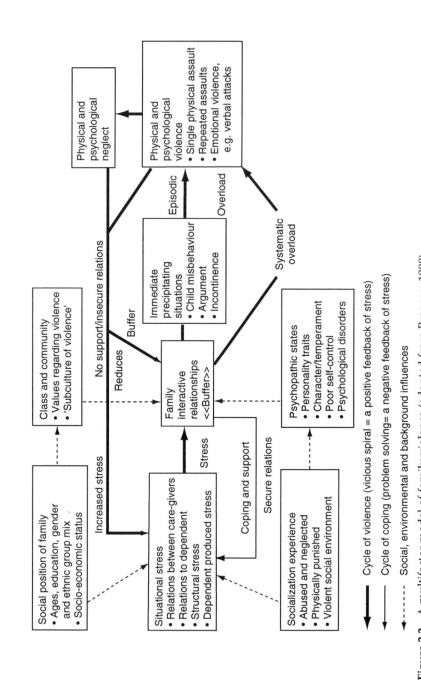

Figure 2.2 A multifactor model of family violence (adapted from Browne, 1988)

could be termed 'The Spiral of Violence'. In some cases violent individuals will cope with their aggressive feelings towards other family members by physical or emotional neglect in order to avoid causing a deliberate injury.

As indicated earlier, culture and community values may also affect attitudes and styles of interaction in family relationships which, in turn, will be influenced by the social position of individuals in terms of their age, sex, education, socioeconomic status, ethnic group and social class background.

According to Rutter (1985), aggression is a social behaviour within everyone's repertoire and he suggests that it is under control when the individual has high self-esteem, good relationships and stress is appropriately managed. However, the quality of relationships and responses to stress in the family will depend on the participant's personality and character traits and the possibility of personality disorder, such as low self-esteem, poor temperament control and gross mood swings. This may be a result of the early social experiences, which may indirectly affect behavioural investment in the family.

CONCLUSION

The causal factors of family violence must be considered within the context of the family's interpersonal network. Affectionate familial relationships act as a buffer against internal and external stress (Belsky, 1980; Browne and Saqi, 1987). An awareness and concern for other family members characterizes affectionate relationships (Browne, 1986; Hinde, 1979). It is important to consider maltreatment in the light of these family dynamics.

Two main features of violent families may be described as a lack of skill in handling conflict and discipline and high rates of aversive behaviour. These coercive family interactions have been previously described by Patterson (1982) and are seen as the primary focus for intervention as described in the next chapter.

In conclusion, the authors suggest that stress factors and background influences are mediated through the interpersonal relationships within the family. Indeed, it is these relationships that should be the focus of work on prevention, treatment and management of family violence and it is at this level that health and social service professionals can make a significant contribution in the short term by promoting positive interactions and 'inoculating' relationships against stress. The prevention of stress factors is a long-term process even in the most optimistic circumstances.

CHAPTER 3 Coercive family relationships

The previous chapters have challenged the stereotype of the family as a safe haven of care and protection. For health and social service professionals endeavouring to assess and intervene in families that have a history of family violence, there is no escape from the uncomfortable reality of hostile, coercive interaction between family members so frequently cited in newspapers, magazines and the professional literature. While there *is* much to be concerned about in what some think of an increasing phenomenon, it is vital to maintain a sense of proportion. The moral panic so cynically exploited by the media is not helpful in understanding what is a complex problem. An attempt to evaluate the available evidence in an objective manner may be of more value.

Let us look, for example, at parents who abuse their children. They tend to complain, threaten and criticize endlessly and often make plain their dislike for their children. They are described as intrusive and insensitive (Crittenden, 1988); also as 'blame-oriented' and inclined to attribute the worst of motives and intentions to their offspring (Wolfe, 1985, 1987). Such punitive characteristics, as Frude (1991) observes, 'predispose the parent to become angered by the child's behaviour, or increase the likelihood of a disciplinary response'. All too often discipline—because of the lack of knowledge of alternatives, or for 'ideological' reasons or the need to give vent to fury and frustration—takes the form of physical punishment. Furthermore, its essential ineffectiveness leads to an escalation which may reach dangerous levels of intensity.

In the literature on what are so often referred to collectively as 'abusive parents', such generic labelling is likely to encourage stereotyping and 'pathologizing' and thus blind us to their individuality and the essential normality (in the sense of being commonplace) of some of their predicaments. This is *not* to condone abuse, but to argue for keeping a sense of balance. A majority of the cases of physical abuse involve relatively minor physical injuries; and most of these take place in what parents perceive to be *disciplinary encounters* (Wolfe, 1991). This is a critical consideration in setting a realistic, but optimistic, agenda for one's interventions. Frude (1991) expresses it clearly:

> The high level of concern both by public and by professionals regarding the serious and dramatic injuries sustained by relatively few children may prove to have the most welcome subsidiary effect of increasing the general societal support available for the very large number of troubled parents and their children. This is unlikely to happen, however, if undue attention is drawn to those very parents who systematically and sadistically torture their children. It is this distorted image of the abusing parent which may lead to the withdrawal of any sympathy towards all parents involved in non-accidental injury and their stigmatization as 'monsters', 'inhuman' and 'a race apart'.

The hard-pressed social worker is often faced with a 'chicken–egg'—which came first?—dilemma. Many abused children behave in an antisocial, provocative manner. Indeed, they may manifest serious disorders of conduct which spill over into delinquent activities (Herbert, 1987a). Frude (1991) makes the point that although disturbance may be the result—in part or in whole—of a history of parental mishandling and abuse (and as such acknowledged), this fact is, in the final count, of limited relevance. In the 'here and now', which is the overriding concern of social and other professional workers, the child's behaviour (which frequently takes an aggressive form) triggers an incident that results in an aggressive counter-attack by the parents or siblings (see Straus, Gelles and Steinmetz, 1980). Abused children harass their peers and parents far more frequently than non-abused children (George and Main, 1979).

The question is: can we turn to any theory (or theories) for assistance in understanding and mitigating these awesome family problems?

THEORETICAL MODELS AND INTERVENTION

The picture which emerges from a plethora of studies of the different forms of aggression expressed between family members, is that family violence is a many-sided phenomenon, caused and maintained by a widely diverse number of mechanisms which are associated with a variety of physiological, psychological and social factors (see Chapter 2).

In the domain of psychology, researchers and clinicians have used theoretical frameworks as diverse as psychoanalysis, social learning, family process, social exchange and many other general or specific theories. Accordingly, they propose divergent explanations which lead to very different types of intervention. For example, an approach based on psychoanalytic theory will focus on the exploration of intrapsychic conflicts and ego lacunae; an approach based on family process theory might lead to a family therapy intervention. A behaviour therapist would look to social learning principles and place the emphasis on behavioural and cognitive contingencies and the availability of adequate models (exemplars) of social behaviour. All these approaches have generated a considerable amount of theoretical and empirical research and have, at least in some cases, provided the basis for successful interventions (see Frude, 1991; Herbert, 1993; Webster-Stratton and Herbert, 1994). It is sadly true, however, that none of them alone provides a complete explanation. Nevertheless, the present authors have attempted in Chapter 2 to formulate a multifactorial integrated model to account for much of the diversity of dysfunctional attributes that constitute the far from unitary phenomenon referred to economically, but simplistically, as 'family violence'.

It may be that a particular model accounts more elegantly, parsimoniously or heuristically for a particular type of family dysfunction, or for a specific category of hostile or hurtful relationship (e.g. spouse abuse, elder abuse, parent abuse or child abuse) than another. However, little effort has been made to assess which of the different models provides the best predictors of abusive interactions between family members or which type of intervention (if any) is most cost-effective for a particular type of family violence. Furthermore, apart from a few exceptions (e.g.

Gerald Patterson's model of coercive family processes), research in this field has tended to neglect, at least theoretically, the *systemic* ramifications of aggression, and the reciprocity (recursiveness) of the use of coercive power as it affects the family *qua* family (see Patterson, 1982).

Coercion and Social Learning Theory

The concept of coercive power has led to the formulation of a theory concerned with the crucial role of coercive interactions in the lives of certain families. It is particularly salient to families whose members are mutually abusive. For example, this theory (developed and tested notably by Patterson) illuminates the manner in which adults' and children's aggressive behaviours can serve to instigate and maintain (particularly through the operation of negative reinforcement) the antisocial, hostile behaviour of other family members. In his book *Coercive Family Process*, Patterson (1982) provides evidence for the coercion theory which he applies to the events that escalate from low-key incidents of an aversive kind (so common in social interaction and, indeed, family life) to the high-density, high-intensity acts of violence which characterize child and spouse abuse.

Before exploring these ideas in more detail it would seem appropriate to touch on social learning theory—the wider theoretical framework within which the coercion hypothesis is firmly rooted. Social learning theory is one of the 'middle-range' theories that Gelles and Straus (1988) and the present authors suggest are needed to account for *some* (certainly not all) of the phenomena of family violence (see Herbert, 1987a; Patterson, 1982). A consistent theoretical framework is of vital importance to the social or health worker trying to make sense of, predictions about, and intervention plans for, the dysfunctional interactions of children and their parents. Social learning theory, with its emphasis on the active nature of learning, the social context in which it takes place, and the role of cognition and meaning, is well-suited to such a remit in social and clinical work (see Bandura, 1977). The view put forward here is that much abnormal behaviour in children and adults (our particular concern is the caregivers) does not differ greatly from *normal* behaviour in its development, its persistence and the way it can be changed.

APPLIED SOCIAL LEARNING THEORY: BEHAVIOURAL WORK

Social learning theory as a basis for a theory of behavioural and cognitive *change* (therapy/modification) is broadly conceived. Behaviour therapy, or to use our preferred term (for its interdisciplinary and systemic connotations) 'behavioural family work', represents a philosophy of change rather than a technology or collection of 'ad hoc' techniques. It is based upon a *broad* and empirically based theory of normal and abnormal behaviour.

The discipline of behavioural work has diversified beyond recognition since its formal beginnings in the late 1950s and early 1960s. It is no longer the monolithic entity it once was, and although the approach emphasizes the principles of classical and operant conditioning, it is not restricted to them. In the light of this statement, and given that several varieties of learning are central to the applied social learning theory paradigm, it is worth reviewing some of them, albeit briefly

Learning by Direct Reinforcement

This perspective begins from a focus on the stimulus which impinges on the person; the person then responds with behaviour. Learning may be said to have taken place when a given stimulus regularly elicits a given response. The stimulus–response association is generally established by reinforcement which may be stimulus-contingent or response-contingent, providing two different learning paradigms:

1. *Stimulus-contingent reinforcement* is referred to as classical conditioning. A previously neutral stimulus (say, a tone) is repeatedly paired with an 'unconditioned stimulus' (say a puff of air to the eye) and gradually acquires its response-eliciting properties (it brings about an eye blink). The response of the indi-

vidual (the eye blink) has, in technical parlance, been 'conditioned' to the tone (the 'conditioned stimulus').
2. *Response-contingent reinforcement* is referred to as instrumental or operant conditioning. A mother wishes to teach her young child a particular skill—for example, asking to go to the toilet. After explanations and prompts the child's behaviour is 'shaped' by positive reinforcement such as words of encouragement and praise whenever it approximates to the required skill sequence. When this skilled response has been mastered it may be elicited repeatedly by making reinforcement contingent on its correct performance.

All forms of learning which are generally functional (adaptive) in their effects—i.e. they help children to adapt to life's demands—can in certain circumstances contribute to maladjustment. In such circumstances learning is dysfunctional in its effects. Thus a youngster who learns usefully on the basis of classical and operant 'conditioning' processes to avoid dangerous situations, can also learn (maladaptively) to fear and avoid school or social gatherings. A parent may unwittingly reinforce temper tantrums by attending to them. The operant equations, which are commonly discussed with parents in training groups, are simple but powerful:

Acceptable behaviour + Reinforcement =
More acceptable behaviour

Acceptable behaviour + No reinforcement =
Less acceptable behaviour

Unacceptable behaviour + Reinforcement =
More unacceptable behaviour

Unacceptable behaviour + No reinforcement =
Less unacceptable behaviour

For all the usefulness of these theories of learning, it is obvious that, as children develop, the speed and complexity of their learning are difficult to explain in terms of direct reinforcement and punishment alone. It became apparent to psychologists in the 1950s that their behavioural/learning theories were inadequate to deal with the subtleties of normal and abnormal behaviour. Social experience and the opportunity to observe another's

There are two categories of contemporary influence to consider in an assessment leading to a formulation and eventually (if appropriate) an intervention in an abusive family: Firstly, circumstances (e.g. physical or verbal attacks, deprivation, frustration, conflict and exposure to disruptive models) which *instigate* or *maintain* (by direct, vicarious and self-reinforcement) activities of a violent kind. Secondly, over the longer term, the individual's *reinforcement history* is of significance. The findings (Herbert, 1987a) suggest that a combination of lax discipline (especially with regard to the offspring's acts of aggression) combined with hostile attitudes in the parents produces very aggressive and poorly controlled behaviour in the offspring. A number of factors are likely to contribute to such inept parenting and an unsatisfactory level of care and control. Among these are poor models of parenting in the parents' families of origin, social disadvantage and the child's temperament (Herbert, 1991).

DEVELOPMENTAL ASPECTS OF AGGRESSION

Looked at developmentally, one observes that children are born with a repertoire of 'aversive' behaviours which they elaborate as they grow up. These behaviours have survival value when age-appropriate, but are signs of maladjustment when used intensively or persistently when the child is older, becomes potentially more mature, and is capable of socially modulated behaviour. They contribute to an atmosphere of family distress and hostility when engaged in frequently (see Table 3.1).

The worrying long-term sequence gets under way when parents fail to label (cognitively structure) or sanction effectively non-compliant and coercive (e.g. oppositional) behaviours manifested by their offspring. There is frequently a lack of contingent consequences among the family members; that is to say, the probability of receiving a positive, neutral or aversive consequence for coercive behaviour seems to be independent of the individual's behaviour. In some families there is gross inconsistency; indeed, there may be positive consequences for the child's antisocial behaviours and even punishment for their rare pro-social actions (Patterson, 1976). This is likely to lead to the persis-

Table 3.1   The definitions and mean base rates (per minute) of aversive behaviour for members of distressed families (adapted from Reid, 1978)

Code categories	Definitions	Problem boys $N=27$	Mothers $N=27$	Fathers $N=18$	Siblings $N=54$
Command negative	Command in which immediate compliance is demanded, aversive consequences threatened, sarcasm or humiliation directed towards receiver	0.008	0.046	0.023	0.008
Cry	Whining or sobbing sounds	0.019	0.000	0.000	0.024
Disapproval	Verbal or gestural criticism of another person's behaviour or characteristics	0.134	0.314	0.182	0.120
Dependency	Request for assistance when person is obviously capable of doing task unaided	0.007	0.003	0.000	0.008
Destructive	When a person damages, soils or breaks something	0.031	0.000	0.000	0.011
High rate	Physically active repetitive behaviour which is likely to be annoying	0.044	0.000	0.000	0.042
Humiliate	Embarrassing, shaming or making fun of another person	0.020	0.011	0.015	0.015
Ignore	Intentional and deliberate non-response to an initiated behaviour	0.005	0.023	0.019	0.010
Non-comply	A person does not do what is requested in response to a command, command negative, or a dependency within 12 seconds of the request being made	0.092	0.011	0.009	0.064
Negativism	A neutral verbal message delivered in a tone of voice which conveys an *attitude* of 'Don't bug me'; also included are defeatist statements	0.115	0.019	0.012	0.059
Physical negative	Physical attack or attempt to attack another person	0.042	0.019	0.003	0.021
Tease	Act of annoying, pestering, mocking or making fun of another person	0.050	0.001	0.014	0.028
Whine	A slurring, nasal, or high-pitched voice; the content of the statement is irrelevant	0.036	0.001	0.000	0.052
Yell	Shouts, yells or loud talk	0.057	0.009	0.000	0.036
	Sum of means for all 14 aversive behaviours	0.660	0.457	0.277	0.498
	Mean total aversive*	0.047	0.033	0.020	0.036

*This mean is obtained from the sum of the 14 means. Typically, this score is obtained by summing up 14 scores for each subject and calculating the mean of that distribution.

tence of antisocial and coercive actions as part of the child's behavioural repertoire (see Figure 3.1).

THE COERCIVE SPIRAL

What is proposed with regard to particular incidents within dyads (parent–child; sibling–sibling) is that an aversive stimulus such as hitting, teasing or crying is applied contingently and repeatedly by one member of the dyad to increase or decrease certain behaviours displayed by the other member. The impact of these aversive behaviours is reflected in changes in the ongoing behaviours of *both* members involved in the aggressive inter-changes. It is hypothesized that it is the immediate shift in the ongoing behaviour of one individual that is reinforcing for the other.

A typical parent–child example is the confrontation between a mother and her wilful toddler. When the child is commanded to do something or desist from doing something he or she is quite likely to react with rage—a frightening display of temper. The parent insists, so the child escalates the tantrum. A vicious circle is often set in motion, the stage being set for increasingly provocative and prolonged exchanges. If the tantrum is intense or persistent enough the parent may acquiesce. Conceding to the child's defiance, however, tends not to happen every time, pro-ducing what is in effect an 'intermittent schedule' of reinforce-ment for coercive, non-compliant actions. This makes for an intractable pattern of difficult behaviour in future situations of a similar kind. The parent's *capitulation* is also reinforced by the relief engendered by the termination of the child's tantrum. This process of reciprocal reinforcement by the removal of aversive stimuli has been described as the 'negative reinforcer trap' (Wahler, 1976).

Now let us look at a coercive sequence between siblings:

(a) John annoys Sophie by taking her toy.
(b) Sophie reacts by hitting John.
(c) John then stops annoying Sophie, thus negatively reinforc-ing her aggressive response.

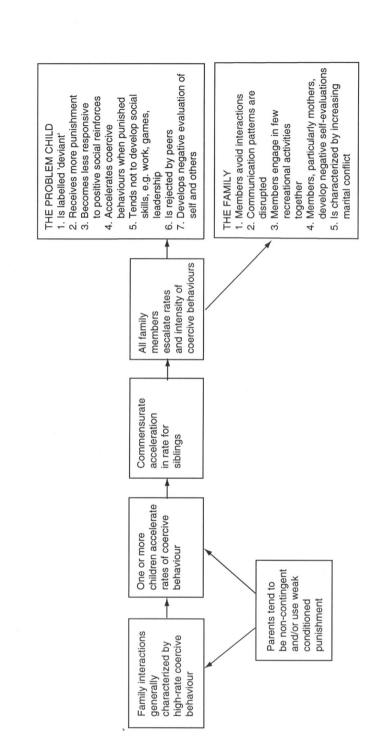

Figure 3.1 Coercive family interactions (adapted from Patterson, 1982)

Sophie has coerced John into terminating his annoying behaviour. A coercive spiral is quite likely to be set in motion, an escalation of attack and counter-attack. To continue the sequence:

(d) John may, of course, react to Sophie's hitting, not by desisting from hijacking Sophie's toy, but by hitting back in an attempt to terminate Sophie's aggression.
(e) Sophie now responds to John's aggression with more intense counter-aggression.

This exchange could continue until it is interrupted by mother and father or until one of the parties is negatively reinforced by the other child submitting. We can see how, over time (if not firmly managed by caregivers), this pattern carries within it the seeds for the perpetuation of aggressive behaviour as a fixture in the child's behavioural repertoire.

Conflict between siblings has been implicated in the exacerbation and maintenance of conduct disorders. The siblings of aggressive children are very likely to initiate and sustain aggressive interactions within the brother/sister context, the most pronounced effects of such exchanges being observed in middle childhood and early adolescence (see Gelles and Cornell, 1990; Herbert, 1987b). Specifically, in that age group, aggressive sibling exchanges contributed so much to the prediction of antisocial behaviour, that irritable exchanges of the mother and the target child added little to prognoses.

A child's oppositional behaviour is often maintained by the contingent application of positive social reinforcement in the form of parental attention. Such attention can come in a variety of forms, including verbal reprimands (scolding, nagging), reasoning with the child, or simply trying to be caring and understanding by discussing the misdemeanour at great length. In response to parental actions of this kind, the child may behave in a cooperative manner, thus reciprocally reinforcing the parental intervention. Wahler (1976) calls this process the 'positive reinforcer trap'. In most cases, oppositional behaviour is maintained by a combination of both positive and negative reinforcement.

PAIN CONTROL

Interestingly, parents of aggressive children display a significantly greater proportion of what have been called pain control methods—commands, criticisms, high rates of threats, anger, nagging and negative consequences—than parents of non-clinic-referred children. Patterson (1982) found that parents of 'anti-social' children issue more negative and vague commands than normal control counterparts; their most common failures in parenting skills consisted of inept discipline—scolding, threatening, 'nattering' and nagging (toward the child)—and the use of frequent and intense physical punishment.

Johnson and Lobitz (1974) have reported that the best discriminating factor between 'normal' children and children referred for psychological treatment was a parental negativeness score. There was also a clear trend for parents of referred children to give more commands. They were actually able to provide conditions (by instruction) in which parents in 12 families could manipulate the deviancy level in their children (aged from 4 to 6) according to prediction. They did this by increasing their rate of ignoring or commanding their offspring and of being negative, restrictive, disapproving and non-compliant.

It is clear that early learning and development are important in the evolution of hostile styles of behaviour; knowledge of such factors may well influence the method adopted when planning an intervention with a violent family. It is certainly likely to be systemic in approach. The reasons are plain when one looks at Patterson's (1982) list of possibilities for children's failure to substitute more adaptive, more mature behaviour for their infantile and primitive coercive repertoire:

- The parents are neglectful in teaching pro-social skills (e.g. they seldom reinforce the use of language or other self-help skills).
- They provide rich schedules of positive reinforcement for coercive behaviours.
- They allow siblings to increase the frequency of aversive stimuli which are terminated when the target child uses coercive behaviour.

- They use punishment inconsistently for coercive behaviour. They tend to use weak-conditioned punishers as consequences for coercive activities.

How a family-orientated programme might be planned to deal with such problems is discussed in Chapters 9 and 12.

From Coercion to Violence

Patterson (1982) reports that inspection of observational data suggests that children's aversive behaviours tend to come in bursts. For example, given the occurrence of one response, there tends to be a significant increase in the probability that the same response will recur or persist. Children who are described as highly aggressive are characterized by a longer duration of such behavioural bursts and also by shorter time intervals between them. Comparing non-problem boys with socially aggressive children, the latter are more likely to make a second noxious response, having just presented one perhaps only a few seconds before.

Observations suggest that mothers and siblings in abusive families are the ones most affected in the coercive spirals described earlier, because their own rates of aversive behaviour are significantly higher than those manifested by their counterparts in non-problem families (Patterson, 1982). As coercive sequences lengthen in duration, there is an increased likelihood of physical aggression by the parents and among the siblings. Although the parents escalate their threats and nagging in response to the child's coercive behaviour, they are unlikely to follow through on their threats. However, at unpredictable intervals, they may explode and use extreme forms of physical punishment. Children with conduct disorders are, not surprisingly, at risk of being physically abused (Herbert, 1995).

Wahler and Dumas (1985), addressing the question of why coercive parent–child interactions persist and indeed escalate, put forward two hypotheses: the compliance hypothesis and the predictability hypothesis. Together they help to explain how some parents and children ratchet up their aversive exchanges into progressively more 'painful', coercive (and sometimes dangerous) interactions. The 'compliance hypothesis' (as we have seen) proposes that the mother's or father's submission to the child's demands and aversive behaviour acts as a *positive (intermittent) reinforcer* for the child's aggression and there is thus a major influence on the maintenance of this kind of behaviour. The parent complies to 'turn off' the child's temper tantrum, hitting, screaming or whatever. The pay-off of relief from painful stimuli, with its escape and avoidance implications, makes further parental compliance more and more likely (*negative reinforcement*).

The 'predictability hypothesis' suggests that aversive behaviour of aggressive children may be maintained in some cases by the consistency of their parent's aversive reactions to it. At least they know where they stand because parental reactions to their positive behaviour are so unpredictable.

The ramifications of aggressive behaviour are ever-widening if persistent: children exhibiting high rates of aggressive and coercive behaviour (having learned it in the home) are likely to be rejected by their peers. Engaging in non-compliant, coercive behaviours in the classroom is likely to result in decreased opportunities for the child to learn, in lowered academic competence and in costly confrontation with teachers (see discussion of bullying in Chapter 8).

A THERAPEUTIC APPROACH TO FAMILY VIOLENCE

The approach to interventions in cases of family violence is dealt with elsewhere; nevertheless, we can summarize some of the issues in a therapeutic agenda. As a general principle, we can confidently claim that the maintenance of aggressive behaviour is in large part dependent on its consequences. Aggressive actions that have 'rewarding' consequences (and this might include 'letting off steam' by a frustrated parent) tend to be repeated, whereas those that are unrewarded or punished are likely to be reduced in frequency or eliminated. In the case of habitually coercive families the cues or messages are frequently negative, with the 'sound and fury' of incessant criticism, nagging, crying, shouting and so on.

The position taken by Patterson (1982)—and he qualifies it carefully—is that the control of antisocial behaviour requires the contingent use of some kind of punishment. This claim seems, on the surface at least, to run counter to the many studies from developmental psychology that investigated parental reports about their punitive practices. They consistently show a positive correlation with antisocial child behaviour (Feshbach, 1964). Parents of problem children report that they use punishment *more frequently* than parents of normal children; also their punitive practices are more likely to be extreme. As we have seen in this chapter, the parents of socially aggressive children do punish more often in reaction to sibling and problem child aggressive behaviour.

The *modelling-frustration hypothesis* is formulated by Bandura (1973). He maintains that in exercising punitive control, prohibitive agents model aggressive styles of behaviour not unlike those they wish to discourage in others. Recipients may, on later occasions, adopt similar aggressive solutions in coping with the problems confronting them. He adds that although the direction of causal relationships cannot be unequivocally established from correlational data, it is clear from controlled studies that aggressive modelling breeds aggression. Here then is the seedcorn for intergenerational violence, but why does aggressive behaviour that is punished not diminish or disappear, as would be predicted from learning theory?

Berkowitz (1993) emphasizes the likelihood that it is *the kind of punishment* used by parents of aggressive children that may be ineffective. He makes a case for the necessity of punishing aggressive child behaviours, but in the context of being a warm, loving parent, who uses reasoning or explanations in conjunction with *non-violent punishment*, such as time out. This view reflects the Patterson team's conclusion from a decade of intervention studies with families of aggressive children. Time-out and analogous consequences (such as work details or loss of privileges) are definitely aversive; however, they are *not* violent. Patterson vouches for their relative effectiveness—a matter we explore in Chapter 9. Certainly, there is overwhelming evidence that extremes of physical punishment, perpetrated against a background of uncaring indifference or outright rejection, constitute the slippery slope for the creation of a violent youngster (Herbert, 1991).

Communication

Communication between members in dysfunctional families may not be so much aversive as impoverished or almost non-existent. Given that all social interaction involves mutual influence because of human interdependence, and given the key role of cooperation in human societies, something has to be done to change the way in which coercive family members try to influence or control one another. Mutual influence is most potent when it has its source within a happy and cohesive family. Indeed, the presence of family cohesion has a marked effect on the psychological well-being of family members. The criteria of cohesiveness provide us with some important if difficult intervention goals for families where such attributes are absent or low in frequency:

- Members frequently indulge in shared activity.
- Interactions that are warm are common and interactions that are hostile are infrequent among members.
- There is full and accurate communication between members of the family.
- Valuations of other members of the family are generally favourable; critical judgements are rare.
- Individuals tend to perceive other members as having favourable views of them.
- Members are visibly affectionate.
- They show high levels of satisfaction and morale and are optimistic about the future stability of the family group.

When these features are absent, the family members who are particularly at risk are those already vulnerable for other reasons: the young, the elderly and those coping with stress.

CONCLUSION

This brief review of the theoretical perspectives on assessment and intervention issues with regard to coercive family relationships sets the scene for an examination of each type of family violence in turn, together with relevant concepts of prevention specific to each type.

CHAPTER 4 Predicting spouse maltreatment

The most intense of all personal relationships is that between two sexually intimate partners. Intimate partner or spouse refers to a broad category of relationships usually, but not exclusively, between similarly aged adults who are married or unmarried, who live together or apart and who are of the same sex or opposite sex. Indeed, these intimate relationships are extremely complex, involving a series of interactions at a conscious and an unconscious level between two people. These interactions affect expectations, judgements and feelings about each other which, in turn, affect the overt behaviour shown to one another. The events surrounding the formation, maintenance, breakdown and termination of intimate relationships have dominated both professional and non-professional literature (Duck, 1986).

Being involved in an intimate relationship is associated with experiencing strong emotional feelings of belonging and commitment towards another individual. This close attachment means that the individual is missed when absent and that emotional distress is caused if the relationship is ended. Indeed, the most intense of human emotions arise during the formation, maintenance, disruption and renewal of intimate relationships to which there is some emotional attachment (Bowlby, 1977).

RELATIONSHIP DIFFICULTIES

A large number of factors influence the breakdown of intimate relationships. For example, Jacobson and Gurman (1986) identified the following difficulties and psychological disorders affecting relationships for their *Clinical Handbook of Marital Therapy*:

- *Relationship difficulties* surrounding, unmarried and remarried couples, separation and divorce, jealousy and extra-marital affairs, cross-cultural relationships and homosexual partnerships.
- *Psychological disorders* involving agoraphobia, depression, alcoholism, schizophrenia, narcissism and abnormal eating.

In addition, significant personal loss in terms of loved ones (bereavement), physical or mental health (disability) and economic well-being will also seriously 'stress' close relationships.

To further complicate the issue, the stage of the relationship at which these difficulties emerge will influence the prognosis for adaptive change and the probability of the couple remaining together. In addition, Reichman (1989) describes the way people unconsciously sabotage intimate relationships by constant criticism, by being tyrannical or jealous, by sulking, by playing the martyr, being overly clinging or constantly trying to please (see Chapter 10). These may be egocentric individuals with high achievement motivation, competitiveness, individualism and ambition, who have as a result high levels of marital breakdown (Bentler and Newcomb, 1978).

Spouse maltreatment may be said to have occurred in the breakdown of an intimate relationship when there is evidence of physical or psychological injury, material deprivation, emotional and sexual abuse, marital rape, pornography or forced relation that has been inflicted upon the victim by the partner (London, 1978). This differs from earlier definitions of spouse abuse (e.g. Gayford, 1975; Martin, 1976) which purely focused on acts of physical damage directed towards the partner. It should be pointed out that the asexual language of this definition is deliberate. Studies of randomly selected families have shown that women report themselves to be at least as violent as men in terms of hitting or throwing things at their partners (Steinmetz, 1977a; Bland and Orn, 1986; Smith et al., 1992) and this has been supported by studies on college students on both sides of the Atlantic (Deal and Wampler, 1986; Browne and Slater, 1997).

Physical aggression, abusive violence and sexual assault have become accepted as male rather than female attributes in intimate relationships, and official reports on the topic reflect this belief (e.g. House of Commons Home Affairs Committee, 1993a, 1993b; Victim Support, 1992). However, there is some evidence to show that this is not always the case: Brand and Kidd (1986) compared physical and sexual violence in heterosexual and female homosexual partners and found that, in 'committed relationships', forced sex (9%, 7%) and physical abuse (27%, 25%) had a similar percentage of occurrence for both groups. The existence of dating and spouse abuse with lesbian relationships is now well established (Levy and Lobel, 1991; Renzetti, 1992). In heterosexual relationships Straus, Gelles and Steinmetz (1980, 1988) found that 12.1% of husbands versus 11.6% of wives had inflicted at least one violent act during an argument with their partners in the year covered by their National US Survey. A Mori poll, commissioned by the BBC television programme 'Here and Now' (1994), constituted the first nationwide survey in the UK looking at domestic violence towards men and women. The poll also found similar rates to the US Survey and also no gender differences in the use of violence to partners.

Thus, violence is not always unidirectional (men to women). Indeed, Gelles (1987a) and Straus (1993) suggest that 'marital violence' is often bidirectional, with similar rates of aggressive behaviour for husbands and wives. Female anger, hostility and violence are now generally recognized but are still largely condemned as psychological abnormalities in women (Kirsta, 1994).

THE EXTENT OF SPOUSE MALTREATMENT

Violence

Research on the prevalence and incidence of spouse abuse, often referred to as 'domestic violence', has been hindered by a general lack of awareness about the problem, a general acceptance and normalization of family violence, and a denial that a problem exists (Dobash and Dobash, 1979; Star, 1980; Finkelhor and Yllö, 1985; Yllö, 1993). Nevertheless, a number of sources have been used to measure the amount of spouse abuse reported, such as police records, medical case notes, divorce applications, family interviews, and surveys of violent crime (Morley and Mullender, 1994).

In the UK there are no regularly updated statistics on wife abuse other than the British Crime Survey (Mayhew, Maung and Mirrless-Black, 1993) which shows that the problem is extensive (see Chapter 1, Figure 1.2). The survey showed that 56% of all assaults on women were domestic, compared to only 8% of assaults on men. Surveys in the USA and the UK, specifically concerned with domestic violence, show that at least one in four married women say they have been hit by their husband (Straus, Gelles and Steinmetz, 1980, 1988; Painter, 1991). As many as one-third of women in the UK experience severe physical violence from a male partner at some time during their adult lives. Furthermore, one in ten report such violence annually, 75% from their current partner and 25% from their former partner (Mooney, 1993).

Severe violence to wives on a regular basis is estimated to occur in 7% of USA families (Dutton, 1988). A rather disturbing finding is the abuse of pregnant women and teenagers (McFarlane, 1991; Newberger et al., 1992). In a study of 290 pregnant women, Helton (1986) found that 15.2% reported a battering before their current pregnancy and 8.3% reported a battering during their current pregnancy.

From the perpetrator perspective, a Canadian survey revealed that one man in ten committed at least one serious assault against his female partner (MacLeod, 1989). Much higher figures have been reported in a London sample (Andrews and Brown, 1988), showing that 37% of men would resort to violence in a conflict situation, and that twice as many would psychologically abuse their partner.

From police records in England, McClintock (1978) reported that 15% of all indictable crimes against the person were committed within the family. For spouse and parent abuse combined, he found the victims to be 74% women and 26% men. From police records in Scotland, Dobash and Dobash (1979, 1987) reported that the second largest category of interpersonal violence was assault on wives (25.1%), the most common form of violence being between unrelated males (37.2%). Of the 1051 cases of violence within the home recorded by the police, 'wife beating' represented 76.8%, 'child beating' 10.5%, and 'husband beating'

1.2% of cases. While 97.4% of the offending family members were male, 94.4% of the victims were female with four out of five requiring medical treatment for their injuries. However, domestic incidents represent only 12% of calls to the Liverpool police (Pease et al., 1991) and it is argued that spouse violence is both the most under-reported and under-recorded crime (Smith, 1989). Surveys of victims suggest that between 14 and 27% of domestic assaults are reported to the police (Dutton, 1988; Jones, MacLean and Young, 1986) and only a small minority are recorded (Edwards, 1989).

The under-reporting of domestic violence is exemplified by figures from separation and divorce proceedings. Three-quarters of domestic assaults reported to the police occur after separation (Hart et al., 1990). In the USA, the study reported that 32% of middle-class and 40% of working-class couples mention physical abuse as a major complaint in divorce proceedings. However, a more recent US Harris poll showed that 66% of separated or divorced women report violence in their previous relationships (Browne, 1989c). Similarly in the UK, 56–59% of separated and divorced women had been hit by their previous husband (Evason, 1982; Painter, 1991).

Police figures give markedly different percentages to those reported in national or college surveys. The predominance of male offenders and female victims in police records may indicate that male to female violence is more serious.

Not surprisingly, there has been much less emphasis on men as victims of spouse violence with only Murray Straus and his colleagues, at the University of New Hampshire, taking a more holistic approach to violence in the home. Their large survey in the US (Straus, 1979; Straus, Gelles and Steinmetz, 1980, 1988) has shown that 'marital violence' occurs once a year or more in 16% of families. Overall, 28% of marriages reported experience of marital violence at some time. Within these violent homes approximately a quarter of the couples had just a male offender, a quarter had just a female offender and in half the couples both partners were reported to be violent.

In terms of 'abusive' violence, the same study revealed that 3.8% of the wives and 4.6% of the husbands were battered by their partners during the previous 12-month period. When these data were first reported as evidence of a 'battered husband syndrome' (Steinmetz, 1977b), they received much criticism, as the survey did not detect whether the wives' violence was in retaliation or self-defence and therefore the data may have been misinter preted (Pleck et al., 1978).

Indeed, for a number of women who have killed their husbands, the US courts have declared the act legally justified as self-defence, especially when the act of killing the man occurred after a long period of violent suffering by the woman (Browne, 1987; Ewing, 1987). However, repeat victimization is extremely common in spouse maltreatment. Indeed, the vast majority (66–90%) of women who experience violence by their partners report regular incidents of aggressive behaviour from them (Hanmer and Stanko, 1985; Andrews and Brown, 1988). In quantitative terms, surveys have shown that one-third of women in violent relationships are attacked more than six times a year and, on average, the female victim is seriously injured four times a year (Mooney, 1993). Pease et al. (1991) outlined the probability of a repeat attack in the violent home. Their Manchester survey showed that after an initial violent incident, 35% of victims suffer a second attack within five weeks of the first, and after a second violent incident 45% of victims suffer a third attack within five weeks of the second.

Domestic homicide is thought to be the end result of a long history of escalating violence, ending in the man killing his wife or the wife finally 'taking her revenge' or 'defending herself' after years of suffering (Browne, 1987; Ewing, 1987). The incidence of domestic murders has been reported to be 40% of all homicides in the US (Curtis, 1974); 45% of the domestic homicide victims were men and 55% were women. In the UK, there is a greater difference in the disproportionate number of male and female homicide victims, which suggests that where male and female spouse violence is interactive, the woman suffers most. From 1983 to 1990, approximately one-fifth of all homicide victims were women killed by current or former male partners. This represented between 42 and 49% of all female homicide victims. By contrast, only 7–11% of male homicide victims were killed by their female spouse (Home Office, 1992; Morley and Mullender,

1994). In approximately one-third of domestic homicides, the couple were no longer living together when the partner was killed (Edwards, 1989). A similar finding has been reported for marital rape, in that one-third of victims are separated from their husband at the time the rape occurred.

Rape

Finkelhor and Yllö (1982, 1985) put the question 'Has your spouse ever used physical force or threat to try to have sex with you?' to a randomized sample of 323 women in Boston. The response was that '10% said yes'. An analysis of the cases of 'marital rape' revealed that the majority (82%) occurred after the spouses had separated. A UK survey of 1236 women living in London (Hall, 1985) revealed a similar finding in that 9% had at some time been forced by their spouse to have sex. Russell (1982, 1990) in her work on this subject interviewed 930 women in San Francisco, 644 of whom were married. For respondents who were married, 4% had experienced forced sex but no other physical violence, 14% had been raped and battered and 12% had been battered but not raped.

Until the 1980s, few professionals considered the concept of 'marital rape' and the public generally minimalized forced sex in marriage as not 'real' rape. However, Finkelhor and Yllö (1985) categorized forced sex in marriage into three types, based on Groth's (1979) classification of 'men who rape'.

1. *Battering rapists.* In 50% of cases, forced sex is a part of the repeated attacks on their partners and could be considered as Groth's 'Anger Rape'. 'These men hit their wives, belittled them, took their money and, as another way of humiliating and degrading them, resorted to sexual violence.' Often the rape was an extension of the beatings. Four out of five such rapes would involve the man stripping his spouse after an attack and then sexually assaulting her, sometimes with an object.
2. *Force only rapists.* Consistent with Groth's 'Power Rape', in 40% of cases the male partner used only as much force as necessary to obtain sex from his spouse. Violence outside of sexual inter-

action was unusual. It was used only to express mastery, strength, control and authority when the man felt inadequate and incapable.

3. *Obsessive rapists.* One in ten marital rapists have bizarre and perverse sexual interests and will use force to fulfil them. Without their partner's consent, these men would tie and bind their spouse and/or insert objects into her vagina and anus, often recording the activities on film or video to create their own pornography. Such activities were likened to Groth's 'Sadistic Rape'. However, it was the element of obsession, not sadism, that stood out as the most common feature of the last 10% of marital rapists. Obsessed with one type of sexual act (e.g. anal or oral intercourse), most of these men would demand, by force, their preferred activity at the exclusion of all other forms of sexual intercourse.

Of course, physical and sexual aggression is not an exclusive problem of married couples; partners cohabiting are just as likely to experience violence and rape outside marriage despite the common use of the terms 'Marital Violence' and 'Marital Rape'. Indeed, similar rates of physical and sexual violence have been reported for homosexual and lesbian relationships (Renzetti, 1992).

COURTSHIP RAPE AND VIOLENCE

The occurrence of physical and sexual violence is not restricted to married or cohabiting couples. Studies have shown that many of the behaviour patterns found in violent spouse relationships emerge long before partners get married or live together. This violence is often termed 'courtship' or 'dating' violence (Levy, 1991) and 'date' or 'acquaintance' rape (Parrot, 1988; Parrot and Bechhofer, 1991; Koss and Cook, 1994).

In the UK, Dobash et al. (1978, 1985) found that 20% of battered women claim that the first violent assault occurred prior to marriage or cohabitation. Similar research in the USA by Roscoe and Benaske (1985) found that 51% of battered women reported being abused before living together. Indeed, college surveys in the USA reveal that between 14 and 15% of female students report having 'forced sex' during a date (Wilson and Durrenberger, 1982; Levine and Kanin, 1987) with 7 to 9% experiencing 'date rape' (Pirog-Good, 1992; Mufson and Kranz, 1993). In addition, US research shows that between 21 and 52% of unmarried student couples report at least one episode of physical violence in their dating history as either the victim or the aggressor (Sugarman and Hotaling, 1989, 1991; Browne, 1989c; DeMaris, 1992).

As with other types of intimate violence, the milder forms of violence (pushing, slapping, shoving) were the most common and interactive. For example, Archer and Ray (1989) found an incidence rate of pushing and shoving as high as 87% in an English student population. However, researchers (e.g. Browne and Slater, 1997; Arias, Samios and O'Leary, 1987; Makepeace, 1981, 1983) have found that the rate of severe 'abusive' violence among dating relationships varies between 1 and 27%.

With respect to current relationships, 21% of the violence is reciprocal with no significant difference between the sexes (DeMarris, 1987; Browne, 1989c). However, gender differences are evident in some studies with males reporting victimization more than females, while the violence reported by the offender is similar for both sexes (Deal and Wampler, 1986; Arias, Samios and O'Leary, 1987).

Finn (1986) states that traditional sex role attitudes are the most powerful predictor of attitudes supporting marital violence, while the person's race and sex play a relatively unimportant role. According to research on high school dating violence, between 12 and 35% of adolescent couples are aggressive. One-quarter of the victims and one-third of the offenders interpret the violence as a sign of love (Henton et al., 1983). The study of courtship violence suggests that the patterns of spouse abuse emerge long before a person gets married. Research clearly demonstrates similarities between courtship and marital violence and suggests that for many women, both young and old, physical abuse alone is not a sufficient reason to terminate a relationship (Roscoe and Benaske, 1985; O'Keefe, Brockopp and Chew, 1986).

It is interesting that some of the studies support the notion of males as victims and Steinmetz's (1977b) 'battered husband syndrome'. She claims that female rather than male aggression is the most under-reported form of intimate violence. Browne (1989c) disagrees and states that aggressive acts by women are not in keeping with a 'feminine' stereotype of 'normal' behaviour and are therefore more likely to be recalled and reported, consequently creating an artificially high level of reported male victimization; whereas attacks by men are more likely to be viewed as 'normal' violence and be quickly forgotten.

Deal and Wampler (1986) first developed this argument, proposing that since women are stereotypically seen as less aggressive than men, it may take less aggression on the part of a woman for her to be labelled 'violent'. This may then lead to an over-reporting of women's aggression by men. Murphy (1988) suggests that a further explanation for these differences is that a woman's acts of defence may be interpreted by both males and females as acts of aggression. Therefore, women may actually use more violent forms of behaviour, but as a defence, not an offence. Therefore, the prevalence rate of courtship violence does not give a true picture of the nature of violence between intimate partners. Even if the same number of males and females are reported to be aggressive, males tend to engage in repeated attacks.

There is now considerable evidence for the interactive nature of spouse abuse (Saunders, 1986; Frude, 1994). It must be pointed out, however, that 'When men hit women and women hit men, the real victims are almost certainly going to be the women' (Gelles, 1981: 128). The data available on dating violence tell us nothing of the outcome of that violence. As in the case of marital violence, the damage caused by violent men is likely to be greater than that caused by violent women because males are usually stronger and larger than their female partners and resort to more dangerous and injurious conflict tactics, such as threatening with or using a knife or gun. This notion is confirmed by Straus (1993) who reported a 42% greater frequency of severe attacks by husbands compared to wives. In addition, men usually have more social resources at their command, so the physical or social consequences of courtship and marital violence are limited when the male is the victim. Therefore, spouse abuse is primarily a problem of victimized women (Pagelow, 1981, 1984; Dobash and Dobash, 1979, 1987; Yllö and Bograd, 1988;

Hampton et al., 1993; Jukes, 1993) although, at least in the beginning, the violence may have been reciprocal.

VICTIM CHARACTERISTICS

In their book *Leaving Violent Men*, Binney, Harkell and Nixon (1981) reported a survey of 150 refuges in England and Wales. The majority of the 656 women had left home to escape physical violence to themselves (90%) and sometimes to their children (27%). Other forms of ill-treatment were also mentioned, such as psychological abuse and not being given enough money. Many of the women had experienced several kinds of ill-treatment. Of the women they interviewed, 68% claimed that 'mental cruelty' was just one of the reasons they left; usually this happened in conjunction with physical violence, although 10% said they had suffered mental cruelty on its own. In some cases the women had been kept virtual prisoners and in others they had been verbally tormented and threatened until they were confused about their own sanity. Dobash and Dobash's in-depth interview (1979) with 106 'battered' women shows that violence during a typical physical assault falls into the following categories: punching the face and/or the body, 44%; kicking, kneeing or butting, 27%; pushing into a non-injurious object, 15%; hitting with an object, 5%; and attempted smothering or strangling, 2%. In some cases it was only when the violence also began to be directed at the children that the woman felt justified in leaving home.

The majority (81%) of the women interviewed in Binney, Harkell and Nixon's (1981) sample were aged between 20 and 34 years with an average of two to three children. The violence these women suffered had often occurred for a considerable length of time, the average length of time being seven years (ranging from a few months to 40 years). Over half the sample (59%) had been abused for three years or more.

Pahl (1985) also carried out detailed interviews with 42 refuge occupants in south-east England. Her study revealed that 36% of the women were *pregnant* when violence began. In most of the cases this was the first child for the prospective parents. In nearly all (90%) cases there was a *child under 5* in the household when the violence was taking place.

To emphasize the desperation of women who seek refuge in the UK, Victim Support (1992) described a number of recent case histories. For example:

> Paula had called the police out on many occasions when her husband's violence got intolerable. They all knew her at the local police station and would sometimes take up to an hour to arrive. She said that they were angry and frustrated with her because she always refused to press charges. She said 'They didn't seem to understand that I just wanted the violence to stop. I didn't want him to go to prison, or to give the kids' father a criminal record, but I did want protecting. I was never told about refuges, and I think that they thought the violence must be no big deal, or I would have prosecuted.

> Zoe called the police the night that her partner locked the children in their rooms and began dragging her about the room by her hair because his dinner was not on the table when he came in from work. He was very abusive to her and then went into the kitchen to get a knife—in his words 'to teach her a lesson'. She called the police and escaped into the garden. When they arrived her husband told them they had simply had a row and it was all right now. Zoe said that he had hit her and she was frightened, but because there didn't seem to be any visible injuries the officers said there was nothing they could do. Zoe felt totally let down and lost all confidence in calling the police.

The disintegration of a spouse relationship is a painful and emotional (as well as physical) experience for victims of domestic violence. Many feel dependent, isolated and confused, unable to deal with the notion of separation and divorce. Those who do, find it difficult to face the legal problems that follow; the custody of the children, maintenance, the division of property and, most importantly, the protection of themselves and their children. Most victims do not fully understand the process of court orders to forbid their violent partner from harassing them or entering their new home. They often see the involvement of a solicitor as a poor use of the minimal resources they command which they may need, in future, to escape. Some victims are unaware that families claiming supplementary benefit from the social services automatically receive 'Legal Aid' in the UK (Law Society, 1987). Even when victims do realize there is 'help', the characteristics of passive coping, social isolation, internalized blame, ambivalent loyalty and compliant behaviour often prevent them taking advantage of the situation (see Table 4.1).

Table 4.1   Victim characteristics in spouse abuse

1. Low self-esteem	7. Compliant behaviour
2. Passive coping mechanisms	8. Ambivalent loyalty
3. High dependence on partners	9. Distorted attributions
4. Anxiety and depression	10. Alcohol and drug abuse
5. Social isolation	11. Stress-related illness
6. Internalize blame	

Passive Coping

Victims usually cope with violence from their partners in a passive way rather than resorting to aggressive or assertive actions. Finn (1985) showed that battered women are typically under serious stress relating to a number of issues, i.e. money, work, children, relatives, physical illness, jealousy, sexual relationship, deciding who's boss, settling arguments, alcohol and drug use. The study demonstrated that as stress increased there was a corresponding decrease in the use of positive coping mechanisms such as acquiring social support. This is despite the fact that intervention by friends, relatives and neighbours, or the threat of such intervention, tends to make spouse abuse less common and less severe (Levinson, 1985; Jaffe et al., 1986a). Finn (1985) reported that battered women were more likely to use passive coping mechanisms of minimal reactivity, or show avoidant strategies such as the use of drugs and social withdrawal, leading to poor health and stress-related illness.

These solutions to the problem result in less control over the situation and psychological problems. Less control results in increased stress and so a cycle develops with a gradually decreasing use of coping techniques. Thus, it is not surprising that Weitzman and Dreen (1982) describe battered women as typically having limited coping mechanisms, high dependence on partners, anxiety, depression and low self-esteem. Women who are continually battered often develop a state of learned helplessness where they perceive themselves to have no control over their lives or environment (Walker, 1979, 1984, 1993). This may lead to alcohol and drug abuse and even suicide (Frude, 1991).

Social Isolation

It has been found that many women experiencing learned helplessness have tried on several occasions to seek outside intervention (Hendricks-Matthews, 1982). Victims generally lack support networks of neighbours, friends or relatives. In addition, agencies such as the police, social services and medical services are very often unwilling to help, which leaves the victim feeling socially isolated. Family life is still often seen as being sacred and neighbours or statutory agencies are reluctant to intrude in private family matters. Police place domestic disturbances at the bottom of their list of priorities and are reluctant to prosecute husbands who assault their wives. Social services often try to keep the couple together, even when the violence is likely to continue. Failed attempts at seeking help only serve to reinforce the abused woman's feelings of helplessness. Very often abused women have a low self-esteem and an external locus of control; they attribute any success to external factors such as good luck. Many of these women regard their failure to seek help as their own fault; and attribute a lack of success to internal factors.

Internalized Blame

An outstanding characteristic of victim behaviour is the degree to which victims internalize the blame and responsibility for the violent encounter (Star, 1980). Many victims believe that they 'cause' the assaults because they argue with the abuser or defy orders. They believe their actions provoke, and in some way justify, the abusive action.

Fincham and Bradbury (1988) emphasize the importance of causal attribution in distressed marriages. 'If she sees the man as the cause of the violence then this may have positive effects on her coping strategies.' However, in a state of learned helplessness the woman will often attribute the blame to herself, thus compounding her feelings of impotence. Abused wives are often persuaded by their husbands that they are incompetent, hysterical or frigid, and as a result of their distorted self-image they may genuinely believe that they provoked the attack.

Compliant Behaviour

Star (1980) states that victims try to avert injury by pacifying their assaulters and removing any cause for violence. 'If I don't argue, I won't get hurt,' they reason. From the victim's viewpoint, compliance is a way to survive.

Ambivalent Loyalty

Despite their pain and anger, victims stand by the abusers and often defend the assaulter's actions. For example, at a hospital in Philadelphia, Martha talked about her stab wound and why she wouldn't have her boyfriend arrested: 'He didn't mean it. Its hard to press charges when you love somebody. It's hard to believe they meant to hurt you' (*The Guardian*, 23 July 1991). Put this way, love is blind and because the same people who hurt them also love them, ambivalence underlies victim motivations. Assaulters are not violent all the time; violence is usually interspersed between periods of calm and affection. Victims want the abuse to end, but often wish the relationship to continue.

Distorted Attributions

Frude (1991) claims that the victims' attributions to the violent partner may be *specific* ('In other ways he's OK'), *unstable* ('He doesn't get drunk very often') or *external* ('He only gets violent when he drinks, I know he cares about me'). These attributions reduce the chances of the victim's leaving. Often the violent partner expresses regret and the couple make up. For some, this may be the only time of intimacy which in turn will have a powerful reinforcing effect on the violence. For many reasons the victim is keen to 'forgive and forget'.

To Leave or to Stay

Learned helplessness is often cited as the reason women remain in an abusive relationship (Barnett and LaViolette, 1993). Walker and Browne (1985) first described how women who are repeatedly abused gradually perceive themselves to have fewer and fewer options. They feel that they can exert no control over their situation and that nothing they do will change anything. Efforts to find ways of escaping the violence cease and, instead, they learn to endure and adapt to the abuse. Gelles (1987a) claims that women are more likely to remain in an abusive relationship if they have a negative self-concept, which may be a result of experiencing violence as a child.

In addition to learned helplessness and negative self-concept, Truninger (1971) suggests that battered women are entrapped in marriage through a lack of resources and economic constraints. They feel they cannot cope alone and that it will be difficult to get a job and make new friends. Some women believe that their children need a father and that divorcees are stigmatized. Overall, most battered women would rather believe that their male partner will reform than consider splitting up and separation (see *Table 4.2*).

Frude (1991) suggests that violence, when intermittent, may be perceived as preferable to constant loneliness. The victims become 'entrapped'; the more they put in, the more they stand to lose. This entrapment is reinforced by the victims' feelings of low self-esteem. They believe that they may never find another partner. Indeed, violent husbands emphasize the benefits of staying, the low probability of repeated violence (mostly untrue), and the accommodation and financial difficulties of separation. By contrast, refuge workers emphasize the benefits of leaving, the high probability of repeated violence, availability of accommodation and financial aid.

For the victim, it becomes a 'cost/benefit' analysis. Not surprisingly, therefore, half of the women who seek refuge continue their relationship with their violent male partner (Frude, 1994) and 34% of those who return home experience further violent assaults (Binney, Harkell and Nixon, 1981, 1985). Frude (1994) emphasizes

Table 4.2   Reasons for remaining in a violent relationship

1. Learned helplessness
2. Negative self-concept
3. Economic hardship of leaving too great
4. Can't cope alone
5. Difficulties getting a job and meeting new friends
6. Children need a father
7. Divorcees are stigmatized
8. Husband will reform

that women who leave and then return home have specific characteristics (Table 4.3). They are more likely to be married with fewer previous separations, have suffered less severe violence (not life threatening), had little contact with police or child protection agencies, are unemployed and economically dependent with shorter stays in refuges and an initial intention to return.

Table 4.3   Women who seek refuge but then return

1. Married women (four times more likely to return)
2. Fewer previous separations
3. Intermittent and less severe violence
4. Little contact with police
5. No involvement with child protection agencies
6. Unemployed and/or economically dependent
7. Shorter stay in refuges
8. Initial intention to return

Thus, there are two types of women who need different types of help: those who have left violent relationships and those who are unable to leave. The first group require assistance in the form of shelters, starting a new life, finding employment, etc.; the second group require counselling to help them overcome feelings of helplessness and inadequacy.

OFFENDER CHARACTERISTICS

Research suggests that men who engage in spouse abuse are very insecure with many anxieties over inferiority, inadequacy and abandonment (Rosenbaum and O'Leary, 1981; Weitzman and

Dreen, 1982). However, they show few personality differences from non-abusive men, other than being less-assertive with low self-esteem and poor social skills (Goldstein and Rosenbaum, 1985). Clinical research has significantly linked spouse abuse to psychiatric disorder (Faulk, 1974; Bland and Orn, 1986; Jacob, 1987), although Coleman (1980) found that less than 25% of the abusive men she interviewed reported a psychiatric history. What has been often observed (Vasell-Augenstein and Ehirch, 1993) is that abusive men have personality and psychological problems such as low self-esteem, alcohol and drug abuse, poor impulse control, cognitive distortions, poor response to stress, violent backgrounds and antisocial behaviour, and these are considered to be 'risk factors' for both spouse and child abuse (O'Leary, 1993; Saunders, 1995).

Table 4.4 Characteristics associated with violent partners

1. Feelings of low self-esteem and inadequacy
2. Feelings of isolation and lack of social support
3. Lack of social skills and assertive behaviour
4. History of psychiatric disorder such as anxiety and depression
5. History of alcohol and/or drug abuse
6. Poor impulse control and antisocial behaviour problems
7. Possessiveness, jealousy and fear of abandonment
8. Externalization of blame, escalation of arguments and showing aggression and violence when provoked
9. Lack of empathy for over-dependent victim, possibly due to poor physical or mental health, sexual problems or difficulties during pregnancy and childbirth
10. Displacement of anger at job dissatisfaction, stress at work or recent aversive life event (e.g. separation from spouse or death of parent or child)
11. Socio-economic problems such as unemployment, poor housing or financial difficulties
12. Exposure to violence as a child
13. Current history of violence, threatening behaviour or use of weapons

Table 4.4 presents the characteristics associated with violent partners compiled from the clinical and research knowledge to date. These characteristics might form the basis of a screening instrument, although the reliability and validity of such 'risk factors' are yet to be determined.

Alcohol and Drug Abuse

The area of research that has attracted the largest amount of interest in relation to spouse abuse is the use of alcohol and drugs (Edleson, Eisikovits and Guttman, 1985). In the UK, Gayford's (1975) sample of battered women described their husband's drunkenness as a contributing factor to violence on a regular (52%) or occasional (22%) basis. In the USA, surveys of battered women typically show that 60% of their partners have an alcohol problem and 21% also have a drug problem (Carlson, 1977; Roberts, 1987). A substantial number of other studies confirm the association of alcohol and drug abuse with violence towards spouse (e.g. Ball, 1977; Bayles, 1978; Gerson, 1978; Hanks and Rosenbaum, 1978; Walker, 1979; Fagen, Stewart and Hansen, 1983; Van Hasselt, Morrison and Bellack, 1985; Gelles, 1987a). Some authors propose that these are the major causes (e.g. Weissberg, 1983; Pernanen, 1991), but Moore (1979) gives a convincing explanation for their frequent representation. She suggests that alcohol consumption relieves the man of the responsibility for his behaviour and gives the wife justification for remaining in the relationship in the hope that he will control his drinking, which will end his aggressiveness. A similar point has been made by Dobash and Dobash (1987) and Ammerman and Hersen (1992).

Indeed, Pahl (1985) states that alcohol is not a cause of violence but an excuse for it and Coleman and Straus (1983) found that extreme levels of alcohol abuse were *not* related to high levels of violence. Physical violence in families actually declined when drunkenness occurred on a regular basis. Therefore, there is no simple link between alcohol use and family violence. The same can also be said of other substance abuse. It appears that, like alcohol, any effects are again mediated by social and personality factors (Gelles, 1994b).

Poor Impulse Control

Most individuals who assault their partner have poor control over their anger and aggressive impulses. Often they have a history of antisocial behaviour with police cautions and legal convictions. Both now and in the past they tend to escalate arguments and show aggression and violence when provoked.

Cognitive Distortions

Violent partners often hold distorted perceptions of their victims. They expect them to meet a wide-range of unfulfilled needs, involving maternal, paternal as well as spousal functions. Abusive spouses regularly *externalize blame* for their anger and place the responsibility for their violent behaviour on others, or on some other factor such as their alcohol intake (Star, 1980): 'It wasn't my fault. I'd been drinking, it was the alcohol talking. I would never have hurt you if I'd been sober.'

Violent partners also rarely accept that their aggression towards their partner was their fault, although they may apologize for the injuries and distress they cause (Star, 1980): 'You made me get mad at you. If you had only done what I told you then I wouldn't have gotten angry and had to hit you.'

Violent partners *lack empathy* and expect others to understand the reasons for their violent behaviour. They cannot empathize with their partner's feelings or perceptions of the abusive relationship or see the situation from the victim's point of view (Star, 1980): 'Why should she be afraid of me? Doesn't she know I love her.' This lack of empathy extends to other problems in the relationship, such as the victim's poor physical or mental health, sexual problems or difficulties during pregnancy and childbirth.

Displaced Anger

This is a familiar aspect of domestic violence. The offender finds it easier to express his aggressive feelings about job dissatisfaction or stress at work once he has returned home. 'Behind Closed Doors' (Straus, Gelles and Steinmetz, 1980, 1988), where there is less social or legal control of violent and assaultive behaviour. Aversive life events, such as a car accident, can also perpetrate violence in the home. The anger associated with a recent bereavement of a friend, relative parent or child might also be taken out on the partner (Browne, 1995c). However, in her random sample Rouse (1988) found that men under stress were more likely to use abusive conflict tactics if they had had some previous exposure to the use of physical force or verbal abuse in childhood or adolescence.

Violent Backgrounds

Many researchers have noted an important association between growing up in a violent home and being in a violent adult relationship either as a victim or as an offender (e.g. Gayford, 1975; Carroll, 1977; Hanks and Rosenbaum, 1978; Rosenbaum and O'Leary, 1981; Walker, 1984; Kalmuss, 1984; Giles-Sims, 1985; Lewis, 1987; Straus, Gelles and Steinmetz, 1980, 1988; Browne, 1993). According to Roy (1977), abusive spouses acknowledge the learning experiences in their childhood, when their fathers taught them 'how to be men' and 'how to be husbands'.

There is evidence that violence between parents and parental attitudes to violence affect the children in the family (Jaffe, Wolfe and Wilson, 1990; Cummings and Davies, 1994). The behaviour and psychiatric problems discovered in children of violent marriages include truancy, aggressive behaviour at home and school and anxiety disorders (Levine, 1975; Hughes and Barad, 1983; Jaffe et al., 1986b; Davis and Carlson, 1987; Carroll, 1994). It is suggested that children learn aggressive behaviour as a general style for controlling their social and physical environments and that this style continues into adulthood (Gully and Dengerink, 1983; Browne and Saqi, 1987). Lewis (1987) claims that some women also learn to accept violent behaviour towards themselves as a result of childhood experiences.

Gelles (1987b) concludes that the family serves as a basic training ground for the development of aggressive behaviour by exposing children to violence, by making them victims of violence and by providing them with learning contexts for the commission of aggressive acts. It transmits the norms and values which condone the use of aggression between family members. However, a violent background does not always predetermine a violent adulthood and not all children who grow up in violent homes become batterers. In fact, many siblings of batterers may live peacefully in non-violent marriages (Dobash and Dobash, 1979). Nevertheless, Spatz Widom (1989) claims that one in six physically abused children grow up to commit violent offences in later life and showed this to be a significantly higher proportion than non-abused children. Hence, the argument that victims of violence often become its protagonists continues to be accepted as a significant factor in the aetiology of abuse and violence in the home and outside it (Spatz Widom, 1989; Browne, 1993). A further discussion of this issue can be found in Chapter 11.

VIOLENT RELATIONSHIPS

Development

Owing to past experiences, some abusing couples tend to establish aggressive relationships because they are familiar with, and therefore comfortable with, violence as an expression of intimate concern and attachment. Indeed, Hanks and Rosenbaum (1978) have commented on the striking similarity between the abused woman's current marital relationship and that of her parents. Jaffe, Wolfe and Wilson (1990) believe that the reason for this intergenerational transmission of violent relationships is that a boy who witnesses his father assaulting his mother is learning that violence is acceptable behaviour and that it is an integral part of intimate relationships. Similarly, a girl witnessing the same event learns about victimization and the extent to which men can utilize violence and fear to exert power and control over family members.

Walker and Browne (1985) also emphasize the way in which males and females are differently socialized during childhood. They state that women typically learn that they are supposed to be weak and unable to cope with violence. They do not develop techniques for avoiding or stopping abuse and, rather than responding assertively, they submit to violence believing that they have no alternative to being abused. By contrast, men are typically socialized to believe that they should be active, aggressive and dominant over women. It is therefore clear that the risk of abuse increases if the couple consists of a dominant male and a passive female. Indeed, these gender differences are seen in teenagers during courtship and dating, so that the use of violent tactics is developed at an early stage. Several studies have shown that teenagers who grow up in violent homes are more likely to abuse their romantic partners than teenagers who grow up in non-violent homes (Bernard and Bernard, 1983; Marshall and Rose, 1988; Follingstad et al., 1992; Browne and Slater, 1997).

It is not only the modelling effects of their exposure to violence that lead to violence in adulthood. People raised in violent environments feel unprotected by the important adults in their life and have come to perceive the world as threatening and hostile. As adults, these persons attempt to master that hostile environment by using physical force. Thus, many battered women and abusive men lack the social competence and personal skills or resources to develop healthy relationships. This may be a result of inadequate parenting and poor socialization in both their childhoods (Walker and Browne, 1985). Hence, spouse abuse is sometimes seen as an interactional process. For example, Gayford (1976) distinguished 10 types of 'battered wives', offering names and descriptions which imply that the cause of violent behaviour lies also with the victim.

Maintenance

Walker (1979) has described a cycle of events which exists periodically in an abusive relationship. This cycle is made up of three phases—a tension-building phase, a period of acute violence and a state of reconciliation. She claimed that once this sequence is entered into it can be very difficult to escape from.

Frude (1980, 1989), as outlined in Chapter 2, takes a similar perspective and puts forward a causal chain leading to an incidence of child abuse which can equally be applied to spouse abuse: firstly, the presence of a stressful situation; secondly, the perception of the situation as threatening (which may be unrealistic); thirdly, an escalation of anger and emotional distress as a response to the situation; and, fourthly, a lack of inhibitions with regard to violent expression in response to a trigger, such as an argument. This finally results in the individual exhibiting aggression and performing a violent act on his or her partner.

After an act of violence, the abusive spouse may continue with his hostile attitude or show a long period of sullen silence. Frequently the abuser expresses regret, apologizing and promising no more attacks. This has been likened to a 'Jekyll and Hyde personality' (Bernard and Bernard, 1984). Nevertheless, it often results in reconciliation and hope for the victim.

From a combination of the ideas proposed by Walker and Frude it is possible to construct a typical 'battering cycle' which maintains violent interactions within a relationship (see *Figure 4.1*).

It is commonly believed that women who are frequently revictimized or move from one violent relationship to another are 'addicted to violence' and seek out violent relationships (Gayford, 1976; Pizzey and Shapiro, 1982). However, the evidence for this is weak. Andrews and Brown (1988) carried out a community study in London and found that 32% of the women who had experi-

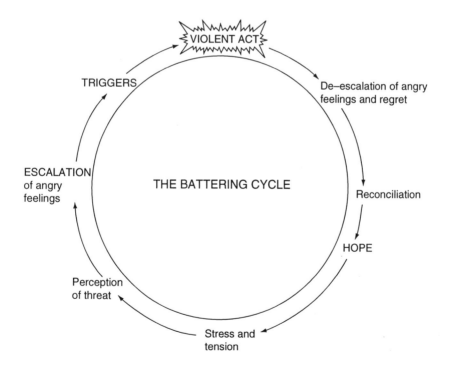

Figure 4.1   The battering cycle

enced or witnessed violence in childhood experienced domestic violence in adulthood. This compared to 22% of women who had no such childhood experiences but had been involved in a violent relationship as an adult. Only 9% of women who had been involved with more than one man had experienced more than one violent relationship. Furthermore, Kelly (1988) suggests that women who experience more than one violent relationship are sexually and physically abused by men who know their history and use it to justify their own violent behaviour.

The evidence indicating that the spouse abuser, rather than the victim, carries his violence from one relationship to another is much stronger. Pagelow (1981, 1984) indicates that 57% of male partners who had been married previously were known to have been violent to another wife.

CONCLUSION

Hodge (1992) claims that violence may be maintained by a process of addiction, but this addiction is not in terms of a substance abuse but an addiction to the violent behaviour and experiences. When individuals are asked about the motive of their violent behaviour many reply that it is not so much the outcome but the experience, such as relief from tension. Therefore, Hodge (1992) argues that it is the experience rather than the event which is of central importance for the perpetrator of violence. This has important implications for prevention, which will be considered in the next chapter.

CHAPTER 5   Preventing spouse maltreatment

The prevention of spouse physical and sexual abuse can be conceptualized in two ways: preventing violence occurring in the first place, or preventing repeat attacks (Morley and Mullender, 1994). However, the majority of current intervention techniques only operate after violence in the family has occurred (treatment or tertiary prevention), with less emphasis placed on strategies that reduce the number of spouse victims of violence (primary and secondary prevention).

PRIMARY PREVENTION

Primary prevention measures, operating at the societal level are comparatively recent approaches to spouse abuse. Telephone helplines and public awareness campaigns have been started by both local and national advocacy groups. These have been mainly directed at women as potential victims, offering them information, addresses and contact numbers on where to find help. The aim of these advocacy groups is to achieve the basic principles of primary prevention outlined in Chapter 1.

Public Awareness Campaigns

At a national level in the UK, the 'zero tolerance' campaign was financed by local authorities to educate the general public about the prevalence of domestic violence and child abuse and to condemn unequivocally a general attitude that accepts violence in the home. The campaign is based on the premise that men have to accept responsibility for the damage they inflict, and it emphasizes that violence is a crime and will not go unpunished.

Messages such 'He gave her chocolate, flowers and multiple bruising' were placed together with a large picture as posters on billboards and other advertising space around local transport systems. An example of a poster used by the Association of London Authorities is shown in Figure 5.1. The poster confronts the myth that domestic violence is a problem found only within the lower socio-economic classes. Nevertheless, some studies have found a higher rate of domestic violence in families from the more disadvantaged classes (Pahl, 1985; Straus, Gelles and Steinmetz, 1980, 1988; Painter, 1991), but critics argue that these groups are simply more visible since they lack material resources to deal privately with their problem (Morley and Mullender, 1994).

BEHIND THESE SUCCESSFUL MEN ARE THE WOMEN THEY PUT IN CASUALTY

Every year 100,000 women in London seek medical help because of domestic violence. It's not just a fact of life, it's a crime.

Figure 5.1 The zero tolerance campaign: poster power getting the message across

The relatively inexpensive 'zero-tolerance' campaign generated a great deal of interest in the media, so that the campaign organizers were able to put their point across in newspapers, radio and television.

Some local authorities and advocacy groups have produced their own pamphlets and newsletters. For example, in 1994 Birmingham City Council set up a special 'Women's Unit' who produced a pamphlet for circulation in health and social service centres outlining facts associated with 'Hidden Violence', 'Hidden Rape' and 'Hidden Sexual Abuse of Children'. They report in the pamphlet that there were 12 151 incidents of domestic violence and 213 rapes recorded by the West Midlands police in 1993. The Birmingham City Council's campaign 'Violence Against Women' also emphasized that violence to women is present in all cultures and communities within the area.

Telephone Helplines

Perhaps the most important aspect of public awareness campaigns is that it gives an opportunity to advertise the telephone helplines that are available locally (e.g. London Women's Aid, 0171 251 6537; Victim Support, 0171 735 9166) or nationally (e.g. Women's Aid Federation National Helpline, 01272 633 542; Rape Crisis Counselling Helpline, 0171 837 1600). In recognition of the smaller number of men that are victims of domestic violence a telephone helpline has also been set up for 'Battered Husbands', although the Male Advice Line and Enquiries (MALE, 0181 543 1102) also confidentially answers calls from men who are violent towards their partner.

Most telephone helplines offer immediate counselling about the potential or actual problem of violence in the home. Indeed, the successful counselling of couples with relationship difficulties could be considered as secondary prevention, as it is these couples who are probably most at risk of violent conflict.

SECONDARY PREVENTION

Marital or cohabitee counselling services, such as 'Relate', contribute a great deal to reducing the probability of violent interactions within a relationship. Counselling, like psychotherapy, is a 'social influence process' (Egan, 1975) which may be defined as:

> The means by which one individual helps another to clarify their life situation and to decide upon further lines of action. (Browne, 1992, p. 12)

Both psychotherapy and counselling may take place on an individual one-to-one basis, or in couples, families or groups. Various modes of counselling are offered. The three principle orientations are 'psychodynamic', 'cognitive-behavioural' and 'humanistic', and these have been recently reviewed to determine the most effective approach in alleviating the problems identified within individuals with relationship difficulties (Browne, 1995c).

Individual Counselling

The psychodynamic approach, derived from Freud (1940, 1949), highlights the relationship between past and present and the unconscious forces that influence behaviour, to encourage the expression of suppressed feelings and emotions. In relationship difficulties resulting from emotional problems, anxiety and an unhappy childhood, this has obvious advantages (see Dare, 1986). Cognitive-behavioural approaches to relationship difficulties (e.g. Bornstein and Bornstein, 1986) may help to improve communication, problem-solving skills and to alleviate depression in the present but will not remove the underlying causes of conflict and negative feelings from the past.

A comparative evaluation of different approaches reveals that the initial therapeutic working alliance or positive professional relationship, as perceived by client and therapist, is the major determinant of success for psychodynamic, cognitive-behavioural and interpersonal humanistic approaches; according to a review of brief psychotherapies by Ursano and Hales (1986).

The beneficial effects of a long-term therapeutic relationship over brief psychotherapy has yet to be shown by empirical research although, in a review of psychotherapy studies, Luborsky et al. (1985) have provided further evidence that the way the therapist and client relate to one another early in treatment is an important predictor of therapeutic outcome regardless of the approach taken (cognitive-behavioural or psychodynamic).

Couple and Family Therapy

Many couples who seek or are referred to therapy to deal with relationship difficulties have children. Sometimes the child's behaviour creates or contributes to the difficulties. In other cases, the parents' problems arise directly from conflicts with each other. Therefore, the line between couple and family therapy is often blurred.

Psychodynamic family therapists consider that relationship difficulties are caused by unconscious impulses, fears and anxieties, and defences against them (Scharff and Scharff, 1987, 1991). The objective of this approach is to free couples of unconscious restrictions to enable them to interact on the basis of current realities rather than images of the past. Transference relationships (i.e. unconsciously interacting and responding in a way that is reminiscent of a previous relationship) with the therapist and other family members reveal and reflect earlier problems within the client's family of origin that contribute to current emotional difficulties. These may be explored during a session using circular interviewing and 'triadic' questioning, following techniques pioneered by the Milan group of therapists for a systemic approach (see Carr, 1991).

Exploring roles is the main purpose of 'Systemic Family Therapy', where the family unit is analysed as a set of interlocking roles (Minuchin and Fishman, 1981; Burnham, 1986). This technique has been used to explore pathological family patterns that damage the development of the children involved (see Bentovim, Gorell-Barnes and Cooklin, 1987; Bentovim et al., 1988).

'Behavioural Family Therapy' (e.g. Wolpe, 1973) has been used primarily to help parents learn about effective rewards and punishments when dealing with conduct-disordered children. More recently, the behavioural approach has broadened to focus on all members of the family, assuming that family conflict is the result of coercion and the use of aversive stimuli (complaints, accusations, etc.) to influence the behaviour of others (Patterson, 1982). The therapy promotes 'reciprocity' and the mutual use of positive reinforcement (praise, compliments, etc.). In addition, cognitive therapy is sometimes used to promote positive perceptions of other family members and to enhance problem-solving skills (Jacobson and Holtzworth-Munroe, 1986). Such specific applications have been found to be generally successful (see Chapters 9 and 12).

Humanistic approaches based on Rogers (1951, 1973) aim to establish an honest dialogue between the two partners, especially where there are communication problems. Individual roles in the family are explored to help clients identify any imbalance in their relationship (e.g. strong vs weak partner).

Few comparative evaluations of the effectiveness of various approaches to couple and family therapy have been carried out.

An exception being a study by Snyder and Wills (1989) that compared behavioural marital therapy with a psychodynamic approach. The study found that both approaches resulted in a significant improvement after therapy and no differences were found at a six-month follow-up. However, at a four-year follow-up (Synder, Wills and Grady-Fletcher, 1991) couples that had experienced psychodynamic therapy had fewer divorces and maintained their improvement better than those who had received the behavioural approach. Johnson and Greenberg (1985) have also shown that Gestalt marital therapy, focusing on uncovering unacknowledged feelings and needs, was more successful than a problem-solving behavioural approach.

Overall, couple and family therapies appear to be more successful than group therapy or individual therapy with one partner (Barker, 1986). In fact problems worsen for approximately 10% of partners seen individually for relationship difficulties whereas 73% of clients find couple and family therapy more helpful (Gurman and Kniskern, 1978; Gurman, Kniskern and Pinsoff, 1986). A meta-analysis of 20 outcome studies has shown that family therapy of various kinds is more effective than no treatment or alternative treatments when measured by either family interactions or behaviour ratings (Hazelrigg; Cooper and Bordun, 1987). Indeed, some therapists have claimed for some time that counselling couples jointly should be the preferred mode despite the increased complexity in dealing with transference (Dicks, 1967).

Group Therapy

Group therapy, like other therapies, can be based on a number of different theoretical approaches, although Yalom (1975) has identified 11 factors that help promote therapy in most orientations: hope, universality, information, altruism, corrective recapitulation of the primary family group, development of social skills, imitative behaviour, interpersonal learning, group cohesiveness, catharsis, and existential factors. Of course, many of these factors are relevant to individual, couple and family therapy.

Psychodynamic approaches emphasize 'interpersonal learning' and 'corrective recapitulation of the primary family group' where leaders may represent parents and other members reflect siblings. Thus the group may help to heal wounds and ease inhibitions resulting from the client's family of origin. By interacting with other members of the group the clients may gain insight into themselves and the relationships they develop. In much the same way as psychodynamic couple and family therapy; defence mechanisms, resistance and transference are analysed within the group. The therapist pays attention to unconscious motives and conflicts among group members and offers interpretations to clarify current problems within the group and of the group members. The main focus is on how clients interact with others to reveal the roots of their personal conflict and offer them insights into how the past is affecting the present (Wolfe, 1949).

Behavioural group therapy is less concerned with group process and is directed towards a specific goal (Lazarus, 1968). Instructions and exercises provided by the group leader constitute the therapy, and social support from group members functions as a valuable source of reinforcement. Relevant to individuals with relationship difficulties are social skills and assertiveness training in these groups. Here it is even more important than usual to promote group 'cohesiveness' through careful preparation and selection for the group, as the clients use one another to rehearse new skills. In general, behavioural groups concentrate on 'information', 'development of social skills' and 'imitative behaviour'.

Humanistic perspectives have produced the greatest number of variations in group therapy with an emphasis on 'altruism' and 'interpersonal learning'. The therapy concerns itself with the development of intimacy and cooperation between individuals within a mutually supportive group. Again the clients explore their own emotions by interacting with others.

The humanistic approach was pioneered with encounter groups and T groups (sensitivity training). The aim of T groups is to examine self-behaviour and to experiment with new ways of behaving, to learn about people and to be honest in relationships, to be cooperative rather than dominant or submissive and to develop the ability to resolve conflict through rational thought rather than force, coercion or manipulation of others (Yalom,

1975). Hence, this technique also has relevance to individuals with relationship difficulties and domestic conflict. In recent years an increasing number of 'peer self-help groups' have developed where the members are people who share special problems that they discuss at regular intervals without the help of therapists and counsellors. The group processes outlined above would be present but without professional direction or containment, which sometimes causes concern among professionals.

Evaluation on group therapy outcome has concluded that it generally results in greater improvement than is seen in clients who are offered no therapy, and some improvements are long lasting (Bednar and Kaul, 1978; Kaul and Bednar, 1986; Dobash and Dobash, 1996). Nevertheless, the outcome measures are based on positive changes in attitude and self-concept which does not necessarily reflect changes in actual behaviour.

Outcome studies on the different approaches to group therapy present a confusing picture. The results from social skills and assertiveness training, using a behavioural model, are generally good (e.g. Rose, 1986) whereas outcome from groups with a psychodynamic or humanistic approach are mixed (Lieberman, Yalom and Miles, 1973). A tentative conclusion was drawn from a study by Piper et al. (1984) that short-term group work was less effective than long-term group or individual work.

Suitability for Counselling

Given the importance of the therapeutic working relationship for future outcome, it is important to assess in the first few sessions whether the client–counsellor relationship is 'good enough' for client cooperation in the therapeutic process (Hill, 1989). The counsellor should address his or her own 'commitment' and 'optimism' for a particular client as these are also very significant influences on positive outcome (Swensen, 1972; Bednar, 1970).

The motivation and determination of the client should be assessed very early as research and clinical evidence show this to be essential for helping people to change (Malan, 1979). Hence, clarifying client expectations concerning the counselling is very important (Heine and Trosman, 1960).

The mental health of the clients is probably the next most important criterion to assess from medication, referred case notes, contact with other agencies and the initial interview. This is especially important for psychodynamic approaches as interpretive counselling can trigger psychosis in borderline personalities (Jacobs, 1985). Clients prone to affective disorders such as depressive illness may also show a poor response to individual therapy. In addition, Ratigan (1989) observes that clients suffering from psychotic illness and severe depression will not benefit from group therapy until they have been helped in other ways (e.g. psychiatric medication). He explains that for group work the schizophrenic is too cut off from other people, the narcissistic are too egocentric, and the paranoid are too suspicious. Similarly, these phenomena would interfere with couple and family work, as a certain minimal level of self awareness, communication and understanding of others is required for therapy. In couple therapy, it should be recognized that partners compete for the therapist's attention. Both partners should be encouraged to temporarily put to one side their own needs so that the other's need can be addressed (Schroder, 1989). The major advantage of couple and family work is that clients living together have the opportunity to negotiate change outside the therapeutic session (Brown and Pedder, 1991). As a result, Skynner (1987) suggests that the spacing between sessions can become longer, making this mode of counselling both effective and economical. However, James and Wilson (1986) warn that working with both partners conjointly must begin soon after the initial referral, as individual therapy may promote a move towards separation. Where couples present with spouse violence they present special concerns to counselling services (Walker, 1990).

Men and women are often reluctant to admit relationship problems and may feel ashamed of their violent interactions. Victim and offender characteristics (Chapter 4) are helpful, therefore, in identifying the possibility of violence both for the family and the therapist (Saunders, 1995; Browne and Howells, 1996). Where there is undue concern about the possibility of spouse violence, the problem should be referred to a more appropriate professional who may fully assess the couple's relationship and adverse factors affecting the family, such as stress and conflict at work (Barling and Rosenbaum, 1986).

Assessment Measures

Barling et al. (1987) claim that the most frequently used measurement of marital and courtship violence is the 'Conflict Tactics Scales' (CTS—Straus, 1979). This is a self-administered 20-item scale assessing the behaviours that an individual might exhibit during an argument with his or her partner (e.g. reason, hostility, threats, violence and severe violence). The last 10 items (ranging from throwing an object to using a knife or gun) make up a violence index. Studies using the CTS have found it to be valid with regard to whether a relationship is violent or not, but usually both men and women report more violence for their partner than for themselves. Husbands tend to see their marriage as mutually violent, whereas wives call it 'husband violent' (Browning and Dutton, 1986). A criticism of the CTS is that it does not consider the consequences or context of violence and so tends to equate male and female aggressive acts.

The Index of Spouse Abuse (ISA) accounts for some of these shortcomings, as it is a 30-item scale designed to measure the severity of abuse inflicted on a woman by her partner (Hudson and McIntosh, 1981). Indicators of individual differences in impulsive aggression have also been developed, such as the Irritability and Emotional Susceptibility Scales (Capara et al., 1985). A cognitive approach to assessment is found in the Novaco Anger Inventory (Novaco, 1975), a 90-item inventory of hypothetical anger inducing situations, such as being called a liar, being called a 'stupid idiot' in an argument, being criticized in front of others, being teased or joked about, being called names, being the subject of personal remarks, and so on.

From a behavioural perspective, Goldstein and Keller (1987) give a comprehensive list of rating scales to assess the following components of aggressive behaviour.

- Interpretation of external stimuli (arousal heightening)

- Heightened affective arousal
- Malcommunication
- Mismanagement of contingencies
- Pro-social skill deficiencies
- Pro-social value deficiencies

However, Edmonds and Kendrick (1980) conclude from their study of the measurement of aggression that indices of social interaction are required. Indeed, the ratio of positive to negative comments is an important indicator of affection in relationships (Patterson, 1982; Browne, 1986). These data can be derived from the Marital Interaction Coding System (MICS), which is an observational measure of spouse interaction developed by Weiss, Hops and Patterson (1973). The MICS technique consists of three assessment stages: (1) videotaping a couple's interaction during a discussion of relationship conflict, (2) coding the observed interaction according to 30 behavioural items and (3) scoring the interaction. Scoring is based on the relative frequencies of behaviour, classified into positive and negative verbal and non-verbal categories. A 'Positivity Index' is obtained for the couple that represents the ratio of positive to negative behaviours. The MICS procedures have been shown to successfully discriminate distressed couples from happily married couples and have also been used to evaluate the effects of behavioural marital therapy (Weiss and Summers, 1983). A more economical observational measure of spouse interaction has been developed by Floyd and Markman (1984) entitled the Communication Skills Test (CST). In contrast to the relatively minute behavioural units coded with the MICS, the observer judges the degree to which an entire statement represents either disruptive or facilitative communication and rates the statement on a 5-point scale, i.e. (1) very negative, (2) negative, (3) neutral, (4) positive and (5) very positive. Relative frequency scores are then obtained by dividing the number of statements in each category by the total number of statements. However, the validity of this test is in question as comparative scores derived from the MICS and the CST do not significantly correlate (see Floyd, O'Farrell and Goldberg, 1987).

Other measures of spouse relationships can be obtained from marital and family questionnaires. These should not be seen as alternatives to observational techniques for marriage and family assessment, but should be used in conjunction with behavioural methods. This is because both indirect and self reports of events may not correspond to actual events. Nevertheless, how a respondent thinks or feels may be crucial. Thus, when time and finances permit, assessment should contain data collected using both approaches, as a multi-method technique allows interview/questionnaire data to be validated against directly observed behaviour and vice versa (Browne, 1986).

A major review of marital and family questionnaires, together with some observation techniques for marriage and family assessment has been compiled by Filsinger (1983). To give just one example, the Positive Feelings Questionnaire (PFQ) is designed to assess positive affection and love for one's partner. The PFQ has been shown to be reliable and sensitive to treatment changes, and its validity has also been demonstrated in terms of high correlations with other measures of relationship satisfaction (O'Leary, Fincham and Turkewitz, 1983).

Measures of stress in the family can also be obtained by questionnaires and checklists. McCubbin and Patterson (1983) have developed the Family Inventory of Life Events and Changes (FILE). This is a 71-item self-report instrument designed to record the hardships, stresses and strains a family has experienced within the past year. These are grouped into nine subscales:

1. Intrafamily strains, such as parental problems
2. Marital strains, such as sexual difficulties or separation
3. Pregnancy and childbearing strains
4. Finance and business strains
5. Work/family transitions and strains, such as periods of unemployment
6. Illness and family care strains
7. Family losses or breakdowns
8. Family transitions, such as family members moving in and out
9. Family legal strains, such as court appearances

The total number of family demands is referred to as the 'family pile-up' score, which may be useful as both the reliability and validity of this instrument has been demonstrated to be high.

CONTROL AND TREATMENT OF SPOUSE MALTREATMENT

At the tertiary level of prevention, interventions are employed when violence between the spouses has actually been determined. Without secondary prevention this will be only after many repeated episodes of spouse violence have occurred. Tertiary prevention aimed at reducing the chances of a repeat attack is, by far, the most common form of intervention for controlling and treating spouse abuse. The control and treatment of spouse violence may be classified into four categories:

1. Refuges and shelters
2. Legal controls
3. Police intervention
4. Psychological treatments

It should be pointed out, however, that owing to the increased recognition of links between spouse abuse and child maltreatment, social work practice is beginning to embrace the problem of spouse violence. In addition, health professionals such as health visitors and general practitioners are beginning to develop guidelines for responding to domestic violence (Pahl, 1995; Lloyd, 1995).

Most of these interventions are aimed at battered women, although it is well recognized that both spouses contribute to the cycle of family violence (Bolton and Bolton, 1987; Gelles, 1987a, 1987b; Straus, Gelles and Steinmetz, 1988; Browne, 1993). Of course, this may be a result of men being reluctant to identify themselves and seek treatment for violent relationships. A small number of refuges in the UK (e.g. Swindon Refuge) will now accept male victims as well as female victims for shelter. These refuges are usually independent of those run by the National Women's Aid Federation.

Refuges and Shelters

In 1971 the first refuge for battered women opened its doors (Pizzey, 1974). Twenty-five years later there are about 290 local refuges in the UK, two-thirds of which are affiliated to one of the four National Women's Aid Federations in England, Wales,

Scotland and Northern Ireland. Each year approximately 25 000 women and children use these shelters and 100 000 contact Women's Aid for support (House of Commons Home Affairs Committee, 1993b). The main objective of the refuges is to provide women and their children shelter on an emergency basis from further abuse for an indefinite period (Martin, 1976). They also offer protection, accommodation, support and advice (Pahl, 1978). Conditions in the shelters are not really suitable for long-term stay owing to overcrowding and the general communal nature of the houses, but they do provide a 'breathing space' which is necessary for the women to come to terms with separation and sort out financial, legal and housing matters. The average length of stay in British refuges is five-and-a-half months but many stay for over a year (Binney, Harkell and Nixon, 1981, 1985). The effectiveness of the shelters is difficult to assess but Binney, Harkell and Nixon (1981, 1985) found that 75% of the women considered that the refuge had helped them.

Most refuges help battered women through 'group house meetings'. These support groups aim to combat isolation and 'empower women to shift from being victims to being survivors' (Morley and Mullender, 1994). The women learn that they are not the only ones to suffer violence, reducing their guilt and stigma. They are encouraged to discuss their victimization in relation to the general position of women in society and consider preventive steps to remain safe in future (Clifton, 1985). A minority of refuges operate a counselling service on an individual basis. The purpose is to get the woman to understand the relationship she was in and to make her feel positive about herself. For example, Whipple (1985) described the use of 'reality therapy' with battered women in a refuge. She identified eight steps to helping a battered woman (see Table 5.1).

It has been claimed that the provision of shelters for battered women breaks the cycle of violence (Berk, Newton and Berk, 1986). Indeed, Pizzey (1974) stated that '. . . in providing refuge today we may remove the need for refuge in the future'. However, this view is over-optimistic as one-third of women return home to their abusive husbands and further violence. Repeat assaults included being kicked, pushed into fires or through glass, thrown against walls or down stairs, being

Table 5.1   Reality therapy received by battered women in shelter

---

1. Client is made to feel accepted and cared for:
   - she is allowed to relate details of experiences
   - assurance is given that she is not different
   - help is offered.
2. Client is asked what she did to end abuse in the past?
   - A change in her own behaviour is emphasized.
3. Each description is evaluated.
4. Client's goals for change are identified.
5. A realistic and immediate plan is formulated.
6. Client's commitment is evaluated.
7. Independence and self-help is emphasized.
8. Repeated therapeutic contact is recommended.

Source: Whipple (1985).

punched or having their hair pulled out (Binney, Harkell and Nixon, 1981, 1985). Nevertheless, in a US study, Stout (1989) found that states with a high number of refuges reported fewer killings of female partners than those states with a low number of refuges. Therefore, refuges are regarded as the central and most important service for battered women (Wharton, 1987). Indeed, the recent House of Commons Home Affairs Committee (1993a) inquiry into domestic violence stated that the first priority for government action on domestic violence should be the establishment of a central, coordinated policy for refuge provision throughout the country (para. 124).

Legal Controls

Under the 1976 UK Domestic Violence Act, there are two main types of injunction: Non-molestation Orders and Exclusion Orders. A Non-molestation Order says that the husband must not use violence against the woman or the children. This incorporates assault, pestering, or otherwise interfering (mental cruelty is also included). An Exclusion Order means that the husband must leave the matrimonial home and stay away from it. The court is also empowered to attach subsidiary orders to the main one, for example an interim Custody Order, or the Penalty of Arrest.

As a result of the 'marital rape exemption' being recently abolished in Great Britain (following Israel, New Zealand, Canada, and most parts of Australia and the USA), men can now be prosecuted for raping their wives (Allison and Wrightsman, 1993). Encouragingly, conviction rates are much higher than for only physical assault of a spouse, with half of the men charged being convicted of an offence (Russell, 1991).

For physical assault the police do have the power to arrest the husband for 'actual bodily harm' or for 'behaviour likely to cause a breach of the peace', but the attitudes of the police in general are not very helpful in this respect, although the Criminal Evidence Act (1986) now allows the police to compel women assaulted by their husbands to give evidence against them (Horley, 1986). Nevertheless, if the husband is imprisoned, it is usually not for the violence but for contempt of court.

Dutton (1987) estimated that the probability of 'wife assault' being detected by the criminal justice system in Canada is about 6.5%. If detected, the probability of arrest is 21.2%. Overall, the offender has a 0.38% chance of being punished by the courts. More recently, there has been a number of encouraging changes in legal responses and police interventions with domestic violence (Hilton, 1993).

Police Intervention

The police are the only 24-hour emergency protection service available in every locality to respond to violent attacks. Therefore, they are uniquely situated to provide immediate aid to victims of domestic violence (Morley and Mullender, 1994). However, studies show the police are rated by victims of domestic violence as one of the least helpful agencies. This is despite the fact they are one of the most frequently contacted (Dobash and Dobash, 1979; Binney, Harkell and Nixon, 1981; Evanson, 1982; Pahl, 1985; Leighton, 1989).

The dissatisfaction with police responses appear to be a result of two major factors: firstly, a reluctance to intervene in domestic violence viewed as a civil (private) rather than criminal matter (Edwards, 1989; Bourlet, 1990); secondly, an assumption that victims of domestic violence withdraw charges (Stanko, 1985, 1989; Hanmer, 1989), even though some researchers claim the extent of withdrawal is questionable (Faragher, 1985; Sanders, 1988). These factors have begun to change following the establishment of Domestic Violence Units within British police forces which have been influenced by evaluations of North American police practice.

Arrests were shown by the 'Minneapolis Experiment' (Sherman and Berk, 1984; Berk and Newton, 1985) to substantially decrease the incidence of wife battering and apparently deter the abuser from rebattering. Since 1984, five similar studies have been carried out, but only two have found a deterrent effect of arrest (Sherman, 1992). Nevertheless, arrest emphasizes to the abuser that domestic violence is both illegal and unacceptable. At the same time, arrest indicates to the victim that she is being protected (Buzawa and Buzawa, 1990). A Canadian study in London, Ontario (Jaffe et al., 1986a), also found that police intervention was effective in reducing repeat spouse violence. Furthermore, it was demonstrated that charging was more effective than not charging the assailant.

Domestic Violence Units

These were first established in London (1987); now over half the police forces in England and Wales have a Domestic Violence Unit (DVU). Guidelines circulated in London by the Metropolitan Police (1989) describe the aims of the units as follows:

(i) To produce a readily accessible service to individuals who have experienced violence in the home and assist them in making reasoned choices.
(ii) To help coordinate social, voluntary and caring agencies, to pool ideas and to ensure a consistency of approach to dealing with Domestic Violence.
(iii) To raise the level of consciousness of police officers and the public to the lonely and vulnerable plight of women subjected to this type of violence.

(Cited in House of Commons
Home Affairs Committee, 1993a)

As a result of the development of DVUs, arrests were made in 45% of 9800 recorded domestic violence incidents in London during 1992. This compares to 770 recorded incidents in 1985 (Morley and Mullender, 1994). Even so, there is still room for a great deal of improvement. In addition to better liaison and coordination with other agencies, Morley and Mullender (1994) offered some practical recommendations to police DVUs on how to treat victims of domestic violence (Table 5.2).

Table 5.2   Recommendations to police 'Domestic Violence Units' on how to treat victims (adapted from Morley and Mullender, 1994)

1. Give prompt and sensitive response to calls
2. Ensure victim's (and children's) safety
3. Never attempt conciliation
4. Interview victim away from perpetrator
5. Provide accurate and precise advice, supplemented by multilingual advice leaflets for women
6. Transport victim and children to a place of safety if requested
7. Policy encouraging arrest when evidence allows
8. Victim's wishes should always be considered

In addition to police support from trained officers, it is essential that those battered women who are unable to leave, or wish to remain with their abusive husbands, receive expert psychological help for themselves and their partners.

Psychological Treatments

Goldstein (1983) has identified three main strategies for psychological intervention:

1. Treating the battered woman.
2. Treating the abusive man.
3. Conjoint treatment.

The complex nature of assessing treatment needs for spouse violence is represented diagrammatically in the decision tree (Figure 5.2) devised by Rosenbaum and O'Leary (1986) to determine the best strategy.

Multiple strategies for treating spouse abuse (e.g. Rosenbaum and O'Leary, 1986; Geller, 1992) have come about through neces-

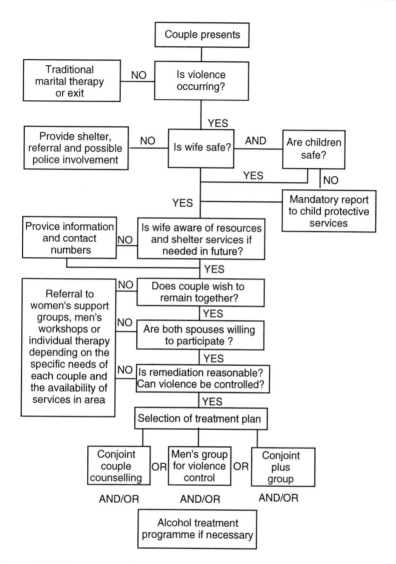

Figure 5.2 Treatment of spouse violence: assessment decision tree (from Rosenbaum and O'Leary, 1986)

sity. Violent men are often reluctant to be involved in counselling and interventions for their aggression (Meth and Pasick, 1990). Even techniques for helping the reluctant client to engage in counselling (Manthei and Matthews, 1989) rely on the individual attending.

Where male partners have been willing to participate in therapy, results in the reduction of their violence have been encouraging when couple therapy is supported by individual and group therapy (Long, 1987; Edleson and Tolman, 1992). Group therapy made up of violent men alone may produce a collusive defence (Skynner, 1976) encouraging macho values to avoid examination of their violence. However, in support of other modes of therapy, groups will help individuals concentrate on their anger (Bion, 1961).

Given the high association between the heavy use of alcohol and family violence (Steinglass, 1987; Pernanen, 1991), related problems may sometimes need to be addressed before or at the same time as the spouse violence. This can be determined in the initial assessment together with other important factors that may trigger violence, e.g. economic problems or sexual difficulties. In addition, personal values and experiences may need to be evaluated as they may enhance the victim/victimizer roles. The coping strategies of the victim during intense conflict may be useful in assessing the dangerousness of the situation and the influences of spouse violence on the children must not be neglected. Indeed, the children's responses may indicate the need for family therapy or individual and group counselling for the children (Jaffe, Wolfe and Wilson, 1990; Cummings and Davies, 1994).

Treating the battered woman

This has included both individual and group psychotherapy. The aim of this therapy is to help the woman achieve a realistic goal and build or restore her self-esteem and sense of competency. If the goal is to leave her husband then it is hoped that by following certain steps (Table 5.1), and having repeated contact to maintain support, the woman will gain independence (Whipple, 1985; Kirkwood, 1993).

Psychotherapy may also help the woman to recognize her feelings of anger at being abused and finally help her to plan her changes in the future, whether she stays or leaves her male partner. During the course of therapy it is sometimes necessary to challenge the commonly held myths that violence is a 'normal' part of intimate relationships and to readdress the woman's causal attributions that it is all her own fault (Goldstein, 1983).

Hendrick-Matthews (1982) suggest that when a battered woman is being counselled it is important to assess how receptive she may be to intervention, as her helplessness can vary from being limited to the abusive relationship to being present in all aspects of her life.

Marital rape victims can resemble battered women who exclusively suffer physical violence. They are characterized by feelings of humiliation, anger, depression, self-blame, poor self-esteem, negative reactions towards men and lack of interest in or enjoyment of sex. Although many victims are in need of counselling for rape, they do not seek help or seek help for a different marital problem. Many of the reasons for this are similar to those for battered wives—for example, learned helplessness, fear of retribution, stigmatization and fear of being blamed. They may see the marital rape as a part of battering and not as a problem in its own right (Hanneke and Sheilds, 1985).

Treating the abusive man

The instigation to spouse violence is usually to be found in the aggressor's social environment. However, Luckenbill (1977) suggests that it is the aggressor's *perception* of events which is important—the way in which the violent person has learned to view and understand the actions of others. Therefore, in order to understand and treat violent behaviour a model is needed which includes environmental, social and individual factors. Novaco (1976, 1978) has offered such a model (see Figure 5.3) which seeks to incorporate both external and internal events in explaining hostility and violence from a cognitive-behavioural perspective.

As outlined in Chapter 2, the determinants of anger are seen by Novaco as a combination of physiological arousal and a cognitive labelling of that arousal. These cognitions are themselves influenced by internal and external factors and the behavioural responses to the situation. The interrelationships between these factors are illustrated in Figure 5.3. Hence, it is suggested that cognitive restructuring of a violent person's perceptions of social

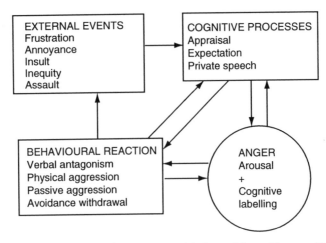

Figure 5.3   Determinants of anger arousal (adapted from Novaco, 1978, with permission)

events, and their relationships with others, can help to reduce aggressive behaviour and hostility (Hollin and Howells, 1989; Browne and Howells, 1996; Dobash and Dobash, 1996).

Cognitive-behavioural approaches to treatment can be divided into those that change cognitions of the violent individual and those that change behaviour (Hollin, 1993). This is exemplified respectively, by 'anger-management' techniques (Feindler and Ecton, 1986; Howells, 1989) and social skills training (Henderson and Hollin, 1983; Howells, 1986). Both these methods of treatment have met with moderate success. A systematic evaluation of such techniques has been provided by Glick and Goldstein (1987) in their 'Aggression Replacement Training' (ART) programme, which uses three main approaches to violent American men:

1. Anger control training
2. Structured learning training, including social problem solving and social skills training.
3. Moral education.

They report that the programme results in greater self-control, lower rates of violence and improved skills. The clinical implications of research on the control of aggression has been reviewed by Goldstein and Keller (1987) and have been applied to the study of spouse abuse (Steinfield, 1986).

An essential feature of anger-management, or anger-control training with violent people, is the attempt to convey to the client an understandable model of anger and its relationship to triggering events, thoughts and violent behaviour itself. Novaco (1978, 1985) labels this the cognitive preparation phase. Cognitive-behavioural methods then focus mainly on the modification of anger-inducing appraisals and on the constructive use of self-instructions (private speech) in order to deal with provoking situations successfully (see Chapter 7).

Social skills training methods (Hollin and Trower, 1986) are used to produce change in overt aggressive behaviour in angry situations. This includes instruction, modelling, video-feedback and role-play rehearsal, to change the violent individual's social repertoire in response to provocation and to reduce the frequency of the escalating verbal and non-verbal threats. Social skills methods have been used as part of a problem-solving orientation (D'Zurilla and Goldfried, 1971; Platt, Pont and Metzger, 1986), with an emphasis on generating alternative strategies for achieving goals and on evaluating the short- and long-term advantages and disadvantages of particular ways of behaving. In practice, maintaining low voice-volume and eliminating verbal threats proved to have the most obvious impact on actual angry encounters, in terms of reducing the probability of a violent outcome (Browne and Howells, 1996).

Group Treatment Programmes for Men

These have concentrated on cessation of violence and the restructuring of attitudes towards the use of violence in the family (e.g. Hall and Ryan, 1984; Stordeur and Stille, 1989). It is generally agreed that a husband's unwillingness to admit to, or work on, the problem of his aggression is a major stumbling block in preventing further abuse (Meth and Pasick, 1990; Jukes, 1993). However, there has been emphasis on increasing group treatment programmes available for abusive men (e.g. Getzel, 1988; Storder and Stille, 1989) to challenge their belief that they 'don't have a problem'. An example of a group programme aimed at teaching abusive men to observe themselves and change their violent behaviour has been described by Edleson and Tolman (1992), who used the following techniques in combination:

1. *Self-observation.* For many men the events leading up to a violent incident are unclear. They cannot connect prior events with the violent act. While aggression may have satisfying effects for the man in the short term, he may fail to see the long-term effects on the relationship. Self-observation helps abusive men to clarify behavioural chains of events and identify precursors of violence in the future.

2. *Cognitive restructuring.* This is a process in which individuals are helped to analyse thought patterns and then change the assumptions and attitudes on which they are based. An abusive man often has a rigid set of beliefs relating to how his partner should behave. This justifies confrontation over his wife's behaviour and allows him to put blame on his wife for causing him to lose his temper.

3. *Interpersonal skills training.* As we have already seen, abusive men and abused women are often deficient in coping skills and so have difficulty diffusing stressful situations before they lead to violence. This type of training is therefore very beneficial to both men and women. It may begin by identifying a specific situation in which a person has experienced difficulties. It is then analysed to find the 'critical moment', that is, the point during the interaction when a different behaviour might have produced a more positive outcome. With the help of others, the appropriate type of behaviour is decided upon and the situation acted out as a role-play to enable the person to practice.

4. *Relaxation training.* A major link in the chain of events leading to a violent outburst is increased tension. If this tension can be recognized and dissipated, another link in the chain has been broken.

5. *Small group format.* Although many men who batter express regret about what they may have done, they continue to blame their partners for the abuse (Bernard and Bernard, 1984) and sometimes receive mixed messages from male peers condoning their actions, e.g. 'Sometimes you've got to keep them in line.' The small group format provides counter-conditioning for such men as they are surrounded by others who want to change their aggressive behaviour.

It must be pointed out, however, that there is a need for systematic evaluation of the effectiveness of most of the above approaches when applied to abusive partners (Gondolf, 1987, 1993). So far, results have been promising (Dobash and Dobash, 1996)

Conjoint Treatment

Given the reciprocal nature of spouse violence, it is thought that abused and abuser integrated programmes for couples, seen together or in groups, help both men and women to perceive the similarity of their concerns and hence enable them to solve their problems together. This approach to marital violence is controversial as it regards both men and women as victims of stress and deficient coping abilities (Hansen and Goldenberg, 1993; Margolin and Burman, 1993). Therefore, stress management techniques (see Meichenbaum, 1985; Boss, 1988) could be suggested for the treatment of couples. Indeed, anger control training for battering couples has shown an 85% success rate, with no further violence up to six months later (Deschner and McNeil, 1986).

There is universal agreement, regardless of theoretical orientation, that conflict is inevitable in long-term relationships. Thus, 'frequent, intense quarrels over long periods of time are not uncommon in marriages' (Retzinger, 1991). Freud (1926) and Bowlby (1973) both consider that anger can be functional or dysfunctional depending on whether the way it is used strengthens the relationship or destroys it. Indeed, Wile (1988, 1993) proposes that 'conflict can improve your relationship' although this view is generally considered appropriate only when anger is adequately controlled by the individual (Beech, 1985).

Problems arise in unhappy couples when one partner denies his or her part in the conflict and projects responsibility and blame onto the other (Horowitz, 1981; Holtzworth-Munroe and Jacobson, 1985). Couple counselling can help these individuals take responsibility for their own negative behaviour. It can also encourage them to explore and question their own negative feelings and emotions (Retzinger, 1991).

CONCLUSION

Help for spouse maltreatment has concentrated on removing the immediate threat of violence by providing shelters, safe homes and refuges for the battered woman, followed by helping her leave the violent relationship. However, many women choose to remain in the relationship and see violence as being only one of a number of stressors. For these women the level of stress can be reduced by increasing the repertoire of coping skills available to both the male and female partner.

The major problem of offering intervention is that most instances of violence go unreported and undetected. This may be due to a fear of retribution by the husband, fear of stigma, fear of being blamed and an absence in the belief that the situation can change. It is often only when a sensitive helping profession-al asks the right question that the victim will admit to the prob-lem. Sensitive methods for interviewing violent families are dis-cussed by Gelles (1987b) and Bolton and Bolton (1987).

In the past, there has been much criticism of both the quality and quantity of services provided for the prevention and treatment of abusive men and battered wives. Traditional sources of help have been accused of aggravating problems by failing to provide assis-tance, deflecting blame onto the woman seeking help and increas-ing her sense of isolation. More recently, professionals have taken a more responsible and informed attitude to spouse violence, but resources available to the health, social and law enforcement ser-vices are still too limited to deal appropriately with the issue. This fact alone will inhibit the adoption of the recommendations made by the House of Commons Home Affairs Committee in their third report on *Domestic Violence* (1993a, 1993b).

CHAPTER 6   Predicting and preventing child maltreatment

Every day in the United States five children die as a result of child maltreatment, homicide being one of the leading causes of death to individuals under the age of 18 years (Durfee and Tilton-Durfee, 1995). Child abuse and neglect is also one of the most common causes of death to young children in Australia and Britain today, with at least one to two children dying at the hands of their parents and relatives every week and a similar number being crippled for life in both countries (Creighton and Noyes, 1989; Creighton, 1992, 1995; Strang, 1992; Central Statistical Office, 1994). Parents and step-parents were responsible for 50–60% of the deaths with relatives and friends responsible for the majority of the remaining fatal cases. However, for children under 10 years, three-quarters of them were killed by the parents or step-parents (Strang, 1992).

These grim statistics highlight the fact that not enough is being done to protect children as exemplified by the increasing number of child-maltreating families in England without social work support (Social Services Inspectorate, 1990). As a result, many children are growing up physically and emotionally scarred for life. This is despite the fact that research shows that the majority of child abuse and neglect is preventable and treatable (see Chapter 7).

THE EXTENT OF CHILD MALTREATMENT

Incidence

In the USA, the National Committee to Prevent Child Abuse and Neglect (1993) calculated from agency reports that 45 children in every 1000 under 18 years of age are abused and/or neglected. In Europe the figure obtained from investigating agencies is much lower, ranging from 1 in 1000 children in Scandinavian countries to 4 in 1000 children in the UK (Department of Health, 1995a). In Australia the rate of child maltreatment is 5 in 1000 children aged 0–16 years (Australian Institute of Health and Welfare, 1995).

It may be argued that such estimates are difficult to compare owing to international variations in reporting practices and that the difference in incidence rates are an artifact of these practices. Nevertheless, similar differences between countries are observed for child homicide rates, which gives some support to the fact that these comparisons may be valid.

Since 1990, the Department of Health in England (DOH) has accurately assessed the number of children and young persons on child protection registers. The estimates are based on annual statistical returns from all 109 local government authorities. Between 1994 and 1995, 48 100 children were the subject of initial child protection case conferences and 63% of them were placed on a register. Figure 6.1 shows the rate per 10 000 children for boys and girls of various age groups and category of abuse, currently on the register in England at 31 March 1995. The overall rate was 3.2 children per thousand under 18 years of age, which represented 34 954 children in need of protection. The highest rates related to very young children under 5 years (4 to 5 per 1000).

According to the Department of Health (1995a), 70% of children on child protection registers are under 10 years of age (including unborn children), with more boys than girls in this age group (12 700 and 11 600 respectively). The opposite is true for the 30% registered between the ages of 10 and 18 years. Here girls outnumber boys to nearly the same extent (5700 and 4900 respectively). This is due to registrations for sexual abuse in adolescent girls. Overall, girls account for 61% of children registered for 'sexual abuse' and boys represent 53% of those registered for physical injury. The boys on the register are generally a little younger. Indeed, NSPCC figures show that over 80% of the physical abuse most likely to cause death or handicap (i.e. head injury) occurs to children aged less than 5 with an over-representation of boys. Over half of all head injuries occur to infants aged less than 1 year (Creighton and Noyes, 1989; Creighton, 1992).

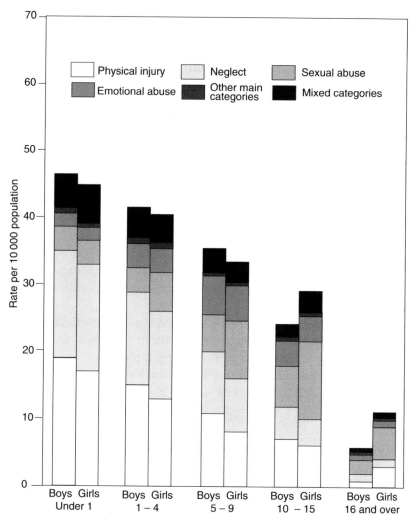

Figure 6.1 Children on child protection registers at 31 March 1995 by age, gender and category of abuse. (Source: Department of Health, 1995a. Reproduced with permission from the Department of Health)

Registration Criteria

The definitions of child abuse recommended as criteria for registration throughout England and Wales by the Departments of Health, Education and Science, the Home Office and Welsh Office (1991) in their joint document *Working Together under the Children Act 1989* (pages 48–49) are as follows:

- *Neglect:* 'The persistent or severe neglect of a child or the failure to protect a child from exposure to any kind of danger, including cold and starvation or extreme failure to carry out important aspects of care, resulting in the significant impairment of the child's health or development, including non-organic failure to thrive.'
- *Physical injury:* 'Actual or likely physical injury to a child, or failure to prevent physical injury (or suffering) to a child, including deliberate poisoning, suffocation and Munchausen's syndrome by proxy.'
- *Sexual abuse:* 'Actual or likely sexual exploitation of a child or adolescent. The child may be dependent and/or developmentally immature', where 'sexual exploitation' represents the involvement of dependent, developmentally immature children and adolescents in sexual activities they do not truly comprehend, to which they are unable to give informed consent or that violate social taboos of family roles (Kempe and Kempe, 1978).
- *Emotional abuse:* 'Actual or likely severe adverse effect on the emotional and behavioural development of a child caused by persistent or severe emotional ill-treatment or rejection.' All abuse involves some emotional ill-treatment. This category is used where it is the main or sole form of abuse.

All the above categories are used for both intrafamilial and extrafamilial abuse and neglect, perpetuated by someone inside or outside the child's home. Mixed categories are also recorded, which register more than one type of abuse and/or neglect occurring to a child. This is especially important when considering 'organized abuse', which is defined in the same document (op. cit.: 38) as: 'Abuse which may involve a number of abusers, a number of abused children and young people and often encompasses different forms of abuse. It involves, to a greater or lesser extent, an element of organization.' For further discussion on the definition of 'organized abuse', see La Fontaine (1993).

Using the above criteria, Table 6.1 shows, for each category of abuse, the number, percentages and rates of children and young people, aged under 18 years, on the registers at 31 March 1995 (Department of Health, 1995a). Thirty-seven per cent of children

Table 6.1   Numbers, percentages and rate of children and young people on English registers at 31 March 1995, by category under which recorded (adapted from Department of Health 1995)

Category of abuse	1994		
	Numbers	%*	Rates[†]
Neglect	11 200	32	10
Physical injury	13 000	37	12
Sexual abuse	9 200	26	8
Emotional abuse	4 700	13	4

* The total of the percentages will exceed 100 because children in the 'mixed' categories are counted more than once.
[†] Rates are per 10 000 population aged under 18.

were considered at risk of physical injury, 32% at risk of neglect, 26% sexual abuse and 13% emotional abuse. The figures show that 8% of children were considered at risk on more than one type of maltreatment.

Overall, 17 300 girls, 17 600 boys and 125 unborn children in England were considered to require protection from maltreatment on 31 March 1995 (32 in 10 000 children) and one in five (23%) of them were 'looked after' by local authorities (in care). Of the 8100 children in care on 31 March 1995, 65.5% (n=5300) were placed with foster parents and 12.5% (n=1000) were living in residential homes or hostels; 16% (n=1300) were placed with a parent and other arrangements were made for a further 6% (n=500). In total, 6800 children on the register were *not* with their own families (Department of Health, 1995a).

Similar registration rates for child abuse and neglect (30 in 10 000 children) were reported previously by the NSPCC (Creighton and Noyes, 1989; Creighton, 1992). Furthermore, the NSPCC claim that their figures for reported physical and sexual abuse were not increasing (Creighton, 1992), although the Department of Health admit to a 7% increase in the number of registrations from 1994 to 1995 (Department of Health, 1995a). During the year, 16% of registrations involved children who had previously been registered and perhaps taken off the register prematurely.

Prevalence

Some researchers claim that new cases of child abuse and neglect which are reported (the incidence rate) represent only a small proportion of the actual number of maltreated children in society at any one time (the prevalence rate). As 9 out of 10 children are hit by their parents (Department of Health, 1995b; Smith et al., 1995), it is suggested that a lot of child abuse and neglect may go undetected (Hallett, 1988; Berger et al., 1988; Hallett and Birchall, 1992; Knutson and Selner, 1994). For example, Straus and Gelles (1986) conducted a prevalence study on a nationally representative selection of American families with at least one child living at home. They obtained information from the parents on their own 'conflict tactics techniques' with their children. They then assessed the number of parents who had used abusive violence. On the basis of the findings they estimated that 1 in every 10 American children aged between 3 and 17 years was subjected to severe physical violence during 1985.

Finkelhor's (1994) international review of 21 countries found a minimum of 7% of females and 3% of males reporting a history of child sexual abuse. He concluded that women were between 1.5 to 3 times more likely than men to have suffered this form of maltreatment. Repeat victimization is also a common finding through the child abuse literature (Fryer and Miyoshi, 1994; Hamilton and Browne, 1997), yet this is apparently little appreciated by those who intervene in child-abusing families. Physical abuse recurs in as much as half of all cases referred to child protection agencies in the USA (Magura, 1981) and sexual abuse will recur in the majority of cases where the offender remains in the family (Bentovim, 1991).

It should be recognized that it is not just the 'procedures' but also parental attitudes and behaviour that require change in order to prevent children being impetuously attacked. If these facts were faced honestly, and if parents who were unable to cope were offered education and training, then the recurrence if not occurrence of child maltreatment might actually be prevented. Nevertheless, it may be unrealistic to offer such services to all parents given current resource limitations. Hence, the ability to predict child maltreatment would be helpful in identifying those families most in need.

PREDICTING CHILD ABUSE AND NEGLECT

As with other problems in child health and development, the risk approach to child maltreatment can be seen as a way of targeting the services that exist and using resources to maximal effect. This is based on the assessment of children and their families as high or low risk for child abuse and neglect. The aim of the risk strategy is to give special attention to those in the greatest need of help in parenting before child maltreatment occurs (Browne, 1995a). In the short term, intervention techniques aimed at the early prediction and identification of potential or actual child abuse and neglect are more realistic. This is considered to be the starting point for secondary prevention that includes professionals involved in counselling, home visits and clinic, health centre or hospital care. Such professionals can be instructed to routinely screen for predictive characteristics in all families who come in contact with the service they are providing.

Checklists of Risk Factors

A number of articles have been written on the prediction of child abuse (see Starr, 1982; Leventhal, 1988; Ammerman and Hersen, 1990; Ammerman, 1993), many of which have presented a list of characteristics common to abusing parents and to abused children (e.g.: Browne and Saqi, 1988a). For example, it has been suggested that an 'early warning system' could begin in the labour room, and that abusing parents can be predicted with 76% accuracy from characteristics noted during the first 24 hours after birth (Gray et al., 1977). Community nurses have been significantly influenced in their work by such articles using the characteristics as 'early warning signs' ever since they were first published in British journals (Lynch, 1975; Lynch, Roberts and Gordon 1976; Lynch and Roberts, 1977). However, recent reviews of the relative value of these characteristics for the practical and routine monitoring of potential child-abusing families have emphasized a need for caution (Barker, 1990; Howitt, 1992).

The danger of predictive claims was demonstrated by Browne and Saqi (1988a) and Browne (1995b), who retrospectively evaluated a typical checklist completed by community nurses around the time of birth. The checklist was developed from a number of demographic and epidemiological studies carried out in the UK, with special reference to non-accidental injury to children in Surrey, England (Browne and Saqi, 1988a).

To facilitate ease of administration, no more than 12 items of information were selected on the basis that they could be routinely and easily obtained by the community nurses. Items included: age of mother, time period between pregnancies, post-delivery separation, evidence of prematurity/low birth weight/handicap, family with separated or single parent, socio-economic problems, history of violence, record of psychiatric problems or socialization difficulties. Characteristics that were more difficult to assess, such as pre-natal experiences, were omitted from the checklist to enhance reliability, and not because they were unimportant.

The idea behind the use of the checklist was that, when applied to all families with a newborn child in a given locality, exceptional families with a high number of adverse characteristics (risk factors) would be identified and offered intervention. It was assumed that the higher the number of factors present, the greater the intervention required and the more 'at risk' the child. Evidence for the high prevalence in abusing families of risk factors used for screening had been already established (see Browne and Saqi, 1988a).

Prospective Evaluation

A prospective evaluation has now been carried out by one of the authors (KB). Community nurses completed the 12-item checklist on all children born in 1985 and 1986 in three health districts of Surrey, England. In total, 14 252 births were screened for the potential of child abuse and neglect and 7% (964) were identified as 'high risk'. This population cohort was then followed up for five years and, in 1991, 106 families had attended a case conference for suspected or actual maltreatment of their newborn child, giving an incidence rate of 7 children in every 1000. This figure is slightly higher than the national estimate of 5 per 1000 for children under 5 years (Department of Health, 1995a). Table 6.2 presents the percentage of abusing and non-abusing families that possessed the checklist characteristics (risk factors), in order of relative importance for prediction. In addition, it shows the percentage of families with a particular characteristic that later abuse and/or neglect their newborn in the first five years of life (conditional probability).

It was found that fully completed checklists, with the relative weighting for each factor taken into account, could correctly classify 86% of cases. The screening procedure was sensitive to 68% of abusing families and correctly specified 94% of the non-abusing families. Surprisingly, nearly one-third of the abusing families had few risk-factor characteristics of any weight and were incorrectly identified as 'low risk' around the time of birth. The most worrying aspect of the checklist is that 6% of the non-abusing families were incorrectly identified as high risk for potential child abuse as they were found to have a number of heavy weighted risk factors. Figure 6.2 shows the grave implications of these statistics in terms of the number of families affected in the population studied.

The Effect of Screening on the Population

The low prevalence of child abuse combined with even the most optimistic estimates of screening effectiveness implies that a screening programme would yield large numbers of false positives (Daniel et al., 1978). The checklist detection rate would mean that for every 14 252 births screened it would be necessary to distinguish between 72 true risk cases and 892 false positives in the 964 cases identified as high risk. This would indicate the requirement of a second screening procedure to be carried out with the high-risk families based on the significant differences found between abusing and non-abusing parent–child relationships (Browne and Saqi, 1987, 1988b). Thus, a second screening could possibly distinguish the true potential NAI cases from the false positives by the use of behavioural indicators.

A more difficult problem would be to distinguish the 34 missed cases of potential child abuse from the 13 254 correctly identi-

Table 6.2 Relative predictive value of screening characteristics for child abuse as determined by discriminate function analysis. (Ranked in order of importance with percentage prevalence)

Checklist characteristics n = Parents with a child under 5 (baseline)	Abusing families (%) (n = 106)	Non-abusing families (%) (n = 14.146)	Conditional probability* (%) 0.7
1. History of family violence	30.2	1.6	12.4
2. Parent indifferent, intolerant or over-anxious towards child	31.1	3.1	7.0
3. Single or separated parent	48.1	6.9	5.0
4. Socio-economic problems such as unemployment	70.8	12.9	3.9
5. History of mental illness, drug or alcohol addiction	34.9	4.8	5.2
6. Parent abused or neglected as a child	19.8	1.8	7.6
7. Infant premature, low birth weight	21.7	6.9	2.3
8. Infant separated from mother for more than 24 hours post-delivery	12.3	3.2	2.8
9. Mother less than 21 years old at time of birth	29.2	7.7	2.8
10. Step-parent or cohabitee present	27.4	6.2	3.2
11. Less than 18 months between birth of children	16.0	7.5	1.6
12. Infant mentally or physically handicapped	2.8	1.1	1.9

* 'Conditional probability' refers to the percentage of families with a particular characteristic that later abuse and/or neglect their newborn in the first five years of life.

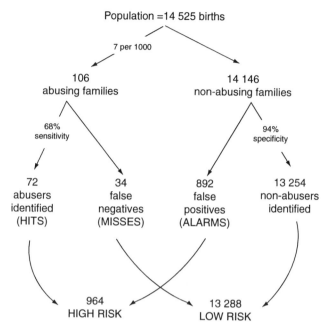

Figure 6.2 Screening effects on a population

fied non-abusers, as they would be mixed up in a population of 13 288 low-risk families.

Therefore, when the checklist was applied prospectively to a large population of births, 7% of English families with a newborn child showed a high number of 'predisposing' factors of child abuse. On follow-up, only one of 13 of these 'high risk' families went on to abuse their children within 5 years of birth. On the basis that approximately half of all abused children are under 5 years of age (Creighton, 1992), this figure should have been considerably higher in order to prevent the majority of child maltreatment. However, it must be recognized that risk factors, which are thought to predispose families to child abuse, are not a sufficient causal explanation (Browne, 1989b).

As outlined in Chapter 2, the chances of situational stressors (risk factors) resulting in child abuse and other forms of family violence are mediated by and depend on the interactive relationships within the family. A secure relationship between the parent and child will 'buffer' any effects of stress and facilitate coping strategies by the parent. In contrast, insecure, or anxious relationships will not 'buffer' the parent under stress and any overload, such as an argument or a child misbehaving, may result in a physical or emotional attack. Overall, this will have a negative effect on the existing parent–child relationship and reduce any 'buffering' effects still further, making it easier for stress to overcome the parent once again. This may lead to a situation where stress results in repeated physical assaults on the child. Indeed, stress in family functioning has been shown to be an important predictor of child abuse potential (Abidin, 1990).

The aetiology of child abuse and neglect is complex. It is now universally acknowledged that the causes of child maltreatment are multifactorial (see Ammerman and Hersen, 1990, 1992), involving characteristics of the parent and child, the social system of the family and demographic and cultural situation of the community (see Chapter 2). Indeed, Ammerman and Hersen state that the prediction and assessment of child maltreatment must take account of the fact that a non-accidental injury to a child rarely takes place in the absence of other inextricably linked events, situations and states—for example, unemployment, mental illness, poverty, alcohol abuse, poor parenting skills or marital discord.

In the USA a number of assessment and screening tools (for example, the 'Child Abuse Potential Inventory') have taken a multifaceted approach (Milner, 1986). Indeed, the CAP inventory is one of the few self-report questionnaires (160 items) that has been evaluated in terms of its reliability (internal consistency and temporal stability) and construct validity. However, the relevance of checklists and inventories for the prediction of child sexual abuse remains questionable, especially when the epidemiological differences between sexual and physical abuse are considered (Jason et al., 1982; Browne, 1994). Nevertheless, certain risk factors are the same, such as step-parenting, marital conflict, poor relationship with parents, etc. (Finkelhor, 1980a; Bergner et al., 1994).

Leventhal (1988) provides evidence from longitudinal cohort studies that suggests that prediction is feasible. However, he concludes that improvements in the assessment of high-risk families are necessary, including the further development and use of a standardized clinical assessment of the parent–child relationship.

THE ASSESSMENT OF PARENT–CHILD RELATIONSHIPS

The move away from socio-demographic to clinical approaches of assessment for pathological parenting requires detailed knowledge of parent–child interaction and attachment in child-maltreating families (Schaffer, 1990).

Belsky (1988) concetualizes child maltreatment as a social psychological phenomenon that is 'multiply determined by forces at work in the individual, the family, as well as in the community and the culture in which both the individual and the family are embedded' (Belsky, 1980: 320). Given a particular combination of these factors, an interactional style develops within the family and it is in the context of this interaction that abuse occurs. The detection of early signs indicating a malfunction in the caretaker-infant relationship has been considered by Crittenden (1988a) who discusses the role of the parents' thought processes in the distortion of interactive patterns in maltreating families. She discovers that two patterns—cooperation/interference and involved/withdrawn—significantly discriminate abusing and non-abusing families. Stratton and Swaffer (1988) also state, 'there are good theoretical grounds for supposing that the beliefs that abusive parents hold about their children are an important factor in determining whether, and in what ways, a child will be abused'. The results of their work show that abusing mothers attribute more control and more internal causes to their children and less to themselves in comparison with non-abusing mothers or mothers of handicapped children. This finding has also been found by Wiehe (1987) who demonstrated that abusing mothers have less empathic ability and an external locus of control in comparison to non-abusing mothers. They all go on to suggest that causal attributions held by abusive parents, both in general and with respect to their children, should be a powerful indicator of the chances of child maltreatment.

Assessing Parent–Child Relationships in High-Risk Families

There are six important aspects to the assessment of high-risk parent–child relationships and the child's need for protection (Browne 1995a).

1. The evaluation of the caretaker's knowledge and attitudes to parenting the child.
2. Parental perceptions of the child's behaviour and the child's perceptions of the parent.
3. Parental emotions and responses to stress.
4. The style of parent–child interaction and behaviour.
5. The quality of child to parent attachment.
6. The quality of parenting.

Knowledge and attitudes to child rearing

Research suggests that abusing and non-abusing families have different attitudes about child development. Martin and Rodeheffer (1976) commented that abusers have unrealistic and distorted expectations of their children's abilities. They are said to have very high expectations of their children and this influences discipline and punishment (Feshbach, 1980). For example, abusing parents may have unrealistic beliefs that babies should be able to sit alone at 12 weeks and take the first step at 40 weeks. More importantly, they may expect their infants to be able to recognize wrong-doing at 52 weeks. Therefore, a significant proportion of sexual and physical abusive incidents involve senseless attempts by parents to force a child to behave in a manner that is beyond the child's developmental limitations.

Research also suggests that these deficits in parental knowledge or understanding are due to low adult intelligence (e.g. Smith, 1975), but this has been refuted (Hyman, 1977; Altemier et al., 1979, 1984). The parents know what to expect and what to do when caring for young children; they just do not apply this knowledge to their own children. Starr (1982) found that one of the differences between abusing and non-abusing parents is that the abusing group see child rearing as a simple rather than a complex task. Many of them show a lack of awareness of their child's abilities and needs.

Parental perceptions of child behaviour in abusing and non-abusing (high-risk and low-risk) families

It is believed that abusing parents have more negative conceptions of their children's behaviour than non-abusing parents; they perceive their children to be more irritable and demanding. This may be related to the fact that abused children are more likely to have health problems and eating or sleeping disturbances. Alternatively, it may be a direct result of the unrealistic expectations often reported for abusing parents (Rosenberg and Reppucci, 1983). A study conducted by Browne and Saqi (1987) examined maternal perceptions in abusing families compared with high-risk and low-risk control groups. The control families with an infant of the same age and sex were designated high or low risk on the basis of their scores on the checklist of risk factors described earlier. The families were also matched for ages and occupation of parents, ethnic origin of child, and type of housing.

The mothers completed a questionnaire based on the 'Behaviour Checklist' devised by Richman, Stevenson and Graham (1983) which covered four main areas of child behaviour: sleeping and eating patterns, activity, controllability and interaction with others. Table 6.3 shows that the abusers accumulated higher scores than both the high-risk and the low-risk families, which reflected a greater number of negative perceptions. The low-risk mothers were the most positive and scored the least.

Dangerous perceptions that might act as triggers for violent parental acts—for example, 'my child is frequently very difficult to manage and control' or 'my child is frequently irritable and miserable'—were never reported by low-risk mothers and only stated by 6% of high-risk mothers (approximately the number that eventually abuse their child). However, half of the abusing mothers held such beliefs. Thus, a parent under stress requires a certain level of misconception and/or negative evaluation of her child to become a child abuser. As exemplified in Table 6.3, the majority of the high-risk group have more positive perceptions about their

Table 6.3 Maternal perceptions of child behaviour as reflected by behaviour checklist scores: high scores = negative perceptions (Browne and Saqi, 1987)

	Low-risk families ($n=39$)	High-risk families ($n=35$)	Abusing families ($n=16$)
Score: 0 to 7	64.1%	40.0%	31.2%
No. of cases	25	14	5
Score: 8 to 14	35.9%	57.1%	43.8%
No. of cases	14	20	7
Score: 15 to 28	0.0%	2.9%	25.0%
No. of cases	0	1	4

Chi-squared = 18.79, df = 2, p <0.001.

children than do the abusers, and these perceptions may help prevent abuse, despite the presence of risk factors. The importance of positive parental perceptions as a protective factor also has been confirmed in the work of Wood-Shuman and Cone (1986).

It has previously been suggested that child factors contribute to the risk of abuse (Kadushin and Martin, 1981). Browne and Saqi (1987) do not support this notion; for example, they found no significant differences in children's health records. The abuse may be attributed to the fact that the parents have unrealistic expectations of their children. They interpret certain age-appropriate behaviours as deliberate or intentional non-compliance, concluding that this behaviour is an indication of the child's inherent 'bad' disposition. Thus abusive parents may see their child's behaviour as a threat to their own self-esteem, which then elicits a punitive attitude and an insensitive approach to parenting.

Children's perceptions

A small project carried out by Hyman and Mitchell (1975) compared physically abused with deprived children using the Bene–Anthony Test of Family Relations. This test consists of cut-out figures representing family members. Into boxes attached to the figures the child posts messages which reflect his or her feelings for family members. Battered children avoided the mother's box, expressing significantly fewer feelings for her, either of a positive or negative kind than the control children. Equally they denied that their mothers had positive feelings or negative feelings for them. These lack of feelings were found among previously battered children who had been receiving help for two years. This was markedly different to other deprived but not physically assaulted children, who did express their feelings towards their mother, both positive and negative.

Assessing Parental Emotions and Responses to Stress

A factor common to many child abusers is a heightened rate of arousal in stressful situations. Frodi and Lamb (1980) showed videotaped scenes of crying and smiling infants to abusive parents and matched controls. It was found that abusers show greater discomfort, irritation and emotional arousal in response to infant cries and smiles. Abusive parents also showed greater physiological arousal, such as increased blood pressure and heart rate and reported more annoyance, indifference and less sympathy to both the crying and smiling infants.

In a similar study conducted by Wolfe et al. (1983) abusive and non-abusive parents were presented with scenes of videotaped parent–child interaction, some of which were highly stressful (such as children screaming and refusing to comply with their parents) and some of which were non-stressful (for example, a child watching television quietly). As expected, the abusive parents responded with greater negative psychophysiological arousal than did the non-abusive comparison group to the stressful scenes. Thus, it may be suggested that poor responses to stress and emotional arousal play a crucial role in the manifestation of child abuse and neglect.

Indeed, abusing parents score high on measures of stress, such as the 'family stress checklist' (Orkow, 1985) and the 'Parenting Stress Index' PSI (Browne and Saqi, 1987). The PSI is a screening instrument that provides scores related to the parent's sense of attachment, competence, social isolation, relationship with spouse, mental and physical health. In addition to an assessment of life stress events, it also provides scores on the child's demands, mood, activity, adaptability and acceptability, as perceived by the parent (Abidin, 1990).

Trickett and Kuczynski (1986) studied the techniques of discipline chosen by parents and their effectiveness. She found that abusive parents reported using punitive approaches, such as yelling and threatening, regardless of the type of child misbehaviour. Non-abusive parents on the other hand used a variety of disciplinary techniques depending on the situation. Consequently it was found that abused children were less likely than non-abused children to comply with their parents' commands.

Observing Parent–Child Interaction and Behaviour

Rohner (1986) presents behavioural descriptions of parental acceptance, hostility, indifference and rejection (see Chapter 11, Figure 11.1) but measures these concepts using a questionnaire for adolescent children and young adults rather than using direct observation in their assessment, which is essential for younger children. One method of assessment using direct observation involves looking at the amount of interactive behaviour occurring between parent and child (Browne, 1986). At this basic level the interest is in whether or not there is any interaction and whether it receives a response (regardless of its content). Types of interaction have been analysed in the following manner. If a general interactive initiative is shown (i.e. behaviour directed towards another), it can have one of three possible outcomes:

- It may result in the respondent reacting with another interactive initiative (mutual or reciprocal interaction).
- It may result in the respondent reacting with a non-interactive behaviour (causal interaction).
- It may receive no reaction at all (failed interaction).

For example, if the mother is eating and the child reaches for the food (interactive initiative), the mother may give the child some food (mutual interaction), stop eating and attend to the child (causal interaction) or continue to eat (failed interaction).

Interaction assessments demonstrate that abused infants and their mothers have interactions that are less reciprocal and fewer

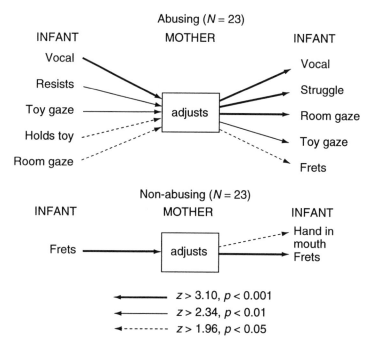

Figure 6.3 Diagrams showing the probabilities of different acts by an infantt preceding and following 'adjusts' by their mother, for mothers suspected of child abuse and control mothers (from Browne and Saqi, 1987)

in number than their matched controls, whether in the presence or absence of a stranger (Burgess and Conger, 1978; Hyman, Parr and Browne, 1979; Browne, 1986; Browne and Saqi, 1987, 1988b).

The reciprocal nature of the parent–child behaviour also can be assessed by methods broadly based on the 'strange situation procedure' (Ainsworth et al., 1969). The methods used involve at least three phases of observation: the infant's behaviour and interaction before separation from the mother, during separation, and on reunion.

Overall, research studies (Hyman, Parr and Browne, 1979; Lewis and Schaeffer, 1981; Gaensbauer, 1982; Browne and Saqi, 1987, 1988b) indicate that prior to separation there is less positive affect between abusing mother–infant dyads, in comparison with non-abusing dyads. During separation, abused infants show less interest in strangers and objects around the room and are less upset than their matched controls. However, abused infants who do display distress and discomfort persist in this, long after their mother's return. By contrast, the matched non-abused infants show immediate recovery. On reunion, the abused infants show less positive affect and greeting behaviour, and again mother–infant interaction in abusing pairs is less reciprocal than controls, with fewer visual and vocal exchanges.

In addition to reporting the frequency of interactions, Browne and Saqi (1987) also examined interactive sequences for the mothers and their children. They found that abusive mothers were more likely to disrupt an interactional sequence by physically adjusting the infant's posture or clothing, whereas non-abusive mothers extended interactive sequences by offering a toy or smiling at their child. Using sequential methods (see Browne, 1986), it can be demonstrated that a lack of sensitivity shown by abusing mothers can enhance aversive behaviour in their infant rather than inhibit it. In *Figure 6.3*, for example, non-abusing mothers significantly respond with ADJUST only to the signal of 'FRETS' from their infants, which may result in a change of behaviour and the cessation of fretting, if they successfully attend to the needs of their infant. By contrast, abusing mothers respond to a wide range of behaviours with 'ADJUST', none of which are indicative of the infant's distress. Ironically, the abusing mothers sometimes induce distress from their infants in the form of 'STRUGGLE' and 'FRETS', as a result of their insensitive and untimely interventions.

In a study of abusive mothers interacting with their young infants, Dietrich, Starr and Weisfield (1983) also noticed that abusive mothers would actively interfere with the baby, poking it and preventing its play. They were also occasionally openly hostile. By contrast, neglectful mothers were found to be generally uninvolved and passive. Observational studies provide evidence that social behaviours and interaction patterns within abusing and non-abusing families are different. Abusing parents have been described as being aversive, negative and controlling, with less pro-social behaviour (Wolfe, 1985, 1987, 1991). They also show less interactive behaviour both in terms of sensitivity and responsiveness to their children. This may result in infants developing an insecure attachment to their abusive caretakers, which in turn produces marked changes in the abused children's socio-emotional behaviour in accordance with the predictions of attachment theory (Browne and Saqi, 1988b). Nevertheless, the consequences of maltreatment are not the same for all children. Findings suggest that there are more behaviour problems in children who are both abused and neglected (Crittenden, 1988b). Abusing and neglectful parents suffer from confusion and ambivalence in their relations with their children. This is not the same as simple parental rejection; it reflects more an uncertainty in the relationship which leaves the child vulnerable and perplexed about what is expected.

Assessing Infant Attachment to the Parent

The view that children are predisposed to form attachments during infancy (Bowlby, 1969) has considerable importance for the study of child abuse. The literature contains numerous reports regarding the high number of abusive parents who were themselves victims of abuse as children (e.g. Egeland, 1988). It has been suggested that in some cases the link between experience of abuse as a child and abusing as a parent is likely to be the result of an unsatisfactory early relationship with the principal caretaker and a failure to form a secure attachment (Browne and Parr, 1980; DeLozier, 1982; Bowlby, 1984; Crittenden and Ainsworth, 1989).

Evidence for this notion has been provided by Egeland and Sroufe (1981) and Crittenden (1985), who found that all of the abused and neglected infants in their study showed an insecure pattern of attachment towards their mother. However, Browne and Saqi (1988b) have demonstrated that only a significantly greater proportion of maltreated infants are insecurely attached to their caregiver (70%) in comparison with infants who have no record of maltreatment (26%). Table 6.4 shows that, despite the maltreatment, 30% of abused children are resilient to their experience and are securely attached.

Schneider-Rosen et al. (1985) report similar findings and suggest that, even for abused infants, compensatory background factors

Table 6.4 Attachment patterns derived from the brief separation and reunion of mother and infant in a strange environment

Attachment pattern	Ainsworth category	Abusing families (N=23)	Non-abusing families (N=23)
Anxious/avoidant (insecure)	A1 A2	10	3
Independent (secure)	B1 B2	4	11
Dependent (secure)	B3 B4	3	6
Anxious/resistant or ambivalent (insecure)	C1 C2	6	3
Total number of insecure attachments		16	6

(Chi-square = 9.04; df=3, p < 0.03)
Source: Browne and Saqi (1988b).

will increase the probability of a secure attachment, while in normal circumstances stressful environmental factors will increase the likelihood of an insecure attachment.

Classification of Infant Attachment Patterns

Each individual infant can be assessed for the quality of attachment to the parent. This is based on the infant's behaviour throughout pre-separation, separation and reunion with the parent. The final assessment of infant to parent attachment can be described using four broad categories of the infant's response to the presence and absence of the mother (adapted from Ainsworth et al., 1978; source, Browne and Saqi, 1988b).

1. *Anxious/avoidant infants* (Insecurely Attached Type I) show high levels of play behaviour throughout and tend not to seek interaction with the parent or stranger. They do not become distressed at being left alone with the stranger. On reunion with their parent, they frequently resist any physical contact or interaction.

2. *Independent infants* (Securely Attached Type I) demonstrate a strong initiative to interact with their parent and to a lesser extent, the stranger. They do not especially seek physical contact with their parent and are rarely distressed on separation. They greet their parent upon reunion by smiling and reaching.

3. *Dependent infants* (Securely Attached Type II) actively seek physical contact and interaction with their parent. They are usually distressed and often cry when left alone with the stranger. On their parent's return, they reach out and maintain physical contact, sometimes by resisting the parent's release. Generally they exhibit a desire for interaction with the parent in preference to the stranger.
4. *Anxious/resistant or ambivalent infants* (Insecurely Attached Type II) show low levels of play behaviour throughout and sometimes cry prior to separation. They demonstrate an obvious wariness of the stranger and intense distress at separation. They are also more prone to crying while left alone with the stranger. They are ambivalent and frequently mix contact-seeking behaviours with active resistance to contact or interaction. This is especially evident on the parent's return: on reunion, these infants continue to be distressed as usually the parent fails to comfort them.

Assessing the Quality of Parenting

Ainsworth et al. (1978) have examined the relationship between the infant's response to separation and reunion and the behaviour of both mother and child in the home environment. Their findings suggest that maternal sensitivity is most influential in affecting the child's reactions. In the homes of the securely attached infants, sensitive mothering was exhibited to the infant's behaviour, while insecurely attached, anxious and avoidant infants were found to have their interactive behaviour rejected by the mothers. It was suggested that the enhanced exploratory behaviours shown by these infants were an attempt to block attachment behaviours that had been rejected in the past. In the home environments of the insecurely attached anxious and resistant infants a disharmonious and often ambivalent mother–infant relationship was evident. The resistant and ambivalent behaviours shown were seen as a result of inconsistent parenting. A summary of Ainsworth et al.'s conclusions with regard to parenting and infant attachment in a heterogeneous population of US families is presented in Figure 6.4.

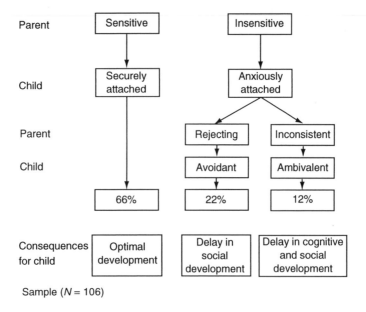

Figure 6.4 Patterns of infant attachment and parenting in a heterogeneous population of US families (adapted from Ainsworth et al., 1978)

Maccoby (1980) concludes from the above findings that the parents' contribution to attachment can be assessed and identified within four dimensions of caretaking style:

1. *Sensitivity/insensitivity.* The sensitive parent 'meshes' her responses to the infant's signals and communications to form a cyclic turn-taking pattern of interaction. In contrast, the insensitive parent intervenes arbitrarily, and these intrusions reflect the parent's own wishes and mood.
2. *Acceptance/rejection.* The accepting parent accepts in general the responsibility of child care. He or she shows few signs of irritation with the child. However, the rejecting parent has feelings of anger and resentment that eclipse his or her affection for the child. The parent often finds the child irritating and resorts to punitive control.
3. *Cooperation/interference.* The cooperative parent respects the child's autonomy and rarely exerts direct control. The interfering parent imposes his or her wishes on the child with little concern for the child's current mood or activity.

4. *Accessibility/ignoring.* The accessible parent is familiar with the child's communications and notices them at some distance, hence the parent is easily distracted by the child. The ignoring parent is preoccupied with his or her own activities and thoughts and often fails to notice the child's communications unless they are obvious through intensification. The parent may even forget about the child outside the scheduled times for caretaking.

The four dimensions above are heavily influenced by parental attitudes, emotions and perceptions of the child as discussed earlier. The dimensions are interrelated and together they determine how 'warm' the parent is to the child and the possibility of rejection (see Chapter 11).

The implications of parental rejection and appropriate interventions with emotionally abused and neglected children are discussed more fully in Chapter 7. In addition, Iwaniec (1995) offers practical approaches to the assessment and treatment of families in need of help because of emotional abuse and neglect, from the perspective of child growth, development and well-being.

PREVENTING CHILD ABUSE AND NEGLECT

Effective intervention strategies to prevent child maltreatment have recently been reviewed (Willis, Holden and Rosenberg, 1992; Gough, 1994). The majority of interventions described operate at the third level of prevention, i.e. after violence to the child has occurred. However, when verbal abuse and denigration of children are considered, then it might be argued that prevention should be directed to most parents and guardians.

Primary Prevention

Techniques of intervention which attempt a fundamental change across society, to prevent child abuse before it occurs, are termed 'primary preventions'. Usually these operate at a community level and offer support to all families. The three main approaches to the primary prevention of child abuse are: firstly, to adapt existing services to enhance parental competence, and promote change through parental education by, for example, community nursing programmes; secondly, to mobilize community resources and offer voluntary help through networks and crisis contact services that reduce social isolation such as telephone helplines; and thirdly, to educate the public through specific projects, such as publicity campaigns which aim to raise public awareness about the prevention of child abuse and neglect.

Publicity campaigns

A nationwide advertising campaign to educate people about emotional abuse was carried out by the US National Committee for the Prevention of Child Abuse (1988–1992). Television, post and magazine adverts used catch phrases such as:

'words hit as hard as a fist'; 'stop using words that hurt'; 'start using words that help'. One advertisement went on to give examples of phrases considered to be emotionally damaging to the child:

- 'Children believe what their parents tell them.'
- 'You disgust me.'
- 'You're pathetic. You can't do anything right.'
- 'You can't be my kid.'
- 'Hey stupid! Don't you know how to listen?'
- 'I'm sick of looking at your face.'
- 'I wish you were never born.'
- 'Stop and listen to what you're saying, you might not believe your ears!'

In Australia, the Queensland Centre for Prevention of Child Abuse in Brisbane also mounted a poster campaign on 'Verbal Abuse' with phrases like 'your words can tear a child apart', 'emotional abuse scars the mind (not the body) leaving your child with painful memories'.

Recently, a similar but more positive approach has been taken in the UK by the Lincolnshire Area Child Protection Committee (1990), who developed a local radio, poster and leaflet publicity campaign entitled 'What do Children Hear?'. Figure 6.5 shows

Figure 6.5   Poster campaign (Lincolnshire Area Child Protection Committee, 1990)

the poster used in the campaign. They followed this with leaflets available to all parents in the area which contained thought-provoking statements about the good and bad aspects of parenting and the problems of coping with young children (*Figure 6.6*).

Publicity campaigns aimed at emotional abuse will involve most parents and few parents will be able to say that the advertisements do not concern them. These primary interventions, therefore, will probably be much more successful than others that aim directly at the minority of parents who physically or sexually abuse their children.

An advertisement stating 'Child Sexual Assault: It's often closer to home than you think' (New South Wales, Government Child Protection Council, 1989) can do little more than heighten awareness. Primary prevention, through the education of parents, must aim at understanding the problems of parenting and at the same time offer positive suggestions for coping.

Research in Chicago has shown that such publicity campaigns have influenced the self-reported behaviour, attitudes and beliefs of parents who viewed the advertisements (Daro, 1989, 1991). Primary preventative strategies are essential to inhibit the kind of parental behaviour that is not identified as abuse by statutory agencies, but which seriously affects the way children feel about themselves and the way they feel about their parents. Furthermore, emotional outbursts and 'verbal' abuse are highly associated with physically and sexually abusing parents and therefore may potentially lead to serious injury of the child.

Indeed, Belsky and Vondra (1987) argue that broad-based interventions for *all* parents are most effective for reducing the rates of child abuse and neglect. Using existing services, they suggest 'mini-interventions' to improve parents' knowledge and attitudes to children. The school system could be used for educating pupils with regular lessons on parenting skills and realistic expectations for parenthood. Pre-natal craft classes provide another ideal opportunity for educating prospective parents. The present physical care focus of pre-natal classes might be broadened to include psychological aspects of child care and appropriate coping strategies for family stress and the transition to parenthood.

BEING A PARENT OR A CARER OF A CHILD CAN BE:

Rewarding Wearing
Fun Tiring
Exciting Boring
Great Horrible
Wonderful Terrible

Being a parent is never an easy job. We all know of things that can make us feel stressed and tired. Here are a few:

- Having to cope alone
- Money may be short
- Feeling trapped and alone
- Having housing problems
- Trying to juggle both a job and being a parent

ON TOP OF THIS WE MAY HAVE TO COPE WITH:

- A child who is unhappy
- A wet, rainy or windy day
- The shopping and cleaning to do
- Not feeling well yourself
- A thousand and one other things

It is not surprising that at times we lose our patience or say things to children that can hurt them and that later we regret.

There are times when we have to say no, but if that is all a child hears then he will feel that he is not loved or needed.

? Have you ever stopped to think how that feels to your child?

? Have you ever put yourself in your childs' shoes?

CHILDREN NEED TO BE TOLD THAT THEY ARE:

LOVED
NEEDED
WANTED

STOP AND LISTEN

TO WHAT YOU'RE SAYING

TO YOUR

CHILD

BEING A PARENT IS NEVER AN EASY JOB:

BUT REMEMBER —
YOU MATTER TOO

It is just that sometimes we are:

Under Pressure
Busy
Tired
Angry
Anxious
Unhappy
Worried
Scared

OR WE FEEL WE JUST CAN'T COPE

It's at times like these that we may say things we wish we could take back.

? WHAT CAN WE DO ABOUT IT?

TAKE TIME OUT - TALK TO A FRIEND
TAKE A DEEP BREATH - COUNT TO 10

IF YOU WISH YOU CAN TALK TO

Your Health Visitor, Family Doctor, School Nurse, Social Worker.

Figure 6.6 Leaflet for ALL parents (Lincolnshire Area Child Protection Committee, 1990)

In the long term, employment environments may be changed to include 'family bulletin boards'. This could be used for posting details of births, birthdays, baby sitters and childhood articles for sale. Such parent enhancement techniques can still be seen in Eastern Europe and are common in Japan. More 'universal' changes in society can be promoted by government legislation (Frude, 1991)—for example, banning the use of corporal punishment by parents and teachers (EPOCH, 1990) with information available to parents on alternative methods of controlling children.

Educational approaches also have been directed at children in schools to enable the potential victim to avoid the dangers from potential sexual perpetrators (e.g. KIDSCAPE—Elliott, 1985). For understandable reasons, training programmes have tended to concentrate on extrafamilial abuse such as sexual assault and bullying, yet according to responses to telephone helplines intrafamilial abuse is probably a greater problem.

Telephone helplines

The figures from Britain's Childline (Browne and Griffiths, 1988) show that a vast variety of topics are discussed over the telephone. Intrafamilial abuse (including those 'at risk') represent 47.6% of the calls. Telephone calls that require counselling children and adolescents with non-abusive problems within or outside of their families represent 24.8 and 11.5% of callers, respectively. For extrafamilial abuse cases (10.3% of calls), the telephone call may be of immense significance to the child. Obviously, children abused outside the family can be advised to confide in their parents about their problem, in order to seek further help.

However, the usefulness of telephone helplines with abuse inside the family is questionable. The majority of abuse and neglect occurs to children under 10 years of age, who are not able or not willing to use the service. Indeed, 94% of calls to Childline are from children aged 10 years or older. When those who do call admit to being abused they rarely give their name and address. Thus of the 28 000 phone calls to Childline involving specific help in the first year of operation, only 270 children (1.0%) were referred to other agencies for help. This, at best, means that telephone helplines are an extremely limited prevention service, especially when some of the children referred are already known to the health and social services agencies.

A more useful method to reduce isolation and prevent child abuse is seen in voluntary agencies that offer help through direct contact with the distressed parent. NEWPIN (Pound and Mills, 1985), for example, runs support groups for depressed mothers in impoverished parts of London, while HOMESTART has a nationwide service of volunteer experienced mothers ready and willing to help and befriend less experienced parents (Van der Eyken, 1982).

However, owing to the scarcity of effective primary prevention programmes aimed at intrafamilial child abuse, and in view of the possible prevalence of child abuse within the family, an objective and systematic means of family assessment to identify parents most at risk, may be more beneficial in the short term.

The inability of potential child-abusing parents to interact adaptively with their children is seen by many researchers as being representative of their general lack of interpersonal skills. Abusive parents share a common pattern of social isolation, poor work history, and few friendships outside the home. This isolation means that child-abusing parents are not willing or able to seek help from outside agencies which could provide assistance or emotional support at a primary preventative level. If they do seek help from other people, abusive parents are most likely to choose people in similar situations to themselves, so they gain no experience of alternative parental styles or coping strategies and continue to be ineffective in controlling their children. Therefore, parents who are already showing poor parenting skills may not be susceptible to primary preventative techniques. They are best offered help at a secondary preventative level.

Secondary Prevention

Interventions that are designed to prevent child abuse and neglect at an early stage of inadequate parenting are termed 'secondary preventions'. Families identified as high risk for child maltreatment by screening may be offered treatment before any serious harm has occurred to the child, therefore reducing the chance of the child being taken into care and the family breaking up. Furthermore, when resources are scarce, high-risk families can be given priority over others for primary prevention services, such as health visits, social work visits, self-help groups, home helps, nursery placements, etc. Of course, such services should be available to *all* families but in reality most are not. Cuts in local and national services have limited the universal nature of work in health and social welfare and professionals are required to prioritize families in need of intervention.

Intervention is based on the same principles as primary prevention but is enhanced by personal contact. A home visit to the parents may encourage the development of appropriate routines of feeding practices and childcare. The home visitor may demonstrate non-violent methods of discipline and provide advice on stress management and anger control (see Chapter 7). Parents' knowledge and attitudes can be modified, as before, with the use of pamphlets and video films but with the added advantage of personal discussion.

The results of home visit interventions are modest owing to the lack of community resources. Barker (1990) claimed some success in enhancing parenting skills and reducing child abuse and neglect by the use of health visitors trained in specific interventions. However, Stevenson et al. (1988) found little evidence of change in parenting style and child behaviour problem after health visitor interventions with high-risk families. It must be pointed out, however, that the health visitors only received two weeks' training.

More encouraging were the findings of Olds and his colleagues (1986, 1989, 1994). They found that high-risk mothers who were visited differed from comparison (control) groups of high-risk mothers who were offered little intervention. The visited mothers had more positive perceptions of their infants and punished them less, which resulted in fewer incidents of child abuse and neglect compared to the control groups. It follows, therefore, that the parent–child relationship should be the focus of work on prevention, treatment and management of child abuse and neglect; and those involved in the treatment of abusive families should be concerned with the development of a 'secure' relationship between parent and child. It is not sufficient to evaluate intervention programmes on the basis of the occurrence or non-occurrence of subsequent abuse. Helping parents to inhibit violence towards their children may still leave the harmful context, in which the initial abuse occurred, quite unchanged.

Work at the family relationship level is essential if prevention is to be achieved. At present, in many casework situations social workers are sometimes forced into wrong decisions, having to withhold support from the least 'dangerous' cases which might have been those most able to profit from secondary prevention strategies, while continuing to work intensively with highly violent families where full physical and psychological rehabilitation can in no way be guaranteed at a tertiary level of intervention.

Tertiary Prevention

Unfortunately, tertiary prevention programmes (i.e. intervention after the child has been maltreated, usually for some time) are by far the most common forms of help offered to distressed and disorganized families, and place children at unnecessary risk of death and handicap. Even at this level there is no guarantee of help as an investigation of child protection practices in London revealed. There were 846 families in London alone with children placed on the child protection register but *without* an allocated social worker to help (Social Services Inspectorate, 1990).

Treatment and control of child-abusing families only after the abuse has been determined is no solution to the problem and will have little effect on the abused to abuser intergenerational cycle (see Chapter 11). This is because, without screening techniques for high-risk families and secondary prevention, intervention takes place only after many repeated episodes of abuse and neglect and violent patterns of coping with stress will by then have become firmly established within family relationships.

As a quarter of children on child protection registers are in care (Department of Health, 1995a), it seems that all too often intervention and treatment fails at the tertiary level. Studies have shown (e.g. Hyman, 1978) that between 40 and 70% of physical abuse and neglect cases of child abuse coming up for case conference have already been known to the relevant authorities either on account of previous injury to the child under review or to one of his siblings. This claim is also supported by follow-up studies after intervention with sexually abusing families (Bentovim et al., 1988; Bentovim, 1991).

For those abused children separated from their families there is the added cost of going into care, which includes stigmatization, bewilderment and feelings of abandonment, a change of school, family, friends and possibly social class. Often children in care also experience diminished contact and increased (both physical and emotional) distance from natural parents. Furthermore, there may be a lack of continuity of care (1 in 10 children have 10 or more placements) and foster home breakdown for 40% of these children (Berridge and Gleaver, 1987; Roberts, 1993). Newspaper reports on Leicestershire careworkers and the Pindown scandal also highlight the fact that there is risk of further abuse for children in care.

It is recognized that new families are required for abused children if their parents are manifestly unable to take on responsibility and to change appropriately. Long-term alternative care is needed, with adoption if necessary. Nevertheless, children must be prepared for fostering or adoption. Counselling preparation should help the child handle feelings of loss, guilt, failure, anger and let down. Foster and adoptive parents may also need to be offered specific counselling if they are to feel confident in their own parenting skills. This is especially the case when they are caring for psychologically damaged children (Roberts, 1993).

Abused children need to be helped to relearn non-violent and non-coercive interpersonal skills. Unfortunately, only a small minority of children placed in long-term care are given any practical help to deal with their abusive experiences. Hence, children fostered by relatives do better in all aspects of physical and emotional recovery and are more likely to remain in touch with their natural parents (Rowe et al., 1984).

CONCLUSION

The aim for all those involved with child abuse work must be the prevention of physical and sexual violence in the family and not just the inadequate control of the problem. This means trained health and social service professionals being available, with suitable resources, to help families with serious problems *before* child abuse and neglect occurs. Even for parents who were maltreated as children, prognosis may be good if effective intervention and therapy (as described in the next chapter) are provided.

CHAPTER 7

Treating parents who abuse and neglect their children

There are many potential therapeutic goals for health and social service professionals to consider when dealing with the emotional and physical abuse of children by their parents. Parents' perceptions of their offspring, and their ideologies and attributions with regard to child rearing, make for an important area of assessment; attention to child management skills constitutes another. These are accessible to social workers and other professionals given a social and developmental psychology knowledge-base and training in appropriate therapeutic skills (see Frude, 1991; Herbert, 1993; Hollin, Wilkie and Herbert, 1987).

CHILDREN IN CONTROL

Parents who abuse their children frequently complain of the sense of intense frustration and anger that causes them to lash out at their offspring when they are (as so often they appear to be) defiant and disruptive (see page 192, Chapter 3). Where this is the case, intervention objectives such as enhancing child management skills, increasing self-control and the related ability to cope with anger, come to the forefront.

From the moment of birth, children have an enormous potential for wielding power over their parents. They can deliver 'aversive stimuli' if things are not to their liking; and while certain expressions of distress or discontent are painful only for the child's own parents, others are universally aversive. The cry of the infant, for example, has been shown to be maximally pitched and varied so that it is both impossible to ignore or get used to. Clearly, it is functional, which is to say that it has survival value for most children. In some contexts (as we shall see) crying is a risky activity. Many, if not most, parents will do a great deal (even get out of bed repeatedly, or prepare a new meal for a faddy child) if the child has 'taught' them in the past that such behaviour will bring the crying or screaming tantrum to a halt. It is in successfully coercing the tired or uncertain parent that the child begins to sense and use his or her power. The discovery of the extent of this power is one of the earliest and most 'traumatic' insights of parenthood. Parents of older children find that some of them (particularly at adolescence—see Chapter 9) make such good use of coercive power in the form of threats and/or physical intimidation, that they feel helpless to control them.

Failure is costly for parents and, in the long run, emotionally bankrupting for their undisciplined children (Herbert, 1989). While disobedience and defiance are common problems as children grow up—and are consequently frustrating, irksome, even exhausting and debilitating for caregivers—they can sometimes prove dangerous if they persist and intensify (for example, in homes at risk of child abuse). There are other potentially serious consequences. Obedience is critical if the complex processes of socialization are to work. Parents have the task of turning helpless, asocial and self-centred infants into sociable, self-controlled children and eventually into mature, responsible members of the community. In the early years—from birth to 7 or 8—a reasonable level of compliance to parental requests and instructions is vital if the child is going to learn the social, intellectual and physical skills he or she will require for a reasonably contented journey towards maturity. The toddler period is particularly sensitive if social training is going to proceed smoothly.

Among the reasons for enforcing certain rules are:

- the need for safety—the child has to learn to avoid dangers;
- harmony within the family—an aggressive, defiant 'brat' sets the scene for an unhappy home and disharmony between the parents;
- the social life of the family—uncontrolled, destructive children are not welcome visitors and contribute to the social isolation of their parents.

Parents achieve compliance partly through example because their children (usually) identify with them, if they love and respect them, seek their approval and want to be as much like them as possible. It is also achieved by consciously steering children in the 'right direction'. A firm but loving framework of discipline helps children to develop their own guidelines and controls, symbolized by what we call 'conscience', so that they can look ahead to the consequences of their actions and 'discipline' themselves. The external words of control uttered by parents in the name of social (community) life become the inner voice of conscience (Herbert, 1987a).

The development of self-control in childhood follows three discrete stages:

- the child's behaviour is controlled by the verbal community;
- the child's own overt speech regulates his or her behaviour;
- the child's covert or 'inner' speech governs his or her actions.

A failure to progress through this developmental sequence results in ineffectual regulatory self-talk (referred to technically as self-statements). Associated with this is a lack of self-control and impulsive behaviour—in sum, a child who is unable and/or unwilling to comply with the rules at the various levels at which they operate in society (see Herbert, 1987a). Many parents find discipline one of the most difficult parts of their responsibilities. They are quite likely to ask practitioners not only awkward questions, but also for specific advice. It does not help matters that this is largely an area, not of scientific facts, but of value judgements, and guidelines, rather than 'formula' prescriptions, will be the kind of support professionals can provide (see Herbert, 1989, 1993). Professionals can also help parents to work out their own coping strategies by teaching them how to solve problems.

OPTIONS FOR INTERVENTION IN CASES OF CHILD ABUSE

There are, in fact, many options; so many that there is insufficient space to deal with all of them here. The potential targets of a plan of work, might be:

- characteristics of the parents (e.g. deficits in bonding and child-rearing skills);
- characteristics of the child (e.g. non-compliant aggressive problems; incontinence);
- interactions of the child and his or her parents (e.g. coercive/aversive communications; mutual avoidance; inappropriate, inconsistent (perhaps non-contingent) reinforcement/ punishment);
- the effects of significant others in the family (interference, subversion of maternal authority by grandparent; sexual/physical abuse by relative/lodger, etc.);
- environmental factors (poverty, overcrowding, social isolation).

Practitioners are likely to be faced with any of the following *specific problems*:

Excess/surplus problems

1. Use of aversive (negative, coercive, punitive) means of influencing/changing others (criticism/physical assaults).
2. Parental shouting, nagging, threats, complaints.
3. High levels of parental stress (marital discord, inadequate income, poor housing, lack of emotional/social support).
4. Alcohol/drug abuse.
5. Acting out, antisocial, conduct problems.

Deficits

1. Skill deficits (poor problem-solving skills, ineffective communication skills, ineffective reinforcement skills).
2. Social isolation.
3. Withholding attention (ignoring).
4. Failure to track minor incidents before they become major confrontations (e.g. fighting).
5. Failure to acknowledge/notice/reward pro-social behaviour.
6. Few family recreational activities together.
7. Poor self-esteem/low perception of self-efficacy.

Inappropriate beliefs/attitudes/knowledge/behaviour

1. Faulty attributions (cause-and-effect inferences).
2. Reinforcement of inappropriate/deviant actions.
3. Unpredictable/inconsistent behaviour.
4. Mutual avoidance.
5. Faulty expectations due to absence of basic knowledge about child development.
6. Inflexible actions in response to child-disciplinary situations.

DEALING WITH 'EXCESS' PROBLEMS

Developing self-control

Poor self-control, characterized by impulsive behaviour, is described as the omission of thought between impulse and action: it is manifested by a failure to stop and think, a failure to learn effective ways of thinking about social situations, and a failure to generate alternative courses of action. This is often what happens in the case of violent outbursts. It is important, of course, to be clear about the meaning of terms such as 'anger' and 'aggression'. Definitions of anger vary, but most describe it as a primary emotion which ranges in intensity from mild irritation to rage, and which occurs when an individual is thwarted from obtaining a goal or fulfilling a need. It could also be said to be a stressful emotional reaction to aversive events (e.g. provocations). Not surprisingly, research evidence shows that the presence of frustration and/or anger increases the likelihood of aggressive action (Patterson, 1976).

As outlined in the Introduction to this book, aggression is used in a broad sense to include any behaviour involving either physical and or psychological harm that is directed against a person. Anger-motivated aggression, in which the victim serves the function of reducing an aversive emotional state, is distinguished from instrumental or incentive-motivated aggression which is directed at achieving some other goal. Violence—an extreme form of aggression—denotes the threat or application of force which has physically harmful consequences and a connotation of social undesirability. It is usually associated with intense anger.

There are several broad therapeutic approaches, originating in different theoretical models, which incorporate some or all of the specific treatment objectives and techniques described above and the methods to follow. Some of these therapeutic approaches have already been discussed in relation to violent spouse relationships and marital breakdown in Chapter 5.

FAMILY THERAPY APPROACHES

Family therapists conceptualize child abuse as emerging from a complex network of personal and family relationships, any aspect of which may have a bearing on the present problem and, indeed, provide clues to the violent episodes. This approach is systemic and embraces the concept of circular reciprocal causation. An individual's behaviour is both stimulus and response. What we have is a recursive sequence in which each action can be considered as the consequence of the action preceding it and the cause of the action following it. No single element in the sequence controls the operation of the sequence as a whole because it is itself governed by the operation of the other elements in the system. Thus any individual in a family system is affected by the activities of other members of the family, activities which his or her actions or decisions (in turn) determine.

Family therapists put particular emphasis on the *process* (subtle and unsubtle) of what is happening within the family as a whole and between its members as individuals or as part of changing 'alliances'. Thus the problem may be formulated in terms of unsatisfactory patterns of dominance, unclear roles and boundaries for members, poor communication and ineffective decision-making. The family members are encouraged by a variety of therapeutic strategies and homework tasks to think, feel and act differently; to look at themselves from a fresh perspective and to try alternative solutions to their dilemmas.

There are several stages in the family therapy process:

1. *The joining stage.* The family and the therapist are originally isolated from each other, but the therapists use their skills to enable them to become absorbed into the family through a process of accommodation. This process creates a new system—family and therapist—which may take several sessions to create.
2. *The middle therapy stage.* This is the phase during which the major restructuring 'work' occurs. Restructuring interventions are made during sessions and consolidating homework tasks are set between sessions.
3. *The termination stage.* This phase tests the family's ability to 'fire' the therapist and do it themselves. The 'ghost' of the therapist is left behind by getting the family to simulate its ability to solve new problems and to deal with old problems if they recur.
4. *The follow-up.* A follow-up session after three months, six months or a year enables the therapist to evaluate the impact of therapy and test whether it has been successful in achieving second-order change, which means enabling family rules and family functioning to change in such a way that the family generates effective solutions to problems.

The techniques for putting the family on to a new and harmonious path are many and varied.

- *Enactment* is the direct illustration by the clients (as opposed to mere description) of the problems that exist between them. Clients are encouraged, where appropriate, to talk directly to one another rather than to (or through) the therapist.
- *Boundary clarification* is the creation or clarification of boundaries between family members, and is a feature of structural work. A mother who babies her teenager may hear with surprise her daughter's answer to the question 'How old do you think your mother treats you as—three or thirteen?'
- *Changing space*—i.e. asking clients in the therapy room to move about—can intensify an interaction or underline an interpretation being made about a relationship. For example, if a husband and wife never confront one another directly but always use their child as a mediator or channel of communication, the therapist blocks that manoeuvre (called triangulation) by ensuring that the child is not placed between the

parents. Here the therapist may comment: 'Let's move Claire from the middle so you can work it out together.'

- *Reframing* is an important method in fulfilling the objective of helping clients change in a covert—less directed—manner. It is an alteration in the emotional or conceptual viewpoint in relation to which a situation is experienced. That experience is placed in another 'frame' which fits the facts of the situation as well (or more plausibly), thereby transforming its entire meaning. Giving people different 'stories' to tell themselves about themselves or about events—stories that are less self-defeating or destructive—is also a feature of behavioural work.

An example of the use of reframing with parents who abuse their children might be in altering negative schema or attributions. There is a conceptual difficulty for some parents whose attributions reflect an axiom that assumes (at least in their own case) that 'there are no problem parents, only problem children'. Problematic behaviours are reified into entities which reside within the child. ('There's a little demon in him'; 'He's always trying to get at me'; 'It's his father's bad blood'). The parents do not share, in any way, in the 'ownership' of the problem. Such a disengagement from any role in the child's negative behaviours can be risky for the child (punitive attitudes are encouraged); it is also very difficult to deal with clinically.

It might be possible by means of reframing (cognitive restructuring) to modify such attributions—by encouraging parents to make 'connections' ('Do you see anything of yourself in your child's behaviour?' 'Were you like Jan at her age?'), and to think about behaviour sequentially and contingently. (The ABC functional analysis which teases out antecedents to behaviour and its consequences and which is central to learning theory, are matters to which we shall return.)

Problems are not unidirectional; there is two-way traffic—powerful reciprocal influences—in the interactions between parents and children. A family therapy perspective illuminates this fact but in a manner that is non-judgemental. Post-mortems of the chicken–egg (which came first: adverse parental influences or difficult child behaviour?) type are not helpful when carrying out interviews with parents who abuse, and who are often suspicious, even cynical, about the possibility of being helped. It requires sensitivity and carefully framed explanations (formulations) if they are to be helped to gain, or regain, insight and confidence in the management of their children and, in addition (in many instances), a reversal of hostile, rejecting attitudes they have towards them (see Webster-Stratton and Herbert, 1994).

PSYCHODYNAMIC APPROACHES

As outlined in Chapter 5, the term 'psychodynamic' is a generic and somewhat vague concept which embraces several methods involving the ventilating and interpretation of intrapsychic events (unconscious motives, conflict, ego defence mechanisms, etc.) leading variously to catharsis, insight and a hoped for resolution of problems. There are different nuances and emphases, indeed schools of psychoanalysis, which make it sometimes difficult to know who does what for whom (i.e. particular client or problem) (see Lee and Herbert, 1970). The common theme running through all dynamic approaches is the achievement of 'insight'. Of course, what constitutes an insight is a moot point, and as Murgatroyd and Wolfe point out, in their book *Helping Families in Distress* (1985):

> . . . it is difficult to know what to do when one has found insights. Many helpers from many backgrounds will be only too well aware of the family whose response to their help is, 'OK, we've now got some insight or awareness into what led to our present difficulties; we can see that we are too aggressive/passive, or controlled/spontaneous, or rigid/anarchic, etc., and that it would help us if we could move to a different point on the continuum, but how do we go about it?'

Murgatroyd and Wolfe (1985) state that awareness is more than just an intellectual event, but involves an emotional process of 'owning' one's own feelings. Thus, admitting that one is aggressive may have little effect if that knowledge is held consciously (in the intellect) while subconsciously there is a strong emotional resistance to accepting the fact (accepting these feelings of anger and aggression as part of oneself—i.e. owning them). The trouble is that fantasies and (say) aggressive impulses may be projected onto other persons in the family. Such defensive strategies require interpretation and the sort of insight that leads to liberation from such self-deluding and potentially dangerous ideas, and is reflected in action (behaviour).

COGNITIVE APPROACHES

Cognitive behavioural treatments—an amalgam of cognitive and behavioural approaches (see Chapter 2)—have proved to be effective in treating anger management problems: reflecting the concept of anger as an emotional arousal with cognitive determinants and behavioural consequences. Cognitive behavioural theory, as we saw in Chapters 2 and 3, is closely allied to social learning theory (e.g. Bandura, 1977). This theoretical perspective stresses the importance of the environment while also seeking to incorporate 'inner' processes as mediators between the outer world and overt behaviour.

There is a wide range of cognitive-behavioural procedures but they share a common assumption: that children (and their parents) can be taught to eliminate their maladaptive behaviours by changing external contingencies and by challenging their irrational beliefs and faulty logic; also by encouraging them to instruct themselves in certain ways.

Self-control procedures

In order to train or modify self-control, techniques have been developed to change the individual's private speech or self-statements.

Self-instructional training

Training moves through a series of stages: firstly, the therapist models the performance of a task, making appropriate overt self-statements; secondly, the client practices the same behaviour, gradually moving to whispered self-instruction; finally, he or she progresses to covert, silent self-instruction. The client is encouraged to use self-statements to self-observe, self-evaluate, and self-reinforce appropriate overt behaviours (Herbert, 1987b; Meichenbaum, 1985).

Anger control

An extension of self-control procedures lies in the development of therapeutic programmes which aim at the self-regulation of anger (e.g. Novaco, 1975, 1985). There are two key ideas behind Novaco's conceptualization of anger:

1. Cognitive processes influence how each individual perceives and structures his or her environment; the person is, in this sense, proactive (an agent) rather than an organism passively *reacting* to an objective world.
2. Stress, of which anger is one form, represents an imbalance between environmental demands and an individual's ability to meet them. If a person is exposed to manageable doses of the stressor (the aversive event), amounts that are sufficient to arouse but not overwhelm him or her, the ability to cope can be increased and the resulting stress reduced. There are three phases to what might be called a process of *'inoculation'*: *cognitive preparation*; *skill acquisition*; and *application practice*. Several demands are made of the client which need to be considered if the intervention is to be effective:

- intellectual abilities, such as being literate and able to fill in forms and keep records;
- ability to reflect and evaluate information (convergent logical thought);
- the need for divergent, imaginative thinking for role-play and rehearsal;
- physical abilities to learn muscle relaxation and breathing control;
- certain personality factors such as a degree of extraversion to enable thinking aloud in front of the therapist;
- sense of humour and ability to take others' perspectives;
- sufficient motivation to tackle the homework tasks, interviews and to complete the course.

Novaco's Anger Management Programme (Novaco, 1975)

Stage 1: Cognitive preparation

- Introducing the meaning and functions of anger and the rationale of the programme (client is given an instruction manual).
- Homework—involves keeping a diary of anger experiences: to facilitate awareness of the relation between anger and self-statements and between the stages of an anger experience (preparing for a provocation, impact and confrontation, coping with arousal and agitation and reflecting when the conflict is over).
- Reviewing with the client the conditions which elicit anger and teaching him or her to discriminate between justified and unjustified anger.

Stage 2: Skill acquisition

- Teaching the client to reappraise anger-eliciting events.
- Promoting a shift from a personal orientation to a task orientation in confronting difficulties.
- Teaching the client to use self-instructions in the course of an angry exchange—statements which guide coping attempts and which provide self-reinforcement.
- Relaxation training.
- Teaching behavioural skills—communication and assertion are taught using modelling and role-play.

Stage 3: Application practice

- Developing skills are applied and tested in graded situations involving simulated anger, both in imagined and role-play scenarios.

A key element of this approach is to alter irrational styles of thinking which have become habitual for the aggressive person. Research findings indicate that the approach is particularly relevant to chronic anger; also for use with problems of 'anger-associated-with-depression' (see Novaco, 1985).

A helpful literature is available for the design of anger management programmes for adolescents; it also provides evidence of their effectiveness with violent offenders of all ages (see Howells, 1989).

Counter-conditioning

Counter-conditioning of angry reactions can result in positive therapeutic outcomes. For example, Smith (1973) found that systematic desensitization alone was not effective in inhibiting angry responses, but it was successful when the hierarchy was embellished with humour. It was suggested, however, that the humour exerted its effects at least partly by modifying cognitive mediational processes. For example, subjects reported being able to see anger-eliciting situations from a new perspective. Others have also demonstrated the anger-reducing properties of humour in their studies (see Baron, 1976). Other incompatible responses have been successfully used to reduce angry expressions, such as gift-giving and the solicitation of sympathy (see Baron, 1976).

Relaxation

Relaxation training has also been applied to anger control treatment. Several reviews conclude that only modest support can be found for the effectiveness of relaxation training alone (e.g. Smith, 1973). One suggestion is that no impact is made on the violent tempers or automatic rage reactions because of the intensity and explosiveness of the client's anger. However, relaxation training can be useful when used in conjunction with other methods.

Life Skills Training (Social Problem-Solving)

Social problem-solving refers to the process, in a given social situation, of generating feasible courses of action, considering the various outcomes that might follow and planning how to achieve the preferred outcome (Hopson and Scully, 1980). There is a multitude of social graces and nuances, communication skills and sensitivities which make family life (indeed social life) pleasurable for all concerned (see Table 7.1).

Table 7.1   A list of parenting skills

Me and my child	Me and significant others
Skills I need to relate effectively to him or her:	*Skills I need to relate effectively to others (e.g. my partner, teachers, friends) involved with my child:*
• How to communicate clearly • How to 'listen' carefully so as to understand • How to develop my relationship • How to give help and care and protection without 'going over the top' • How to teach and discipline • How to show and receive affection • How to manage/resolve conflict • How to give and receive feedback • How to maintain a balance between extremes (e.g. loving without being possessive) • How to negotiate sensible compromises • How to set limits—reasonable ones—and stick to them	• How to be reasonably objective about others • How not to be possessive • How to be assertive (without being intrusive or bossy) • How to influence crucial people and systems (e.g. school) • How to work in groups (e.g. parents' groups, pressure groups) • How to express my feelings clearly and constructively • How to inspire confidence and strength in others • How to see my child's friends from his or her point of view • How to resist/cope with jealousy

Source: Adapted from Hopson and Scully (1980).

Parents and children often lack (owing to temperament and/or a variety of experiences of social deprivation) the skills of confidence, forming accurate impressions and engaging in kindly communications with others. They find it difficult to choose between alternative courses of action in person-to-person situations. In addition, they lack knowledge of the social actions ('solutions') they can take, plus some means of choosing between those they do have. Alternatively, they are locked into narrow, rigid and perhaps self-destructive behavioural repertoires, aggressiveness being a classic example. In such cases the therapeutic aim is to increase the child's or caregiver's repertoire of possible actions in person-to-person situations, making their relationships with others more constructive and more creatively benign.

The *social problem-solving model* assumes that some persons are unskilled or deskilled (i.e. lose proficiency at problem solving) because of a lack of opportunity to learn or practise them in various social settings, or a loss of confidence brought about by various circumstances (Shure, 1981). In problem-solving skills training, cognitive techniques (particularly self-instructional training) are blended with modelling, role-play and discussion in order to train clients how to *recognize* problems, how to *unravel* and *define* them and then how to *generate solutions* and *plan outcomes* (Spivack, Platt and Shure, 1976).

Assertiveness training

Self-assertion training is an approach which assists the individual to cope constructively with provocation and anger arousal by restraining the hostile/impulsive expression (e.g. accusation or emotional display). This might involve a calm, modulated *assertion* of his or her true feelings. Instead of the angry form of response being reinforced due to a decrease in physiological arousal (drive reduction), it is the new and more socially acceptable assertive behaviour that is strengthened.

Social skills training

The social skills training (SST) model views effective social functioning as being dependent upon the client's:

- knowledge of specific interpersonal actions and how they fit into different kinds of person-to-person situations;
- ability to convert knowledge of social nuances into the skilled performance of social or self-restrained actions in various interactive contexts; and
- ability to evaluate skilful and unskilful behaviour accurately and to adjust one's behaviour accordingly.

If children (and indeed their parents) can be helped to become more competent socially, the hope is that they may have less recourse to maladaptive antisocial actions such as violence. These skills include improving powers of observation and accurate judgement; basic conversational skills such as listening, asking questions and talking; expressive skills such as the use of body language; social techniques for special occasions, and so on.

All in all the results of SST research are only mildly encouraging (Herbert, 1986). The evidence suggests that the younger or less mature children and the more aggressive children are relatively unaffected by the existing child social skills training pro-grammes. Because few studies have actually employed direct observational measures of aggression or non-compliance, it is not possible to tell whether those children who do show improvements in cognitive processes, social skills and sociomet-ric ratings will also show reductions in conduct problems. There has been a failure to demonstrate convincingly whether improvements in social or cognitive skills in the laboratory or in analogue situations generalize to the real world, or that the long-term effects of child treatments are maintained.

Parent training/coaching

Parent training, on an individual or group basis, has proved a fruitful enterprise in work with families (see Patterson, 1982; Webster-Stratton and Herbert, 1994). As a reaction, in part, to the large numbers of conduct disordered children and the shortfall of professional personnel, agencies have looked increasingly to parent training to mitigate and prevent family disruption.

Parent-training programmes involving the modification of *both* antecedent events and consequent events appear to produce a better generalization of effects (Forehand and McMahon, 1981). This is not surprising as variables at either end of the ABC equa-tion contribute to aggression and non-compliance in children. Attention to both provides the parents with constructive skills (see Herbert, 1994; Callias, 1994). There are several ways to alter proximal and distal antecedent events (see Figure 7.1) in order to increase (say) the parent's stimulus control in disciplinary situations:

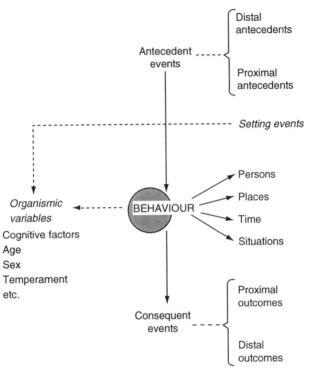

Figure 7.1   General assessment guidelines

(a) examining rules and expectations in the home;
(b) assessing and altering setting events;
(c) attending to the nature of caregiver commands, instructions, requests;
(d) training caregivers in giving instructions.

The 'Child-Wise' Parent Skills Programme (Herbert and Wookey, 1997), in its session on compliance, incorporates instruction in setting up house rules, making effective requests, use of positive consequences for obedience, negative consequences for disobedience (loss of privileges and time-out) and procedures for special times and places.

Proximal and Distal Antecedents

Proximal and distal antecedents need to be considered in any intervention with defiant and/or aggressive children.

Proximal antecedents

Parental requests, instructions and commands are vital antecedent events in caring for and training children. The immediate or proximal command has been studied in the laboratory and in treatment studies. Such investigations illustrate the importance of the nature and manner of parental commands in influencing whether the child will or will not comply (see Forehand and McMahon, 1981). For example, parents of oppositional children give their children significantly more instructions or commands than compliant children and do not allow them enough time to comply with the commands. Instead they interrupt them with repetition of the command, softening of the command, or coaxing.

Forehand and McMahon (1981) identify five general types of beta commands: chain commands, vague commands, question commands, 'lets' commands and commands followed by a rationale or other verbalizations. In contrast, alpha commands are characterized by being specific and direct, being given one at a time and being followed by a wait of five seconds. Parents of normal children generally give more time-limited and activity-specific (alpha) commands, whereas parents of oppositional children typically give more vague (beta) commands and stop commands. Beta commands are the best predictor of the child's non-compliance. Even though the mothers of oppositional children are aware that beta commands are less effective, they reported feeling unable to control the frequency of issuing such commands.

These findings suggest that training parents to use alpha commands should result in an improvement in the child's level of obedience. Indeed, the McMahon and Forehand team have demonstrated that when mothers are trained to use specific unitary commands (alpha commands) rather than vague, interrupted commands (beta commands), the rate of compliance increases from 35.2 to 63.9%. The quality of the command in eliciting child compliance is also of significance. Hudson and Blane (1985) investigated the non-verbal elements of (i) distance from child, (ii) body orientation of mother, (iii) eye contact between mother and child, (iv) tone of voice and (v) mother's orientation towards objects involved in the instruction. All were found to be related to the rate of child compliance.

Distal antecedents: rules

McIndoe (1989) makes the point that while a good deal of attention has been given to both verbal and non-verbal aspects of giving instructions, little attention has been given to more distal antecedents such as non-compliance to long-standing rules about expected behaviour. In a pilot study of parents' expectations of children's behaviour, she used a structured interview and questionnaire to obtain information about types of rules, methods of conveying rules, reasons for rules, frequency of rules being broken and consequences for rules being followed and broken. Twelve categories of rule were established, two of which were meta-rules. One related to respect and cooperation (Meta-rule 1) and the other to compliance to rules (Meta-rule 2). The other categories related to manners, chores, behavioural prohibitions, safety and responsibility. Meta-rule 1—rules about personal responsibility and chores—were the ones most often of concern to parents. Rules were usually conveyed verbally and three levels were established (Instructed, Reminded, Discussed). Data on the frequency of rules being broken was not sufficient to draw many conclusions. However, the most frequently reported rules were those most frequently broken. Consequences for breaking rules were, like methods of conveying rules, largely verbal (Reminder, Rebuke, Discussion). When rules were followed parents most often praised the child or did nothing; overall positive consequences were twice as frequent as 'neutral' (did nothing) reactions.

Altering Consequences

Most of the early behavioural work on behaviour problems concentrated on the consequence side of the ABC equation (see Figure 7.1, page 162), modifying (inter alia) parents' usual responses to the child's opposition or aggression by means of training in the employment of time-out from positive reinforcement (TO) and differential attention (DA). There have been reports of successful interventions along these lines (see Herbert, 1987a and 1995 for reviews of the literature) and reports of failure when DA was used on its own. It is worth noting that the addition of DA was generally sufficient to bring about a positive outcome.

Unfortunately, time-out has a number of counter-productive effects for the child. He or she is in the limelight, possibly acting the buffoon and therefore still the centre of attention. Or he or she is avoiding some unwelcome scholastic task or is away from a sarcastic, frightening teacher. If this is the case, teachers should have a hard look at their teaching and/or their interactions with this child. Behaviour techniques such as time-out, which are designed to eliminate inappropriate or undesirable behaviour, are unlikely to succeed unless supplemented by the reinforcement of an alternative and more appropriate behaviour pattern.

A critical determinant of the effectiveness of time-out is the extent to which the child actually enjoys the situation from which he or she is removed. If that situation is positively frightening, anxiety-provoking or boring, it is possible that the time-out procedure might involve removing the child to a less aversive situation and thereby actually *increase*, rather than decrease, the frequency of the inappropriate behaviour.

IMPLICATIONS OF DIFFERENT THERAPY MODELS

Webster-Stratton and Herbert (1993) make the point that the different therapeutic models come with different sets of assumptions about the therapist's role with clients, the causes of problems, family violence and the level of responsibility the client or therapist assumes for resolving problems. For example, in quasi-medical models such as psychoanalytic psychotherapy, clients are not thought of as 'responsible' for their problems. Nor are parents responsible for finding solutions. The therapist, who is the expert in the relationship, gradually uncovers the problems hidden in the unconscious areas of the client's psyche, in past experiences, and/or in the dynamics of family life. He or she interprets them to the individual client, or to the entire family in the case of psychodynamic family therapy. The client is seen as a relatively passive recipient of the therapist's analysis and interpretations.

The advantage of the medical model is that it allows parents to accept help for their own or their child's problems without feeling that they are to blame for the problems; its disadvantage is that it fosters dependency on the therapist for a long period of time and, in the case of child play therapy, isolates parent from the therapeutic process.

Other models appear to blame parents for the family problems. This happens most often in social casework in areas of child abuse. It is not uncommon at professional case conferences to hear a tragic case of child abuse explained in terms of a failure, absence, or distortion of the mother's attachment to her child. Emotional and physical abuse have been linked causally with a failure on the part of the mother to become 'bonded' to her child (Iwaniec, 1995). These assumptions may lead to guilt-laden parents 'submitting' to therapy rather than seeking it while harbouring a negative self-image and a lack of feeling of self-control.

By way of contrast, cognitive-behavioural therapists, working from an assumption that behaviour is intrinsically as well as extrinsically determined, encourage parents to focus not on the past, but on the present and future, directing their energies forward to solve their own problems and to learn new skills. They are allowed to take credit for their improvements and, as a result, begin to feel more competent. This and the provision of performance skills, facilitates an increase in parents' perceived self-efficacy (Bandura, 1977). Webster-Stratton and Herbert (1993) suggest that such an approach has several possible disadvantages. Firstly, it may suggest there are panaceas (quick fixes) for children's problems. Secondly, it may create feelings of failure or guilt if the raised expectations brought about respectively by high levels of initial success and subsequent reversals of gains come crashing down. Thirdly, any therapist may implement parent training in a directive or prescriptive fashion which may not only foster parents' dependency and a lack of self-reliance, but also may impart a scapegoating message of parental inadequacies being to blame for their children's problems.

At the other extreme from these models are humanistic-existential models (e.g. Rogers, 1957) which reject the notion of conducting treatment on the basis of deficit motivation. The assumption, rather, is that people have it within themselves to find solutions and change. Rogerian theory, which epitomizes the humanistic approach, is client-centred, non-directive, non-intrusive and supportive. The Rogerian therapist's unconditional positive regard for the client helps people to help themselves by searching for their own answers, moving towards self-actualization and maturity. The advantage of this approach is that it promotes clients' positive self-esteem and self-direction; on the other hand, this type of therapy can be a lengthy process and may not be appropriate for clients who do not have solid communication and problem-solving skills.

THE COLLABORATIVE APPROACH

The theoretical approach of Webster-Stratton and Herbert (1993, 1994) for working with parents in coercive families falls within the cognitive social learning model, while integrating some of the core elements of the humanistic model. They have chosen not to call their approach 'parent training' because this term may imply a model based on a hierarchical relationship between the therapist and the parent wherein the expert therapist is 'making good some deficit' within the parent. A term such as 'parent coaching' is preferable. Regardless of terminology, the underlying helping model they advocate for working with parents follows a collaborative process.

Collaboration implies a non-blaming, reciprocal relationship based on utilizing equally the therapist's knowledge and the parent's unique strengths and perspectives. It implies respect for each person's contribution, a relationship built on trust and open communication; parents actively participate in the setting of goals and therapy agenda. Collaboration also implies that parents provide ongoing evaluation of each therapy session so that the therapist can use these evaluations to refine and adapt the intervention to ensure that it is sensitive to the family's needs.

In a collaborative relationship the therapist works *with* the parents by actively soliciting their ideas and feelings, understanding their cultural context and jointly involving them in the process of sharing their experiences, discussing ideas and problem solving.

The therapist does not assume the role of 'expert' dispensing advice or lectures to parents about how they *should* parent more effectively, rather, he or she invites parents to help write the 'script' for the intervention programme. The therapist's role, then, is that of collaborator, attempting to understand the parents' perspectives, to clarify issues, to summarize important ideas and themes raised by the parents, to teach and to interpret in a way that is empowering to them. An illustration of the collaborative approach applied to emotional abuse problems at the Centre for Behaviour Work with Families is given below.

Non-organic failure to thrive is a term to describe infants and children whose growth and development are significantly below age-related norms and in whom no physical causes can be detected. These abnormalities are frequently associated with emotional abuse and neglect and family disorganization. The problem area overlaps significantly with child physical abuse.

There is no clear differentiation between neglected and abused children; in fact, many children initially identified as victims of physical abuse are later discovered to be seriously neglected as well. While physical abuse is relatively easy to recognize (if severe) because of distinct physical marks, neglect can go unnoticed for a long time, especially that of an emotional kind (Iwaniec, Herbert and McNeish, 1985a; Iwaniec, 1995).

Difficulties of Feeding and Their Sequelae

Some parents spend excessive periods of time struggling to feed the child with poor results. This provokes anxiety, frustration and anger in both parties. Others give up and retreat into inertia—passive neglect and emotional indifference. Seeing a child who looks seriously undernourished, withdrawn and apathetic, suggests neglect and poor parenting ability. Parents meet with frequent criticism and rebukes, not only from health and child-care agencies, but also from their partners, families, friends, neighbours and, at times, complete strangers. Parents often feel that they are being blamed unjustly for their child's condition. Some turn their anger on the child for causing them so much misery. Some caregivers become forceful in their feeding and child management, hostile and abusive; their offspring, in turn, become more anxious, fearful and withdrawn. They actively avoid feeding situations and a vicious circle is created.

There are some children whose poor physical growth and appearance has nothing to do with the food-avoidance behaviour consequent on emotional deprivation and abuse, as described above. They are the victims of parental ignorance of the requirements for adequate child nourishment; there is inadequate calorific provision and poor quality of care and attention generally.

Active Rejection

Any child will find it particularly difficult to cope with palpable, ongoing parental rejection. Some fathers and mothers did not want the pregnancy in the first place; others may become rejecting for a variety of reasons: their babies are perceived as unresponsive or, indeed, in some of their attributes, quite 'unlovable'. The infant's mere presence may lead to disharmony between the mother and a jealous partner.

Of course, rejection is not a *fixed* characteristic—feelings can and do change. An understanding of 'affectionless' parents requires a more general understanding of the so-called affectionless personality in people who are often described as psychopathic. It is quite likely that adults who are capable only of relating to other adults (spouses for example) in a superficial, exploitive and hostile manner, show similar relationships with their children (Gil, 1970).

Child-to-Parent Attachment

It is a fairly reliable generalization that punishment leads to self-control only when children are on the side of (i.e. identify with) the person doing the punishing (see page 148). This implies an attachment to the parent that indicates respect and affection. As emphasized in the previous chapter, the child's attachment to the parent is disrupted in the majority of child-maltreating families. Investigations (see Belsky, 1988) have established a clear link between early insecure attachments and later development of behaviour problems, bringing attachment research into the domain of the clinical and social work practice (see Chapter 12). It is hypothesized that many 'conduct problems are strategies for gaining the attention or proximity of caregivers who are unresponsive to the child's pro-social communications'.

It is important to remember that the patterns of behaviour described above do not necessarily persist and they are not necessarily indicators of a serious rift in the relationship between parent and child. However, they are worthy of following up in an assessment (see Herbert (1991, 1992) for assessment protocols, questionnaires and rating scales). There is always the danger that if the child is unloved, he or she will become unloving and this child and parent will become mutually antagonistic.

INTERVENTION

A psychosocial intervention developed at the Centre for Behavioural Work with Families (Iwaniec, Herbert and McNeish, 1985b) consists of two phases.

Phase 1: Crisis intervention
- Ensuring that the child is safe.
- Organizing a case-conference for more serious cases and putting these on the Child Protection Register in order to involve the statutory agencies.
- Arranging attendance at a day nursery (in part, a safety measure), which (a) provides an opportunity for the child to be monitored for a substantial part of the day, (b) provides the mother with a 'break' and the space for the social worker to elucidate and work on her problems with her and other members of the family and (c) provides the child with what may be much needed social stimulation.
- Arranging, where appropriate, for health visitors, volunteers, family aides and neighbours, to assist mothers with feeding and child-care (following the initiation of the therapeutic programme) and, not least, to provide moral support.

- Assisting parents with problems of housing, finances, welfare rights, etc., where appropriate.
- Providing supervision by regular visits and phone calls.
- Beginning and supporting a self-help parent group to which new clients are introduced.

Phase 2: The treatment package
There are several strands to the family-oriented interventions:

- Counselling for parents (in their own right).
- Cognitive restructuring.
- Developmental counselling.
- Desensitizing (where necessary) the mother's tension, anger and resentment when in the child's company. It is almost always necessary for the mothers of these children to learn to control hostile feelings and to deal with high levels of anxiety. This is dealt with (before any formal work on the child's feeding can be initiated) by training in relaxation, stress management and self-control.
- Management of the disturbed feeding patterns.

The methods evolved at the *Centre for Behavioural Work with Families* in order to improve the caregiver's interactions and relationship with the child (Herbert, 1987a, 1987b, 1994; Iwaniec, Herbert and McNeish, 1985a, 1985b), also have relevance for parents where anxiety, panic and resentment (rather than rejection and hostility) have undermined the child's confidence and the parent's relationships and feeding skills. Direct observation of parent–child interactions, in an investigation of 17 non-organic failure-to-thrive children (including 12 hours of meal time observations per family) revealed four different interactional and management styles on the part of the caregiver (Iwaniec, 1995):

- forceful, anxious and impatient;
- neglectful, chaotic and unconcerned;
- angry, hostile but essentially indifferent;
- determined and coaxing, but anxious.

This classification (approximate and sometimes overlapping though it is) was helpful in explaining the process of problem development and influenced the choice of appropriate treatment strategies based upon individual feeding style and its ramifications for the feeder (see Table 7.2).

Table 7.2   Feeding style and consequent choice of treatment

Feeding style	Feeding process	Child's reaction	Treatment
(a) Forceful, anxious, impatient	Force feeding; screaming and shouting; hurrying; panicking; anxious confused, attitudes	Food avoidance behaviour	Changing to calm – free patterns of feeding and other activities; self-control strategies; systematic desensitization
(b) Neglectful, chaotic and unconcerned	Irregular feeding; inadequate calorie intake; missed meals, wrong food; signals of hunger ignored or mis-understood; uncaring attitudes	Wasting away; starvation; passive withdrawal	Improving quality of care; introducing informed diet; increasing amount of food; providing stimulation
(c) Angry, hostile, indifferent	Neglectful and unresponsive early on, then frequent withdrawal of food as punishment; restrictive provision of food; hostile rejective attitudes	Initial poor intake of food; vomiting and diarrhoea; changing when able to feed themselves to over-eating and bizarre eating behaviour	Reducing overtly hostile and rejective interactions and relationship between the caregiver and child
(d) Determined and coaxing but anxious	Encouraging flexibility in a routine and type of food given; patience in managing difficulties; caring attitudes	Long feeding periods, faddiness, spitting; storing food in the mouth; heaving; poor chewing	Support and advice re feeding and eating, helping to cope with caregiver anxiety

In order to bring parent and child closer together and to feel more comfortable in each other's company, a structured progressive interaction, based on play and other activities, is introduced. This phase is always discussed in detail with parents; rationale and methods are explained simply and carefully. As a rule the programme is scripted and given to parents to refresh their memories. In situations where parent–child interactions are highly (and sometimes mutually) aversive—a frequent finding— the caregiver is asked to play exclusively with the child each evening after his or her partner returns from work, or at a convenient time. The play sessions last 15 minutes during the first week, for about 20 minutes during the second and third weeks and, eventually, if things go well, some 30 minutes during the fourth and subsequent weeks. After the session with the child, the rest of the family joins in for a family play session or indeed other joint activities.

The play sessions are modelled by the worker to start with; then the caregiver plays and the worker observes and helps if there are difficulties. The toys and the play materials are carefully chosen and first sessions are fully discussed and, at times, rehearsed with the caregiver. It is essential, where mutual aversion/avoidance is extreme, not to begin play sessions in close proximity, but rather at some distance (e.g. using two toy telephones placed in different corners of the room). As time goes on, the closeness of play is increased. As always, the caregiver is encouraged to talk to the child in a soft, reassuring manner, encouraging participation in the play. She is prompted and cued (if needed) to smile at the child, look at the child, hold its hand, stroke its hair and praise it for each response. This may require careful programming if the child's behaviour is very timid. The tentative approaches towards the caregiver are shaped by a series of successive approximations. The caregiver is encouraged to be proactive *as well* as reactive. Once the child and the caregiver show signs of being more at ease with each other, they enter into the next stage to promote more intimate proximity.

The caregiver is encouraged to sit the child on her lap for increasing periods of time, hugging the child while holding her or him closely but gently. People cannot grow to love each other if they seldom meet or only interact with confrontational circumstances. Where there is mutual avoidance, parent and child are brought into unthreatening contact by a process referred to as exposure-training or systematic desensitization. The caregiver is asked to read a story, describe pictures or watch a television programme during these sessions. The objective is to achieve feelings of pleasure, security and reassurance—of being wanted and loved. Some rejecting caregivers have found that this is not only difficult but, at times, distasteful. This extreme aversion tends to lessen gradually when the child begins to smile back, seeks the caregiver's presence and, in other ways, responds to the overtures by the mother. Needless to say, it does not work in all cases. However, it is progress to move parents on from active dislike to reluctant acceptance (Iwaniec, Herbert and McNeish, 1985b). This task requires time and the process cannot be rushed. The key worker can share the task with a trained volunteer or family aide. Frequent visits and telephone calls should be made to monitor the programme. Reinforcing the reinforcer is critical to this work.

There is a final consolidating stage, planned to include two weeks of deliberately intensified caregiver–child interaction. The carers are asked to have the child near them much of the time, to talk softly and lovingly, to smile at, hug spontaneously, and to cuddle and praise the child and to encourage their attempts to seek help. An important element is brought to this stage of casework—improving the target child's relationship with siblings. They are sometimes scapegoats for sibling hostility (see Chapter 8).

The caregiver is asked to spend some time playing with *all* the children. The bedtime story (if absent) is introduced for all children. A formal programme is faded out gradually (over a period of several weeks—depending on the particular case) after discussion with the parent(s). The case is terminated when there is evidence of the child's continued satisfactory growth (checked out at the clinic) and evidence of improved family interactions, eating performance and change of attitudes towards the child (carefully monitored and evaluated in terms of explicit behavioural criteria, see Herbert, 1991).

The results of the methods evolved by Iwaniec (1995) in a collaboration between the Social Services, Leicestershire, the Health Services (Leicester DHA) and Leicester University and drawing on the assistance of day nurseries, family aides and volunteers (justifying the philosophy of close inter-agency cooperation in cases of child abuse) produced encouragingly high success rates with regard (inter alia) to weight gain (see Figure 7.2) and useful, if more moderate improvements (see Tables 7.3(a) and 7.3(b)) in parent–child relationships and child behaviour problems.

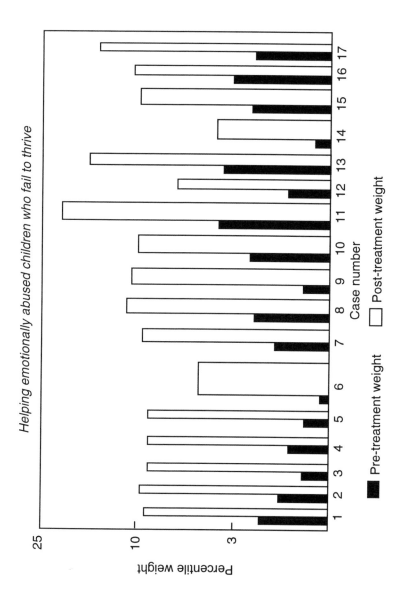

Figure 7.2 Weight gains in 17 failure-to-thrive children following behavioural family therapy (adapted from Iwaniec, Herbert and McNeish, 1988). The width of the histograms represents time taken in treatment and is not pertinent in the present discussion

Table 7.3(a)   Mother–child interactions *(N = 12)*

Satisfactory improvement	Moderate improvement	No improvement
6 (50%)	4 (33%)	2 (17%)

Source: Iwaniec, Herbert and Sluckin (1988).

Table 7.3(b)   Ratings of change in behaviour problems (e.g. non-compliance, coercive actions, etc.) manifested by 12 children

Satisfactory improvement	Moderate improvement	No improvement
11 (44%)	11 (44%)	3 (12%)

Source: Iwaniec, Herbert and Sluckin (1988).

GROUP WORK

Mention was made of the value of groups in working with the parents of emotionally abused children. There are several advantages in working with a group manifesting similar difficulties. They include the following functions:

- experiential
- dynamic
- social
- didactic

Many adults feel that they have failed miserably as parents and that their child is uniquely difficult to understand and manage. Sharing experiences with other parents can be comforting, indeed reassuring. The opportunity to express feelings of apprehension, resentment and anger (the latter aimed, not uncommonly, at the helping agencies) in a group setting can be beneficial if handled sensitively by the group organizer.

COLLABORATIVE GROUP THERAPY

Webster-Stratton and Herbert (1993) have published a paper that describes the process of working with parents who have conduct-disordered children—the kind of children who are particularly at risk of being abused by caregivers. The processes they describe there are complementary to the content and methods described in the Parents and Children Videotape Series, which is a series of videotapes developed for use by therapists working with groups of parents. This videotape modelling therapist-led group discussion treatment programme has been shown to be effective in promoting more positive parent attitudes and parent–child interactional behaviours and in reducing child conduct disorders in comparison to untreated control families and families who received only the parent group discussion treatment (Webster-Stratton, 1982, 1984). Showing these videotapes only comprises 20% of a group or individual session (20 minutes); the remaining time is spent engaged in discussion. A knowledge of parent training and a familiarity with the videotapes are necessary but not sufficient for producing success in working with most parents of conduct-disordered children; the second requirement necessary for positive outcomes is a high degree of clinical skill in working with parents, whether individually (Herbert, 1987b) or in groups (Webster-Stratton, 1988).

For example, it is clear that the therapist's conscious use of a variety of roles such as collaborator, empowerer, supporter, teacher, interpreter, leader, and prophesizer helps to change parents' behaviours and attitudes, to alter attributions about past and present behaviours, and, most importantly, to increase their perceived self-efficacy and persistence of effective coping skills. In a sense, the therapist's role with parents is a model for the kind of relationship Webster-Stratton and Herbert are encouraging parents to develop with their children. Moreover, just as parents get tired of the hard work of parenting, the therapist may tire of the hard work of filling these roles. The implementation of these roles with a group of parents, especially in the face of parent confrontations and resistance, can at times be a formidable task.

It is important that the therapist also has a support system in which he or she can analyse a difficult situation or group problem with other colleagues and rehearse the cost-effective use of a role. By discussing the situation with another therapist it is possible to brainstorm and determine how to reframe it, interpret it, or explain it in a different way so that it makes sense to the parent. The added support and objectivity of another person can be of immense help to the therapist to renew enthusiasm and keep trying in the face of highly resistant families. In sum, it is important for the therapist also to view himself or herself in a coping model—capable of making mistakes with parents, learning from the mistakes, being realistic about treatment goals, not expecting magical solutions and feelings refuelled from each family's gradual successes. One important advantage of the collaborative group therapy model, from the therapist's point of view, is that this process itself creates a feeling of support for the therapist because of the joint ownership of solutions and outcome. Besides reducing the dependency of families on the therapist, collaboration is reinforcing for the therapist in that it is gratifying to see parents coping independently. Lastly, the collaborative process constantly provides new learning for the therapist.

CONCLUSION

With regard to the overlap between physical and sexual abuse of children (see Chapter 1), the therapist must also consider the prevention of sexual as well as physical revictimization and maltreatment of children in the family. If sexual abuse is present on referral of a family, the prognosis for the family remaining together is poor. Bentovim (1991) describes 'clinical' work with families in which sexual abuse has occurred. He states that only 15% of families were able to work fully with the treatment process and remain together without the child suffering further. In the vast majority of cases the family members were separated. For 30% of cases, the mother sided with the child and they continued to live together in the absence of the father. In the remaining 55% of cases the mother was unsupportive and the child left home (30%) or was placed in care (25%). A description of assessment and treatment approaches to child sexual abuse in the family is beyond the scope of this book but may be found in Bentovim et al. (1988).

CHAPTER 8   Predicting sibling abuse

The researchers Gelles and Cornell, in their book *Intimate Violence in Families* (1990), observe that the raised consciousness brought about by an intense public and professional scrutiny of child and spouse abuse has had the unanticipated effect of many people assuming that male violence to women and children is the most common and most problematic aspect of violence in the home. Yet, women and children are far from being the only, or most common, victims of family violence. For example, violence between siblings (and siblings will often have shared a common experience of abuse) is so frequent that the public rarely perceives these events as family violence. This is puzzling given the mounting tide of public concern about violence by children, and more particularly adolescents, on the streets *and* in the schools. Although this is a book about family violence it would be short-sighted to neglect the repercussions of aggressive patterns of behaviour, nurtured often in the home, but also at school. Social systems within which children learn and behave are not insulated from each other.

Accounts in the media of violence at school (bullying and blackmail of peers, attacks on teachers), the flouting of norms and laws in the form of vandalism and hooliganism on the streets, sound a note of hysteria and moral panic. Patricia Morgan, in the 1970s, painted a sombre picture of growing numbers of poorly socialized individuals who have scarcely acquired the rudiments of human culture. She was of the opinion that the most alarming aspect was probably the sharp increase in crime, violence and aimless destruction of all kinds and larger proportionate increases as one goes down the age scale (Morgan, 1975). Such apocalyptic rhetoric continues to be a feature of press reports in the 1990s.

BULLYING: SIBLING AND PEER ABUSE

Although the apocalyptic school of thought may exaggerate the situation, there *is* cause for concern, especially with regard to the abuse by bullying of a growing number of victims in the home and classroom. Sibling violence involves an aggressive or violent act directed by one sibling against another; it is the most common form of family violence. Frude (1991) states that aside from the pushing, shoving and hair pulling that are very common in children's attacks on one another, several cases of extreme aggression—babies being thrown down the toilet, assault with knives and scissors—have been reported. The greater the difference in age between the members of a dyad involved in hostile interactions, the more likely is the assault and its consequences to approximate abuse of the kind that occurs between adults and children. Indeed sibling violence is often found in families where there is child physical, sexual and emotional maltreatment by the parents (Bolton and Bolton, 1987) or child sexual abuse by brothers and sisters (Finkelhor, 1980a, 1980b; Johnson, 1988, 1989; DeLong, 1989).

Much physical aggression in families is occasional, uncontrolled and (in that sense) a one-off response to provocation or frustration, administered in the heat of the moment, especially in what are perceived as disciplinary encounters (Wolfe, 1987, 1991) or hostile manifestations of sibling rivalry (Herbert, 1989). In statistical terms such aggressive outbursts are 'normal', if unpleasant, side-effects of the frictions inherent in family life. To call these manifestations family 'violence' would seem to smack of hyperbole when applied to most childhood quarrels. Frude (1991) raises the question of the role of hatred in aggression. The association is not clear: children may or may not be aggressive towards those whom they hate, and aggression may or may not be the outward and visible sign of hatred. Certainly, the intensity of feelings between siblings who are jealous of one another, or the rivalry of step-siblings in reconstituted families, can give every appearance of unmitigated hatred. The intensity and frequency of what is referred to as bullying may well deserve the designation 'violence'.

Bullying

Bullying, with its intention to *hurt* the victim tends to be a systematically repetitive activity, involving physical and/or psychological (often verbal) harm, instigated by one or more persons against another person—one who lacks the power, strength or will to resist. Merciless taunting and teasing may be as damaging over the longer term as physical assaults.

Thus, Lane (1989) defines bullying as 'any action or implied action, such as threats or violence, intended to cause fear or distress' on more than one occasion.

It is difficult to obtain reliable figures for the prevalence of bullying in the home among children, but they are worryingly high according to surveys carried out on such activities in schools. A study of some 2000 pupils in several middle and secondary schools in South Yorkshire (Ahmed and Smith, 1989) suggests an incidence of up to 1 in 5 children being bullied, and up to 1 in 10 children bullying other children. There are resonances with the mute suffering of many children who are abused in the home. Smith refers to the 'silent nightmare' to describe the fact that half of the victims of bullying kept their suffering to themselves.

Bullying is a subset of aggressive behaviour. I have taken only one example of an aggressive activity outside the family to illustrate how widespread interpersonal violence can be. But what of aggression by children within the family? It would be naive to think that all (or most) bullies limit their aggression (which in some cases reaches a sadistic level) to the school campus and its environs. Children who are aggressive at school tend to be aggressive at home; after non-compliance (the flouting of authority) aggression is one of the most common complaints of adults who have to rear, care for, or teach difficult children (Herbert, 1987a).

Parents (and teachers) tend to become worried about the children in their care when their behaviour appears (a) to be out of control, (b) to be unpredictable, or (c) to lack sense or meaning. If these tendencies are extreme and/or persistent they are likely to be thought of as 'problematic' or 'abnormal' and the growing concern they engender may result in a referral to a social worker or general practitioner and possibly to a clinical child psychologist or child psychiatrist. These criteria particularly fit aggressive behaviour which includes destructiveness, physical attack and verbal assault.

Sibling Conflict

Sibling rivalry, which can take the form of destructive behaviour, physical and verbal assault, is considered a 'normal' part of relations between brothers and sisters (Dunn and Kendrick, 1982; Dunn, 1984). Indeed many parents believe that such rivalry provides a good training ground for the successful management of aggressive behaviour in the real world. American parents generally feel that some exposure to aggression is a positive experience that should occur early in life; 7 out of 10 Americans agreed with the statement 'When a boy is growing up it is important for him to have a few fist fights' (Stark and McEvoy, 1970).

There is a view, which is both popular and respectable (although unproven), that childhood fighting and games of murder and mayhem, and also the watching of portrayed violence, can exert a positive effect through 'catharsis'. Emotions (according to this theory) are purged because of the release of tension involved in sibling quarrels or in identifying with the participants in a representation of violent events. Anger is 'drained off', so to speak, by 'living through' (in imagination) or 'acting out' these situations. Some parents argue that it is in order for children to express aggression towards their parents (or siblings) because they frustrate them. This channellized and direct expression of anger is supposed to be 'healthier' than its inhibition. Here is the instinct energy model—the pressure-cooker metaphor (Lorenz, 1966).

McCandless (1967), a developmental psychologist, finds at least two reasons to question the assumptions underlying such notions. The first is that there is little place in civilized, cooperative living for direct and primitive expression of aggression, when aggression is thought of as either physical or verbal attack. Certain 'disguised' verbal aggression, such as gossip or 'frankness', are condoned to a greater degree than physical attack or direct verbal abuse; but even gossip and frankness that conceal hostility are more likely to produce complications in human relations than to ease or facilitate social interaction. Secondly, learning theory predicts that the expression of aggression and its consequent momentary tension-relief strengthens rather than weakens the tendency to behave aggressively. McCandless provides evidence to support this prediction. By contrast, evidence does not indicate that behaving aggressively reduces tendencies to be aggressive. If anything, available studies suggest that the opposite is true. Whatever the evidence, public opinion seems remarkably 'philosophical', indeed complacent about manifestations of aggression in children.

The sociologist Suzanne Steinmetz (1977a), in her study of sibling conflict in a representative sample of 57 intact families in Delaware, USA, found that it was sometimes difficult to get parents to discuss sibling violence, not because they were ashamed or embarrassed to admit such behaviour, but because they simply did not view their children's actions, much of the time, as abusive or even worthy of mentioning. She discovered frequent incidents of sibling conflict. The parents in 49 families recorded the frequency and types of aggressive interaction between their offspring during a one-week period. Steinmetz found that a total of 131 sibling conflicts occurred during this period, ranging from short-lived arguments to more serious confrontations. This figure, although high, is probably a considerable underestimation of the true extent of sibling aggression. She notes that there are many problems inherent in relying upon parents to record the frequency of sibling conflicts. For example, in most of the families in Steinmetz's sample both parents worked, reducing the amount of time the parents actually spent with their children. This, in turn, reduced the opportunity for parents to observe and record aggressive behaviour between children. Steinmetz also found that parents would often record a series of events as one incident because the events were all related to the same causal circumstance. The way in which parents chose to record conflicts eventually affected the total number of conflicts observed. Finally, parents were at times too busy to record their children's behaviour; recording the aggressive incidents at a later time increased the probability that some occurrences of sibling conflict could have been forgotten.

Most parents view conflict among siblings as an inevitable part of growing up and rarely discourage wholeheartedly expressions of aggressive behaviour between their offspring. When Steinmetz asked the parents 'How do your children get along?', she received statements such as:

> Terrible! They fight all the time.
> Oh, it's just constant, but I understand that this is normal.
> I talk to other people and their children are the same way.
> (Steinmetz, 1977a: 43)

Steinmetz (1982) found that between 63 and 68% of adolescents in the families she studied used physical force to resolve conflicts with their brothers and sisters. Sociologists who have studied aggression (or what they tend to call violence) between brothers and sisters report that parents feel it is important for their children to learn how to handle themselves in violent situations. They do not actively discourage their children from becoming involved in provocative disputes with their siblings. In fact, parents may try to ignore aggressive interactions and only become involved when minor situations are perceived as escalating into major confrontations. There is some evidence that, within limits, this may not be a bad policy.

Dunn (1984, 1988) observed directly the interactions of English children—brothers and sisters—in their own homes. In each of 43 pairs of siblings, the younger child was 18 months old. They revisited six months later to make further observations. The mothers' actions were also recorded. They discovered that:

- There was a good deal of quarrelling—an average of about eight fights per hour.
- The mother's intrusion in quarrels led to more conflict over the longer term. In families where the mother tended to intervene often in the first observation period, the children did have longer quarrels and more frequent physical fights in the second observation period (six months later) than in families where the mother intervened less.
- When a mother adopted a style of discussing rules and feelings with the children when they quarrelled, they were apt to develop in their offspring more mature ways of handling con-

flict. These included conciliatory actions such as showing concern for, comforting, helping or apologizing to the other. Their children were more likely to refer to rules ('We have to take turns. Mummy said so').

It is sometimes argued that quarrelling might well increase in frequency if each child observes the other being reprimanded or getting the parent—even temporarily—to take his or her side. The counter-argument is that parental intervention is necessary to teach values of fair play, sharing and compromise. Many parents feel, too, that if they *do not* intervene, injury and/or an injustice could be inflicted on the younger and/or weaker child. Nor do they wish to condone the use of fighting or bullying by default, which means inaction.

Dunn (1984, 1993) has reviewed several studies of parental intervention and non-intervention. On the one hand, studies in which parents were trained to stay right out of brotherly and sisterly quarrels seem to indicate that the frequency of such arguments can be reduced—particularly if ignoring quarrels is combined with rewarding the children for desisting from conflict. On the other hand, other studies indicate that if parents wish to encourage in children an ability to care about what happens to other people, they need to point out clearly and forcefully to their offspring when young, the consequences of being unkind and aggressive. Dunn comments that quarrels between brothers and sisters provide the ideal training-ground to carry out this kind of teaching. It can be an uphill struggle. Interviews with young children indicate that they use far more emotional words to describe their brothers and sisters than to describe friends or even parents. More often than not the words they choose to apply are negative.

A large variety of unpleasant events ('aversive stimuli') can set the stage for the development of conflict and a chain reaction of quarrelsome behaviours—for example, bullying and teasing of a painful, threatening or humiliating nature; depriving the weaker child of his or her property, rights and opportunities. Dunn (1984) found that 2-year-old, second born children were just as likely as their elders to initiate a quarrel, to tease and to hit. Mothers were twice as likely to scold the older children and tell them to stop; with younger children, however, they tended not to scold but to distract them and try to interest them in something other than the source of conflict.

In a nationally representative study by Straus, Gelles and Steinmetz (1980, 1988), sibling conflict was one of several hidden forms of family violence investigated (Table 8.1). More than four out of five (82%) children between the ages of 3 and 17, residing in the United States, and having one or more siblings living at home, engaged in at least one aggressive act towards a sibling during a one-year period. Such acts included pushing, slapping, shoving and throwing things. Even when 'lesser' forms of aggression were excluded and the researchers examined only the more severe forms (such as kicking, biting, hitting with an object and 'beating up'), the rates were still alarmingly high (see Table 8.1). Straus and his colleagues estimate that over 19 million American children engage in acts of 'abusive violence' against a sibling over a one-year period.

Table 8.1 Incidence of hidden forms of family violence (in percentages)

Violent acts	Sibling to sibling	Parent to adolescent	Adolescent to parent
Any violence	82	46	10
Pushed or shoved	74	25	6
Slapped	48	28	3
Threw things	43	4	4
Kicked, bit or punched	42	2	2
Hit, or tried to hit, with an object	40	7	2
Beaten up	16	1.3	0.7
Threatened with a knife or gun	0.8	0.2	0.3
Used a knife or gun	0.3	0.2	0.2

Note: This table is based on data collected by Straus, Gelles and Steinmetz (1980, 1988).

ASSESSMENT: DEVELOPMENTAL ASPECTS

The term violence is emotive and begs the questions of whether it is appropriate to use when referring to children's actions; whether it means the same thing as aggression; or represents, in some way, a more severe form or 'savouring' of aggression. Whatever the answers to such questions, it is important to carry out a comprehensive functional analysis of aggressive incidents by looking at their antecedents (i.e. the circumstances or interactions that preceded or set the scene for their occurrence); the precise nature of the aggressive outburst in words and deeds; and the consequences (interactions, outcomes) that flow from these events (Frude, 1991; Herbert, 1987b).

Precise specifications of aggression in overt behavioural terms are a desideratum of clinical and social work practice because of the possibilities of disagreement over developmental and social definitions of what is acceptable, appropriate or abnormal. Social and cultural attitudes, as well as developmental influences, determine which childish actions are labelled 'violent' as opposed to 'aggressive', or the more socially acceptable 'assertive' behaviour. Aggression in children is most usefully analysed in its developmental and social contact, *not* reified as an entity residing in the individual. The use of the word aggression, or violence, as a noun ('there is a lot of violence in him or her') is misleading. The use of the words 'aggressive behaviour' is more likely to remind us to look at the meaning of aggressive actions on the part of a child (i.e. a child of a particular age).

Most people have heard of the 'terrible' twos. Parents tend to make allowances for children's cognitive immaturity and poorly developed self-control; they distinguish between their actions and intentions. At that tender age the children 'do not really mean to hurt' when they hit out. Parents whose attributions carry more sinister connotations ('It's his bad blood', 'She has the devil in her', 'He's always trying to get at me') are quite likely to be among those who use excessive punishment on their children when they are aggressive and disobedient.

Before the age of 2, children largely fail to differentiate what *they* do from what an *adult* does; in other words, they do not comprehend causal agency. The development of the cognitive ability to differentiate between *self* and *other* leads to a recognition of causal relationships, transforming, in turn, the assimilation of the interesting into a desire for influence over things and people. This increasing awareness of self-identity typically leads to a 'negativistic crisis' around the age of 2—the 'terrible twos'. Children who have previously accepted assistance in their efforts without fuss, insist on doing things themselves and displaying their own competence; they also resist parental requests and commands.

Patterson et al. (1975) trace the developmental history of coercive behaviours. Children display a steady decline in performance rates from a high point shortly before the age of 3 down to more moderate levels at the age of school entrance. Two-year-olds display high rates of whining, crying, yelling as well as high rates from most other coercive actions. By the age of 4, there are substantial reductions in negative commands, destruction and attempts to lash out.

By the age of 5, most children used less negativism, non-compliance and negative physical actions than younger siblings (Reynolds, 1982). There is also a significant decrease in aggression from the age of 4 through to 8 years in classroom behaviour (Hartup, 1974). The older 'aggressive' boy or girl—identified as 'problematic'—is likely to display coercive behaviours at a level more appropriate to, or commensurate with a 3- to 4-year-old child's behaviour; in this sense he or she is an example of arrested socialization (Patterson, 1982). With increasing age, certain coercive behaviours are no longer acceptable to parents. The behaviours then become the target, in normal homes, for careful monitoring and sanctions which, in turn, are accompanied by reductions in their frequency and intensity. What then brings about abusive levels of aggression?

FACTORS THAT INFLUENCE THE EXTENT OF SIBLING VIOLENCE

Many factors are likely to affect and influence the occurrence, severity and extent of sibling aggression—influences such as family factors, disability, gender, age, temperament and empathy.

Influences

Family factors

Family factors certainly influence the development of rivalry and assault. They have been implicated in the manifestation of bullying behaviour, most clearly in Norwegian research (see Olweus, 1979, 1989). Sibling abuse is more likely to occur in a home that already knows child abuse at the hands of the parent. Exposure to a violent parent and a general background lacking warmth or positive affect, can result in children experiencing difficulty in controlling their aggressive impulses. In the case of children who bully others (inside or outside the home), there seems to be an association with cold as opposed to warm child-rearing, intense levels of discord or violence in the home, and a lack of clear rules about discipline, or monitoring of aggressive or other behaviour (Loeber and Dishion, 1984). Children growing up in such families have bullying behaviours to imitate, with little countervailing affection or training in self-restraint.

Bolton and Bolton (1987) report that the family in which serious physical abuse between siblings occurs tends to be chaotic and disorganized; the balance of care and attention is inappropriate. The child perpetrator is often an only child who has had to accept the intrusion of new half-siblings. The sibling who perpetrates is often on the 'down side' of the family equation. They are seen negatively by the parent(s). The parent tends to be preoccupied with providing attention to the child who is victimized by the sibling. There is a great deal of crisis in the family that is centred, in particular, on the mother; when her time and energy have to be directed elsewhere, the perpetrating child is often asked to serve as 'caregiver' to the child victim. This is just the time when an assault is likely to occur (Green, 1984).

The discrepancy between the quality of care given the children is so extreme, so obvious, and so painful for the perpetrating child that it is reasonable to hypothesize that abuse towards the seemingly 'more loved' sibling is an effort to 'get even', a way to express hostility intended for the mother, a device to gain attention, or a strategy to master their own victimization by adopting a perpetrator role (Green, 1984).

Disability

The likelihood of abuse is increased if there are learning problems, organic dysfunction in the child, or any feature of his or her physical or psychological being that makes the child feel inferior (Green, 1984). Such disabilities also make the child more vulnerable to sibling abuse.

Gender

At all ages girls are less aggressive than boys, but the differences are relatively small (Gelles and Cornell, 1990). Girls' quarrels tend to be more verbal and less physical than boys' quarrels (Herbert, 1987a). Overall, 83% of boys and 74% of girls are physically abusive towards their brothers or sisters (Straus, Gelles and Steinmetz, 1980, 1988).

Age

Research into sibling aggression confirms the belief that, as children grow older, the rates of using aggression or more extreme violence to resolve conflicts between siblings decrease (Steinmetz, 1977a, 1977b; Straus, Gelles and Steinmetz, 1980, 1988). This could be the result of children becoming better equipped at using verbal skills to settle disputes. (At a young age girls are more verbal than boys generally.) Of course, older children do tend to spend more time away from home and this takes them away from potential sibling conflicts.

Steinmetz found that the factors precipitating conflicts varied with age. Younger children were more likely to have conflicts centred on possessions, especially toys. One family reported that, during a one-week period, their young children fought over 'the use of a glider, sharing a truck, sharing a tricycle, knocking down one child's building blocks and taking them', e.g. young adolescent conflicts focused on territory, with adolescents becoming very upset if a sibling invaded their personal space. 'They fuss. They say, "He's sitting on my seat"' (Steinmetz, 1977a).

Temperament

Temperament plays its part on both sides of the coin, being related to the impulsiveness and quick-tempered nature of responses by bullying children (see page 147), as compared with the withdrawal and lack of assertiveness of victims (Herbert, 1991).

Empathy

Children who bully others may be less empathetic to the feelings of others, particularly potential victims; certainly Smith (1990) found that both the typical questionnaire responses, as well as interviews with bullies, reveal that they tend to feel positive or neutral about seeing bullying incidents, whereas most children say they feel bad or unhappy about them. It has been argued that, in children who bully others, it is not so much that they lack social skills in the information-processing sense (Dodge et al., 1986), but simply have different values and goals which give direction (or a lack of direction, some would say) to their social encounters (Smith and Bolton, 1990).

Adaptive/Maladaptive Functioning

Bullying behaviour could be considered as 'pseudopathological' in the sense that Crawford and Anderson (1989) use the term—that is, behaviour which might have been adaptive for the individual performing it at one time, or in certain circumstances, but which is *no longer* socially acceptable, or appropriate *in any circumstance* because of the harm it bestows on others. An example of the latter comes from interviews with bullies which often suggest that they view the playground as a tough place where you need to dominate or humiliate others in order not to be so treated yourself (Smith, 1990).

Cognitive and Social Skill Deficits

Dodge et al. (1986) describe social competence in children in terms of a five-stage processing model: (1) encoding the stimulus situation; (2) interpreting it; (3) searching for suitable responses; (4) evaluating the best response; and (5) enacting the chosen response. Any 'deficit' in social competence would be ascribed to one or more of these stages. Research in the USA suggests that highly aggressive children tend to encode situations as hostile (i.e. more readily attributing hostile intentions to others), and to generate fewer non-hostile responses (Dodge and Frame, 1982; Guerra and Slaby, 1989).

Conduct Disorder

A list of the attributes of conduct-disordered children will indicate why this constellation of behaviour problems looms large in the casework of practitioners dealing with family violence in general and sibling abuse in particular. This is why it is important to be aware of the ramifications of this disorder for their work with regard to assessment, planning and intervention (see Table 8.2).

Table 8.2 Frequently found attributes defining conduct disorders

Fighting, hitting, assaultive
Temper tantrums
Disobedient, defiant
Destructiveness of own or other's property
Impertinent, 'smart', impudent
Uncooperative, resistive, inconsiderate
Disruptive, interrupts, disturbs
Negative, refuses direction
Restless
Boisterous, noisy
Irritability, 'blows up' easily
Attention-seeking, 'show-off'
Dominates others, bullies, threatens
Hyperactivity
Untrustworthy, dishonest, lies
Profanity, abusive language
Jealousy
Quarrelsome, argues
Irresponsible, undependable
Inattentive
Steals
Distractibility
Teases
Denies mistakes, blames others
Pouts and sulks
Selfish

Source: Adapted from Quay (1986).

Conduct disorder is very common in children and adolescents, boys being clearly more affected than girls. Its high prevalence is well documented in a series of epidemiological studies or community surveys, although the figures vary from study to study. They range from 4 to 6% (see Webster-Stratton and Herbert, 1994).

The general picture that emerges from various studies is that conduct disorders are a widespread phenomenon that can be found in different countries and have an early onset, sometimes as early as the age of 3 years (see Richman, Stevenson and Graham, 1982). Sadly, the prevalence of these disorders is increasing, generating a need for services that far outstrips available personnel and resources; indeed fewer than 10% of children who need mental health services actually receive them (Hobbs, 1982). For those who do, child conduct disorders make up a lion's share (one-third to one-half) of all child and adolescent clinical referrals. In an epidemiological and longitudinal study involving very young children, Richman, Stevenson and Graham (1982) found that 62% of those with clinically relevant problems at the age of 3 also showed severe disorders at the age of 8, in comparison with only 22% of the children rated as without problems. It was also found that children with conduct disorder at the age of 8 were often described as restless, as more difficult to control and as having poorer peer relations at the age of 13.

Chapter 9 returns to this important matter of prognosis and indeed to the wider issue of the conduct disorders, their role in family violence and the need to assist families with such problems in their midst. These aggressive children are at increased risk of being rejected by their peers (Coie, 1990a, 1990b) and/or abused by their parents (Reid, Taplin and Loeber, 1981).

Sexual Maltreatment by Siblings

Although beyond the scope of this review, the sexual maltreatment of brothers and sisters by their siblings is much more common than once thought. To a certain extent this has been the result of a reappraisal of what was once considered sexual exploration between brothers and sisters, which has been more appropriately described as exploitation where the age difference between the siblings is greater than five years (Finkelhor, 1980a; DeLong, 1989).

In a recent study, as many as 2% of English undergraduate students reported being sexually maltreated by a sibling on at least one occasion (Browne and Hamilton, 1997). Often this sexual maltreatment was associated with physical abuse, a fact that has been confirmed by a number of American studies for both boys and girls (Johnson, 1988, 1989; DeLong, 1989).

Similar to physical and sexual assaults by adults, it is in the context of caregiving or 'child minding' that many of these attacks by adolescents takes place (Margolin, 1990). Indeed, most child sexual offenders begin to take advantage of younger children during their adolescence, with the majority having been physically and/or sexually assaulted themselves by other teenagers and adults (Elliott, Browne and Kilcoyne, 1995). Nevertheless, sibling maltreatment of both a physical and sexual nature has been observed in very young children (Cantwell, 1988). Overall, Johnson (1988) noted that 46% of a sample of 47 sexually abusive boys were involved in the abuse of their siblings. Similarly, Pierce and Pierce (1987) reported that 59 offences had been committed by the 37 juvenile sex offenders in their study, 40% were against sisters and 20% were against brothers.

CONCLUSION

In conclusion, the study of physical and sexual maltreatment by brothers and sisters is limited and prevention is only just beginning. It requires a great deal more research given its prevalence and consequences (Tooley, 1977; Gibbens, 1978; Laviola, 1989). A summary of the knowledge to date on peer relations in maltreated children can be found in Mueller and Silverman (1989).

CHAPTER 9   Predicting and preventing parent abuse

Many of the parents that the authors meet in the course of their research or casework feel bruised and abused (literally and figuratively, physically and emotionally) by their children and teenagers. Others, we suspect, remain silent—too embarrassed to admit the harassment and, not infrequently, fear which is a part of their daily experience. One of the authors (MH) has worked with adolescents whose hatred for their parents spills over regularly into verbal abuse (obscenities, humiliating criticism and threats) and physical assaults (ranging from 'minor' slaps to serious violence).

Can we speak of 'parent abuse' or are we stretching the concept of abuse to such ludicrous limits that we debase its meaning? Gelles and Cornell (1990) are in no doubt about the value of this usage. As they observe:

> Parent abuse is considered almost humorous by those who first hear of it. Researchers who study parent abuse have been teased that they must be running out of victims or asked if 'pet abuse' is next on their list. The large majority of parent victims are so ashamed by their victimization that they are reluctant to discuss anything but the most severe incidents; and when they do report, they, like adolescent victims, are blamed for being hit.

These authors make the point that the very notion of children controlling, and indeed assaulting, their parents is so alien to our ideas about the power relationships between parents and their offspring that it is difficult to believe that such a reversal, and one so subversive, can actually occur. It seems a sacrilege to suggest that the children we love, the children who can be (or have been) so loving, should have in them the seeds of indifference, cruelty and hatred which are the common accompaniments of violence to parents (see Herbert, 1993).

For the purpose of this chapter we are adopting a broad interpretation of the word abuse. It will encompass the type of attitude and behaviour (for whatever reason) that negates the commonly accepted expectations of a child's relationships and interactions with his or her parents. Society vests legal authority and control in the parents of a child. It also enjoins children to respect their mothers and fathers. It is an unwelcome revelation that so many young people usurp this control and show disrespect, indeed contempt, by asserting their wishes, willpower, defiance and/or physical strength.

The family that allows itself to be intimidated by the children to the point of losing control, is one, in the view of Bolton and Bolton (1987), that has abdicated responsibility and authority over their offspring. As they put it: 'The child is the parent. The real parent is emotionally incompetent and over-taxed and the child has long been asked to accept responsibility beyond his or her capabilities. The eventual result is an explosion.'

PREVALENCE AND PERSPECTIVE

Physical Violence

The prevalence of child-to-parent violence is difficult enough to assess; the loss of parental authority, impossible. The former, while less than parent-to-child abuse (see Chapter 8; Table 8.1), is high enough to merit serious academic and professional attention (Gelles and Cornell, 1990; Straus Gelles and Steinmetz, 1988). For all that, the fact is that problems of definition—what constitutes abuse and violence—reduce all statistical estimates to 'informed guestimates'. Professionals know of many examples of small children hurting their parents by kicking their shins, pulling their hair and pinching them. Older children sometimes threaten, indeed lash out at their parents. But, is this abuse? Matters of definition remain unresolved, and this makes a critical review of the evidence difficult.

Of course, there is no mistaking the gravity of some acts of aggression. In some, fortunately relatively rare cases, the violence is so unrestrained that it results in very serious injury and even the murder of the parent (parricide). This is usually an end result of the most dysfunctional relationships within extremely disturbed families (Harbin and Madden, 1979; Mones, 1993; Heide, 1995). It is not only those who are in authority (i.e. the parents) who use extreme forms of violence but also adolescents (grown strong) and even children, despite their lesser size and strength. Table 9.1 shows that mothers are more likely to be victims of serious 'abusive' violence from their children. Fathers are the more likely victims of older male children (Cornell and Gelles, 1982; Agnew and Huguley, 1989). Overall prevalence rates, for any act of violence against parents, were estimated as 7–8% to fathers and 6–11% to mothers (Cornell and Gelles, 1982; Peek, Fisher and Kidwell, 1985), although it has been claimed that 25% of single mothers with teenage children are hit by them (Livingstone, 1986).

Table 9.1 Violence severity towards parents by sex of child

Sex of child	Sex of parent	Overall violence	Severe violence
Son	Mother	11% (157)	4% (166)
	Father	8% (153)	2% (159)
Daughter	Mother	9% (130)	5% (127)
	Father	4% (115)	0% (118)

Source: Cornell and Gelles (1982).

Harbin and Madden (1979) found that the majority of young people who attack a parent are between the ages of 13 and 24, although they also report children as young as 10 years old inflicting injury on their parents. Researchers agree that sons are slightly more likely to be violent and abusive than daughters. The sons' rates of severe aggression against a parent increase with age, while for daughters the rates of extreme aggression tend to decline with age (Agnew and Huguley, 1989).

Most researchers report that the rates at which children 'abuse' their parents range from 5 to 12% (Agnew and Huguley, 1989;

Cornell and Gelles, 1982; Peek, Fisher and Kidwell, 1985; Straus, Gelles and Steinmetz, 1980). The US Department of Justice (1980) reported that of the 1.2 million incidents of violence between relatives, 47 000 involved children's acts of aggression against parents.

Cornell and Gelles (1982) analysed a sample drawn from a nationally representative series of families who had a teenager living at home between the ages of 10 and 17. Nine per cent of parents reported at least one act of 'violence'. This means, on extrapolation to the US population, that approximately 2.5 million parents were struck at least once a year. A statistic was also calculated for the more severe forms of violence. Approximately 3% of the adolescents were reported to have kicked, punched, bit, 'beat up', or used a knife or gun against a parent. While this percentage appears quite small, when it is projected to the total number of adolescents between 10 and 17 living in two-parent households it means that 900 000 parents are being 'abused' each year.

Straus, Gelles and Steinmetz (1988) found that 10% of the children aged between 3 and 17 years in their sample performed at least one act of violence against a parent during a one-year period. Agnew and Huguley (1989) analysed data from the 1972 National Survey of Youth and report that roughly 5% of the adolescents in the survey had hit one of their parents in the previous year. Such acts of aggression, especially the sporadic kind, do not necessarily indicate that parents have completely surrendered their authority or influence. But they often do.

In the UK, general estimates of adolescent and teenage violence to parents give a prevalence rate of 6% (Parentline, 1990; Smith et al., 1992). More recently, the first in-depth study in the UK (Browne and Hamilton, 1997) revealed prevalence rates similar to those found in the USA. Overall, 9% of teenagers report being violent to their mothers and 6% to their fathers. Serious 'Abusive Violence' was reported by 2 and 3% of teenagers to mothers and fathers, respectively.

Bearing in mind the ambiguities of terms such as violence and abuse and the dubious status of the statistics, we nevertheless have a problem that merits serious attention from researchers and practitioners. That is certainly the case if we adopt a broader definition of abuse to include those parents who feel intimidated, shamed and disempowered (indeed 'abused') by their children usurping control in situations which normally come under parental authority.

Loss of Parental Control

Clinical observations of children and adolescents who exert continuing and extreme defiance of, or intimidation (including physical assaults) towards, parents indicate that most families have some disturbance in the authority structure within the family. These children may develop a grandiose sense of self, feel omnipotent, and expect everyone to respond to them accordingly (Herbert, 1987a). It is suggested that they are seeking some kind of structure in a family environment which lacks boundaries, but which does not set limits. But they are not capable of providing those boundaries for themselves in any rational manner. The outcome is insecurity and a series of explosive responses to situations for which no prior family rules exist (Bolton and Bolton, 1987; Paulson et al., 1990).

As children approach adolescence and grow stronger, more assertive and rebellious, what were 'merely' difficult situations for parents can become menacing, and in some cases, dangerous—especially where they have been granted too much control over decisions when young. Such a burden—the assumption of control when immature—is thought to cause a mixture of anxiety and extreme frustration (Harbin and Madden, 1979). Physical attacks on parents are thought often to be an attempt by adolescents to either control the family or to punish the parents for forcing decision making on them prematurely (ibid.).

Of course, many children are disobedient, or go through disobedient phases; some take to an extreme their antagonism to parental requests and commands. So intense is the resistance that at times it becomes quite clear that the child is not merely failing to comply, but is doing precisely the opposite of what is desired—a pattern of behaviour called 'negativism'.

A Developmental Perspective

The perennial problem for the social and health worker assessing the seriousness of non-compliance is the ubiquity of disobedience as a 'problem' of childhood. It is, in a sense, a 'normal' response to the 'rigours' of socialization and one that peaks at certain stages in the child's development, notably during the striving for independence which takes place in toddlerhood and adolescence (Herbert, 1974). Indeed, up to a point, disobedience is undoubtedly adaptive and its absence, or a manifestation of mindless servility, would be a matter of concern. But what is that 'point' at which non-compliance is thought to be excessive, counter-productive and thus maladaptive? Forehand and McMahon (1981), in their book on noncompliance, indicate that the ratio of compliance to parental commands for non-clinic normal pre-school samples ranges from approximately 60 to 80%.

Not infrequently the parent or teacher may concede to the child's disobedience—often a result of the child's coercive response (e.g. with a temper tantrum) to the parent's attempts to insist. Although tantrums are frightening they tend to be intropunitive rather than extrapunitive—that is to say, the child tends to hurt himself or herself rather than others. Giving in to the child's non-compliance (as we saw in Chapter 3) tends not to occur on every occasion, producing what is, in effect, an intermittent schedule of reinforcement for coercive, non-compliant actions. The parent's submission becomes habitual, reinforced by the termination of the child's tantrum. This process of reciprocal reinforcement by the removal of aversive stimuli has been described as the 'negative reinforcer trap' (Wahler and Dumas, 1985).

A child's oppositional behaviour is often maintained by the contingent application of positive social reinforcement in the form of self-gratification (getting one's own way) or parental attention. Such attention can come in a variety of forms, including verbal reprimands (scolding, nagging), reasoning with the child, or simply trying to be reasonable by discussing the misdemeanour at great length. In response to parental actions of this kind, the child may behave in a cooperative manner, thus reciprocally reinforcing the parental intervention. This process (as we saw earlier) is called the 'positive reinforcer trap'.

In most cases, oppositional behaviour is probably maintained by a combination of both positive and negative reinforcement. Where such patterns are frequent, intense, and persist over time, there is a danger of dysfunctional patterns of family life becoming ingrained.

Previous Learning Experience

There seems to be a consensus from a variety of studies that aggressive behaviour in children can be related to broad (long-term) attitudes and child-rearing practices. To summarize the findings, a combination of lax discipline (especially with regard to the offsprings' acts of aggression) combined with hostile attitudes in the parents produces very aggressive and poorly controlled behaviour in the offspring (see Herbert, 1987a). Parents tend to demonstrate their hostile attitudes by being unaccepting and disapproving of their children. They fail to give affection, understanding or explanations to children, and tend to use a lot of physical punishment without giving reasons for exerting their authority—something applied erratically and arbitrarily. Such methods are often referred to as power-assertive (see page 204); the adult asserts dominant and authoritarian control through physical punishment, harsh verbal abuse, angry threats and deprivation of privileges. There is a positive relationship between the extensive use of physical punishment in the home by parents and high levels of aggression in their offspring outside the home (Herbert, 1987a).

Mary Main and Carol George carried out a study of abused children and non-abused children and their mothers. The abused children at the ages of only 1 and 2 had already begun to imitate the destructive ways of their parents. Main and George (1985) reported that abused young children at a nursery hit, slapped, kicked, pushed and shoved their peers more often than non-abused young children. Abused young children acted in a similar way to their parents and caregivers, without provocation. It was reported that 7 out of 10 abused young children harassed their caregivers compared with only 2 out of 10 non-abused young children.

Violence begets violence; what the child appears to learn is that might is right. Furthermore, delinquents have more commonly been the victims of adult assaults—often of a vicious, persistent and even calculated nature—than non-delinquents (Herbert, 1987a). The transition of victim to offender is explored in Chapter 10.

By way of contrast with the adverse life influences described above, the factors that facilitate the development of social awareness and adaptive behaviour (see Hoffman, 1970; Wright, 1971; Staub, 1975) include:

- strong ties of affection between parents and children;
- firm moral demands made by parents on their offspring;
- techniques of punishment that are psychological rather than physical (i.e. methods that signify or threaten withdrawal of approval), thus provoking anxiety or guilt rather than anger;
- an intensive use of reasoning and explanations (inductive methods);
- giving responsibility.

The balancing of these components is perhaps best illustrated in the philosophy of what (on the basis of her investigations) Baumrind (1971) calls the 'authoritative' parent. The parent attempts to direct the child's activities in a rational manner determined by the issues involved in particular disciplinary situations. He or she also encourages verbal give and take and shares with the child the reasoning behind policy. She values both the child's self-expression and his or her so-called 'instrumental attributes' (respect for authority, work, etc.), appreciating evidence of both independent self-will and disciplined conformity. Therefore, this kind of parent exerts firm control at points where he or she and the child diverge in viewpoint, but does not suppress the child with restrictions. The parent recognizes his or her own special rights as an adult, but also the child's individual interests and special ways.

Conscience and Self-restraint

Principles which derive from the study of anxiety conditioning on the one hand, and instrumental learning on the other, are used to explain self-restraint and resistance to temptation (e.g. Mowrer, 1960). Learning theorists consider that behaviours indicative of guilt, such as confession, self-criticism and apology, are learned responses that have been found to be instrumental in reducing the anxiety that follows a child's transgression of, say, the parents' rules. Guilt is but one of several facets of moral behaviour. It is the emotional discomfort or remorse we ascribe to our consciences when we have transgressed the rules.

Prior to the stage of development that comes at about the age of 5, children certainly feel 'bad' when they have transgressed, but primarily because of fears of external parental punishment or disapproval. But, at about 4 or 5 years of age, the locus of anxiety or fear comes from within, and children feel guilt when they have transgressed. Hoffman (1970) observes that:

> . . . the guiding concept in most moral development research is the internalization of socially sanctioned prohibitions and mandates. One of the legacies of Freud, and the sociologist Durkheim as well, is the assumption now prevalent among social scientists that the individual does not go through life viewing society's central norms as externally and coercively imposed pressures to which he must submit. Though the norms are initially alien, they are eventually adopted by the individual, largely though the efforts of his early socializers—the parents—and come to serve as internalized guides so that he behaves in accord with them even when external authority is not present to enforce them. That is, control by others is replaced by self-control.

Substantial deviations represented by authoritarian parenting at one 'extreme' and permissive (*laissez-faire*) parenting at the other, are regarded, if not as pathological, at least as entailing risks for the child's healthy development (Herbert, 1974). Non-conformity is likely to be a consequence of lax, *laissez-faire* parenting (Herbert, 1987a); in extreme form it is prejudicial to good adjustment. The child who refuses to moderate or restrain his or her self-centred impulses, or conform to the accepted standards of the group, is likely to become a social outcast. This is serious for social development because the child is deprived of the satisfaction of belonging to a group and of the learning experiences that come from a sense of belonging and the feelings that go with comradeship.

Disciplinary Encounters

Hoffman (1970) makes the point that all disciplinary encounters that contribute to social and moral development have a great deal in common, regardless of the specific technique used. These are particularly significant because so many abusive incidents occur in the context of what are perceived as disciplinary confrontations (see page 42). The techniques have three components, any one of which may predominate:

- *Power assertion*. Hoffman contends that the most reliable finding in the parent–child area of research is the negative relationship between power assertion and various indices of moral behaviour. It holds up for both sexes and across the entire age range of childhood.
- *Withdrawal of approval*. Anxiety about threatened withdrawal of parent love or approval is not (according to the evidence which runs counter to 'received wisdom') the major contributing factor to the child's internalization of parental values. However, there is evidence that love withdrawal may contribute to the inhibition of anger (see Herbert, 1974). It produces anxiety which leads to the renunciation of hostile and possibly other impulses. While it may contribute to making the child more susceptible to adult influence, this does not necessarily have a bearing on moral development (i.e. guilt and internal moral judgement). The interesting question is, of course, 'What happens when there is no love or approval to threaten to withdraw?' The issue of parental rejection is considered on page 169.
- *Induction*. This is the type of discipline that is most conducive to moral development; it involves pointing out the effects of the child's behaviour, giving reasons and explanations. (The cognitive structuring of aggressive acts is elaborated on page 49.)

A variety of social and family conditions preclude the operation of these factors in the lives of some children. Disharmonious, rejecting home backgrounds, the breakdown of discipline, parental loss, and broken homes are examples of life variables that are often linked aetiologically to disorders of conduct, among which are the acts of violence which are the subject of this chapter (Herbert, 1987a). When the family fails, the child seems to be particularly vulnerable to the development of conduct and delinquent disorders—a fact reflected in empirical studies (e.g. West and Farrington, 1973; Farrington, 1995).

CAUSATION: DISORDERS OF CONDUCT IN CHILDREN WHO ABUSE

Child abuse and spouse abuse have been found to be related to many social, family and situational factors. Child and adolescent aggression or violence, however, cannot be explained simply in terms of the social factors that determine adult violence. The influences that are hypothesized to be important in the prevalence of conduct disorders are remarkably similar to those that vary in relation to the prevalence of abuse by parents. Studies indicate that the frequency of parent abuse is related to the frequency of other forms of family violence in the home (Herbert, 1987a). The more violence children experience or witness, the more likely they are to strike out at a parent. Adolescents who have friends who assault parents, who approve of delinquency in certain circumstances, who perceive the possibility of being arrested as low, and who are weakly attached to their parents have been found to be the most likely to use violence towards their parents (Agnew and Huguley, 1989).

In a recent study on teenage–parent conflict and its relation to child maltreatment (Browne and Hamilton, 1997), 469 English university students completed the Conflict Tactics Scale and a Childhood History Questionnaire giving, respectively, details on tactics employed during the previous year and information about their childhood. The study showed that the conflict tactics used by the respondents were found to be significantly related to the reported tactics of their parents and the experience of maltreatment by the parents in earlier years (see Figure 9.1). For example, Browne and Hamilton (1997) state that for 14% of students who were violent to their parents (4% severely violent), four out of five had been recent victims of their parents' violence.

Furthermore, Browne and Hamilton (1997) found that maltreatment by people outside the family had no significant effect on the likelihood of parents being aggressed against by their children. These findings support the notion that violence being displayed in the 'family of orientation' has a strong influence on the development of aggressive behaviour (Agnew and Huguley, 1989) and are consistent with the hypothesis that families who view violence as a legitimate way to resolve conflict run a greater risk of experiencing all forms of family violence, including parent abuse. Doubtless the intergenerational cycle of disadvantage is at work. Parents who abuse are likely to produce children who abuse, who later become parents who abuse, who in turn . . . and so on. The mystery is why the cycle is broken for some individuals but not for others; and the issue is whether (and how) we can bring a halt to this transfer of abuse from generation to generation (see Chapter 11).

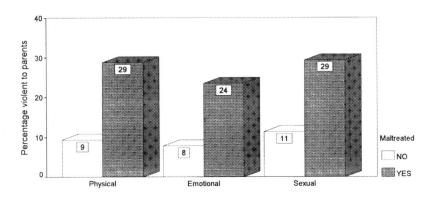

Figure 9.1 The percent of maltreated (intrafamilial) and non-maltreated (N=469 minus n cases) students who were violent by type of maltreatment. (Values have been rounded to the nearest whole number.) (From Browne and Hamilton, 1997)

It is not the case that children who abuse their parents would all be diagnosed as suffering from a conduct disorder. But this condition does figure importantly in the victimization of parents. In considering the conduct disorders of childhood we are moving a good distance from the normal range of non-compliant, oppositional problems which are a feature of the 'growing pains' of so many children, and the child-rearing pains of a multitude of hard-pressed parents. At a higher level of intensity and frequency, the children described as conduct disordered are unpredictable, argumentative with adults, lose their temper, swear, and are aggressive, resentful and easily annoyed by others. They frequently and actively defy adults' requests or rules and deliberately annoy other people (see Webster-Stratton and Herbert, 1994). These criteria are seen to be the defining characteristics of these disorders.

Patterson (1982) is of the opinion that there is considerable overlap among the different types of behavioural problem (variously defined as oppositional-defiant, hyperactivity, attention deficit or conduct disorder) exhibited by children, and that it is advisable to examine the behaviour in the social and other contexts in which it occurs. It is more fruitful to learn the conditions that contribute to the problem manifestation rather than get bogged down in pedantic attempts to narrowly define behaviour in terms of diagnostic criteria. Patterson (1976) concludes, on the basis of naturalistic observations in home settings, that the social experience of some children is so severely restricted that they do not learn the social skills necessary to function effectively within their family or in peer relationships. This may delay the average 10–12 year old at the level exhibited by 3 year olds. These children are likely to receive three times as much punishment from their peers compared with non-aggressive children. Frude (1991) notes the factors other than aggression—low sociability, lack of social skills, immaturity, 'offensive' behaviour—that are commonly associated with a high risk of being rejected by peers (see Chapter 11). These attributes, too, are frequently associated with conduct disorder. These various difficulties do not spontaneously improve without intervention.

PROGNOSIS AND SCREENING

In contrast to normal children who generally outgrow their aggressive antisocial behaviour, children with severe conduct disorders are at great risk of exhibiting similar patterns of behaviour later in adolescence and adulthood (see Herbert, 1989, 1991 for recent reviews). In one of the earliest studies addressing this issue (Morris et al., 1956), a group of 66 children clinically referred for their aggressive behaviour was followed up until the age of 18 or over. It was found that only 14% of them were considered to be well adjusted. The others were described as suffering from several serious types of maladjustment, including seven who had committed criminal offences. The histories show that some young people follow an aggressive path, others a non-aggressive path, and yet others a substance abuse path. These paths are characterized by different types of antisocial behaviour, different ages of onset and different outcomes. For instance, individuals in the aggressive versatile path start early (sometimes in the pre-school period) and present a great variety of antisocial behaviour, particularly of the aggressive type. In contrast with this, what typifies individuals in the non-aggressive category is a relatively late onset (in adolescence or later childhood), absence of aggression and involvement in antisocial behaviours such as truancy, theft or lying.

Since several antisocial behaviours are included in the category of conduct disorder, it is worth investigating whether some specific forms of antisocial behaviour are better predictors of later maladjustment than others. Behaviours such as aggression are not only good predictors of different forms of social and psychological maladjustment later in adolescence and adulthood but they also show stability and continuity over the years. A good illustration of this is provided by Olweus (1979) in a review of 16 longitudinal studies on aggression published between 1935 and 1978, mainly in America and the UK. The studies were very heterogeneous regarding the number and age of subject, the method used to assess their aggressive behaviour, and the period between the first and the last measurement or observation. Recalculating and correcting their original stability coefficients, he found that on average the correlation of the aggression score at time 1 and time 2 was about 0.60. As the same author noted, this coefficient is very similar to the figures for the stability of IQ.

In a series of investigations Loeber and his collaborators (see Loeber and Dishion, 1983), analysed the data from previous follow-up and retrospective longitudinal studies and found that good predictors (inter alia) were lack of parental consistency in the management of children's early antisocial behaviour, a history of antisocial or delinquent behaviour in the family and poor educational achievement. Children with hyperactivity and con-

duct disorder show less improvement than children with conduct disorder only.

There are other stable individual characteristics which may play
a part in the intractability of aggressiveness. Patterson's (1982)
comments on the attributional characteristics that differentiate
aggressive from non-aggressive boys, i.e., the tendency to
attribute hostile intent to peers in ambiguous situations. If
aggressive, children are more likely to perceive ambiguous situations as hostile. Given that they have difficulty in attending to a
situation, or do not usually make careful discriminations, it is not
surprising that the complex interactional flow of the family or
the playground offers a rich field of possibilities for cue distortions or misattributions leading to conflict. Several studies (see
Patterson, 1982) have demonstrated the difficulties that aggressive children experience in decoding social messages given to
them by family and peers, and their tendency to minimize perceptions of their own aggressiveness, while maximizing that of
others (notably peers).

Family Correlates of Antisocial, Aggressive Problems

The impact of family variables on children's antisocial behaviours has been well documented in a number of cross-sectional
and longitudinal studies (see Sines, 1987, for a review). For
instance, researchers report a strong association between marital
disturbance in parents and antisocial behaviour in children.
Some of them have focused on the importance of individual
socio-demographic variables such as family size, number of siblings, socio-economic status, parental absence, parental criminality or other abnormal individual characteristics. Usually they
show significant correlations between these variables and antisocial behaviour, although the way they operate is not clear.

More interesting to the practitioner in search of a formulation
leading to an intervention, have been the studies on the interactional characteristics of these families carried out by Patterson
and his collaborators at the Oregon Social Learning Center
(Patterson, 1982). Observing in great detail the behaviour of
aggressive children at home, they found that the families studied

differed from the families of normal children in a number of ways. Among other things, the parents of aggressive children showed a lack of consistency in disciplining their children. Although they use punishment very often, this is inefficient either because it is not clearly associated with transgression or because, when the child counter-attacks, the parents finally give in to his or her demands (see Chapter 3 for more detail).

Another characteristic of such families is the lack of supervision or monitoring; aggressive children are more frequently left on their own. Furthermore, parents of aggressive children are described as lacking warmth, unable to involve themselves in pleasant shared activities. They tend not to clearly show the children what is right and what is wrong or what is expected of them in social situations.

Webster-Stratton (cited in Webster-Stratton and Herbert, 1994) found that mothers of aggressive children are likely to identify *themselves* as victims of their child's hostile aggression. It is reasonable to propose that if a child is subjected to frequent critical evaluations by family members it could lead to a poor self-image, resulting in a predisposition to act aggressively, particularly in threatening interpersonal situations. In this situation children are likely to use aggressive behaviour to terminate aversive interactions by their parents or other members of the family. In fact this process is neatly described by Patterson (1982) in terms of what he refers to as the 'coercive family process' (see Chapter 3). The theory postulates that aggressive, conduct-disordered children engage in excessive rates of behaviour which are aversive for parents who, in turn, retaliate with equally excessive rates of aversive actions which lead on to an upwardly escalating spiral of unremitting sound and fury. Such interactions are reinforcing both to the aggressive children and to the parents. Children are reinforced by their parents' eventual compliance. It is difficult in these circumstances to know what is cause and what is effect. In terms of the development of anti-social behaviour, these processes can be conceptualized as a series of positive feedback loops. Inept parenting fosters anti-social child behaviour and deficits in the child's skills; these are characteristics which, in turn, make child-rearing more difficult for the parents, and so on.

INTERVENTION

Approximately two-thirds of the children referred for psychological evaluation present aggressive conduct or oppositional defiant behaviour disorders (see Herbert, 1995). Olweus (1979) warns that there is little evidence that children outgrow these problems without intervention; they are likely to need extended therapeutic intervention or end up with potentially serious problems as adults.

Sadly, what evidence there is suggests that only 20–33% of British and American children and young adults with significant psychological problems receive the treatment they require; furthermore, children with less serious difficulties are more likely to receive the scarce resources of therapy than those with the more serious, long-term problems (see Herbert, 1995).

A preventive or remedial plan of work is likely to focus, of necessity, on the child's (or adolescent's) family. The methods include three levels at which interventions might be aimed: systemic, dyadic and individual (see Table 9.2).

Work at the systemic level, e.g. family therapy, has been described on page 151. Among the issues that are likely to be of importance, are those seeking:

- how to bring about more effective disciplinary (i.e. socialization) strategies, based on a foundation of knowledge of child development;
- how to identify variables in the family (including their own actions) which may contribute to the children's antisocial behaviour; and
- how to alter the pattern of coercive interactions frequently observed in the homes of aggressive children.

Developmental Counselling

Developmental counselling on disciplinary issues should—in the light of the literature reviewed in Chapter 7—have both a preventive *and* a therapeutic function. This may occur on an individual or (more economically) a group basis (see Webster-

Table 9.2   Preventive plan of work: potential intervention strategies

1. *Systemic level*
- Written contracts
- Negotiation training
- Settling differences
- Contingency contracting (exchange theory)
- Communication enhancement
- Clarification of roles and rules
- Improvement of physical environment resources (e.g. child-minding/day care)

2. *Dyadic level*
Interactions/relationship
- Enhancing positive interactions
- Operant programmes (increasing positive reinforcement—'catching the child out in good behaviour')
- Decreasing threats, criticism
- Playing with children
- Increasing consistency
- Negotiating fair/few/clear rules
- Marital work

3. *Individual level*
Parents
- Training in more effective child-rearing practices (e.g. use of effective sanctions)
- Developmental counselling to improve knowledge/decrease faulty expectation/attributions
- Cognitive restructuring
- Decreasing inappropriate anxiety/anger reactions:
  - Relaxation
  - Self-talk
  - Self-control training
- Improving skills

Child
- Play therapy
- Behaviour therapy
- Skills training

Stratton and Herbert, 1994). The 'Child-Wise Parenting Programme' (Herbert and Wookey, 1997) has found encouraging evidence of the ability of parents to help themselves and their 'problematic' children over a wide range of difficult problems with the help of developmental counselling and cognitive-behavioural programmes. Patterson and Fleischman (1979) have also shown this to be the case.

The discussion of disciplinary and other child management issues with parents in families or in groups seems to be of particular value in raising parents' confidence. Parents discuss video vignettes, do homework tasks and are given handouts. At the 'Child-Wise Parenting' Groups, various issues are raised for debate and clarification (Table 9.3). This programme is based on the child development and psychopathology literature, also in its practical content, on programmes and material designed by Webster-Stratton and Herbert (see Webster-Stratton, 1988; Webster-Stratton and Herbert, 1994; Herbert, 1987b, 1992). A collaborative model informs the therapeutic aspects of the programme (see page 167).

Table 9.3   Issues for debate and clarification

- The best time to start the disciplinary process is at the very beginning.
- Work out a general strategy on discipline.
- Have clear priorities.
- Work out the 'house rules'.
- Restrict requests and demands to those that are reasonable and fair; appropriate to the child's age and ability.
- Happiness and love (alone) are not enough; detailed training is essential.
- *Show* affection and foster the child's love and respect.
- Set limits for the child.
- Try to be around enough to encourage the child in his or her efforts to learn about and cope with life.
- Explain the reasons behind disciplinary actions.
- Listen carefully to what the child (or teenager) is saying.
- Prepare the child for life by encouraging personal habits and routines.
- Ask what the child is doing rather than why he or she is doing it.
- Make good behaviour worth-while—that is to say, accentuate the positive.
- Judge when to ignore the child's misbehaviour.
- Consequences (positive or negative) should follow *promptly* the behaviour they are designed to encourage or discourage.
- Try to nip misbehaviour in the bud.
- Be consistent.
- Make requests/demands in a clear, firm and confident manner.
- Tell children what they *should* do, as well as what they *should not* do.
- Give them the chance to be responsible by giving them responsibility.
- Include the older child in family discussions.
- Tell the older child how one feels.
- Refrain from sticking negative 'labels' to the young adult's (adolescent's) personality.
- Continue to make firm moral and social demands.
- Teach the young adult the art of compromise.
- Encourage (by example) the young adult to negotiate.
- Keep an eye on things: 'supervision' (if it isn't surveillance) is not a dirty word.

Behavioural Parent Training (BPT)

The generic term covers a variety of programmes made up of various methods designed to enhance parents' coping strategies, skills and self-perceived efficacy (confidence). Among the goals are the reduction of confrontations and antagonistic interactions between the family members, an increase in the effectiveness of positive interactions and a reduction in the violence (in cases where there is abuse) inflicted on one another.

Webster-Stratton and Herbert (1994) prefer the term *working with families* to 'parent training' because the latter seem to suggest a therapeutic model based on a one-way relationship between the therapist and the parent rather than a genuine collaborative partnership designed to develop strategies for coping with difficult family circumstances. Nevertheless, we need to look briefly at the Behavioural Parent Training (BPT) movement to understand its rationale and the validity of its claims.

During the 1960s theorists began to suggest that parents could be taught to use behavioural principles and techniques to manage their children's conduct problems and make good behaviour-deficits themselves. In a typical early individual training programme, Zeilberger, Sampen and Sloane (1968) examined the effectiveness of teaching parents to use outcome control methods such as time-out, extinction, and differential reinforcement in reducing a 4-year-old boy's aggressive behaviour and increasing his willingness to follow instructions. They successfully modified his severe screaming, fighting, negativism, teasing and dominating behaviour.

Treatment was conducted at home with the mother as therapist. The authors trained the parents in the home using daily one-hour sessions, showing them how to apply differential reinforcement. The procedures consisted of ignoring maladaptive behaviour, putting the boy in time-out and giving social rewards paired with food or special toys for compliant behaviour. The parents did not have responsibility for making observations and recording data. Observations were made and recorded by two observers in the home. The training was limited to specific techniques for dealing with the presenting problems rather than a broader framework of discussion, debate, role-play and teaching of life-skills (e.g. communication) and general principles which provide the curriculum for contemporary/family orientated behavioural programmes.

BPT has been used predominantly in the areas of severe conduct disorders in children, especially where there is a disturbed parent–child relationship. BPT utilizes the so-called *triadic model* of therapy in which the therapist mediates the therapy mainly through the caregivers of a referred child rather than (as in the case of the dyadic model) working primarily and directly with the child. In this model, changes in parental behaviour are identified as a prerequisite for changes in children's behaviour, hence the need to work directly with parents rather than with the nominated (i.e. referred) 'client'—the child or adolescent. A further rationale for the triadic model is that parents have a longer term and more intensive contact with their children than any psychologist or social worker could have. Given the crucial need for consistency over time in any behavioural approach, and for painstaking attention to detail in the early stages of a programme, the benefit of training parents to be their own therapists would seem self-evident. Of course, there are other caregivers who may be teachers or social service staff in residential homes, but most often they are the child's parents or substitute (e.g. foster) parents.

Social learning theorists argue that although children may be predisposed to respond to provocation with aggression, the nature, frequency and intensity of aggressive acts are determined through learning in a social context, either from direct experience or by observing other people. The maintenance of aggressive behaviour is seen to be largely dependent upon the consequences that flow from aggressive actions. Parents of aggressive children tend not to sanction aggressive acts; indeed, they tend to reward them.

BPT, on an individual or group basis, has proved a fruitful enterprise in dealing with aggressive and other antisocial actions. An early study by Patterson (cited in Patterson, 1982) evaluated the use of a behavioural parent training programmes at the Oregan Social Learning Center with the parents of 27 'socially-aggressive' boys. He reported that the BPT programme produced an average 60% reduction in deviant behaviours (Baseline v Post-Treatment) in 75% of the sample, and if training families in family management skills effectively produces a reduction in the *coercion levels* for these families, then one might expect the treatment effects to persist. Patterson and Fleischman (1979) have shown this to be the case (see Figure 9.2).

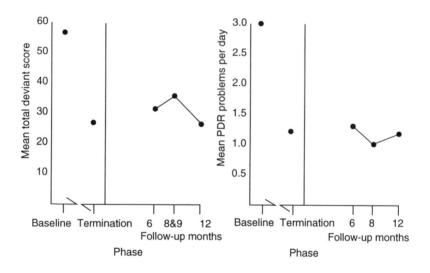

Figure 9.2   Follow-up data for treated children (from Patterson and Fleischman, 1979: 179)

Patterson (1982) states that crises re-emerge after treatment, and if the parents reinstate the family management procedures, they should 'work' for them again. In effect, each success is an example of negative reinforcement, increasing the likelihood that in the future parents will apply family management procedures. In a sense, the mechanism for persistence is 'built in'. Herbert (1987b) has suggested the use of booster sessions to consolidate and maintain improvement as there are other life variables that lead (as in dietary programmes) to a gradual 'slippage' in the rules and limits that have been set, followed by a loss of control.

Patterson (1982), on the basis of experience with over 200 families with extremely aggressive antisocial children, is now able to claim confidently that changing family management styles produces changes in antisocial behaviours. The focus in this treatment is the encouragement (and supervision) of effective family management skills. Such work is viewed as a *necessary* (but also not sufficient) component. There is a second component that has been shown to be necessary (but not sufficient): the therapist must be skilled in coping with the resistance to change that characterizes the majority of the families referred for treatment. Ordinarily, this level of clinical skill requires several years of supervised clinical experience (see Hollin, Wilkie and Herbert, 1986, on training in Applied Social Learning Theory).

Recent research on different clinical populations (see Callias, 1995) has focused upon five issues:

- The extent to which training generalizes.
- The role of cognitive/attitudinal/demographic factors in moderating the effectiveness of training.
- Theory versus technique-based programmes.
- Features of conduct-problem families that are predictive of training outcome.
- Treatment acceptability and consumer satisfaction.

An evaluative study (Scott and Stradling, 1987) examined the Scott programme which was developed for the typical social service clientele of single-parent, low-income or state-benefit families. The programme can be administered by social workers or assistants familiar with the programme manual. The programme consists of six 90-minute sessions run at weekly intervals during which a variety of behavioural techniques (e.g. planned ignoring, social reinforcement, time-out, response cost, teaching new skills) are taught, largely through role-play, with a follow-up session a month later. The groups are made up of five to eight mothers.

A total of 77 mothers were trained to manage the behaviour problems of their children (age range 2–4, mean 3.14 years). Their progress was evaluated by a range of before and after measures on both a treatment group and a waiting list control group.

Maintenance of treatment gains was tested after three months and, for some measures, after a six-month interval. The programme significantly reduced the perceived number and intensity of child behaviour problems; parental depression, inward and outward irritability; and the level of perceived child conduct problems, impulsivity and anxiety. It also significantly improved parents' child management skills. These improvements were maintained over a six-month period.

As with all new therapeutic approaches subjected to rigorous evaluation (and sadly many are not validated), there is certainly no evidence that BPT is a panacea. Studies cast doubt on whether all families with child conduct problems are equally able to benefit from purely behavioural BPT packages. Nevertheless, as a reaction, in part, to the large numbers of aggressive conduct disordered children and the shortfall of professional personnel, agencies look increasingly to *enhanced* parent training for help. The results of the use of more broadly conceived models of collaboration plus effective aids to learning (e.g. the Parents and Children Videotape Series) are sufficiently encouraging to make them a cost-effective investment (Webster-Stratton and Herbert, 1994).

Programme Content

One of the main difficulties in evaluating the large number of studies on BPT is that the term has been used to describe a confusing variety of different treatment *packages*. While these are all based upon the teaching of principles of learning, development and behaviour to parents, the common denominator ends there. Some studies have the psychologist or social worker working individually with a single set of parents, while others use a group format in which two persons work with a group of up to 10 parents. As we saw on page 212, BPT packages make use of a variety of methods which have been used, either individually or in combination, to teach parents (inter alia) contingency management and contracting, conflict resolution skills, parent–child interaction, and household organization.

Some or all of the training might take place at the clinic, in the parent's home or at a family centre. Today there is less emphasis on the contingency management of specific target behaviours, and more on broad principles of child management, the interpersonal interactions of members of the family, the marital relationships (which are often poor in the parents of problematic children), and other relationship and skill-related matters. Variations in the complexity of problems, the family values and attitudes and individual differences in the temperament of the children concerned, require flexibility in the design of individual programmes.

A particularly good example of a comprehensive and carefully evaluated parent training programme for young conduct disordered children is that of Webster-Stratton (1988). The content, which was designed for parents with children ages 3 to 8 years. What is of particular interest about this research is its concern with developing the most effective *methods* of training parents—that is, methods that are cost-effective, widely applicable and sustaining. The programme utilizes videotape-modelling methods. While the examples of parent–child interactions modelled are more positive than negative, the intent in showing negative or ambivalent examples is to demystify the notion that there is such a thing as 'perfect parenting' and to illustrate how one can learn from one's mistakes. There is also an attempt to promote the modelling effects for parents by creating positive feelings about the models shown on the videotapes. The videotapes show models of differing sexes, ages, cultures, socio-economic backgrounds and temperaments, so that parents will perceive the models as similar to themselves and their children.

The basic parent training programme includes a series of 10 videotape programmes of modelled parenting skills (250 vignettes, each of which lasts approximately 1–2 minutes) which are shown by a therapist to groups of parents (8–12 parents per group). After each vignette, the therapist leads a group discussion of the relevant interactions and encourages parents' ideas and problem-solving as well as role-playing and rehearsal. The programme has also been given to over 80 parents of conduct-disordered children as a completely self-administered intervention. (The parents complete the videotape programmes and homework assignments without therapist feedback or group support.) An advance programme (ENHANCE) based on six videotape programmes has been developed to focus on family issues other than parent skills, such as anger management, coping with depression, marital communication skills, problem-solving strategies, and how to teach children to solve problems and manage their anger more effectively. In both these programmes, the children do not attend the therapy sessions, although parents are given homework exercises to practise various skills with their children at home.

Training Formats

Efforts have been made to 'tease out' the specific components which contribute to a successful outcome, and an important issue is how best to train parents. There are three broad approaches to parent training:

1. In the *individual* consultation approach, the parent complaining of specific problems is instructed in how to behave towards the child under various contingencies. Individual instructions can range from enabling parents to carry out simple instructions in contingency management to a full involvement as co-therapists in all aspects of observation, recording, programme planning and implementation.
2. The controlled learning environment, another variant of parent training, involves highly structured individual instruction, with the consultant directly shaping or modelling parent–child interactions. Sophisticated signalling and feedback devices are used while the parent interacts with the child.
3. Another means of training parents is within *educational groups*. Courses vary in duration, intensity and structure. Various aids to learning such as lectures, guides, manuals, role-playing, videotape feedback, modelling, discussion and home exercises have been used.

The consultation format, in which parents receive advice and reading material, has had its successes as has the individual, training approach (see Herbert, 1987b). Parents have also been successfully trained in groups (see Webster-Stratton and Herbert, 1993). Not unnaturally, this approach has been compared for its cost-effectiveness with the other models of training. Christensen et al. (1980) directly compared these three formats. Although parents in all three approaches perceived their children as significantly improved at the end of treatment, behaviour observations recorded by parents demonstrated that the individual and group formats were superior to the 'consultation only' approach. Parents found the individual treatment format most satisfying, however, this format was most costly in comparison studies which have examined the *content* of parent training programmes. Therapists make a distinction between *broad-focus training* which is concerned with teaching general behavioural principles as well as skills for changing the child's particular behavioural problems, and *specific-focus training* which includes only skills training for the problem in question.

Evaluation

Studies of broad-focus content (e.g. Christensen et al., 1980) indicate that parents can learn general principles of behaviour change simply from reading a manual, although individual and group training appear to facilitate actual implementation of skills. Ollendick and Cerny (1981) conclude a review of the evidence on content and formal aspects of parent training by concluding that although training in behavioural principles may not significantly increase parents' intellectual comprehension of child management techniques in the behavioural modality, or their attitudes towards parent training, a grounding in these basic principles does seem to facilitate the implementation and generalization of the newly acquired skills in a non-training situation.

It is important that BPT does not suffer the fate of Social Skills Training and come to be thought of as a panacea. Not all clients benefit from this approach. Of course, negative findings may reflect an erroneous clinical formulation, or perhaps a lack of *ability* on the part of the therapist, or an inability of the parents to conceptualize learning principles or a resistance to perceiving improvement in their children's behaviour. Some practitioners suggest that failure is sometimes a reflection of great stress (social and economic, marital and personal) undermining parents with exhaustion and despair (see Webster-Stratton and Herbert, 1994). The disappointing results may relate to the parents' own previous experiences of parenting and to ideologies of child-care and discipline (in particular punishment) that are at odds with the assumptions of parent 'trainers'. The somewhat poor outcome reported for parents of lower socio-economic status, for parents with strong ideologies or single parents could be due to a lack of perceived relevance, an absence of face validity, in the applied social learning approach. Perhaps such parents, who have tried for many years to manage an intractable child, are looking for 'better' (i.e. more effective) ways to punish their child rather than a 'long' drawn-out programme that emphasizes rewards and the positive side of their offspring—a feature of many programmes. In other words, there is an ideological mismatch; they are sometimes looking for more immediate (and punishment-led) results.

CONCLUSION

For all these cautionary comments, it has to be said that the parent training programmes are our main hope in work with families with highly aggressive children and poor disciplinary practices. A critical review by Webster-Stratton and Herbert (1993) of this area of work concludes that the success of short-term treatment is verified by significant changes in parents' and children's behaviour and in parental perceptions of child adjustment. Also, home observations indicated that parents were successful in reducing children's levels of aggression by 20–60% over reasonable follow-up periods (1 to 4 years). However, the results of studies which assessed generalization of child behaviours from the clinic to the school are less consistent.

With regard to comparison studies, programmes based on changes from Patterson's parent training approach have been shown to be superior to family-based psychotherapy, attention-placebo (discussion) and no-treatment conditions (Patterson, Chamberlain and Reid, 1982). Those from Forehand and McMahon's (1981) programme have been shown to be more effective than a family systems therapy, and a group version of the programme was more effective than a parent discussion group based on the Systematic Training for Effective Parenting (STEP) programme (see Webster-Stratton and Herbert, 1994, for a review of the evidence).

The need for early intervention with adolescents who abuse their parents should not be underestimated. Beyond the teenage years the coercive relationship pattern between parent and child may continue and possibly worsen. This could result in elder maltreatment where the parent, growing increasingly older and dependent, is abused and/or neglected by the child, now adult and 'in power'. Thus, the concept of elder maltreatment, its prediction and prevention, will be the topic of the next chapter.

CHAPTER 10   Predicting and preventing elder maltreatment

Only recently has the concept of elder abuse and neglect become recognized as a widespread problem, even though 'Granny Battering' had been first referred to in 1975 (Baker, 1975; Burston, 1975, 1977). The problem still remains one of the least-researched areas of family violence and this is reflected in the amount of literature that is available on the subject. Nevertheless, a number of review publications have emerged that summarize the current understanding of the problem (e.g. Pillemer and Wolf, 1986; Quinn and Tomita, 1986; Steinmetz, 1988; Breckman and Adelman, 1988; Bennett and Kingston, 1993; Decalmer and Glendenning, 1993; Eastman, 1994; Biggs, Phillipson and Kingston, 1995; Pritchard, 1995).

As with other types of intrafamilial maltreatment, the maltreatment of elderly people incorporates a wide range of phenomena, which include physical injury and pain, mental trauma and anguish, isolation, withholding of basic necessities of life; food, shelter, medicine and personal care, and financial exploitation (see Chapter 1, Table 1.2).

AGEING AND SOCIETY

Major demographic changes in Western societies have been an influencing factor for the increased awareness of elderly maltreatment. Firstly, the life expectancy of the average person has increased by half during this century. Secondly, the number of people aged 65 years and over, which represented 15.6% (8.9 million) of the total UK population in 1989, is expected to increase to 16% (9.2 million) in 2001 and 19% by the year 2030 (Field, 1992). In particular, the population aged over 80 is projected to increase most rapidly from 2 million in 1989 to over 2½ million by 2001, representing 4% of the UK population (op. cit.).

The number of elderly people requiring assistance will also increase due to the positive association between ageing and mental and physical disability. The rate of disability among elderly people aged 75 and over is 63% for women and 53% for men, with approximately 70% of all disabled adults being aged 60 or over (Central Statistical Office, 1989). The majority of help is supplied by members of the elderly person's family, usually a spouse or an adult offspring (Henwood and Wicks, 1984). According to the 1986 General Household Survey, only a very small minority of people over 65 (approximately 5%) permanently live in residential institutions (Field, 1992). The majority of the elderly people (79%) live in the community either alone (34%) or with a spouse (43%), approximately 19% of elderly people share a household with adult offspring. However, only 5% actually leave their own household to move in with their adult offspring (Dale, Evandrou and Arber, 1987), so most elderly people in these circumstances share their own home with their adult children.

The combined effect of demographic changes and present commitments to 'Care in the Community' (DHSS, 1981; Griffiths, 1988) may mean increasing numbers of elderly people could become at risk of intrafamilial elder abuse and neglect, especially when services to support 'informal carers' are limited (Armstrong-Esther, Browne and Esther, 1997).

It is not surprising, therefore, to find that the literature on elder maltreatment suggests that those most at risk are 'frail' elderly people who are usually over 75 or who have physical and/or mental impairments. Hence, the majority of domestic perpetrators of elder abuse and neglect are relatives engaged in a stressful caregiving capacity in their middle age (Kosberg, 1988). Pierce and Trotta (1986) report that it is the stress associated with caring for the elderly relative, which is the precipitating factor for violence in the majority of cases (63%).

FORMS OF ELDER MALTREATMENT

The US Congress Select Committee on Aging (1981) gave a definition as 'The wilful infliction of physical pain, injury or debilitating mental anguish, unreasonable confinement, or wilful deprivation by a caretaker of services which are necessary to maintain mental and physical health'. Of course, this broad description is not confined to domestic settings, and might include actions that may be a direct or indirect result of policies promoted by the government itself.

With respect to elder abuse in the home environment, Eastman (1989, 1994) has identified and provided examples for the following types of maltreatment: physical violence, including threats of physical violence; sexual abuse, including rape and pornography; neglect, such as locking an elderly relative in a room, refusing to provide meals and refusing material or emotional support; abandonment—either to hospital, residential care or the street; psychological abuse, including intimidation, humiliation and the threat of abandonment; exploitation, such as financial abuse of the elderly person's resources for the personal gain of the caregiver.

Some researchers have argued that psychological abuse and neglect should *not* be included in a definition of maltreatment, instead maltreatment should concentrate on physical violence that results in injury, or is intended to do so (Crystal, 1986; Johnson, 1986; Pillemer and Suitor, 1988). However, this ignores the fact that neglect can be also life threatening to a frail and dependent elderly person (Douglas, 1983). It has also been stated that psychological abuse such as the fear of being beaten or punished can cause as much harm to the victim's functioning as the actual physical act (Pedrick-Cornell and Gelles, 1982; Giordano and Giordano, 1984). Abuse and neglect may be aetiologically and conceptually distinct, but any definition of elder maltreatment needs to consider both forms. Valentine and Cash (1986: 22) have attempted to combine the two in a workable definition similar to that given in Chapter 1 for family violence in general.

> Elder maltreatment as a generic term refers to the non-accidental situation in which the elder suffers physical trauma, deprivation of physical needs or mental injury as a result of an act of commission (abuse) or omission (neglect) by a caretaker, guardian or relative.

In the past, the definition of elder maltreatment has often been inconsistent. However, there is now a general consensus about what constitutes elder abuse and neglect. The forms of elder mal-treatment described by Douglas (1983) and Eastman (1989) have gradually gained acceptance among other researchers (e.g. Hudson and Johnson, 1986; McCredie, 1994; Pritchard, 1995), and reflect those outlined in Chapter 1 (Table 1.2) for family vio-lence in general, that is; physical, sexual, psychological and emo-tional abuse, witting and unwitting neglect. One particular cate-gory of elder abuse has been specially emphasised by several authors (e.g. Wolf, 1986), that of material/financial abuse which involves the illegal or improper exploitation and/or use of funds or other material resources. Furthermore, 'Munchausen Syndrome by Proxy' has been described as a form of elder mal-treatment (Smith and Ardern, 1989) in a similar way to that described for young children whose carers consistently give fraudulent clinical histories and fabricated signs (e.g. Meadow, 1982). This results in the dependant undergoing potentially harmful medical investigations and treatment. Nevertheless, physical abuse is believed to be the most common form of abuse (Haviland and O'Brien, 1989).

In a survey conducted by Pillemer and Finkelhor (1988) most of the elders who had been maltreated reported they had experi-enced physical abuse: 45% reported having something thrown at them, 63% had been pushed, grabbed or shoved, 42% had been slapped and 10% had been hit with a fist, bitten or kicked. Earlier research conducted by Lau and Kosberg (1979) reached similar conclusions. However, some studies (Steinmetz, 1978; Douglas, 1983; Hudson, 1986) have found that neglect was the most com-mon form of maltreatment and physical abuse was less common. For example, tying an elderly person who needs constant watch-ing onto a bed or chair in order to complete the housework or shopping, or the excessive use of sleeping medication and alco-hol in order to make the person more manageable. It is important to recognize that this type of neglect may not be intended neces-sarily to harm the elderly person. There is a lack of knowledge about how to care for an elderly dependant, and in some cases abuse is not intentional.

In the United States, Block (1983) showed that the caregivers used a wide range of means to control their elderly relatives; 40% screamed or yelled, 6% used physical restraint, 6% force-fed or used medication, 6% threatened to send them to a nursing home, 4% threatened physical force and 3% used physical force. US police reports have found that 62.7% of all assaults against elderly people are committed by the caregiving relative other than the spouse (Baltimore Police Department, 1978).

Other researchers have concluded that psychological abuse is the most prevalent form of elder maltreatment (e.g. Pratt, Koval and Lloyd, 1983; Wolf, 1986; Eastman, 1994). As indicated in earlier chapters of this book, different forms of maltreatment coexist and such relative comparisons may reflect differences in the line of enquiry of each study. Therefore, the validity of comparisons is questionable. For example, an interview study of health professionals found that most maltreatment cases were physical in nature (Lau and Kosberg, 1979); whereas a study of cases known to social service providers found that most victims were psychologically abused (Block and Sinnott, 1979); and a study focused on legal agencies found that the most commonly reported type of abuse was financial abuse (Sengstock and Barrett, 1986).

Nevertheless, reviewers of the empirical literature (e.g. Rathbone-McCuan, 1980; Taler and Ansello, 1985; Zdorkowski and Galbraith, 1985) have noted two consistent findings: maltreatment of the elderly is rarely limited to a single episode or to a single category of abuse or neglect. The research evidence suggests that many abusive relationships involving elderly people have been ongoing for many years (O'Malley et al. 1984) and that the occurrence of one form of abuse appears to precipitate others (Sengstock and Barrett, 1986).

THE EXTENT OF ELDER MALTREATMENT

Estimates of the number of elderly people who are abused and neglected by family members range from 4 to 10% of all those over 65 years (Pierce and Trotta, 1986; Hudson and Johnson, 1986; Pillemer and Suitor, 1988; Ballantyne, 1989; Ogg and Bennett, 1992). However, there are no accurate statistics to document the scope of elder maltreatment because of a lack of uniformity in reporting, record keeping and empirical research (Salend et al., 1984; Crystal, 1987).

An early attempt to estimate the incidence rate of elder abuse and neglect was made by Lau and Kosberg (1979) and Block and Sinnott (1979). They reported incidence rates of 9.6% and 4% respectively. These figures have been subsequently widely cited by researchers and policy makers alike, both in the USA and the UK (Pillemer and Finkelhor, 1988). Unfortunately, both surveys had low response rates, small sample sizes and limited to parts of the USA.

A more comprehensive investigation of elder maltreatment in 50 states was carried out by Pepper and Oaker (1981) who attempted to extrapolate a national incidence rate. They reported 28 869 cases of elder abuse and neglect and an incidence rate of 4%, confirming Block and Sinnott's estimate (1979).

In 1988, Pillemer and Finkelhor surveyed a large-scale random sample of elderly persons ($N=2020$) regarding their experience of physical violence, verbal aggression and neglect. They reported a prevalence rate for maltreatment of 32 elderly persons per 1000, with an incidence rate of 26 elderly persons per 1000. However, it has been suggested that the estimates quoted are probably conservative and that the true extent of elder abuse and neglect remains hidden (Quinn and Tomita, 1986; Kosberg, 1988). It has been claimed that only 1 in 6 cases of elder maltreatment are ever reported to the authorities (Pepper and Oaker, 1981). Several explanations for the invisibility of elder maltreatment have been suggested. Firstly, family members, including the abuser and the abused, may engage in a conspiracy of silence (Council on Scientific Affairs, 1987). Lau and Kosberg (1979) found that one-third of the elderly who were judged to have been abused denied any problem; a similar finding was reported by Chen et al. (1981). Elderly victims may deny abuse because they fear reprisals from the abuser (Kosberg, 1988); or they may feel too ashamed and embarrassed to admit they are being abused by their own relatives (Quinn and Tomita, 1986); the elderly person may be reluctant to initiate legal or criminal action against a relative for fear the solution will be worse than the problem itself, for example, institutionalization (Fulmer and Cahill, 1984). They may also assume the blame for the abuser's behaviour, a trait that is also common in wife and child abuse victims. Often the love for the abuser is stronger than the desire to leave (Gelles and Cornell, 1990).

Abusive relatives are also likely to deny their abusive behaviour as they may fear informal sanctions from friends, kin and neighbours, and formal sanctions from the police and the courts (Kosberg, 1988). They may feel too ashamed and guilt ridden to admit they lost control and resorted to abusive action (Chen et al., 1981).

Secondly, elder abuse goes undetected because of the failure of professionals to detect the problem or to be aware that elder abuse may have occurred (British Geriatrics Society, 1988; Powills, 1988, Rathbone-McCuan, 1980). Abuse most often occurs within the confines of a private dwelling, hidden from outside scrutiny. Elderly people are not involved in social networks such as schooling or employment. They are, on average, even more isolated from the mainstream of society than younger adults. There is no requirement that necessitates an elderly person leaving their dwelling and being seen by non-family members and professionals (Browne, 1989c). Indeed, case-control studies by Phillips (1983) and Pillemer (1986) have found that abused elderly persons had less social contact than their non-abused controls.

CHARACTERISTICS OF THE VICTIM

The majority (70–80%) of cases concern a female elderly victim aged 70 years or over who shares a household with the abuser (Hocking, 1982; Johnson, 1986; Eastman, 1994). It has been claimed that the risk of maltreatment increases with age (Fulmer and Cahill, 1984). However, Pillemer and Finkelhor (1988) reported that the 'young-elderly' (65–74 years) were equally at risk, and that men in this age group were at more risk than women.

In addition, elderly people with physical or mental impairments run a greater risk of being abused or neglected (Pillemer and Finkelhor, 1988; Eastman, 1994). It has been hypothesized that this is a result of greater dependency of the elderly person on the caregiver (Steinmetz, 1988). Those elders that were dependent were more likely to be victims of neglect, while elders who were considered to be independent tended to be physically abused (O'Malley et al., 1984; Wolf, 1986).

It has been suggested that in some families the elderly dependant becomes the scapegoat for the release of tension, anger,
frustration and resentment within the home setting (Chen et
al., 1981). The vulnerability of the elderly victim is aggravated
by their dependency, isolation, powerlessness and being in
poor physical or mental health (Chen et al., 1981; Anetzberger,
1987), which increases as a consequence of the violence, making the elderly victim more vulnerable to further abuse
(Mindel and Wright, 1982). Thus, a vicious cycle is set up (see
Chapter 2).

CHARACTERISTICS OF THE ABUSER

The most commonly reported abusers of elderly people are relatives of the victims that share the same accommodation
(Hudson, 1986). These abusers are either aged spouses (Pillemer
and Finkelhor, 1988) or middle-aged offspring (Taler and
Ansello, 1985). Other abusive relatives are said to include elderly siblings, children-in-law, grandchildren, nieces and nephews
(Eastman, 1994).

Several studies have reported that a female relative is more
likely to be the abuser (Phillips, 1983; Eastman, 1994); others
have concluded a higher proportion of male relatives are mal-
treaters of their elderly dependants (Chen et al., 1981; Giordano
and Giordano, 1984). By contrast others have found male and
female adults equally likely to abuse an elderly relative
(O'Malley et al., 1984).

A common assumption is that the abusing relatives are usually
involved in a caring capacity and are under a lot of stress looking
after their dependent elders (Steinmetz, 1983; Eastman, 1994).
But this characteristic has not received unanimous support, Wolf
(1986) and Pillemer (1986) have reported that the abusers were
more likely to be dependent on their elderly relative for finances
and accommodation.

Grafstrom, Nordberg and Wimblad (1992) claim that elder maltreatment occurs because the primary carer is suffering from
high levels of stress, either external or internal to the caring
relationship. When it is internal, it relates to the strain or the

burden of caring for a dependent elderly family member. When the source of stress is external to the caring relationship it relates to environmental circumstances of family life crisis (Phillips, 1986). In either case, stress overload occurs when an individual's skills or resources cannot cope with perceived or actual demands.

Burston (1977) suggests that stress may have an accumulative effect over time and a distinction can be made between 'acute stress' and 'chronic stress'. Chronic stress results in various problems over a long period, for example, physical and mental illness, deterioration in carer–elder relations (Anetzberger, 1987). There is considerable agreement that the role of carer to an impaired, dependent elder can be stressful or burdensome (Zarit, Rever and Bach-Peterson, 1980; Steinmetz, 1988; Cicirelli, 1986) and that the nature and frequency of the caregiving tasks can cause both acute and chronic stress for carers (Anetzberger, 1987). Although caring can be a stressful experience only a minority of carers are often severely stressed (Cicirelli, 1983, 1986).

It is suggested that carers who lack social support or who are socially isolated suffer most (Anetzberger, 1987). Isolation forces carers to cope with the burden of caring alone with no support or respite. Their ability to obtain assistance is also severely restricted (Burston, 1977; Kosberg, 1988).

There has been considerable support for an association between intra-individual pathology of the abuser and maltreatment of the elderly victim (Lau and Kosberg, 1979; Taler and Ansello, 1985; Wolf, 1986; Kosberg, 1988). Pillemer (1986) reported that 79% of the victims indicated that the relatives had mental or emotional problems to some degree, compared with only 24% of the controls. The relatives of the abused elderly were also more likely to have been resident in psychiatric hospitals at some point, in comparison to the controls (op. cit.).

Alcohol and/or drug abuse is another characteristic that has gained acceptance as a partial explanation of why elder abuse occurs (Chen et al., 1981; O'Malley et al., 1984; Pillemer, 1986; Wolf, 1986, 1988; Anetzberger, Korbin and Austin, 1994).

INTERGENERATIONAL TRANSMISSION OF VIOLENCE OR CARING

Anetzberger (1987) suggests that some individuals have been socialized to abuse elders (and others) through witnessing and learning to use violence during childhood. This explanation is based on social learning theory, in that a child learns to be violent in the family setting in which a violent parent has been taken as a role model. When frustrated or angry as an adult, the individual relies on this learned behaviour and resorts to abusive action. This theory has led to the concept of a 'cycle of violence' (see Chapter 11) which suggests that abused children grow up to become abusers of their own children, their spouses and possibly their elderly relatives (Renvoize, 1978; Kosberg, 1988; Browne, 1993). Some support for the notion of intergenerational transmission of violence has been supplied by Lau and Kosberg (1979) and Chen et al. (1981), but other studies have found a limited association (Pillemer, 1986; Wolf, 1986; Anetzberger, 1987; Pillemer and Suitor, 1988). Others suggest that a long standing abusive relationship has continued into later life (Homer and Gilleard, 1990; Grafstrom, Nordberg and Wimblad, 1992).

Indeed, violent and disruptive behaviour by the elderly relative, now or in the past, can increase the chances of the carer being violent in return (Pillemer and Suitor, 1992). Suzanne Steinmetz (1988) found in her research that much of the violence was reciprocal with 18% of elderly dependants resorting to physical attacks on their carers, 1 in 10 of whom had been violent to the elderly person.

The extension of attachment theory over the life span has provided a conceptual framework that helps to explain the persistence of abusive parent–child relationships into old age. Attachment refers to an emotional or affectional bond between two people, and constitutes being identified with, in love with, and having a desire to remain in contact with, another person (Cicirelli, 1986). Although usually associated with infant to mother relationships, attachment does not end in childhood but continues throughout the entire life span, along with its proximity seeking and protective behavioural systems (Holmes, 1993). Attachment behaviours in adulthood are utilized to maintain psychological and physical closeness and contact, for example, visiting and telephoning (Cicirelli, 1983), and the attachment behaviours of adult offspring towards an aged parent are manifested by the child's helping and caregiving behaviours to the elderly parent.

A causal path model of adult children's helping behaviour has been developed by Cicirelli (1983, 1986) and consists of a network of variables that predict adult children's helping behaviours to their elderly parents and their commitment to provide further help in the future (see Figure 10.1).

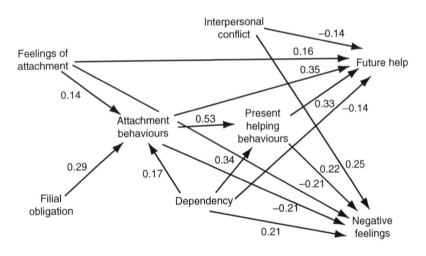

Figure 10.1   The helping relationship and family neglect in later life. Path diagram of adult children's present helping behaviours and future help to elderly mothers. (Path coefficients are standardized partial regression coefficients.) (From Cicirelli, 1983, p. 821; reproduced with permission)

Cicirelli claims that the adult offspring's helping behaviour is a function of attachment towards the elderly parent. Thus, an adult offspring's commitment to help an elderly parent in the future is mainly a function of attachment in the present.

Attachment is also seen as a protective factor against negative feelings (e.g. frustration, bitterness, resentment and anger) as helping behaviours and dependency increases resulting in conflict between elderly parent and adult child. Negative feelings are lessened when the adult child's feelings of attachment are strong and as attachment behaviours increase.

It has been suggested that an adult child who is engaged in conflict with an elderly parent or one who is experiencing intense negative feelings, can engage in one of four possible responses (Cicirelli, 1986):

1. To continue caregiving and endure a great deal of stress and negative feelings until overload occurs resulting in abusive action or eventual avoidance.
2. To avoid the situation completely, which results in physical and emotional neglect.
3. To provide care for a while and when conflict or negative feelings arise withdrawing from the situation. Here there is a possibility of episodic maltreatment.
4. To recognize that there is a problem and takes active steps to resolve the conflict and continue with the caregiving process due to the strong bond of attachment to the parent.

Although attachment theory is a relatively new concept in the field of elder abuse and neglect, indirect empirical support has been provided from studies researching the nature of the caregiving relationship and stress, where it has been suggested that the majority of carers continue caring in the face of adversity due to strong emotional bonds (Horowitz and Shindelman, 1983; Lewis and Meredith, 1988).

As outlined in Chapter 2, the multifactor model of family violence suggests that the effects of situational stress are mediated through the interactive relationships between elderly dependant and the relative. A 'secure/good' relationship between elder and relative will 'buffer' effects of stress and facilitate coping strategies on behalf of the relative (Browne, 1989c). In contrast, an 'insecure/poor' relationship will not buffer the relative under stress and a 'trigger' situation, for example an argument with the elder, may result in 'episodic overload' and an abusive response. This will have a negative effect on the existing interpersonal relationship and reduce any 'buffering' effects still further, making it easier for stresses to overload the system once again. Hence a (positive feedback) vicious cycle, is set up which can lead to 'systematic overload', where constant stress results in repeated mal-

This situation gets progressively worse without ι and has been termed the 'spiral of violence' (see

PREVENTION AND TREATMENT

Primary Prevention of Fundamental Change

Intrafamilial elder abuse and neglect is largely a hidden problem, and in order to help prevent it at a primary level the public and professionals must be made aware that it exists (Rathbone-McCuan, 1980; Kosberg, 1983; Homer and Gilleard, 1990).

The general public and professionals need to be made aware that elder maltreatment can and does happen, they need to be educated about the normal ageing process and resources available to help those elderly people in need (Pierce and Trotta, 1986). It has been suggested that many misconceptions arise from a misunderstanding of the ageing process, for example, 'all old people go senile', and over-reliance on popular stereotypes, which are usually negative (Gray and Wilcock, 1981; Eastman, 1994). These misconceptions and stereotypes may be contributory factors in the maltreatment of elderly people; as they serve to dehumanize and devalue the elderly person in our society. Therefore, for prevention to be effective at this level, community education should be facilitated and conducted by health and social service personnel. Such education should be aimed at all families and also individuals working in the caring professions.

Overviews of the causes and consequences of elder abuse (e.g. Zdorkowski and Galbraith, 1985) suggest that primary interventions should be concerned with the maintenance of rights, safety and health of elderly individuals and the reformulation of 'ageist' attitudes in our society. Furthermore, Giordano and Giordano (1984) assert that changes in health and social policy could reduce elder abuse.

At present, services to the elderly focus on those who live alone without family support and those in institutions. It is also necessary to acknowledge the family's contribution to care of the elderly and to provide services that support and enhance their role. Such services include home nursing, day care and residential care which temporarily may give some relief to the caregivers. The provision of these services are increasingly important with the demographic changes in population. The dependent status of an elderly relative in the family has led to elder abuse being compared with child abuse (Bolton and Bolton, 1987). However, there are some distinct differences.

The knowledge that children gradually become increasingly less dependent as they grow older can be a source of relief to their parents. The care of the elderly contrasts sharply with this: as they grow older they are likely to become more demanding and more dependent (Galbraith and Davison, 1985). The elderly person may be extremely difficult to handle, but more often the stress and frustration is related to the caregivers' unwillingness to devote themselves entirely to that person. This happens frequently where a daughter feels acute distress at having to look after an aged parent, when perhaps for the first time since her own children have grown up, she is seeking self-fulfilment as a woman beyond the family boundaries.

The family needs external resources such as 'day centres' and 'home-helps' to alleviate the intense care of an elderly relative for a number of hours each day. Together with a secure and supportive spouse relationship (itself a buffer to stress, see Chapter 4), the possibility of elder abuse will be considerably reduced.

Secondary Prevention of Prediction and Identification

Elderly people who have undergone abuse are often admitted to hospital with physical injuries which are attributed to falls. Such injuries are treated without suspicion. Thus there is a real need for screening to identify elderly people that are potentially or actually victims of abuse (Rathbone-McCuan and Voyles, 1982). This could be done by Primary Health Care Teams (Bennett and Kingston, 1993).

Case histories which describe elderly abuse appear to associate risk factors with the problem of elder abuse and neglect. These high risk factors are listed in *Table 10.1*. It has been stated that the more risk factors present in a family environment the greater the

Table 10.1 Factors associated with elder abuse

High-risk elderly person
- Physical and/or mental dependency on a 'key member of the family'—the caregiver.
- Poor or negative communication between the elderly dependant and caregiver.
- Demanding and/or aggressive behaviour.
- Past maltreatment of the caregiver by the elderly dependant (role reversal).
- The presence of a triggering behaviour or condition of the elderly dependant (e.g. incontinence, spitting). The 'trigger' can be almost anything that produces a sense of anger or rage in the caregiver.
- The elderly dependant lives constantly with the caregiver(s).
- Frequent periods of hospitalization of the elderly dependant, history of falls, facial bruising.
- Vague explanations given by elderly dependant about their injury.

High-risk relative/carer
- Poor physical health of caregiver.
- Caregiver is inexperienced.
- Unrealistic expectations of elderly dependant.
- Negative feelings and attribution toward the elderly dependant.
- The caregiver is responsible for the support of 'another' member of the family (e.g. husband, dependant, child, etc.).
- The caregiver makes repeated visits to the general practitioner.
- Vague explanations given by the carer about injuries to their elderly dependant.
- Low self-esteem of the caregiver.
- The dependency of the elderly person is perceived by the caregiver as 'childlike' and demanding.
- The caregiver is experiencing multiple stress (e.g. marital conflict, financial problems, etc.).
- The caregiver has a history of mental ill health or impairment.
- Unemployment of either caregiver or significant other in the family.
- Drinking or drug problems of either caregiver or significant other in the family.
- Unwilling carer, economically dependent on elder relative.
- Carer abused or neglected as a child.

High-risk family
- Poor or inadequate health provision in family.
- Lack of support from community and social services.
- Overcrowding and cramped living conditions.
- Socially isolated family.
- Conflict between family members.
- Desire for institutionalization.

likelihood of maltreatment (Pillemer and Finkelhor, 1988; Browne, 1989c). Assessment and recognition of these predisposing conditions may assist the helping professionals in identifying potential abusive situations. Once recognized, help can be targeted at those most in need (British Geriatrics Society, 1988), possibly before serious maltreatment has occurred (Kosberg, 1988). As it is not yet possible to specifically identify conditions that led to maltreatment, it should be remembered that abuse and neglect will not always occur in the presence of a single or some combinations of risk factors (Pillemer and Suitor, 1988).

In response to the need for general guidelines several screening instruments have been devised to help professionals recognize and identify risk factors (Ferguson and Beck, 1983; Kosberg, 1988; Eastman, 1989). In addition, an assessment of the elderly person's relationship with the caregiver would be useful. However, it is most important to assess the mental ability of the elderly relative (Bolton and Bolton, 1987), as impairment severely affects the quality and quantity of social interaction to and from caregivers (Armstrong-Esther and Browne, 1986).

Although many risk factors have been identified, their relative predictive power has not been systematically researched or evaluated. Therefore, there is an urgent need for further research in this area similar to that described for child abuse in Chapter 6.

Tertiary Prevention of Treatment and Control

Diagnosis and assessment

The first step in treating or ameliorating the effects of maltreatment involves learning to recognize the cues that indicate intrafamilial elder maltreatment is occurring (Feinmann, 1988). It has been suggested that victims of maltreatment are overlooked by physicians and that social workers fail to recognize an on-going abusive situation until several months have elapsed, or in some cases several years (Cochrane and Petrone, 1987).

To help practitioners in this task, checklists have been devised by Rathbone-McCuan and Voyles (1982), Quinn and Tomita (1986) and Cochrane and Petrone (1987); the checklists rely on both physical and behavioural indicators. No single indicator identifies maltreatment but any one of them should alert a professional to the possibility of maltreatment, and the need for further investigation.

Physical indicators have been described as 'observable conditions of the elderly person that range from signs of physical neglect to physical injury' (Council on Scientific Affairs, 1987); for example:

- Bruises and welts on the body which may be in various stages of healing.
- Fractures in non-ambulatory elders.
- Cigarette burns and burns from other objects on the body.
- Lacerations and abrasions on the lips, eyes, or other parts of the face.
- Repeated skin or other injuries on the elder's body.
- Evidence of severe malnutrition and/or dehydration.
- Evidence of poor personal care, for example, deep pressure sores.

Cochrane and Petrone (1987) suggest that four other cues could also arouse suspicion; history of elder being 'accident prone'; discrepancy between the nature of the injury and its causal explanation; injuries to an area of the body usually protected by clothing; relative is being unwilling for their elder relative to be examined or interviewed privately.

Certain types of behaviour manifested by the elderly person can provide information on the relationship the elder has with a relative/carer; for example, excessive fear in the presence of an adult offspring may indicate an abusive situation (Quinn and Tomita, 1986). Changes in the elder's affect may be indicative of a maltreating situation, for example, if the elder becomes depressed, withdrawn, passive or even suicidal. Observation of the elder and suspected perpetrator may show whether the relative is unprepared to talk to, listen to, respond to or touch the elderly relative (Rathbone-McCuan and Voyles, 1982). Close attention should be paid to what the elderly person is saying and to the interaction between elder person and their 'caring' relative.

Health professionals, particularly those based in the community, could play a key role in the identification of elder maltreatment cases because they are the individuals whom the elderly person is most likely to see and trust. Health professionals are in a position to thoroughly examine elders and to question them and their families about symptoms or injuries. Social workers involved with families caring for an elderly dependant are also in a position to recognize potential maltreatment, if attention is paid to risk factors and behavioural and physical indicators of maltreatment.

Intervention and Control

The most frequent form of tertiary intervention is the removal of the elderly relative from the family and family counselling, although a high proportion of elder abuse is 'ignored' by the police and social services and goes unreported (Eastman, 1989; 1994).

In the USA, health and social services professionals have a statutory duty to report alleged elder maltreatment cases under mandatory state reporting laws (Thobaben and Anderson, 1985) and agencies have a duty to make preliminary investigations of all alleged cases of maltreatment within 24–72 hours. In Britain there are no such legal obligations to report alleged abuse and neglect to the authorities.

In the UK, there is no legal responsibility for a relative to care for an elderly dependant (Crystal, 1987) and so local authorities and other agencies have no statutory duty to formally investigate or intervene in alleged maltreatment, nor have they powers to summon all parties to a case conference (Greengross, 1986; Stevenson, 1989). In this respect the management of elder maltreatment cases differs fundamentally from that of child abuse cases. Hence, there are no specific practice guidelines or departmental policies on how to intervene in or manage cases of alleged elder maltreatment. Therefore, responses to alleged maltreatment are dealt with by social services staff on an ad hoc basis which varies from one local authority to another, although there has been some progress in recent years (Pritchard, 1995).

Management

A multidisciplinary approach to assessment should always be adopted, as both medical and social assessments are needed before further action can be decided upon (Ansello, King and Taler, 1986; Greengross, 1986). In the USA, specialist multidisciplinary assessment teams have been set up to assess cases of elder maltreatment; for example, the Beth Israel Hospital Elder Assessment Team (1986). During assessment the needs of the elder, the needs of the carer and the needs of the family are assessed to establish whether or not further action is needed (Cicirelli, 1986).

At present a multidisciplinary case conference potentially offers the best forum for gathering and evaluating information and for coordinating the functions and responsibilities of the different agencies involved in providing services (Eastman, 1994). The wishes of the elder and his/her family should always be presented either in person or by a representative at any such gathering of agencies (Stevenson, 1989). According to Eastman (1994) the aims of a case conference are fourfold:

1. To identify the problems and recommend possible solutions and interventions.
2. To ensure case planning and involvement of other agencies.
3. To facilitate and coordinate service provision.
4. To evaluate effectiveness of case conference recommendations through a regular review system.

The elderly person is a consenting adult with a right to refuse any services or interventions that may be offered. Unlike working with children, where authorities can decide what is best for a child, elderly people have a right to determine their own lives, unless judged 'incompetent' to do so, and this right must be respected by all practitioners working with them (Stevenson, 1989).

The abused elderly dependant may deny or be reluctant to admit there is a problem due to fear or embarrassment (Kosberg, 1988) and may exhibit what has been termed the 'Battering Syndrome' with symptoms of marked passivity, low self-esteem, self-blame and indecision which may frustrate the professionals trying to help them (Cochrane and Petrone, 1987).

Treatment

The psychological treatment of elder abuse is still in its infancy. Family therapists have concentrated on educational issues about elderly care rather than therapeutic issues. It has been suggested that the main problem in elder maltreatment is not abuse but neglect, which is a result of not knowing how to cope emotionally or functionally with a dependent elderly relative (Steinmetz, 1983). Therefore families must be trained for these responsibilities (Hooyman, 1983; Bolton and Bolton, 1987). The research into anger control is beginning to be applied to families with elder abuse (Reay, 1996). Cognitive approaches may be useful (e.g. Novaco, 1976) as many relatives claim that their elderly dependants 'deliberately' provoke them (Eastman, 1989).

McCuan et al. (1986) proposes a Task Centred Approach that has been shown to be effective in the early stages of elder abuse. The family is required to sign a contract stating their agreement to a 'stop abuse policy'. Strategies employed within the family include: time out, relaxation, respite, practical support and supervision. Throughout the programme the family is required to maintain a diary to record any abusive behaviour together with their prior Antecedents' Behaviour and later Consequences (The ABC model). Using the diary the family is encouraged to take responsibility for their actions and provide their own solutions to the difficulties and abuse in the family. The strengths of this approach include its emphasis on empowering the carer acknowledging the carer's need for respite, practical help and guidance (Papadopoulos, 1990).

In terms of repairing an abusive relationship, reminiscence therapy is an effective approach to the redevelopment of intimacy and attachment between the carer and the elderly relative. Reminiscence therapy involves the recalling of memories of the past, bringing to mind experiences that are personal to an individual. From photographs, old records, favourite foods or smells, emotion may be triggered such as happiness, sadness, anger, joy or grief. Reminiscing can be therapeutic for elderly dependants, as it can highlight their assets rather than their disabilities and enhance a sense of self-worth. For the carer reminiscence can help in appreciating the elderly person as an individual, learning from and sharing the older person's memories, to regenerate a sense of belonging and attachment (Norris, 1986).

Virtually no research has been conducted on whether current intervention programmes actually benefit those they serve or help modify maltreating behaviour (Pillemer and Suitor, 1988). However, interventions are more likely to be successful if the intervention addresses both the needs of the maltreated elderly person and other family members (Pratt, Koval and Lloyd, 1983; Eastman, 1994). Therefore, whenever possible, a family-oriented approach to intervention is recommended with supportive counselling (Edinberg, 1986; Smith, Smith and Toseland, 1991).

Pillemer and Suitor (1988) suggest that there are two possible types of elder maltreatment cases that require fundamentally different intervention strategies: first, where an elderly person is dependent upon others and the occurrence of maltreatment is related to stresses experienced by the carer; and, second, where an independent elderly person is being maltreated by a dependent or non-dependent relative. The latter type of case may require separation of the elderly person from the abusing relative, not necessarily through institutional care but by encouraging the abusing relative to live independently or by assisting the elderly person in a move to a new living situation (Browne, 1989c). Melville (1987) reports on refuges in Liverpool for elderly victims of violence that are being run along similar lines to the Women's Aid Refuges. Nevertheless, unplanned emergency stays at an institution could translate into permanent residential care. Therefore, such interventions involving separation from family members should be well planned and time limited.

In the case of more dependent elderly relatives most interventions utilize health and social services that help in reducing the strain experienced by many families caring for a dependent elderly person (Pillemer and Suitor, 1988). This is based on the premise that if the strains experienced by the carer can be reduced, then the likelihood of maltreatment may also be reduced. Table 10.2 presents a list of some of the services available to treat families at risk of elder abuse and neglect.

For any form of intervention to be effective it needs to be offered to a family promptly; which requires early identification of spe-

Table 10.2 Services and interventions for the treatment of elder abuse and neglect

---

Home help service: to help with the routine household workload of the carer.
Day care: provides a regular daily break for carers.
Relief care: provides regular breaks for the carer and a chance for the professionals involved to reassess the elderly person's needs.
Permanent care: to be used as a last resort and only if desired by both elder and relative.
District nurse or health visitor: to help with personal care routines and to provide supplies, advice and information.
Community Psychiatric Nurse: to provide advice on the management of persistent difficult behaviours and mental health problems.
Voluntary sitter: to provide carer with short respite periods.
Relative support group: provides an opportunity for carers to share experiences and exchange skills and information.
Relaxation training or anger management techniques: to help carer cope with the frustrations of caring in a non-violent manner.
Counselling services: for the elder and/or relative, giving the opportunity to talk about the situation, themselves and the relationship, etc.
Behavioural programmes: to modify any maladaptive behaviour in the elder, for example, excessive shouting or demanding behaviour, or to increase self-help skills.

---

cific problems. The intervention should then be coordinated, monitored and reviewed regularly to assess appropriateness and effectiveness (Eastman, 1994).

CONCLUSION

In summary, elder abuse and neglect are strongly associated with stress and frustration of the caregiver, particularly those stressors brought about by the elderly person's increasing age and continual presence at home. In such families, carers are under considerable stress from multiple sources. At the same time, they may be deficient in coping skills that might buffer the impact of these stresses, which in turn promotes violent control of the social and physical environment.

One clear distinction can be made between elder abuse and neglect and spouse violence. Stopping elder abuse must involve the promotion of safe dependence for elderly relatives, whereas stopping spouse abuse must entail the promotion of safe independence for the intimate partner.

CHAPTER 11 Preventing the cycle of violence

FROM VICTIM TO OFFENDER

According to research, delinquent and disturbed children are significantly more likely to have been referred for child abuse and neglect than non-delinquents (Takii, 1992; Scudder et al., 1993). In fact, it has been suggested that childhood maltreatment and/or witnessing violence as a child may be a primary cause of delinquency in adolescence (Jaffe, Wolfe and Wilson, 1990; Widom, 1991), although the majority of maltreated children do not become delinquent (Koski, 1987; O'Connell-Higgins, 1994).

In Britain over the last two years the news media have turned their attention away from the child as a victim to highlighting the child as an offender. News reports describe children as murderers, rapists, arsonists and perpetrators of physical and sexual violence both outside and inside the family. Most of the children are aged between 10 and 18, although some have been as young as 8 years old.

Most forms of teenage violence are neither new nor unusual. As Chapter 9 pointed out, in the United States it is estimated that between 5 and 12% of all teenagers show physical aggression towards their parents (Gelles, 1987b; Gelles and Cornell, 1990) and in the UK the estimate is 6% (Parentline, 1990; Smith et al., 1992). There are no simple solutions to preventing teenage violence and the causes and explanations are complex: it cannot be simply the result of watching TV or pornographic and violent videos as some UK Government ministers and moral crusaders suggest (*The Guardian*, 20 March 1993). The physical, social and cultural environments now and during the child's development will all play their part and possibly require psychotherapeutic intervention.

A recognition of the consequences of abuse and neglect on the behaviour of individuals later in life has been one of the factors that has challenged the assumption that delinquent and anti-social acts are in some way inherent in the individual (e.g. Eysenck, 1964). There is an increased awareness that childhood victimization can involve physical, psychological and sexual components (Groth and Burgess, 1979, 1980), any of which can have long-lasting effects on the behaviour and cognitions of the victim (Peters, 1988; Briere, 1992; Kilpatrick, 1992). The effects can include feelings of depression, low self-esteem, powerlessness, loss of control and lack of trust in others (Peters, 1988; Jehu, 1988; Watkins and Bentovim, 1992). Victims may experience difficulties in managing emotions and feelings in relation to others and may show poor social skills (Steele and Alexander, 1981), or may express their distress through abuse of drugs and alcohol (Watkins and Bentovim, 1992).

The fact that some victims may experience difficulties in express-ing emotions and trust is important as this may form the basis of later problems in adulthood. These problems may be triggered by critical events in an individual's life, such as developing a sex-ual relationship, having children, etc. Painful feelings about the past can affect current behaviour, sometimes resulting in the vic-tim becoming an offender (Search, 1988). Thus, questions about the existence of some kind of relationship between early nega-tive experiences and sexual and violent offending are important to address (Falshaw, Browne and Hollin, 1996).

Studies aimed at establishing links between characteristics of child abuse and subsequent trauma displayed by the victim are mainly American in origin. For example, Finkelhor (1986) pro-vides a useful model encompassing characteristics of child sexu-al abuse which result in long-term trauma: traumatic sexualiz-ation, betrayal, powerlessness, stigmatization. Moreover, these dynamics have since been applied more generally to family vio-lence and child physical abuse (Bentovim, 1992).

As each victim's experience of the abuse will differ and the response to it will be determined by the victim's own personal resources and perspective on life, a wide range of different long-term effects can be observed (see Table 11.1).

Table 11.1   Psychological response patterns among victims

Emotional	*Behavioural*
Fear	Aggressive behaviour
Anxiety	Suicidal behaviour
Intrusion	Substance abuse
Depression	Impaired social functioning
Self-esteem disturbances	Personality disorders
Anger	*Interpersonal*
Guilt and shame	Sexuality problems
Cognitive	Relationship problems
Perceptual disturbances	Re-victimization
(hallucinations, illusions,	Victim becomes victimizer
flashbacks, depersonalization,	
de-realization, dissociation)	
Biological	
Physiological hyper-arousal	
Somatic disturbances	

Source: Adapted from McCann, Sakheim and Abrahamson (1988: 538).

Finkelhor (1986) maintains that some effects may be a result of more than one dynamic. For example, depression can be a function of a sense of betrayal or powerlessness. Thus, it is important to understand how victims relate to their abusive experiences and their offenders. This makes the prediction of trauma associated with child abuse and neglect very difficult, and much ambiguity exists as to how abuse characteristics influence trauma.

In relation to victims of child sexual abuse, Rogers and Terry (1984) suggest that some behavioural responses appear to be much more common in male victims. These are: (1) confusion of sexual identity; (2) inappropriate reassertions of masculinity; and (3) the recapitulating victim experiences. Thus, sexually abused boys have a higher probability of homosexual activity (Finkelhor, 1984; Johnson and Shrier, 1987), aggressive and antisocial behaviour (Summit, 1983) and becoming a perpetrator of sexual abuse (Cantwell, 1988; Watkins and Bentovim, 1992).

Indeed, it has been reported that adults with a history of child sexual abuse have more long-term emotional, behavioural and interpersonal problems than victims of any other form of child maltreatment (Bagley and McDonald, 1984; Egeland, 1988; Freud, 1981) and girls are sexually abused 1½ to 3 times more than boys (Finkelhor, 1994; Pilkington and Kremer, 1995a, 1995b). However, significantly more males than females are convicted of offences against the person, which reflects the more pronounced gender differences for conduct disorder, delinquency and criminal behaviour in general.

Summit (1983) claimed that male victims of sexual abuse are more likely than female victims to externalize their inner rage and hostility and hence harm others rather than themselves. This can result in juvenile delinquency and/or crime. A recent review of prospective studies on sexually abused boys indicated that at a later stage 1 in 5 sexually molest other children (Watkins and Bentovim, 1992), while a study of physically abused male children suggests that 1 in 6 commit violent assaults as a teenager (Widom, 1989b).

Retrospective studies of adult sex offenders provide further evidence for the long-term nature of a victim-to-perpetrator cycle. Groth and Burgess (1979) found that one-third of the child molesters in their study ($n=106$) reported some form of sexual trauma in their childhood. Faller (1989) also found that 27% of incestuous fathers and step-fathers had been sexually abused as children.

The victim to perpetrator pattern seems to be particularly relevant to molesters and paedophiles with 56–57% reporting adverse sexual experiences as children in comparison to between 5 and 23% of rapists (Pithers et al., 1988; Seghorn, Prentkey and Boucher, 1987). Furthermore, retrospective studies have also revealed that 60–80% of adult child sex offenders began molesting children as adolescents (Groth, Longo and McFadin, 1982; Elliott, Browne and Kilcoyne, 1995) and it has been estimated that adolescents perpetrate 50% of the sex crimes against boys and 15–20% of offences against girls (Rogers and Terry, 1984). The sex abuse victim-to-offender pattern is not limited to sexual offences, for example 14% of male and 50% of female adolescent firesetters have a history of child sexual abuse (Epps and Swaffer, 1997).

Female perpetrators usually direct their aggression towards members of their own family, especially their children. Their children could be seen as part of themselves, supporting the notion that females direct their rage internally as suggested above

(Summit, 1983). Evidence of this has been provided by Egeland et al. (1987, 1988). In an intergenerational study of US mothers, he found that a cycle existed between the mothers' childhood history and their pattern of care of their own children. The worst care pattern was shown by mothers who had been sexually abused, followed by those neglected and physically abused. Table 11.2 shows, however, that despite these experiences a minority of mothers with a history of abuse and neglect showed supportive patterns of care towards their children, and most just demonstrated inadequate care, rather than repeating the cycle of abuse and neglect.

Table 11.2   Relations of patterns of caretaking from first to second generation

Mother's care history as a child: first generation	Mothers' patterns of caretaking as a parent: second generation				
	Mal-treatment	Other problems	Border-line	Adequate care	Totals
Severe physical abuse	16 (34%)	3 (6%)	14 (30%)	14 (30%)	47
Sexual abuse	6 (46%)	2 (15%)	4 (31%)	1 (8%)	13
Neglect	3 (38%)	0 (0%)	3 (37%)	2 (25%)	8
Emotionally supportive	1 (3%)	0 (0%)	14 (40%)	20 (57%)	35
Control (no abuse and limited emotional support)	7 (9%)	7 (9%)	24 (30%)	41 (52%)	79

Chi-square = 27.15; $p < 0.001$. Reproduced from Egeland (1988).

The concept of a victim-to-perpetrator pattern is helpful to understand both social dysfunction and deviance, and their relationship to delinquency and crime. In particular, it is relevant to the development of offending behaviour.

THE DEVELOPMENT OF DELINQUENCY AND OFFENDING BEHAVIOUR

During childhood, adult–child interaction enhances the child's physical, perceptual, social and linguistic development which in turn promotes the cognitive (intellectual) and moral abilities that are essential to thinking, learning, self-identity and actualization (full development of one's potential). Hence, from responsive parental care comes the sense that:

- 'I can elicit care' (Infant)
- 'I can affect the environment' (Child)
- 'I can cope with the stress of change and challenge the environment' (Adult).

Allport (1961) describes the characteristics of the 'mature personality', and states that an adequate sense of self-worth is fundamental to maturity. Thus, contemporary psychology holds the belief that a child must develop psychologically as well as physically for optimal maturity.

Bowlby (1969) argues that children develop generalized social expectations of their caregiver's behaviour and an 'internal working model' of their parents' accessibility, sensitivity, responsiveness and acceptance. In turn, children build a reflective view of self as worthy or unworthy. Bowlby claims that this 'internal working model of self' heavily influences personality formation, especially the growth of autonomy, initiative and self-identity so important for adolescent resolution of psycho-social conflict, as described by Erikson (1965).

Bowlby contests Freud's (1905) ideas on the nature of the relationship between early experience and later problems. Psychological disorders in individuals are not always a result of sexual seduction or due to their fantasies and secret wishes. He argues that conflicts are the result of actual adverse experiences in the broadest sense, during the formation and maintenance of early social relationships.

Bowlby (1984) claims that insecurely and anxiously attached children have a greater probability of psychological and conduct disorders in adulthood. He proposes that children who experience a rejection of their attachment behaviours can develop 'Affectionless' personality characteristics. This view is of considerable importance to understanding the relationship between child maltreatment and delinquency (Rutter, 1981). The literature on child abuse contains several reports regarding the high number of conduct-disordered antisocial teenagers who were themselves victims of abuse and neglect as children (Grey, 1988; Widom, 1989a; Stein and Lewis, 1992; Widom and Ames, 1994). Indeed, a helpful way of viewing this is to see a teenager's possible experiences of parenting along a dimension of warmth from parental acceptance to parental rejection. Rohner (1986) has provided a conceptual framework for the 'warmth dimension of parenting', as diagrammatically illustrated in Figure 11.1. The dimension ranges from parental acceptance characterized by positive actions of a physical and verbal nature, to parental rejection associated with actions of hostility and aggression moving to indifference, neglect and undifferentiated rejection as an extreme lack of parental warmth.

Of all the stages of life, there is little doubt that adolescent and teenage years are some of the most stressful. A number of developmental changes—physical, psychological and social—place great demands on the individual (see Table 11.3; Havighurst, 1973). By its very nature the process of change carries the potential for crises as the young person struggles with often turbulent emotions to establish a sense of self-identity rather than become confused in his or her role as an individual (Erikson, 1965).

The disturbed adolescent has a tendency to magnify his or her internal conflict and to use violence as a frequent mode of expression (Flavigny, 1988). This is often accompanied by substance abuse (Hollin, 1994b). Adolescents and teenagers referred to secure accommodation have usually expressed violence in the severest of forms, including rape, arson and life-threatening aggression with no regard to the potential of killing someone.

An 'antisocial' tendency is seen by Winnicott (1963) to be an adolescent's need to be defiant in his or her struggle for independence and self-identity. The emotionally disturbed adolescent, as a result of pathological parenting (i.e. negative emotions and actions from the primary caregiver) and a disorganized family background, will have developed feelings of failure and inadequacy and lack self-confidence.

Fears about loss and separation, derived from an insecure attachment to the primary caregiver (Holmes, 1993), will confuse the need for independence and thwart the sense of being in control.

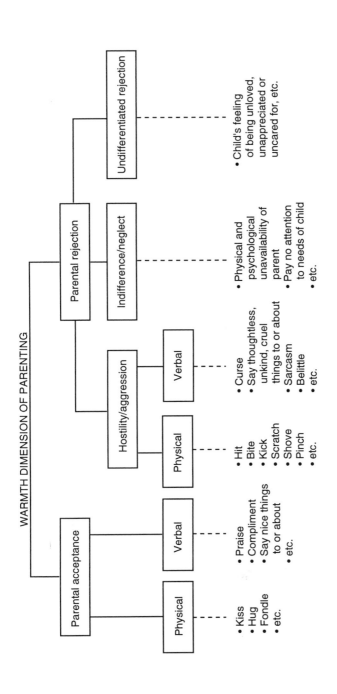

Figure 11.1 Conceptual framework of principal parenting concepts in parental acceptance—rejection theory (from Rohner, 1986). The warmth dimension: foundations of parental acceptance—rejection theory (Beverly Hills, CA: Sage, p. 20, Figure 1). With kind permission of Sage Publications

Table 11.3   Developmental tasks of adolescence (after Havighurst, 1973)

1. Achieving new and more mature relations with age-mates of both sexes
2. Achieving a masculine or feminine social role
3. Accepting one's physique and using the body effectively
4. Achieving emotional independence from parents and other adults
5. Preparing for marriage and family life
6. Preparing for an economic career
7. Acquiring a set of values and an ethnical system as a guide to behaviour—developing an ideology
8. Desiring and achieving socially responsible behaviour

Wanting both dependence and independence may cause the adolescent to feel confused and isolated. These unresolved issues may then become associated with violent 'acting-out' and other antisocial behaviours, perhaps in a primitive attempt to gain power and control over his or her environment (Winnicott, 1956; Rutter and Giller, 1983; Flavigny, 1988).

Indeed, the highest number of convictions occur between the ages of 14 and 21 years, with those from deprived backgrounds showing a greater number of convictions than those from environments with no deprivation (see Figure 11.2; Kolvin et al., 1988).

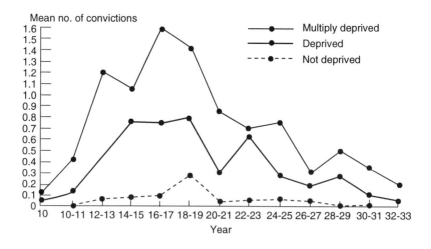

Figure 11.2   Mean number of convictions by deprivation (Kolvin et al., 1988)

The loss or withdrawal of good parental experiences in a child's early life (for example, by death, desertion, neglect, rejection, abuse or inconsistent and insensitive parenting) can have a lasting traumatic effect, leaving deprived adolescents functioning in childlike ways, unable to experience guilt and impulsively controlling what they perceive as a threat (Flavigny, 1988). Without further self-development, these primary processes of coping remain present in adulthood.

A diagrammatic illustration of a developmental progression for antisocial behaviour is presented in Figure 11.3. The model is based on the notion that growing up in a violent family may do serious harm to children. The consequences of such an experience are that a child becomes socially unresponsive, emotionally

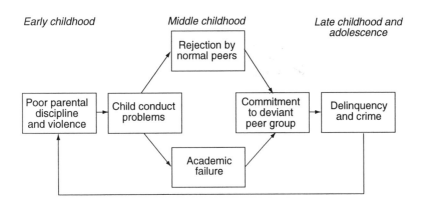

Figure 11.3   Developmental progression for antisocial behaviour (adapted from Patterson, DeBaryshe and Ramsey, 1989)

blunted, passive, apathetic and inattentive (Martin and Beezley, 1977).

Neglected children are insensitive to their social environment, whereas abused children are hyperactive, aggressive and more easily provoked to violent behaviour. As a form of control of the environment, abused children often exhibit aggression. Once violence occurs, it is not easily stopped (Main and George, 1985). Abused children are punitive to other children; they lack empathy and have a poor understanding of others. In fact, if they hit a child and that child cries, the abused child will hit the child even more (op. cit.). Hence, the emotional vulnerability of abused children is often acted out and expressed as bullying and cruel teasing; as a consequence, they are rejected by their peers at school (Szur, 1987). Acting out may also lead to further victimization by teachers and the educational system, which can further contribute towards producing a delinquent child who shows antisocial behaviour to others and commitment to a deviant peer group (Hart, Brassard and Germain, 1987; Lewis, Mallouh and Webb, 1989). Abused children develop an external locus of control, where their problems are seen as being the fault of others. There is little personal responsibility for disruptive behaviour. By contrast, neglected children turn the problems of their social world inwards; they have an internal locus of control, blaming themselves.

Abused and neglected children both have poor impulse control, low self-esteem and are sad and easily depressed, contributing to impulsive behaviour, poor school adjustment, substance abuse, delinquency and crime. It is not surprising, therefore, that when these children develop into adolescents and teenagers they have a greater probability of becoming violent and sexual offenders (see Egeland, 1988; Watkins and Bentovim, 1992). In addition to greater probability of becoming violent, they may also have a greater probability of becoming victims of violence (Lewis, Mallouh and Webb, 1989). However, the implications of these contingencies for the recognition and prevention of juvenile delinquency have yet to be determined.

In early and middle adulthood between 20 and 30% of these disturbed young people will continue the pattern of violent interactions, from one generation to the next, by abusing their own children (Herrenkohl, Herrenkohl and Toedter, 1983; Hunter and Kilstrom, 1979; Silver, Dublin and Lourie, 1969). Therefore, it is important to break this intergenerational 'cycle of violence'.

POOR FAMILY DYNAMICS AND VIOLENT VICTIMS

The idea that family background can have long-term effects on subsequent behaviour is well established. In particular family criminality can encourage a life of crime (West and Farrington, 1973; Blumstein, Farrington and Moitra, 1985; Farrington, 1995). The same can be said of social factors, such as parental unemployment and family breakdown (Hollin, 1992; McCord, 1990). Indeed, the high number of convictions in young people is probably related to the multiple deprivation they have suffered, as Kolvin et al. (1988) have shown that there is a significant positive correlation between the two (Fig. 11.2). Family discord is one of the most influential forms of childhood deprivation in terms of later delinquency and adolescent disturbance. This has been confirmed by studies of children of battered women, which conclude that witnessing spouse abuse is a severe form of emotional maltreatment for the child (Davis and Carlson, 1987; Carroll, 1994).

It is estimated that 3.3 million children in the USA live with violent parents (Carlson, 1984) and children have witnessed between 68 and 90% of wife assault cases (Pahl, 1985; Leighton, 1989). Furthermore, research in the UK on women in shelters report that 4 out of 5 battered women recall witnessing their mother being assaulted by their father during their childhood (Gayford, 1975).

According to research, the effects of witnessing wife assault can result in childhood conduct and personality disorders (Jouriles, Murphy and O'Leary, 1989; Grych and Fincham, 1990). It seems that, regardless of whether children are victims of aggression themselves, witnessing other forms of family violence will still have a very profound effect on children's development and attitudes to social relationships.

In their book *Children of Battered Women*, Jaffe, Wolfe and Wilson (1990) explain that boys and girls learn that violence is an acceptable way to resolve conflict with an intimate partner after witnessing their mother and father fighting. Boys and girls also learn about victimization—the extent that males can use aggression and fear to gain power and control over other family members. This learning results in a change in their own behaviour; indeed, Livingstone (1986) claims that children who have witnessed an adult striking their single-parent mother display more frequent and severe violence towards their mother. His findings indicate that 29% of single-parent mothers suffer such abuse. Intervention programmes have been proposed based on the children's social problem-solving skills (Rosenberg, 1987) and education-based counselling (Wilson, Jaffe and Wolfe, 1989).

Viewing violence directly can affect social behaviour. It teaches aggressive styles of conduct, increases arousal to aggressive situations, reduces restraints on aggressive behaviour, distorts views about conflict resolution and desensitizes individuals to violence. It has also been suggested that viewing violence indirectly, such as on television, may have similar effects (Huston et al., 1992; Newson, 1994a, 1994b). However, this viewpoint is considered controversial as other psychologists claim that television and film violence have little direct effect on children and young adults (Cumberbach, 1994). It may be that the effects of witnessing violence on television and film is not so clear-cut. Recently, Browne (1995e) suggested that the 3–10% of children who grow up in violent families are likely to be those who are most affected by violence in the media. Indeed, they may preferentially select violent material and have a media diet of violence as a way of exploring their own difficult experiences. Understandably, abused children who witness parental violence suffer significantly more distress and behaviour problems than non-abused children who witness their parents fighting (Davis and Carlson, 1987; Hughes, 1988).

The high levels of family violence reported in the backgrounds of children and disturbed adolescents in secure accommodation (Browne, Falshaw and Hamilton, 1995; Boswell, 1995) support the observation that exposure to parental conflict and violence within the family environment is linked to the demonstration of violence outside of the family home (Kruttschnitt, Ward and Sheble, 1987; Widom, 1989a, 1989b; Henry et al., 1993). Therefore, adverse family dynamics can have long-reaching effects on those who experience them.

A recent UK survey commissioned by the Princes Trust (Boswell, 1995) showed that 40% of the 200 juveniles who were sentenced into custody under Section 53, had themselves endured physical abuse earlier in life. Twenty-nine per cent had suffered sexual abuse and 57% cessation of contact with a parent. The findings of Browne, Falshaw and Hamilton (1995) are even higher, with 57% physically abused, 38% sexually abused and 75% loss of regular contact with a parent. The higher figures may relate to the inclusion of young offenders on care-orders (Section 25) in the sample. Overall, the finding of this study—that 74% of young offenders have experienced some kind of physical and/or sexual maltreatment—is remarkably similar to the 72% figure reported in the Princes Trust Survey (Boswell, 1995). Moreover, in a study by Stein and Lewis (1992) of 66 incarcerated youths in Connecticut, it was found that four out of five residents admitted, in an 'extensive personal interview', that severe physical abuse had taken place during their childhood.

However, the study by Browne, Falshaw and Hamilton (1995) did not support the notion that victims of sexual maltreatment had a higher propensity for sexual offending, as suggested by Watkins and Bentovim (1992), or even that victims of physical abuse had a greater chance of violent offending, as suggested by Widom (1989a, 1989b). It appears that other young people who have experienced deprivation but not abuse are just as likely to offend, although a confounding influence in this study may be the heterogeneous sample of males and females analysed together. As pointed out earlier, male victims are more likely to act-out their pain and females direct their pain inwardly (Summit, 1983). Owing to the small sample size ($N=44$), Browne, Falshaw and Hamilton (1995) did not analyse the sexes separately to ascertain whether an association remained for males.

Consistent with the literature on child sexual abuse, which shows that prevalence rates range between 6 and 62% for females and 3 and 29% for males, and that girls are abused 1½ to 3 times more than boys (Finkelhor, 1994; Pilkington and Kremer, 1995a), The study of young offenders by Browne, Falshaw and Hamilton showed that 75% of females had a history of sexual abuse in comparison to 29% of males. Interestingly, these figures are more comparable to the sexual abuse rates reported for clinical populations (Pilkington and Kremer, 1995b) rather than those estimated for community samples (Pilkington and Kremer,

1995a). Conversely, there was no gender difference in the incidence of physical abuse in childhood for the young offenders. This is consistent with literature on physical abuse which shows that girls are just as likely as boys to be placed on child protection registers for physical abuse (Browne, 1995d).

A most disturbing aspect of childhood victimization is its association with self-mutilation (Walsh and Rosen, 1988). It is suggested that sexual abuse in childhood leads to 'body alienation' in adolescence, although body image problems are also associated with physical abuse. Witnessing self-damaging behaviours in parents (e.g. self-mutilation, alcohol and drug abuse) and destructive behaviour in the family (e.g. spouse abuse) is also correlated to self-abuse and neglect (op. cit.). Given the prevalence of childhood maltreatment among adolescent and teenage perpetrators of crime, it was not surprising to find that 9 out of 10 young offenders in secure accommodation have a history of self-damaging behaviour (Browne, Falshaw and Hamilton, 1995). Of more concern are those young people who currently harm themselves. Indeed, Bagley et al. (1995) claim that disturbed behaviours such as self-harm are linked to 'dissociative personality traits' which can be seen in as many as 29% of individuals with a prior history of severe child maltreatment. Hence, the need for counselling young people in care or secure accommodation is without question.

COUNSELLING ADULT VICTIMS

The process of counselling may be defined as the means by which one individual helps another to clarify his or her life situation and to decide upon further lines of action. The counsellor provides the opportunity for a relationship, which may enable the clients to get in touch with their own resources and search for their own solutions to their difficulties.

The psychodynamic approach derived from Freud (1949) highlights the relationship between past and present and the unconscious forces that influence behaviour, to encourage the expression of suppressed feeling and emotions. This has obvious advantages for difficulties resulting from emotional problems, anxiety and an unhappy childhood (Sanderson, 1995). Cognitive-behavioural approaches to relationship difficulties may help to improve communication and problem-solving skills and to alleviate depression in the present, but will not remove the underlying causes of the conflict and negative feeling from the past. However, a comparative evaluation of different approaches (Ursano and Hales, 1986) reveals that the initial working alliance, as perceived by client and therapist, is the major determinant of success for psychodynamic, cognitive/behavioural and interpersonal humanistic approaches.

Egeland et al. (1987, 1988) discovered that the women who had managed to break the cycle of violence were those who had received some form of help with their abusive experiences. Whether it was a relative, a therapist or a social worker, somewhere in their life-history was someone who listened, believed and expressed empathy and understanding about their experiences. As a result they managed to break the cycle of violence by clear factual and emotional recall of their own abuse as children with little dissociation. All the women who broke the cycle had benefited from psychotherapy as adolescents or young adults and were currently in stable, long-term, supportive relationships with a boyfriend or husband. In comparison to abusive mothers, these non-abusive women had lower current life stress, lower anxiety and depression, less apprehension and dependency, higher IQ and stable home environments and social support networks. Similar conclusions have been made by Herrenkohl et al. (1991).

Research evidence suggests that positive improvements as a result of counselling are most frequently seen in clients with extreme feelings of emotional distress (and possibly an inclination to violence) but little psychological disorder (Traux and Carkhuff, 1967). These can be achieved using most approaches and modes of therapy as long as the therapeutic relationship exhibits genuineness and warmth, enhanced by the counsellor's appropriate respect, positive regard and empathy, and the client(s) feeling of being understood (Traux and Carkhuff, 1967). However, studies have shown that these characteristics are not sufficient to induce change in juvenile delinquents (Ollendick and Henson, 1979; Kazdin et al., 1987). Consequently, those working with young offenders must rely on more than a person-centred approach (see Rogers, 1957). The counsellor must develop specific skills that respond to the unique characteristics of the delinquent.

COUNSELLING YOUNG OFFENDERS

Ferrara (1992) suggests that the following are effective approaches for counsellors to use when working with juvenile delinquents and young offenders.

1. *Commitment:* the counsellor must be committed to working with young offenders.
2. *Responsibility:* the counsellor who is irresponsible is discounted by the young offender, who finds it difficult to trust others.
3. *Intensity:* sometimes it takes a great deal of strength and persistence to 'get through' the ego-defence of a young offender.
4. *Scepticism:* since so much of the young offender's life is based on deception the counsellor must be sceptical of what the delinquent says and does. Being sceptical entails suspending judgement.
5. *Leadership:* it is most important for the counsellor to be aware that most young offenders will require a more directive and confrontational style of counselling than many other clients.

It has been suggested (Ferrara, 1992) that the above approaches are effective in group work with juvenile delinquents. Furthermore, Day, Maddicks and McMahon (1993) demonstrated significant treatment effects in 'two plus one' brief psychotherapy sessions where one counsellor works with two young offenders, referred for depression, alcohol and anger problems, while in custody. The permanence of these changes remains in question as there was no long-term follow-up.

The poor structure of the counselling work in secure accommodation contributes to the fact that a quarter of the young resident offenders are not receiving counselling sessions on their most difficult problems (e.g. history of victimization, self-concept, emotional function, problems at home and in care), when they had been assessed as in need of it (Browne, 1995f).

The effectiveness of group therapy in working psychodynamically with young female victims of sexual abuse has been shown

(DeLuca et al., 1995). Results indicate that, following group therapy, self-esteem increased and anxiety and behaviour problems decreased and that the improvements were maintained at a 9–12 month follow-up. It is somewhat disappointing, therefore, that group therapy approaches to child maltreatment are not employed in secure accommodation.

However, the work that needs to be done with young offenders is inhibited by their own mistrust of others and lack of commitment to a therapeutic alliance. Trust might perhaps be built up in time, but an occasional obstacle to long-term counselling is the rapid turnover of residents in secure environments. These are usually young people on secure care orders (Section 25) rather than those convicted (Section 53). Even for the residents with a sentence over six months, therapeutic counselling work can end abruptly, leaving the client psychologically unsupported for his or her return to the community.

The following case study of one male young offender resident in secure accommodation will be presented to illustrate the points raised.

John's Case

John (pseudonym) was aged 15 when he was sentenced under Section 53(2) for two years on conviction of robbery with violence. John had persistently absconded from previous care establishments after being received into voluntary care. He had made allegations of physical and sexual abuse against his father.

On arrival, John was at great risk of physical harm to himself and others. He had a history of alcohol, drug and solvent abuse, had previously overdosed on medication, cut himself, set fire to himself and attempted to hang himself. John also had a history of violent threats and assaults to his parents, careworkers and the general public. Other offences included stealing.

Certain treatment objectives were identified for John and one-to-one counselling was recommended, covering the issues of social skills, anger management and self-esteem. John was initially receiving three sessions a week. The sessions were always conducted in the same room and always involved the same member of staff. The length of the sessions depended on John's mood. These sessions were rarely interrupted and were always conducted in a private room where the participants could be neither seen nor heard.

Sessions would also be conducted on demand as well as being arranged in advance. These ad hoc sessions occurred weekly on average and would not always occur in the same venue. John would only see four particular members of staff for these sessions for any length of time, depending on his needs and mood. John's social worker would travel regularly to John's parents' home and engage them in session work of their own. Although this session work was successful in isolation, efforts to merge John's session work with that involving his parents failed. Nevertheless, he kept in regular telephone contact and received visits from his mother and siblings. There was no contact with his father.

The keyworker who 'counselled' John during the one-to-one session work reported some satisfaction with what John had achieved. When John first arrived, he showed a lack of empathy for other people and had no emotional connection with anyone. However, after six months of his stay he began to open up more. The keyworker believed that the sessions may have allowed John to see things more clearly, especially as feelings and information gathered from John were reflected and paraphrased back to him. The keyworker believes that John showed behavioural change as a result of the sessions. He stopped being so aggressive and also lessened his episodes of self-injurious behaviour.

Overall, the keyworker felt close to John and felt that she gave John the time and attention he needed. In the keyworker's opinion John trusted her and felt understood by her. She believed that John shared her inner thoughts and feelings in a free and open way. However, John was at times hostile towards her and she felt impatient and disappointed with her client, sometimes showing John her annoyance.

After 18 months, John was discharged from secure accommodation and returned to the community, living in his own apartment under the supervision of social services. After a short time, John was arrested 'drunk and disorderly', threatening to kill himself and his father or anyone else who got in his way. John was again remanded to the care of the local authority.

John absconded, became drunk and aggressive and violently threatened members of the general public. Once apprehended, he returned to a local authority care institution. Here he assaulted a member of staff following a phone call from his father.

After a court appearance, John was re-admitted to secure accommodation, where he is continuing with his counselling.

Summary

This sequence of events perhaps reflects the necessity of psychodynamic counselling work for victims of abuse. For individuals with a history of victimization, the benefits of cognitive-behavioural work are short-lived as underlying matters of a more unconscious nature are *not* addressed. However, relapse into offending behaviour is also seen with breaks in psychodynamic therapy (Welldon, 1994). This is associated with feeling abandoned by the therapist at times of need. John may have also felt abandoned and unprotected, moving from a secure environment with regular counselling to a self-contained flat. There was little time for transition.

TREATMENT OBJECTIVES

According to Winnicott (1956), 'it is the environment that plays the essential role in the natural healing of the anti-social tendency'. Severely emotionally disturbed adolescents and young offenders need a safe healing environment which provides them with opportunities to experience separations which they can live through positively and thereby rework earlier difficulties.

Treatment objectives for disturbed adolescents and young offenders need to consider the whole person and not merely be focused on the violent behaviour which is a symptom of their disturbance. The structured environment of a secure therapeutic setting can compensate to some extent for an inadequate and disorganized domestic environment.

Disturbed adolescents need to establish relationships with carers who are capable of imposing meaningful limits to, as well as coping with, anger (Flavingy, 1988). When the young person acts out intense feelings belonging to an earlier stage of life, the carer may be provoked into reacting as an inadequate parent would have done.

The carers have to live through the hate and negative feelings dumped on them while the young person struggles to develop more stable relationships (Winnicott, 1950). Hence, the treatment of disturbed adolescents and young offenders needs to remain at a 'here-and-now' level for a long period of time, declining gradually into issues of the past. Premature in-depth counselling, or insights shared too soon, could prove destructive, increasing the risk of suicide or a delusional crisis (Flavigny, 1988).

Hill (1989) concludes that for change to occur in a counselling/therapeutic relationship, the counsellor has to deliver the appropriate techniques for a particular client within the context of a 'good enough relationship'. This means there must be an attachment between client and counsellor.

In the long-term, the application of Attachment Theory (Bowlby, 1969) to the counselling and psychotherapy of damaged adolescents may be relevant, as described by Holmes (1993, 1994). He sees the main therapeutic tasks as: (1) providing a safe and secure base from which the client can explore feelings and thoughts; (2) listening to the client's narrative with atonement and empathy to enhance a sense of worth; (3) helping the client to consider feelings, thoughts and actions as products of childhood experiences; (4) helping the client recognize that his or her model of self may be distorted by childhood experiences; (5) encouraging the client to consider relationship patterns with significant others in his or her current life; and (6) examining the relationship between client and counsellor in attachment terms. These techniques have special relevance to individuals maltreated in their childhood by trusted caregivers and help to rehabilitate an 'affectionless' character (Bowlby, 1988).

A more permanent approach to achieving change with damaged children is to contain their anxiety by providing a safe forum for exploration and shouldering their feelings of inadequacy

(Mawson, 1994). Because of earlier maltreatment, damaged children often mistrust others and form insecure attachments. Indeed, psychological and behavioural problems related to an insecure attachment often emerge in the relationship between the child and the therapist. The counsellor can intervene in the context of the relationship to enable the child to modify negative and pessimistic beliefs and expectations of self and others (Pearce and Pezzot-Pearce, 1994).

Work with young offenders reveals that they vary in the degree to which they live their delinquent lifestyles. They tend either to be impulsive or to be more power oriented, exploitive and predatory (Walters and White, 1990). Their lives are characterized by the emphasis on 'being a winner'. In this way, they fail to consider the needs of others. They are angry and have limited guilt, unrealistic feelings of pride and avoid responsibility. Welldon (1994) claims that abused clients need to feel in control as they are vulnerable to anything that reminds them of their original adverse experiences. There is also an unconscious need for revenge and for inflicting harm. Furthermore, they may use over-sexualized behaviour as a means of dealing with feelings of insecurity and inadequacy.

Of course, institutional structures and organizational issues are paramount for effective rehabilitation programmes of disturbed adolescents and young offenders, whether in a community or residential setting (Hollin, 1994a). According to Hollin, 'treatment integrity' can only be achieved with (1) staff training, (2) organizational structures that facilitate rehabilitation work and (3) management and supervisory systems that monitor the design, implementation and progress of treatment programmes.

Organizational policies to produce the above must be backed by adequate resources and a stable, chaos-free environment, rather than one that is constantly reorganized or leaps from one crisis to another (Stokes, 1994).

Portraying children and teenagers as perpetrators of violent acts may reduce concerns about their protection. In 1993, the Prime Minister, John Major, was quoted as saying that 'society needs to condemn more and understand less those teenagers who commit violent crimes'. A return to the 'short, sharp shock' of custodial sentences will be futile; the ineffectiveness of such methods was clearly shown by the research of the 1970s. More resources are required for positive intervention programmes with young offenders. Currently any such programmes for violent young-sters are patchy and fragmented, and it is only in the last four or five years that there has been any concerted effort to look at the problem of juvenile sex offences and to coordinate intervention programmes together with their evaluation.

PREVENTION

The treatment, management and control of young offenders is tertiary prevention which intervenes to ameliorate any further adversity *only after* an adverse outcome. This is despite the fact there are two other forms of prevention—primary and sec-ondary—that intervene *prior to* an adverse outcome.

The interrelationship of adverse factors in the background of young offenders resident in secure accommodation is illustrat-ed in Figure 11.4. Each factor warrants both a primary and a secondary approach to prevention. Identifying at-risk groups such as violent or chemically dependent families in order to offer social skills, alcohol and anger management training might be regarded as secondary prevention, but even this is not enough.

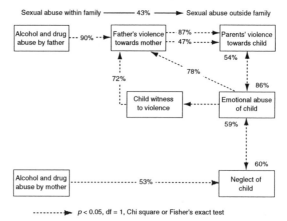

Figure 11.4 The interrelationship of adverse factors in the background of young offenders (N=44) (from Browne, 1995f)

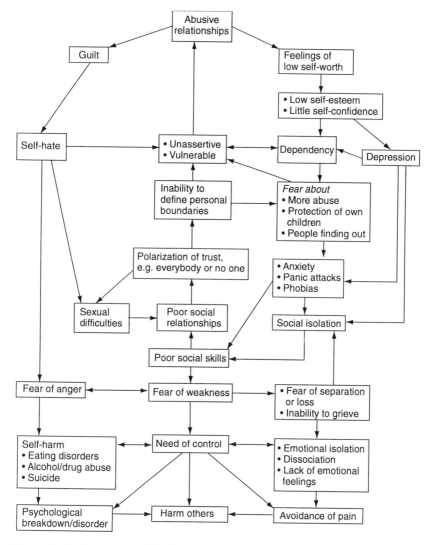

Figure 11.5 Impact of child abuse on adult mental health

Helping parents to inhibit violence towards their children may still leave quite unchanged the emotionally harmful consequences of the initial abuse. Intervention should involve all the members of a family, with therapy going hand-in-hand with the treatment of parent–child interactions. Work at the family relationship level is essential for primary prevention of violence. In addition, psychotherapy for those who are victims may help prevent delinquency and the cycle of violence from victim to offender.

The consequences of child abuse and neglect for the victim are extensive and multi-dimensional, affecting all aspects of adult mental health (see *Figure 11.5*). There are also additional problems when a child is taken into care for his or her own protection, which are:

- feelings of stigmatization, bewilderment and abandonment
- a lack of continuity in family, school and community
- contact with family of origin
- care placement breakdown
- risk of further abuse.

It is not surprising, therefore, to find a high proportion of victims of child maltreatment with a long-term care history in samples of severely damaged young people, who are both delinquent and psychologically disordered.

Threats of violence, bullying and intimidation continue to occur in care and secure accommodation, especially when the institution fails to take the issue seriously and where staff use intimidation to manage and control young people, despite the fact that there are a number of practical ways to intervene and prevent bullying both in schools and care institutions (see Lane and Tattum, 1989; Browne and Falshaw, 1996).

Interestingly, a more in-depth review of this emerging concept of 'Victim as Offender' has been recently provided by Falshaw, Browne and Hollin (1996), which emphasizes the importance of working with violent families.

CHAPTER 12   Working with violent families

It is clear from longitudinal studies of the development of violent patterns of behaviour that *early* interventions of a remedial, or better still, preventive kind, are vital (see Herbert, 1994). Social and health workers often claim to carry out 'preventive' work with families. But what does this mean? It is a common practice in the literature to make use of some variation of the standard classification from preventive medicine to describe preventive social work and clinical practice. Thus, primary, secondary and tertiary levels of prevention describe the differing professional responses that might be made according to the particular stages in the development of a personal or social problem. Primary prevention would prevent the emergence of a problem; secondary prevention would refer to working on a problem in its early stages; and tertiary prevention would limit the damaging effects of a problem already established. Secondary prevention would seem to include *two* sets of circumstances: (i) the early identification of comparatively mild problems with a hopeful outcome, and (ii) the more serious problems in which a degree of amelioration and containment may be all that is feasible, yet may still prevent a violent incident occurring. Tertiary prevention is illustrated by the work of professionals who take therapeutic action in families where violence is recognized and before the point of a child's admission to care. Interventions at this preventive level are designed to forestall repeat victimization and the worst effects of chronic family difficulties and to prevent clients from being drawn into increasingly intrusive interventions.

The sheer complexity of the personal circumstances of many social work and health service clients does not lend itself to neatly compartmentalized descriptions; the reality is that social and health workers are operating at different levels of prevention

MODEL OF WELFARE

LEVEL OF PREVENTION	Residual	Institutional	Developmental	Radical
1. Primary (i) Action to prevent problems from arising (ii) Action to reduce the need for the formal services of the SSD			**1. Primary/developmental** *Localized service bases support for self-help / mutual support systems, Family Centres, etc. advice & information services child care / management education lobbying (eg TV violence)*	
2. Secondary (i) Early identification of and action to resolve problems (ii) Intervention aimed at early restoration of non-client status		**2. Secondary /institutional** *Advice and information services early screening / detection (duty/intake system geared to assessment) short-term intervention (behavioural social work; crisis intervention) social care planning*		
3. Tertiary (i) Action to prevent the worst effects of chronic well-established problems (ii) Action to prevent clients from being drawn into increasingly intrusive and damaging interventions	**3. Tertiary / residual** *'Treatment' response to families whose children are in imminent danger of admission to care; gate-keeping on entry into care; day-care, etc., linked to treatment goals; statutory social work*			
4. Quaternary (i) Action to prevent damage arising from long-term substitute care (ii) Permanency planning				

Figure 12.1 Models of prevention in child care (*Source:* Hardiker et al., 1989)

within any one case at any one time. Prevention can be an objective at all stages of intervention. Indeed, preventive action can go beyond the point of a child's admission to care; this requires, and is seen as, a fourth or *quaternary level* of prevention. This broader perspective is enshrined, in part, in the 1989 Children Act. Rehabilitation is a major concern; attempting to mitigate damage that might be engendered by taking children into care—the loss of self-esteem, threat to identity, to independence and to power over making decisions—is high on the practitioner's agenda. Maintaining links and collaborating with parents (e.g. training them for the child's return to the family) is a goal deserving particular emphasis.

The aims of particular social work interventions cannot be considered in isolation from the *value systems* within which they are located and whose purposes they serve, according to Hardiker, Exton and Barker (1989). Adapting (with permission) an example given by them, let us consider parents who approach a social services department for help because their teenage son is intimidating the family with his violence, and indulging in bullying and other anti-social (possibly delinquent) activities outside the home. They may be offered a variety of 'preventive' strategies ranging from immediate advice with no follow-up, allocation of social worker to provide counselling or behavioural family work, through to 'preventive intermediate treatment' (see Fig. 12.1). It is possible to argue from a *rights model* that there are indications of family dysfunction that could well be remedied by early intervention and therefore have the family allocated a social work service. From a *social rights* or *developmental model* one might contend that an absence of local facilities for teenage recreation, combined with high-profile policing of the area, is placing many young people at risk of delinquent careers. Some practitioners might urge the parents to become involved in a local pressure group which is negotiating with the education and police authorities for different policies in the area. All of these responses could be placed under the rubric 'prevention'.

However, at both agency and practitioner levels, the room for manoeuvre is significantly reduced if this young person is an offender shortly facing yet another substantive court appearance on a charge of assault. The practitioner may continue to bring personal values to bear in the construction of the 'problem', but the agency's social control functions cannot be abrogated, given the seriousness of the offences and the statutory requirement to consider the protection of the general public.

PSYCHOSOCIAL INTERVENTIONS

The social-structural context within which childhood and adolescent conduct disorders and problems of violent familial interactions develop and thrive—poor housing, destitute inner city slum environments, physical and emotional deprivation—cannot be overlooked in our desire to provide individualized or family-based professional help. As we have seen, social and health policy issues represent an important level of analysis and potential intervention which are of concern to social and health workers.

Although these people and their agencies are not in the business of attacking or ameliorating the *structural* causes of social problems directly, their 'front line' knowledge of the effects of poverty and the actual workings of the cycle of disadvantage places them in a unique position to influence social policies. As Hardiker, Exton and Barker (1989) point out, there are several approaches which offer personalized forms of help to people with difficulties without the stigma of becoming a patient or client.

Primary Prevention

Self-help groups and community projects may provide support to parents and families, empower vulnerable people and initiate informal networks in neighbourhoods. Strategies to divert people experiencing minor difficulties from becoming 'clients' or 'patients' are vital aspects of primary prevention, for example, advice, guidance and signposting services provided through attachments to health centres, schools and hospitals or through patch-based social services offices.

Secondary Prevention

Secondary prevention takes place when an individual is accepted as a patient at a clinic/hospital or an entire family as, in a sense, a client of a social work agency. For example, a normally well-functioning family may be thrown into an acute state of crisis through a traumatic event—say a marital breakdown and separation. A social work assessment may indicate the need for an intervention of a short-term nature (a so called 'crisis intervention') with a view to returning the family to its former non-client status.

A variety of casework options is available (see Herbert, 1991, 1995) in high-risk cases involving antisocial and aggressive behaviour. The choice depends upon an analysis of causes of personal and social problems of the kind that can be seen in Figure 12.2.

The diagram illustrates the complexities of a clinical or casework formulation. It shows the multilevel and multidimensional nature of causal influences on problem behaviour. The advantages of working with parents and other caregivers are notably in the areas of primary *and* secondary prevention (Herbert, 1987a, 1993; Webster-Stratton and Herbert, 1993); therapeutic effectiveness and cost effectiveness (see Callias, 1994). In the light of such a claim it seems appropriate to look more closely at the way it works.

ANALYSING AGGRESSIVE AND OTHER AVERSIVE INCIDENTS

To address the question of *why* self-defeating or other offending behaviours such as aggression are initiated and maintained (the issue of causation) behaviourally orientated professionals conduct a comprehensive functional analysis of the child's (or caregiver's) behaviour relating it to events and contingencies in its two environments—external and internal (organismic). A theoretical perspective—social learning theory—for coercive/aggressive behaviour was provided in Chapter 2.

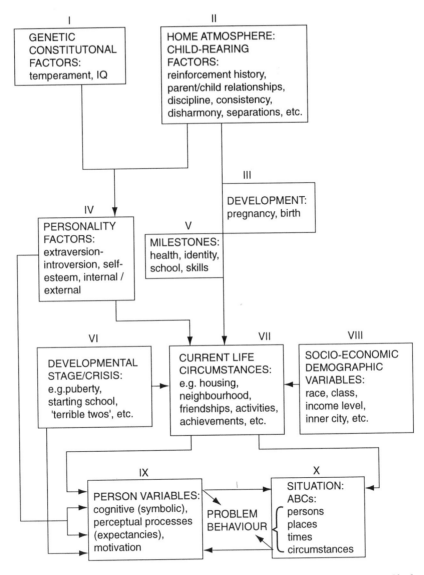

Figure 12.2   The 10-factor clinical formation of causation (adapted from Clark, 1977; reproduced by permission of the British Psychological Society)

THE 'WHAT' QUESTION

Before we can answer the causal 'why' question we must be clear about what it is we are explaining. This requires a painstaking investigation of the parameters of the problem(s), once they have been specified. There are psychological screening/assessment instruments to help us in the task (see Chapter 5 and 6).

Self-monitoring procedures

The self-monitoring of both aggressive responses and the cognitions accompanying those responses is a potentially useful source of information with regard to older children and adolescents. With self-monitoring, the child is required to discriminate and record the occurrence of an actual behaviour, or the thoughts that accompany the behaviour as it occurs. In this respect, self-monitoring is a direct measure of the angry response and is distinct from self-report measures of aggression which involve the report of behaviours that occurred at some earlier time. Of interest is the rapidly developing use of self-statement tests to monitor the cognitions that accompany anger or aggressive outbursts.

Parent and teacher measures

A variety of parent and teacher rating scales and checklists (see Webster-Stratton and Herbert, 1994) have been used in the assessment of (inter alia) conduct problems in children. Among the more frequently used are the following:

Child Behaviour Checklist (CBCL)

The parent form of CBCL (Achenbach and Edelbrock, 1983) consists of 20 social competence items and 118 behaviour problems. Sample items include: cruelty, bullying or meanness to others; argues a lot; sets fires. Parents are asked to report the occurrence of these items generally over the previous six months. It has been shown to discriminate clinic-referred from non-referred children. The items constitute multiple behaviour-problem scales derived separately from boys and girls in different age groups. The scales form two broad-band groupings in all sex/age groups: Externalizing Behaviour (aggressive, antisocial, and undercontrolled) and Internalizing Behaviour (fearful, inhibited, overcontrolled). The Social Competence score and the Externalizing,

Internalizing and Total Behaviour Problem scores are of primary relevance to treatment. The CBCL has established norms; intraclass correlations were 0.98 for interparent agreement and 0.84 for test–retest reliability.

Eyberg Child Behaviour Inventory (ECBI)

The ECBI (Robinson, Eyberg and Ross, 1980) is one of the more well-investigated measures of conduct problems. It is a 36-item behavioural inventory of child conduct problem behaviour of 2–16-year-old children. The response format yields two scores: a total problem score, which indicates the total number of behaviour problems parents are concerned about, and an intensity score which indicates the frequency or intensity with which conduct problems occur. Sample items include: verbally fighting with friends, refusing to do chores when asked, destroying objects, yelling or screaming. Most of the items reflect oppositional behaviours rather than serious antisocial behaviours.

The Revised Behaviour Problem Checklist (Quay and Peterson, 1983)

This consists of 89 problem behaviours that are also rated on a three-point scale ranging from 'not a problem' to 'mild problem' to 'severe problem'. Factor analysis of the scale yields the following six dimensions: conduct problem, socialized aggression, attention problem-immaturity, anxiety-withdrawal, psychotic behaviour and motor excess. Like the CBCL the Problem Behaviour Checklist is a reliable and valid tool with which to assess significant-other reports of children's aggressive behaviour and its relationship to other deviant behaviour.

Rutter Behaviour Rating Scales (Rutter, 1967)

The parent and teacher versions of the Rutter scales (for children aged 3 to 10) have been standardized in the UK and possess sound test–retest and interjudge reliability; their validity has also been confirmed in many studies. They generate scores which, above a certain criterion, indicate conduct or emotional disorder.

A recent review of the tests has been published by Elander and Rutter (1996).

Behavioural observations

The most direct way to assess fearful and anxious behaviours in children and adults is to observe these behaviours in the situation in which they occur (see Chapter 6). In behavioural observation systems, specific behaviours indicative of aggression are defined, observed, and recorded. These systems are highly individualized and tailored to the measurement of specific phobias. For example, Patterson (1982) has detailed a set of operationally defined behaviours reflective of aggressive, coercive activities.

It is important to obtain assessments from the teachers' perspective because teachers have the unique advantage of comparing the children against a large background of many other children and can provide valuable information about children's peer relationships, social skills, and academic success or failure. Their perspective of comparing the child to his/her peers is a perspective usually not available to parents. They also observe children for long periods of time during structured and unstructured activities as well as academic, social and recreational settings. In addition, teacher assessments provide us with the knowledge as to whether the child's conduct problems have spread from the home to the school, across settings.

Behar Preschool Questionnaire (BPQ)

The BPQ (Behar, 1977) includes 30 items, each rated on a 0–2 point scale, and is completed by teachers of children aged 3–6 years. Test–retest reliabilities have ranged from 0.60 to 0.99. Factor analyses have yielded three subscales (Hostile–Aggressive, Anxious–Fearful, and Hyperactive–Distractible). In addition, there is a Total Behaviour Problem Scale which reflects a summary score of all three subscales. Of these scales the Total Behaviour Problem Scale is of most importance because it samples a broad range of conduct problems.

A resource pack of checklists and proforma for assessing problematic (e.g. violent) behaviours and attitudes in children *and* their caregivers has been published by one of the authors (Herbert, 1992).

THE 'WHY' QUESTIONS: THE FORMULATION

It is useful, in a *formulation*—the putting forward of hypotheses to explain personal and social problems—to draw a distinction between proximal and distal, direct and indirect causal influences. These are illustrated below:

Direct Causal Influences

Proximal (current) influences are direct in their effects and close in time to the actions they influence. They are *functionally* related to behaviour and can thus—as hypotheses about causation—be tested directly in behavioural casework using single case experimental designs. The relative temporal relationships of the elements can be specified in ABC terms (see page 161).

The formulation is directed towards the precise identification of the antecedent, outcome and symbolic conditions which control the maladaptive behaviour or undesirable interactions. Target problems, so-called, are chosen for analysis and intervention because of their hypothesized significance as undesirable features in the child's (possibly the parent's) repertoire, or in their relationships. The functional relationship would be formulated in hypothetical form. Thus an assessment and formulation might indicate particular *antecedent conditions* which directly *elicit* or *signal the reinforcing potential* of (say) aggressive actions.

In practice, a child (or caregiver) who indulges in frequent and/or intense aggressive actions would be observed in order to determine the specific circumstances and conditions in which the violence is manifested. Such conditions may involve antecedent organismic and/or environmental stimulus events (A) which actually *precipitate* or *set the stage* (discriminative stimuli) for the aggressive outbursts (B) and the consequent events (C) that are generated by them and indeed, maintain them through their reinforcement value (see page 52). Other conditions involve some lack of appropriate stimulus control over the individual's behaviour:

(a) *Inappropriate stimulus control of behaviour:* a situation in which a normally neutral stimulus configuration (e.g. constructive/ helpful comment) acquires the capability of eliciting a dysfunctional response like verbal abuse. This might arise—in part—from a history of denigration and unremitting criticism which has the effect of *conditioning* anger to *any* verbal comment.

(b) *Defective stimulus control over behaviour:* this indicates the inability of a stimulus (say friendliness), normally associated with a pattern of behaviour (reciprocated friendliness), to cue this pattern in a person. An example might be the child who reacts invariably to imagined 'provocation' from friendly peers by acts of aggression.

This pattern of defective control in children might stem from the experience of *laissez faire* parenting: extreme permissiveness, or lack of clear and consistent disciplinary outcomes to actions.

Any of these inappropriate forms of antecedent control might be operating through the person's symbolic processing, rather than via his or her external environment. In the case of what are referred to as 'aversive self-reinforcing systems' the person sets high standards in evaluating himself/herself, thus leading to continued self-depreciation and criticism rather than self-approval. Such punitive cognitions may have originated from an early history in which the individual was unremittingly criticized and thus taught rigidly stern standards of self-appraisal. An example might be frustrated, unhappy children who lash out to cover their lack of self-confidence and self-esteem. They operate on the principle 'attack is the best means of defence'.

A formulation might also reveal:

(c) *Defective incentive systems* which are characterized by the failure of reinforcers, normally capable of acting as incentives, to influence an individual. Defective incentive systems are to be seen in the aloof and isolated parent, the person who is indifferent to affection, achievement and learning. Inappropriate incentive systems are to be found in some violent delinquents. These developments may have their origins in gross hostility and rejection (emotional and physical abuse) in the early reinforcement history of the individual (Iwaniec, Herbert and McNeish, 1985a).

(d) *Behavioural deficits* are observable in the absence of skills normally expected in a child of a particular age, or indeed, the parent. These could also be an impairment in the child's (or caregiver's) problem-solving capability. These deficits stem, sometimes, from physical and/or intellectual disability, the absence of appropriate parental models, the suppression of prosocial behaviour through punitive attitudes, or the lack of encouragement of social and problem-solving skills. Aggression may substitute for a lack of social skills in some children—a way of ensuring attention and other 'pay-offs' (Herbert, 1987a).

(e) *Cognitive distortions.* Cognitively orientated practitioners accept as primary data the phenomenology of problems. These might include verbal reports of *internal* cognitive states, such as the parent's descriptions of his or her feelings of helplessness or temptations to hurt the child. An example of a cognitive approach is Ellis's (1982) RET (Rational Emotive Therapy) with its notion that certain core irrational ideas are at the root of much emotional disturbance, and that such dysfunctional cognitions can be altered. The basic ABC paradigm becomes ABC-DE in the RET model: antecedents, beliefs, consequences; disputation and effect— the last two referring to the intervention.

Historical (Distal) Influences

These are factors removed (or distant) in time from the current life-situation, but significant as predisposing causes, e.g. early learning, traumatic experiences and so on. Such influences obviously cannot be modified or manipulated directly. An analysis of these factors is not necessarily a condition of successful interventions. It is not possible to reverse history, nevertheless when people bring their past into the present through the attitudes and attributions they have learned, they *can* be 'liberated' from their negative influence by cognitive restructuring and therapeutic conversations.

THE 'HOW' QUESTION

How do I help my client? This brings us the question about choice of interventions. The behavioural approach is particularly well suited to the kind of aggressive problems we have been discussing. Some of the most effective behavioural methods, especially those applied to adults who physically abuse, were described in Chapter 6. Most of the early behavioural work on specific items of children's problematic behaviour such as non-compliance and aggression concentrated on the consequence side of the ABC equation (see page 161) modifying (inter alia) the parent's usual responses to the child's opposition or aggression by means of training them to employ (inter alia) time-out from positive reinforcement and differential attention. There have been reports of successful interventions along these lines as we shall see.

Antecedent Control

On the antecedent side of the equation there are several strategies that are useful in reducing aggressive behaviour:

Reducing aversive stimuli

Violent reactions whether by children or adults may be triggered by a large variety of aversive stimuli: it is reasonable to expect that a reduction of such aversive stimuli might be accompanied by a decrease in aggression. One technique is to resolve conflicts before they flare up into violence. Another is to defuse aversive stimuli by diminishing their power to arouse anger in the child. This can be achieved by using humour, by cognitive restructuring (reframing 'provocative' stimuli), or by using desensitization procedures.

Stimulus change: reducing discriminative stimuli for aggression

Certain stimulus conditions provide signals to the child that aggressive behaviour is likely to have rewarding consequences.

A careful situational assessment and training discussions are planned to reduce discriminative stimuli for such aggression.

Desensitization

There is a choice of three procedures which have been designed to reduce anger: systematic desensitization, desensitization with cognitive relaxation and desensitization in the absence of relaxation training.

Systematic desensitization has typically involved imaginal representation of the fear or anger-producing stimuli and has employed muscular relaxation as the competing, inhibiting response. Although these procedures appear to work reasonably well with adolescents and older children, younger children appear to have difficulty in acquiring the muscular relaxation response and in being able to image clearly the fear-producing stimuli (see Herbert, 1987b, 1994). As a result, in vivo desensitization and emotive imagery have become increasingly popular, at least with younger children. Although mainly designed for fear-provoking situations these approaches can be adapted to anger-eliciting circumstances.

Settling differences (conflict resolution)

There are two broad approaches to conflict resolution: (a) arbitration or mediation of specific conflicts, and (b) modification of communication processes (see Herbert, 1987a). Behavioural contracting is the most common example of the negotiation and arbitration approach; it involves the worker in the role of a mediator or arbitrator who facilitates discussions to seek compromises and mutual agreements between opposing parties. Contracts about reciprocal exchanges of specific behaviours and reinforcers can be drawn up to enhance the likelihood of a positive outcome (see Chapters 3 and 7).

Reducing the exposure to aggressive models

Exposure to other people behaving aggressively may facilitate the imitation of such behaviour by the observer. An attempt to reduce the exposure of children to such models (e.g. aggressive peers) is likely to decrease the likelihood of their behaving similarly.

Providing models for non-aggressive behaviour

Acceptable alternatives to aggression may be demonstrated by exposing youngsters to influential children or adolescents who tend to manifest non-aggressive behaviours, especially when they are instrumental in obtaining favourable outcomes for the 'models'.

Cognitive change with regard to antecedent events

The instigation of aggression may be influenced by antecedent cognitive events such as aversive thoughts (e.g. remembering a past grudge), or being incapable of solving problems mentally instead of 'lashing out' reflexly. The child's or adolescent's search for various possible courses of action in the fact of provocation and frustration can be made more flexible by attention to the thinking processes that precede, accompany and follow violent actions. A skill that hostile children sometimes lack is the ability to identify and label the precursors (physiological, affective and cognitive) to an aggressive outburst, so that they can bring into play more adaptive solutions to their problems.

Self-instruction (self-talk)

Self-instruction training—the development of children's skills in guiding their own performance by the use of self-suggestion, comments, praise and other directions—has proved invaluable with hyperactive, aggressive (impulsive) children (Meichenbaum and Goodman, 1971; Schneider, 1973). More cognitively orientated methods have proved useful with older children and adolescents, e.g. self-control training (assertion and relaxation training, role-play, behaviour rehearsal (Herbert, 1991, 1994).

Outcome Control

Sanctions

Aversive consequences (penalties and punishments) are another contemporary influence on the performance of aggressive behaviour and a contentious issue in any intervention repertoire. In general, punishment tends to decrease aggression but the effects are complex and often paradoxical. Patterson (1982) is unequivocal on this subject. He concludes that the findings from studies analysing punishment have direct relevance to the treatment of families with antisocial children.

Parents of non-aggressive children tend to ignore most coercive child behaviours of a relatively minor kind. As a result, the episodes tend to be of short duration. When they wish to, these parents are able to use punishment to halt or suppress these behaviours. By contrast parents of antisocial children *ignore less* and *nag or natter more*. Not only are they unable to stop coercive behaviours, but their nattering actually contributes directly to extended coercive episodes.

After years of treating samples of extremely difficult, delinquent and abused children, Patterson and his colleagues are convinced that training parents to use a *non-violent* form of punishment like time-out is a *necessary component* of successful intervention. At the *Centre for Behavioural Work with Families*, our findings confirm Patterson's conclusions (Sutton, 1988).

Patterson (1982) admits frankly that this position was reluctantly accepted, it was certainly not in keeping with his earlier views on punishment (e.g. Patterson, 1965). Previously it was thought that positive reinforcement of pro-social responses that competed with the deviant responses would serve as the rationale for the intervention. However, clinical experience quickly underscored the fact that this was not the case. The studies showed that extinction, per se, was not successful even when combined with reinforcement of competing responses. (For a discussion of the myths and misunderstandings about 'discipline' see Herbert, 1989a.)

Modifying self-perceptions/reinforcers

Given the low self-esteem and under-achievement commonly found in aggressive, conduct-disordered youngsters, it is worth bearing in mind potent sources of reinforcement for aggressive behaviour—the aggressors themselves. To some extent, children regulate their actions by self-produced consequences. They tend to repeat behaviour which has given them feelings of satisfaction and worth. Conversely, they tend to refrain from behaviours that cause them mental pain or anguish.

Differential reinforcement

There is sound evidence that procedures based on reduction of reinforcement identified as maintaining aggressive behaviour, can reduce its frequency and/or intensity. In some studies, aggressive behaviour is consistently ignored; in others it is ignored while a competing pattern of pro-social conduct is rewarded. We have seen that differential attention alone is not always effective; in such cases not only should pro-social behaviour be positively reinforced, but aggression specifically punished by psychological as opposed to physical methods (Patterson, 1982).

Planned ignoring, time-out and response cost have been systematically applied in programmes designed to provide stimulus conditions which signal to the child that his or her aggressive behaviour will not only fail to have rewarding consequences but, indeed, will result in punitive consequences. The provision of such discriminative stimuli brings aggression under control while more acceptable alternative behaviour is being encouraged (Herbert, 1987a).

TO, or time-out from positive reinforcement to give it its full name, is a particularly potent aid to behavioural change and improvement in fiercely oppositional children (e.g. Day and Roberts, 1983; Roberts, Hatzenbuehler and Bean, 1981) and is particularly valuable in cases of child abuse when non-compliance is a major complaint by parents. It allows parent and child the opportunity to 'cool down' and it tends to have face-validity for those parents (during the early stages of a programme) who demonstrate a punitive ideology of child-rearing and who find it difficult to engage in the positive aspects (so vital) of finding opportunities to encourage and praise their offspring. The essentially punitive quality of TO gives it credibility for parents who have not yet moved on, in treatment, from an authoritarian view of discipline and either ineffectual verbal complaints (nattering) or self-defeating and child-abusive power-assertive practices to more realistic attributions and effective methods. It is not simply an ethical matter to counterbalance TO with positive attention (play, praise, additional contact), it is also good practice. The best outcomes are obtained when *both* praise and time-out are employed (Herbert, 1987b).

A BROADLY CONCEIVED APPROACH

The training described above was limited to specific techniques for dealing with the presenting problems rather than a broader framework of discussion, debate, role-play and teaching of life-skills (e.g. communication) and general principles which provides the curriculum for contemporary behavioural family therapy (see Herbert, 1995) or behavioural parent training (BPT) programmes (see Webster-Stratton and Herbert, 1994).

The therapeutic process which we use in group and individual family settings is one of the therapist collaborating with parents in multiple roles so that parents can gradually gain knowledge, control and competence to effectively cope with the stresses of having an aggressive, conduct-disordered child. The script for the therapy evolves around collaborating with parents to help them learn more effective coping strategies and parenting skills so that ultimately the child's antisocial problems are reduced and his/her pro-social behaviour increased. Several themes emerge throughout the therapy process as part of this coping model.

The Script for Parents: Learning to Cope more Effectively

(Webster-Stratton and Herbert, 1993)

Promoting parents' problem solving

Problem solving and collaboration between the therapist and parent go hand in hand throughout the sessions. Often we find that parents have initially come to us with the belief that there is a single cause for the child's aggression and consequently a single solution for the problem. By the end of the programme the goal is for parents to come to realize there is no single, simple prescription, no panacea for parenting. Rather, parents have to become confident in their own ability to think sequentially and analyse parent–child interactions, to search for external causes of misbehaviour (as opposed to scapegoating the child for the sole ownership of his/her badness) and to generate a well-stocked 'menu' of possible solutions. They then have the problem-solving strategies necessary to sort out which solutions they will try and to evaluate whether or not these solutions are working.

Parents coming to terms

Parents are helped to come to terms with the realistic facts concerning the temperamental nature of their child. This means helping parents to manage their anger (and grief) related to their dashed hope for an 'ideal' (or at least a normal) child. It also means learning to accept their child's difficulties.

Because many of these children's problems are to some degree, chronic, characterized by unpredictable relapses, constant vulnerability to changes in routine, and the emergence of new problems whenever the child faces new settings, parents have to be helped to face the fact that they must invest a great deal of time and energy in the hard work of anticipating, monitoring and problem solving for many years to come.

The therapist can prepare parents for this, partly by helping them focus on long-term rather than short-term goals. For example, one common mistake is for parents to go for short-term pay-offs (i.e. giving into the child's tantrum to stop worse aggressive behaviours) at the expense of long-term consequences (the child learns to have tantrums to get what he or she wants). Parents need to be reminded of their long-term goals. In the long term, punitive physical approaches are likely to teach a child to hit or yell when frustrated, thereby fostering more aggression. We emphasize that the strategies taught in our programme, such as play, praise and patient problem solving, need to be repeated hundreds of times for them to be effective.

It is sometimes useful to depict the environment provided by parents for these children as a sort of 'prosthetic environment' of parent reinforcement, attention, discipline and monitoring for a persistent problem. As with the diabetic child, if parents withdraw the treatment there is a return to 'symptoms'.

Parents gaining empathy for the child

It is important to help parents gain understanding, empathy and acceptance of their child's unique personality as well as sensitivity to the child's efforts to master particular developmental tasks. It is especially hard for parents of 'difficult' and demanding children to remain patient, to constantly be 'on guard' for monitoring and to consistently limit-set. Parents can do this more easily and can be more supportive if the therapist has helped them to understand that some of the child's oppositional behaviours are really needs for independence or needs to test the security of their environment. Parents can also learn to reduce some of their unnecessary commands and criticisms if they have been helped to understand that children need the opportunity to learn from their own mistakes.

Parents aren't perfect

Coping effectively implies not only coming to accept and understand their child's strengths and difficulties, but also their own imperfections as parents. The therapist helps parents learn to stop belittling and berating themselves for their 'mistakes' and 'inadequacies'.

EFFECT OF WITNESSING OR EXPERIENCING VIOLENCE

As indicated in Chapter 11, children who witness violence suffer from a number of effects (Lynch and Roberts, 1992; Carroll, 1994). Such experiences teach aggressive styles of conduct, increase arousal to aggressive situations, reduce aggressive restraint, distort views about conflict resolution and desensitize them to violent behaviour. It is therefore not surprising to find that 29% of single mothers in the USA are hit by their teenage children (Livingstone, 1986), perhaps as a way of controlling the parent or punishing her for being divorced. Harbin and Madden (1989) identified four ways in which parents would deny the existence of the violent behaviour of their children.

1. Avoidance of confrontation or discussion of the violent action.
2. Attempt by all the members of the family to minimize the seriousness of the violent behaviour.
3. Avoidance of punishment or inconsistent responses to inappropriate aggression.
4. Refusal to ask for outside help either for themselves or for their child.

Perhaps the reluctance to accept that parental abuse by children occurs is partly because the less powerful are taking on the more powerful (Charles, 1986). However, not all children remain in a violent home.

Runaways

During 1988, it was estimated by The Children's Society that there were 98 000 reported incidents of young persons under 18 years of age going missing in the UK (Newman, 1989). More recently, Abrahams and Mungall (1992) have claimed that 43 000 children under 18 run away every year and account for an annual total 102 000 reported runaway incidents in England and Scotland alone. Additional research carried out by The Children's Society in Leeds suggested that one in seven under 16 year olds run away for at least one night and approximately 2% of these young people ran away 10 times or more from home or a care setting (Rees, 1993). It is claimed that many of these runaway incidents involve issues around family violence and child abuse (Stein, Rees and Frost, 1994).

In the USA it is claimed that 1 out of every 8 adolescents between the ages of 12 and 18 run away at least once from home (Young et al., 1983). If 'runaway' is defined as 'children who leave home without permission and stay away overnight or longer' then as many as one in five run away from home, with girls leaving home for longer periods than boys (Cairns and Cairns, 1994). What is certain is that many young people are at risk in their homes as well as on the streets, with as many as 78% of those in shelters reporting that physical and/or sexual abuse is the primary reason for leaving home and running away (Farber et al., 1984; Stiffman, 1989). In other studies of adolescent runaways, 73% of the girls and 38% of the boys report being sexually abused (McCormack, Janus and Burgess, 1986) and 44% of runaways report being physically abused (Stiffman, 1989).

In fact, three-quarters of adolescents running away from home are attempting to escape and 'retreat' from family conflict and violence in the home and/or significant problems at school such as peer pressure and bullying (Nye, 1980; Straus, 1994). Some researchers claim that 40–50% of runaways are escaping from severe sexual and physical violence or emotional neglect (Adams and Gulotta, 1983). This group of vulnerable children and adolescents have been termed 'endangered' runners (Roberts, 1982), 'terrified' runners (Greene and Esselstyn, 1972), 'victim' runners (Miller et al., 1980), or just 'push-outs', 'exiles', 'castaways' and 'throwaways' (Nye, 1980; Janus et al., 1987; White, 1989). Nevertheless, a significant minority of runaways are 'social pleasure seekers', 'explorers' or 'manipulators' (Roberts, 1982; Lappin and Covelman, 1985) who place themselves at the unnecessary risk of becoming victims and/or offenders in crime.

Young people with a history of adverse experiences in childhood are especially vulnerable to further revictimization and are more likely to commit offences in an attempt to control their environment and maintain a life outside society, living on the street. For example, research has shown that 1 in 5 sexually abused boys go on to sexually offend against others by the time they are teenagers (Watkins and Bentovim, 1992; Browne, 1994) and that, during their teenage years, 1 in 6 physically abused children go on to assault others violently (Widom, 1989a, 1989b, 1989c; Browne, 1993).

Straus (1994) claims that after one month, 50% of runaway children resort to prostitution, stealing, drug dealing or other crime to support themselves. Pessimistically she proposes that children who have spent more than six months on the street are nearly impossible to rescue by promoting interest in continuing education, looking for employment, working on family problems and giving up drugs.

Counting the number of adolescents on the street and the number of associated criminal acts at any given time is an impossible task as many return home temporarily to run away again, as they see the problems of street life preferable to the problems within the family home. Without intervention these young people will join the swelling ranks of homeless adolescents that may resort to crime in order to maintain an existence divorced from society. The number of children in such circumstances is estimated at one million in the USA (Dryfoos, 1990) and 90 000 in the UK (Children's Society Central London Teenage Project 'Safe House').

It has been recognized for some time that a safe temporary place was needed for young people often fleeing from abusive, uncaring parents and broken relationships, or alternatively from the stress of foster families and care placements. These children feel rejected and thrown away by society, making them more likely to commit criminal acts to feel in power and control. To date projects run by the Children's Society, Barnardos and Centrepoint have found it difficult to work with alienated children and young people who assume a 'don't come near me' attitude to survive. Those that are 'apprehended' may be returned home without any serious attempt to address the issues leading the young persons to place themselves at risk on the street and of becoming involved in criminal activity. Indeed, a recent study of 202 sexually abused children in London (Prior, Lynch and Glaser, 1994) showed that 37% received no therapy, yet all these children had described contact abuse and there was a professional consensus that the abuse had occurred. Therefore, this book concludes by considering the costs of domestic violence to victims in terms of physical and psychological well-being.

CONCLUSION The cost of domestic violence

The costs of family violence to the individual and society as a whole are immense. Gelles (1987b) reports figures from a national crime survey in the USA and estimates that 192 000 incidences of family violence resulted in:

- 21 000 hospitalizations
- 99 800 days in hospital
- 28 700 emergency department visits
- 39 000 physician visits

For the individuals concerned the economic costs were 175 500 lost days from paid work; with regard to the economy of society as a whole, $44 million were spent in direct medical costs in order to provide the necessary services to victims of family violence. Thus, it is possible to justify putting resources into the prevention of family violence, not only from a philanthropic viewpoint but also from an economic one. Furthermore, the notion that a variety of negative life experiences or 'life events' may adversely affect psychological well-being and precipitate psychiatric disorder is well established (Andrews and Brown, 1988) and there are many papers on the impact of child abuse on adult mental health (e.g. Davenport, Browne and Palmer, 1994; Briere, 1992). A summary of their conclusions is presented in Figure 11.5 (see Chapter 11). The cost of psychiatric morbidity is immense. Croft-Jeffreys and Wilkinson (1985) estimated that 'conspicuous minor mental disorder' seen in primary care and out-patient settings cost the British Government £404 million annually, 10 years ago. Most of these patients (90%) present with depression and anxiety, and given the cost and extent of psychological disorder, a preventative approach has received less attention than would be expected. If policing and social services are taken into account, the cost of family violence runs into billions of dollars or pounds (Muller, 1994). In parallel to this, social policies in the UK between 1979 and 1991 have resulted in increasing disparities in health and wealth (Smith and Egger, 1993). Inequalities in income have grown dramatically with 24% of the population now living on less than 50% of the average income (Department of Social Security, 1993).

Households receiving the lowest 10% of income have suffered a 14% loss between 1979 and 1991, while higher earning households have benefited to as much as 20% (Smith and Egger, 1993). This has mainly been a function of tax cuts and shifts from direct to indirect taxation, with the poorest 10% £1 a week worse off and the richest 10% £87 per week better off (Oppenheim, 1993). Together with increased unemployment, highly associated with family violence (see Krugman, 1986), it is not surprising that the incidence of family violence and child abuse is increasing. Of course, 'structural stress' associated with the family's situation—such as poverty, unemployment and social isolation—are just part of the picture, as Chapter 2 outlined. There are many stressors that may trigger family violence which may be characteristics of the offender or the victim (see Chapter 4). Stress has been emphasized at the individual level by psychologists and at the social level by sociologists. However, the integration of both approaches and intervention aimed at family relationships offer the most promising solution (see Figure C.1).

FAMILIES COPING WITH STRESS

Families under stress should be encouraged to recognize and value the factors in the home that compensate for and buffer stress, such positive and supportive relationships. Communication of worries and problem solving as a family often promotes coping strategies and self-esteem. Families can learn to engage their problems by active measures rather than avoiding the problem and disengaging from each other (see Figure C.2). In this way intervention aimed at the family level can 'inoculate' family members against acute crises and enhance their management and tolerance for stress. The Family Homes and Domestic Violence Bill (1996) in Britain will give further powers to exclude

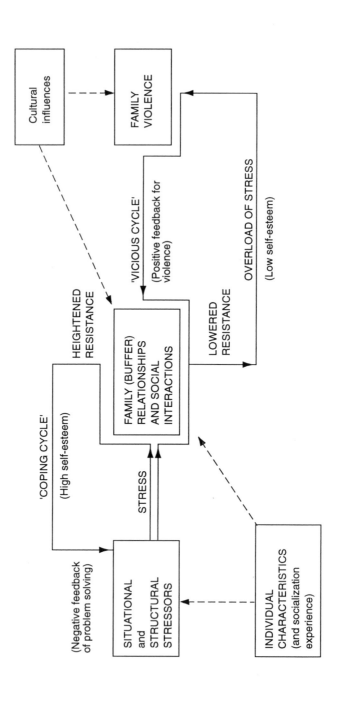

Figure C.1 The causation of family violence (from Browne, 1989c)

the violent offender from the home (rather than the victim) if an improvement in family interaction cannot be achieved.

Successful prevention is dependent on the way the problem of family violence is approached. All too often, statutory services are only concerned with the situational and structural stresses facing a violent family, instead of helping with social relationship problems within the family. It seems that the social and health services in Great Britain work on the basis of damage limitation, trying to control the situation of family violence in the short term rather than offering help with personal relationships to prevent family violence in the long term.

Policies and practice need to be concerned with primary prevention—that is, intervention strategies which change the fundamental situation for most families, such as education for parents and teenagers and reducing poverty and isolation (Parton, 1985; Howitt, 1992).

The British government has acknowledged the need for much more preventive work with families (White Paper: *The Law of Child Care and Family Services*, 1987, Cm 62). As a result of these recommendations, there are numerous provisions in the Children Act 1989, which was implemented on 14 October 1991, intended to ensure that local authorities address this need.

The Children Act 1989 (schedule 2, paragraph 4(1)) imposes a duty on all local authorities to take reasonable steps through the provision of services to prevent children suffering from 'Significant Harm' (see Figure C.3). The Act also imposes a duty on local authorities to provide a wide range of services to all families of 'children in need' and a definition of 'in need' is also supplied. Clearly, local authorities may find difficulty in meeting these needs without additional funding.

Policies and practice must also be concerned with secondary prevention, where high-risk families are identified, and offered help and resources (such as nursery placements, adequate housing, support groups) before the violence starts. Most of the time, families are offered help and resources only after abuse or neglect has taken place and, sometimes, only when it involves a child. Such tertiary prevention or treatment is too late if the

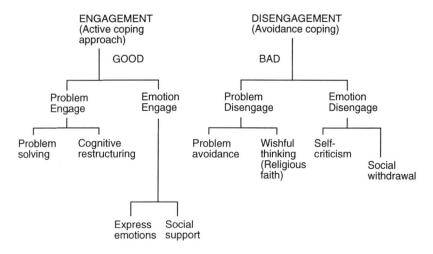

Figure C.2   Coping (adapted from Tobin et al., 1989)

child has already witnessed violence in the family or become a victim of violence. In terms of promoting an intergenerational cycle of family violence, you simply wait for the child to be abused before you intervene. Indeed, intervention at this stage offers minimal help as evidence shows that, after tertiary prevention, families have a high rate of re-abuse (Hamilton and Browne, 1997). For persistently violent families, the prognosis for the child is separation, foster care and possible adoption. Might this have been avoided with primary or secondary preventions?

In a book called *Long-term Foster Care*, Rowe et al. (1984) report what happened to children after they were taken into long-term care. They concluded that being fostered by relatives was by far the best hope for these children. However, it was disturbing that their follow-up report showed that only 10% of children in long-term foster care were actively reconsidered for rehabilitation with their family (p. 50, op. cit.). Once taken into long-term care, 90% of the children remain separated from their family for the rest of their childhood and few receive any therapy for their experience. The Children Act 1989 attempts to address this much criticized feature of practice. It imposes on the local authority the duty to maintain links between children (cared for away from

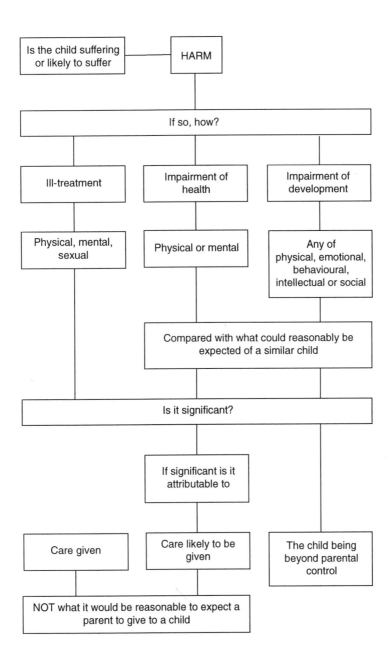

Figure C.3 Significant harm (from White, 1991)

home) and their natural parents with a presumption in favour of rehabilitation. Witnessing the results of these significant changes must be encouraged and evaluations carried out.

After reading this book, *Preventing Family Violence*, there should be no doubt that the prevention of violence in the family, in general, begins with the prevention of child abuse and neglect.

PREVENTION STARTS WITH PARENTS

In the past 20 years there has been much debate about what services can be delivered in order to minimize the maltreatment of children. This debate has been limited by a poor understanding of intervention strategies for child abuse and neglect and what constitutes a desirable outcome. Reviews on the causes of maltreatment (see Browne, 1988) have emphasized a growing recognition that child abuse and neglect are products of a poor parent–child relationship. This interactive perspective places less emphasis on individual problems of the parents. Therefore, interventions that strengthen the parent–child relationship are considered to be more promising for prevention than those aimed at parental psychopathology (Wolfe, 1991).

Wolfe (1993) observes that there have been promising developments in early interventions which address parental competency and family support in order to promote more positive parental knowledge, attitudes, skills and behaviour. He claims that personalized programmes such as home visits over a period of 1 to 3 years stand out as the most successful interventions in achieving desired outcomes in terms of fewer child injuries, emergency room visits and reports to protective agencies.

A number of countries in the world have statutory government sponsored home visitation schemes, usually using health professionals such as community nurses. Most of these schemes were set up with the aim of preventing ill health in families with young children and reducing the rates of morbidity and mortality in young children. It has been emphasized in the United Kingdom (e.g. Browne, 1989b, 1995b) that community nursing services such as 'Health Visiting' could be used to prevent child abuse and neglect at a primary and secondary level through the promotion of positive parenting. Indeed, follow-up research by

Gibbons et al. (1995) showed that parent–child interactions were the most significant factor for those children showing present poor functioning. Thus, the Department of Health Research Programme on Child Protection (Department of Health, 1995b) concludes that an effective system of child protection needs to be complemented and balanced by well-targeted family support services. However, few countries have systematically used home visitation practices in this way and even fewer have evaluated the effectiveness of home visits on the incidence and prevalence of child maltreatment. An exception has been the work of David Olds and his colleagues in the USA. They have shown that 'Nurse Home Visitation Schemes' (a) have lasting effects in the promotion of positive qualities of parenting (Olds, Henderson and Kitzman, 1994); (b) improve the development of socially dis-advantaged mothers and their children (Olds et al, 1988); and (c) save on government spending in relation to these families both in the short and long term (Olds et al., 1993).

Despite this knowledge, health visitor staffing levels in England have been falling steadily from 1988 to 1994. Hence, caseloads of 0–4-year-old children have risen by 22%. The aver-age caseload of children in this 0–4 age group is now estimated to be approximately 400 per health visitor. In the last four years, the number of families contacted per health visitor also have risen by 13.5%, while at the same time there has been a 4.2% drop in staffing levels (Health Visitors' Association, 1994). This is 'cause for concern' when the majority of children who require protection are under 5 years of age, with 5 in every 1000 children in this age group currently listed on Child Protection Registers (Browne, 1995d). Indeed, it is this age group which has the highest number of deaths from non-accidental injury (Creighton, 1995). Therefore, limitations in resources have made it essential for health visitors to prioritize families on the basis of need. Hence, health visitors use a variety of decision-making methods to identify and target 'at-risk' families.

THE RISK APPROACH

As stated in Chapter 6, the risk approach to child protection can be seen as a tool for the flexible and rational distribution of scarce resources and their maximal utilization. This is based on the assessment of children and their families as high or low risk for child abuse and neglect. The aim of the risk strategy is to give special attention to those in the greatest need of help in parenting before physical or psychological damage to the child occurs.

The surveillance and monitoring of child health, growth and development is regarded as good practice throughout the Western world (Hall, 1995). However, there is a paucity of research into the specific components and methods used in various screening and assessment programmes.

Screening and assessment programmes have to be sensitive to the needs of parents as well as children. Parents expect to be consulted about and participate in decisions that involve their children (Hall, 1995). The recommendations laid down in the Children Act 1989, the 'Patient's Charter' and the United Nation's Convention on the Rights of the Child, all reflect a move towards parent participation (Cleaver and Freeman, 1995), and the Department of Health (1995b) have recently issued 15 essential principles for working in partnership with parents on child protection issues. Nevertheless, it is difficult to introduce the concept of child protection in Parent Held Records due to the sensitive nature of the topic (see Armstrong-Esther et al., 1987).

The joint evaluation of a child's need for protection requires a personal (home visit) approach with parents, involving experienced health professionals, who are in regular contact with families and where there is no stigma attached to the home visit.

SCREENING EFFECTIVENESS

The relatively low prevalence of child abuse and neglect in the population as a whole, combined with even the most optimistic estimates of screening effectiveness, implies that a screening programme would yield large numbers of false positives. Indeed, this has been shown to be the case by Browne and Saqi (1988a) who retrospectively evaluated a typical health visitor 'checklist' of risk factors, completed on just one occasion. The checklist detection rate of 82% of cases compared to 12% false alarms within the population suggested that for every 10 000 births screened it would be necessary to distinguish between 33 true risk cases and 1195 false alarms. Hence, this research has often been quoted to emphasize the futility of attempts at early prediction (e.g. Howitt, 1992). Equally, however, this research could indicate the requirement for a 'second' screening procedure. Assessments could be carried out jointly with parents, based on the significant differences found in parent–child interaction studies (Browne, 1986). Thus, a second screening could possibly distinguish true child protection cases from false positives, by the use of behavioural indicators such as infant attachment to the parent and parental sensitivity and expectations (see Chapter 6).

It must be pointed out, however, that the use of health visitors in England for the prediction and prevention of child maltreatment remains controversial as it is seen to be the role of the social services. Hence, it is difficult to obtain funds from the Health Service Agencies to evaluate a primary health care approach to child protection.

Browne and Saqi (1988a) suggest that the behavioural responses of the parent and the infant to a researcher will be similar to their reactions to a community worker. Thus, the precise determination of behavioural characteristics of violent families is considered to be of value, to provide indicators that will help to recognize families needing extra support and help in parenting.

SCREENING FOR POTENTIAL CHILD ABUSERS

For social and background risk factors to be of use in the recognition and prediction of family violence they must be considered within the context of the family's interpersonal network and compensatory factors. Therefore, screening for child abuse should have at least three stages to eliminate false alarms.

1. All families with a newborn should been screened at the time of birth for stressful social and demographic risk factors of the child, the parent and the family. This will identify a target group for further screening. However, the remaining population cannot be considered immune to family stress and child abuse. Any change in family circumstances leading to increased stress should be assessed and, if applicable, the family added to the target group.

2. All parents in the target group should be screened 3 to 6 months after birth on their attitudes and perceptions of the child and those aspects of parenting and family life they consider to be stressful.
3. Approximately 9 to 12 months after birth, the infant's attachment to the primary caregiver or parent should be assessed, together with parental sensitivity to the infant's behaviour.

Those parents with risk factors who are under stress with negative perceptions about the child's behaviour need help with parenting. Those parents who, in addition, have a poor relationship with their child, as measured by the quality of attachment and their sensitivity to the child's behaviour, must be considered as a potential risk for child abuse and neglect and treatment for the family should immediately be offered before any aggressive incidents occur.

As stated in Chapter 1, for this approach to be reliable and to correctly classify families as high risk for child abuse with few false alarms, the process requires resources for each local community to (1) develop methods for detecting risk factors, (2) train health care workers in the sensitive use of these methods, and (3) provide intervention strategies to prevent or ameliorate undesired outcomes.

The above approach has recently been implemented in the Southend Community NHS Trust with an assessment of need and a child protection targeted service developed for Health Visitors and Public Health Nurses called the Child Assessment Rating and Evaluation (CARE) Programme (Browne, Hamilton and Ware, 1996). A pilot study of the programme (Ware and Browne, 1996) has revealed that the use of behavioural observations of parent–child interaction in conjunction with an Index of Need containing factors pertinent to psychosocial family development do indeed demonstrate those families that require a targeted service in order to minimize the risk of child abuse and neglect.

TOWARDS A CARING FUTURE!

Prevention needs to be aimed at any interaction or lack of interaction between a child and his or her caregiver which results in preventable harm to the child's physical and psychological development. The relevance of this family systems approach to sexual abuse is controversial. Nevertheless, many sexually abused children (approximately one-third) have been previously physically abused and even more emotionally abused (Finkelhor and Baron, 1986). Therefore, comprehensive approaches to the screening and prevention of emotional/physical abuse and neglect early in the child's life may also help prevent sexual abuse within the family and/or revictimization by others outside the family (Hamilton and Browne, 1997).

The book *Preventing Family Violence* has indicated that it is not sufficient to evaluate intervention on the basis of occurrence or non-occurrence of aggressive behaviour. Helping family members to inhibit violence towards each other and their dependants may still leave unchanged the emotionally harmful environment in which the initial abuse occurred. Therefore work on interpersonal relationships is essential if prevention of family violence is to be achieved both in this generation and the next.

The aim for all those involved in work with violent families must be the prevention of physical and sexual violence in the family. This means being available, with suitable resources, to help families with serious problems before violence, abuse and neglect occurs. Even for individuals who were maltreated as children, prognosis may be good with effective intervention and therapy.

Perhaps, in order to prevent family violence, child abuse and neglect, we have to first challenge the unrealistic expectations of service managers, politicians, policy makers and society in general of what limited resource can achieve. We must inform them of the consequences of underestimating the investment required in the prevention of family violence, child abuse and neglect for the next generation and future society.

REFERENCES

Abidin, R. (1990). *Manual of the Parenting Stress Index (PSI)* (3rd edn). Charlottsville, VA: University of Virginia, Pediatric Psychology Press.

Abraham, C. and Mungall, R. (1992). *Runaways: Exploding the Myths*, London: National Children's Home Action for Children.

Adams, G.R. and Gulotta, T.S. (1983). *Adolescent Life Experiences*, Monterey, CA: Brooks & Cole.

Achenbach, T.M. and Edelbrock, C.S. (1983). *Manual for the Child Behavior Checklist and Revised Child Behavior Profile*. Burlington, VT: University Associates in Psychiatry.

Adler, A. (1965). *Superiority and Social Interest*. London: Routledge & Kegan Paul.

Agnew, R. and Huguley, S. (1989). Adolescent violence towards parents. *Journal of Marriage and the Family*, 51(3): 699–711.

Ahmad, Y. and Smith, P.K. (1989). Bully/victim problems among schoolchildren. Poster presented at conference of the Developmental Section of the BPS, Guildford.

Ainsworth, M.D.S., Blehar, M.C. Waters, E. and Wall, S. (1978). *Patterns of Attachment: A Psychological Study of the Strange Situation*. Hillsdale, NJ: Lawrence Erlbaum.

Allison, J.A. and Wrightsman, L.S. (1993). *Rape: The Misunderstood Crime*. London: Sage.

Allport, G.W. (1961). *Patterns and Growth in Personality*. New York: Holt, Rinehart & Winston.

Altemeier, W.A., O'Conner, S., Vietze, P., Sandler, H. and Sherrod, K. (1984). Prediction of child abuse. A prospective study of feasibility. *Child Abuse and Neglect*, 8: 393–400.

Altemeier, W.A., Vietze, P.M., Sherrod, K.B., Sandler, H.M., Falsey, S. and O'Conner, S. (1979). Prediction of child maltreatment during pregnancy. *Journal of the American Academy of Child Psychiatry*, 18: 205–218.

Ammerman, R.T. (1993). Physical abuse and neglect. In T. Ollendick and M. Hersen (Eds), *Handbook of Child and Adolescent Assessment*. Boston, Allyn & Bacon, pp. 439–454.

Ammerman, R.T. and Hersen, M. (Eds) (1990). *Treatment of Family Violence*. New York: Wiley.

Ammerman, R.T. and Hersen, M. (Eds) (1992). *Assessment of Family Violence: A Clinical and Legal Sourcebook*. New York: Wiley.

Andrews, B. and Brown, G.W. (1988). Marital violence in the community: a biographical approach. *Journal of Psychiatry*, **153**: 305–312.

Anetzberger, G. (1987). *The Etiology of Elder Abuse by Adult Offspring*. Springfield: Thomas.

Anetzberger, G., Korbin, J.E. and Austin, C. (1994). Alcoholism and elder abuse. *Journal of Interpersonal Violence*, **9**(2): 184–193.

Ansello, E., King, D. and Taler, G. (1986). The environmental press model: a theoretical framework for intervention in elder abuse. In K. Pillemer and R. Wolf (Eds), *Elder Abuse: Conflict in the Family*. Dover: Auburn House, pp. 314–330.

Archer, J. (1988). *The Behavioural Biology of Aggression*. Cambridge: Cambridge University Press.

Archer, J. (ed.) (1994). *Male Violence*. London: Routledge.

Archer, J. and Browne, K.D. (1989). Concepts and approaches to the study of aggression. In J. Archer and K.D. Browne (Eds), *Human Aggression: Naturalistic Approaches*. London: Routledge, pp. 3–24.

Archer, J. and Ray, N. (1989). Dating violence in the United Kingdom: a preliminary study. *Aggressive Behaviour*, **15**: 337–343.

Armstrong-Esther, C.A. and Browne, K.D. (1986). The effect of mental impairment on nurse–patient interaction in the elderly. *Journal of Advanced Nursing*, **11**, 379–387.

Armstrong-Esther, C.A., Lacey, B., Sandilands, M. and Browne, K.D. (1987). Partnership in care. *Journal of Advanced Nursing*, **12**: 735–741.

Armstrong-Esther, C., Browne, K.D. and Esther, C. (1997). Is there a future for informal care in a changing society? *Ageing and Society* (in revision).

Arias, I., Samios, M. and O'Leary, K. (1987). Prevalence and correlates of physical aggression during courtship. *Journal of Interpersonal Violence*, **2**(1): 82–90.

Australian Institute of Health and Welfare (1995). *Child Abuse and Neglect, Australia 1992–93*. Child Welfare Series, No. 9, Canberra: AGPS.

Averill, J.R. (1983). Studies on anger and aggression. *American Psychologist*, **38**: 1145–1160.

Bagley, C. and McDonald, M. (1984). Adult mental health sequels of child sexual abuse, physical abuse and neglect in maternally separated children. *Canadian Journal of Community Mental Health*, **3**(1), Spring: 15–26.

Bagley, C., Rodberg, G., Wellings, D. and Moosa-Mitha, M. (1995). Sexual and physical abuse and the development of dissociative personality traits. *Child Abuse Review*, **4**(2): 99–113.

Baker, A.A. (1975). Granny battering. *Modern Geriatrics*, **5**(8): 20–24.

Baker, A.W. and Duncan, S.P. (1985). Child sexual abuse: a study of prevalence in Britain. *Child Abuse and Neglect*, **8**(4): 457–467.

Ball, M. (1977). Issues of violence in the family casework. *Social Casework*, **58**: 3–12.

Ballantyne, A. (1989). 500,000 old people 'At risk of abuse'. *The Guardian*, 10 May 1989.

Baltimore Police Department (1978).

Bandura, A. (1973). *Aggression: A Social Learning Analysis*. Englewood Cliffs, NJ: Prentice Hall.

Bandura, A. (1977). *Social Learning Theory*. Englewood Cliffs, NJ: Prentice Hall.

Bandura, A. and Walters, R. (1963). *Adolescent Aggression*. New York: Ronald Press.

Barker, P. (1986). *Basic Family Therapy* (2nd edn). London: Collins.

Barker, W. (1990). Practical and ethical doubts about screening for child abuse. *Health Visitor*, **63**(1): 14–17.

Barling, J., O'Leary, K., Joumiles, E., Vivian, D. and McEwen, K. (1987). Factor implications. *Journal of Family Violence*, **2**(1): 37–54.

Barling, J. and Rosenbaum, A. (1986). Work stressors and wife abuse. *Journal of Applied Psychology*, **71**: 346–348.

Barnett, O.W. and La Violette, A.D. (1993). *It Could Happen to Anyone: Why Battered Women Stay*. Newbury Park, CA: Sage.

Baron, R.A. (1976). The reduction of human aggression—a field study of the influence of incompatible reactions. *Journal of Applied Psychology*, **6**: 260–274.

Baumrind, D. (1971). Current patterns of parental authority. *Developmental Psychology Monograph*, **1**: 1–102.

Bayles, J.A. (1978). Violence, alcohol problems and other problems in disintegrating families. *Journal of Studies on Alcohol*, **50**: 253–262.

Bednar, R.L. (1970). Persuasibility and the power of belief. *Personality and Guidance Journal*, **48**: 647–652.

Bednar, J.V. and Kaul, T.J. (1978). Experimental group research: current perspectives. In S.L. Garfield and A.E. Bergin (Eds), *Handbook of Psychotherapy and Behavior Change: An Empirical Analysis* (2nd edn). New York: Wiley.

Beech, R. (1985). *Staying Together: A Practical Way to Make Your Relationship Succeed and Grow*. Chichester: Wiley.

Behar, L.B. (1977). The Preschool Behavior Questionnaire. *Journal of Abnormal Child Psychology*, **5**, 265–275.

Belsky, J. (1980). Child maltreatment: an ecological integration. *American Psychologist*, **35**: 320–335.

Belsky, J. (1988). Child maltreatment and the emergent family system (Chapter 17). In K. Browne, C. Davies and P. Stratton (Eds), *Early Prediction and Prevention of Child Abuse*. Chichester: Wiley, pp. 267–287.

Belsky, J. and Vondra, J. (1987). Child maltreatment: prevalence, consequences, causes and prevention. In D.H. Crowell, I.M. Evans and C.R. O'Donnell (Eds), *Childhood Aggression and Violence: Sources of Influence, Prevention and Control*. New York: Plenum.

Bennett, G.C.J. and Kingston, P.A. (1993). *Elder Abuse: Concepts, Theories and Interventions*. London: Chapman & Hall.

Bentovim, A. (1991). Clinical work with families in which sexual abuse has occurred. In C.R. Hollin and K. Howells (Eds), *Clinical Approaches to sex Offenders and their Victims*. Chichester: Wiley, pp. 179–208.

Bentovim, A. (1992). *Trauma Organised Systems: Physical and Sexual Abuse in Families*. London: Karnac Books.

Bentovim, A., Gorell-Barnes, G. and Cooklin, A. (1987). *Family Therapy: Complementary Frameworks of Theory and Practice*. London: Academic Press.

Bentovim, A., Elton, A., Hildebrand, J., Tranter, M. and Vizard, E. (1988). *Child Sexual Abuse Within the Family (Assessment and Treatment)*. London: Wright.

Bentler, P.M. and Newcomb, M.D. (1978). Longitudinal study of marital success and failure. *Journal of Consulting and Clinical Psychology*, **46**: 1053–1070.

Berger, A.M., Knutson, J.F., Mehm, J.G. and Perkins, K.A. (1988). The self-report of punitive childhood experiences of young adults and adolescents. *Child Abuse and Neglect*, **12**: 251–262.

Bergner, A.M., Delgado, L.K. and Graybill, D. (1994). Finkelhor's risk factor checklist: a cross validation study. *Child Abuse and Neglect*, **18**(4): 331–340.

Berk, R.A. and Newton, P.J. (1985). Does arrest really deter wife battery? An effort to replicate the findings of the Minneapolis spouse abuse experiment. *American Sociological Review*, **50**: 253–262.

Berk, R.A., Newton, P.J. and Berk, S. (1986). What a difference a day makes: an experimental study of the impact of shelters to battered women. *Journal of Marriage and the Family*, **48**(3): 481–490.

Berkowitz, L. (1984). Some effects of thought on anti and pro-social influences of media events: a cognitive-neoassociation analysis. *Psychological Bulletin*, **95**: 410–427.

Berkowitz, L. (1989). Laboratory experiments in the study of aggression. In J. Archer and K. Browne (Eds), *Human Aggression: Naturalistic Approaches*. London: Routledge, pp. 42–61.

Berkowitz, L. (1993). *Aggression: Its Causes, Consequences and Control*. New York: McGraw-Hill.

Bernard, M. and Bernard, J. (1983). Violent intimacy: the family as a model for love relationships. *Family Relations*, **32**: 283–286.

Bernard, J. and Bernard, M. (1984). The abusive male seeking treatment: Jekyll and Hyde. *Journal of Applied Family and Child Studies*, **33**(4): 543–547.

Berridge, D. and Cleaver, H. (1987). *Foster Home Breakdown*, Blackwell: Oxford.

Besharov, J.D. (1982). Towards better research on child abuse and neglect: making definition issues an explicit methodological concern. *Child Abuse and Neglect*, **5**: 383–390.

Beth Israel Hospital Elder Assessment Team (1986). An Elder Abuse Assessment Team in an acute hospital setting. *The Gerontologist*, **26**(2): 115–118.

Biggs, S., Phillipson, C. and Kingston, P. (1995). *Elder Abuse in Perspective*. Buckingham: Open University Press.

Binney, V., Harkell, G. and Nixon, J. (1981). *Leaving Violent Men*. London: National Women's Aid Federation.

Binney, V., Harkell, G. and Nixon, J. (1985). Refuges and housing for battered women. In J. Pahl (Ed.), *Private Violence and Public Policy: The Needs of Battered Women and the Response of the Public Services*. London: Routledge & Kegan Paul.

Bion, W.R. (1961). *Experiences in Groups and Other Papers*, London: Tavistock/Routledge.

Blackburn, R. (1993). *The Psychology of Criminal Conduct: Theory, Research and Practice*. Chichester: Wiley.

Bland, R. and Orn, H. (1986). Family violence and psychiatric disorder. *Canadian Journal of Psychiatry*, **31**: 129–137.

Block, M.R. (1983). Special problems and vulnerability of elderly women. In J.I. Kosberg (Ed.), *Abuse and Mistreatment of the Elderly*. Boston: C.S.G.

Block, M. and Sinnott, J. (1979). The Battered Elderly Syndrome: an exploratory study. Unpublished Manuscript. Centre for Ageing, University of Maryland. In M. Hudson and T. Johnson (1986), Elder abuse and neglect: a review of the literature. *Annual Review of Gerontology and Geriatrics*, **6**: 81–134.

Blumstein, A., Farrington, D.P. and Moitra, S. (1985). Delinquency careers: innocents, desisters and persisters. In M. Tonry and N. Morris (Eds), *Crime and Justice: An Annual Review of Research*, Vol. 6. Chicago: University of Chicago Press, pp. 187–219.

Bolton, F.G. and Bolton, S.R. (1987). *Working with Families: A Guide for Clinical and Legal Practitioners*. Beverly Hills, CA: Sage.

Borkowski, M., Murch, M. and Walker, V. (1983). *Marital Violence*. London: Tavistock.

Bornstein, P.H. and Bornstein, M.T. (1986). *Marital Therapy: A Behavioural Communication Approach*. London: Pergamon.

Boss, P. (1988). *Family Stress Management*. Beverly Hills, CA: Sage.

Boswell, G. (1995). *Violent Victims*. London: Prince's Trust.

Bourlet, A. (1990). *Police Intervention in Marital Violence*. Milton Keynes: Open University Press.

Bowlby, J. (1958). The nature of the child's tie to his mother. *International Journal of Psychoanalysis*, **39**: 350–373.

Bowlby, J. (1969). *Attachment and Loss*. Vol. 1, *Attachment*. London: Hogarth.

Bowlby, J. (1973). *Attachment and Loss*. Vol. 2, *Separation*. London: Penguin.

Bowlby, J. (1977). The mating and breaking of affectional bonds. *British Journal of Psychiatry*, **130**: 201–210.

Bowlby, J. (1984). Violence in the family as a disorder of attachment and caregiving systems. *American Journal of Psychoanalysis*, **44**(1): 9–31.

Bowlby, J. (1988). *A Secure Base—Clinical Applications of Attachment Theory*. London: Routledge.

Brand, P.A. and Kidd, A.H. (1986). Frequency of physical aggression in heterosexual and female homosexual dyads. *Psychological Reports*, **59**: 1309–1313.

Breckman, L.S. and Adelman, R.D. (1988). *Strategies for Helping Victims of Elder Mistreatment*. London: Sage.

Briere, J.N. (1992). *Child Abuse Trauma: Theory and Treatment of Lasting Effects*. Beverly Hills, CA: Sage.

British Geriatrics Society (1988). Abuse of the elderly: aetiology, natural history and the doctor's role. *Geriatric Medicine*, **18**(11): 33.

Brown, D. and Pedder, J. (1991). *Introduction to Psychotherapy*. London: Tavistock/Routledge.

Browne, A. (1987). *When Battered Women Kill*. New York: The Free Press.

Browne, A. (1991). *Women who Kill*. Beverly Hills, CA: Sage.

Browne, K.D. (1986). Methods and approaches to the study of parenting (Chapter 12). In W. Sluckin and M. Herbert (Eds), *Parental Behaviour*. Oxford: Blackwell, pp. 344–373.

Browne, K.D. (1988). The nature of child abuse and neglect: an overview. In K. Browne, C. Davies, and P. Stratton (Eds), *Early Prediction and Prevention of Child Abuse*. Chichester: Wiley, pp. 15–30.

Browne, K.D. (1989a). The naturalistic context of family violence and child abuse. In J. Archer and K. Browne (Eds), *Human Aggression: Naturalistic Approaches*. London: Routledge, pp. 182–216.

Browne, K.D. (1989b). A health visitor's role in screening for child abuse. *Health Visitor*, **62**: 275–277.

Browne, K.D. (1989c). Family violence: spouse and elder abuse. In K. Howells and C. Hollin (Eds), *Clinical Approaches to Violence*. Chichester: Wiley, pp. 119–154.

Browne, K.D. (1992). *Communication with Patients* (Practice Management Tutorial Two). Beckingham: Publishing Initiatives.

Browne, K.D. (1993). Violence in the family and its links to child abuse. *Bailliere's Clinical Paediatrics*, **1**(1): 149–164.

Browne, K.D. (1994). Child Sexual Abuse. In J. Archer (Ed.). *Male Violence*. London: Routledge, pp.210–230.

Browne, K.D. (1995a). The prediction of child maltreatment. In P. Reder (Ed.), *The Assessment of Parenting*. London: Routledge, pp.118–135.

Browne, K.D. (1995b). Preventing child maltreatment through community nursing. *Journal of Advanced Nursing*, **21**: 57–63.

Browne, K.D. (1995c). Alleviating spouse relationship difficulties. *Counselling Psychology Quarterly*, **8**(2): 109–122.

Browne, K.D. (1995d). Child abuse: defining, understanding and intervening. In K. Wilson and A. James (Eds), *The Child Protection Handbook*. London: Bailliere Tindall, pp. 43–65.

Browne, K.D. (1995e). Possible effects of video film on the behaviour of young offenders. *Proceedings of the British Psychological Society*, **3**(2): 114.

Browne, K.D. (1995f). *Aspects of Counselling Used by The Youth Treatment Service and the Characteristics of Young Offenders Who Receive Counselling in a Secure Environment*, Unpublished MEd thesis, University of Birmingham: Faculty of Education and Continuing Studies.

Browne, K.D. and Falshaw, L. (1996). Factors related to bullying in secure accommodation. *Child Abuse Review*, **5**: 123–127.

Browne, K.D. and Griffiths, P. (1988). Can telephone helplines prevent child abuse? *Changes*, **6**(4): 119–122.

Browne, K.D. and Hamilton, C. (1997). Physical violence between young adults and their parents: associated with a history of child maltreatment. *Journal of Family Violence* (in press).

Browne, K.D. and Howells, K. (1996). The violent offender. In C. Hollin (Ed.), *Working with Offenders*. Chichester: Wiley, pp. 118–210.

Browne, K.D. and Lynch, M.A. (1994) Prevention: actions speak louder than words. *Child Abuse Review*, **3**(4): 240–243.

Browne, K.D. and Lynch, M.A. (1995). Guessing at the extent of child sexual abuse. *Child Abuse Review*, **4**(2): 79–83.

Browne, K.D. and Parr, R. (1980). Contributions of an ethological approach to the study of abuse. In N. Frude (Ed.), *Psychological Approaches to Child Abuse*. London: Batsford, pp. 83–99.

Browne, K.D. and Saqi, S. (1987). Parent–child interaction in abusing families: possible causes and consequences. In P. Maher (Ed.), *Child Abuse: An Educational Perspective*. Oxford: Blackwell, pp. 77–104.

Browne, K.D. and Saqi, S. (1988a). Approaches to screening families high risk for child abuse. In K. Browne, C. Davies and P. Stratton (Eds), *Early Prediction and Prevention of Child Abuse*. Chichester: Wiley, pp. 57–85.

Browne, K.D. and Saqi, S. (1988b). Mother–infant interactions and attachment in physically abusing families. *Journal of Reproductive and Infant Psychology*, **6**(3): 163–282.

Browne, K.D. and Slater, R. (1997). The conflict tactics of romantic partners and their relationship to early experiences. *Journal of Interpersonal Violence* (in revision).

Browne, K.D., Davies, C. and Stratton, P. (Eds) (1988). *Early Prediction and Prevention of Child Abuse*. Chichester: Wiley, pp. 15–30.

Browne, K.D., Falshaw, L. and Hamilton, C. (1995). Characteristics of young persons resident at the Glenthorne Centre during the first half of 1995. *Youth Treatment Service Journal*, **1**(2): 52–71.

Browne, K.D., Hamilton, C. and Ware, J.R. (1996). The Child Assessment Rating and Evaluation (C.A.R.E.) Program Manual. Unpublished, University of Birmingham/Southend Community NHS Trust.

Browning, J. and Dutton, D. (1986). Assessment of wife assault with the Conflict Tactics Scales: using couple data to quantify the differential responding effect. *Journal of Marriage and Family*, **48**: 375–379.

Brutz, J. and Ingoldsby, B.B. (1984). Conflict resolution in Quaker families. *Journal of Marriage and the Family*, **46**: 21–26.

Buchanan, A. (1996). *Cycles in Maltreatment*. Chichester: Wiley.

Burgess, R.L. and Conger, R.D. (1978). Family interaction in abusive, neglectful and normal families. *Child Development*, **49**: 1163–1173.

Burnham, J.B. (1986). *Family Therapy: First Steps Toward a Systemic Approach*. London: Tavistock.

Burston, G. (1975). Granny Bashing. *British Medical Journal*, 3(5983): 592, 6 Sept.

Burston, G. (1977). Do your elderly patients live in fear of being battered? *Modern Geriatrics*, 7: 54–55.

Buss, A.H. and Durkee, A. (1957). An inventory for assessing different types of hostility. *Journal of Consulting Psychology*, 21: 343–349.

Butler, J. (1989). *Child Health Surveillance in Primary Care*. A critical review for the Department of Health. London: HMSO.

Buzawa, E.S. and Buzawa, C.G. (1990). *Domestic Violence: The Criminal Justice Response*. Newbury Park, CA: Sage.

Byles, J.E. (1978). Violence, alcohol problems and other problems in disintegrating families. *Journal of Studies on Alcohol*, 39: 551–553.

Cairns, R.B. and Cairns, B.D. (1994). *Lifelines and Risks: Pathways of Youth in Our Time*. New York: Harvester Wheatsheaf.

Callias, M. (1994). Parent training. In M. Rutter, E. Taylor and L. Hersov (Eds), *Child and Adolescent Psychiatry: Modern Approaches* (3rd edn). Oxford: Blackwell.

Cantwell, H.B. (1988). Child Sexual Abuse: very young perpetrators. *Child Abuse and Neglect*, 12(4): 579–582.

Capara, G., Cinanni, V., D'Imperio, G., Passerini, S., Renzi, P. and Travaglia, G. (1985). Indicators of impulsive aggression: present status of research on irritability and emotional susceptibility scales. *Personality and Individual Differences*, 6(6): 665–674.

Carlson, B.E. (1977). Battered women and their assailants. *Social Work*, 22: 455–460.

Carlson, B.E. (1984). Children's observations of interparental violence. In A.R. Roberts (Ed.), *Battered Women and their Families*. New York: Springer, pp. 147–167.

Carroll, J. (1977). The intergenerational transmission of family violence: the long term effects of aggressive behaviour. *Aggressive Behaviour*, 3: 289–299.

Carroll, J. (1994). The protection of children exposed to marital violence. *Child Abuse Review*, 3(1): 6–14.

Carr, A. (1991). Milan systemic family therapy: a review of ten investigations. *Journal of Family Therapy*, 13: 237–263.

Central Statistical Office (1989). *Social Trends*, Vol. 19. London: HMSO.

Central Statistical Office (1994). *Social Focus on Children '94*. London: HMSO.

Charles, A.V. (1986). Physically abused parents. *Journal of Family Violence*, 4: 343–355.

Chen, P., Bell, S., Dolinsky, D., Doyle, J. and Dunn, M. (1981). Elder abuse in domestic settings: a pilot study. *Journal of Gerontological Social Work*, 4(1): 3–17.

Christensen, A., Johnson, S.M., Phillips, S. and Glasgow, R.E. (1980). Cost effectiveness in parent consultation. *Behavior Therapy*, 11: 208–226.

Cicirelli, V. (1983). Adult children's attachment and helping behaviour to elderly parents: A path model. *Journal of Marriage and the Family*, 4(4): 815–825.

Cicirelli, V. (1986). The helping relationship and family neglect in later life. In K. Pillemer and R. Wolf (Eds), *Elder Abuse: Conflict in the Family*. Dover: Auburn House, pp. 49–67.

Clarke, R.G.V. (1977). Psychology and Crime. *Bulletin of the British Psychological Society*, 30: 280–283.

Cleaver, H. and Freeman, P. (1995). *Parental Perspectives in Cases of Suspected Child Abuse*. London: HMSO.

Clifton, J. (1985). Refuges and self-help. In N. Johnson (Ed.), *Marital Violence*. London: Routledge & Kegan Paul.

Coccaro, E.F. (1995). The biology of aggression. *Scientific American: Science and Medicine*, 2(1): 38–47.

Cochrane, C. and Petrone, S. (1987). Elder abuse: the physician's role in identification and prevention. *I.M.J.*, 171(4): 241–246.

Coie, J.D. (1990a). Adapting intervention to the problems of aggressive and disruptive rejected children. In S.R. Asher and J.D. Coie (Eds), *Peer Rejection in Childhood*. Cambridge: Cambridge University Press, pp. 309–337.

Coie, J.D. (1990b). Toward a theory of peer rejection. In S.R. Asher and J.D. Coie (Eds), *Peer Rejection in Childhood*. Cambridge: Cambridge University Press, pp. 365–398.

Coleman, K.H. (1980). Conjugal violence: what 33 men report. *Journal of Marriage and the Family*, 6: 207–213.

Coleman, D. and Straus, M. (1983). Alcohol abuse and family violence. In E. Gottheil, K. Druley, T. Skoloda and H. Waxman (Eds), *Alcohol, Drug Abuse and Aggression*. Springfield, IL: Thomas.

Cornell, C.P. and Gelles, R.J. (1982). Adolescent to parental violence. *Urban and Social Change Review*, **15**: 8–14.

Council on Scientific Affairs (1987). Elder abuse and neglect. *Journal of the American Medical Association*, **257**(7): 966–971.

Council of Europe (1986). *Violence in the Family*. Recommendation No. R(85)4 adopted by the Committee of Ministers of the Council of Europe on 26 March 1985 & Explanatory Memorandum. Strasbourg.

Crawford, C.B. and Anderson, J.L. (1989). Sociobiology: an environmentalist discipline? *American Psychologist*, **44**: 1449–1459.

Creighton, S.J. and Noyes, P. (1989). *Child Abuse Trends in England and Wales 1983–1987*. London: NSPCC.

Creighton, S.J. (1995). 'Fatal child abuse—how preventable is it?' *Child Abuse Review*, **4**(5): 318–328.

Creighton, S.J. (1992). *Child Abuse Trends in England and Wales 1988–1990*. London: NSPCC, 80pp.

Crittenden, P.M. (1985). Maltreated infants: vulnerability and resilience. *Journal of Child Psychology and Psychiatry*, **26**(1): 85–96.

Crittenden, P.M. (1988a). Distorted patterns of relationship in maltreating families: the role of internal representation models. *Journal of Reproductive and Infant Psychology*, **6**: 183–199.

Crittenden, P.M. (1988b). Family and dyadic patterns of functioning in maltreating families. In K.D. Browne, C. Davies and P. Stratton (Eds), *Early Prediction and Prevention of Child Abuse*. Chichester: Wiley, pp. 161–192.

Crittenden, P.M. and Ainsworth, M.D.S. (1989). Child maltreatment and attachment theory. In D. Cicchetti and V. Carlson (Eds), *Child Maltreatment: Theory and Research on the Causes and Consequences of Child Abuse and Neglect*. Cambridge: Cambridge University Press, pp. 432–463.

Croft-Jeffreys, C. and Wilkinson, G. (1989). Estimated costs of neurotic disorder in UK general practice 1985. *Psychological Medicine*, **19**: 549–558.

Crystal, S. (1986). Social policy and elder abuse. In K. Pillemer and R. Wolf (Eds), *Elder Abuse: Conflict in the Family*. Dover: Auburn House, pp. 331–341.

Crystal, S. (1987). Elder abuse: the latest crisis. *The Public Interest*, **88** (Summer): 56–66.

Cumberbatch, G. (1994). Legislating mythology: video violence and children. *Journal of Mental Health*, **3**: 485–494.

Cummings, E.M. and Davies, P. (1994). *Children and Marital Conflict*. London: Guilford Press.

Curtis, L. (1974). Criminal violence. *National Patterns and Behaviour*. Lexington, MA: Lexington Books.

Dale, A., Evandrou, M. and Arber, S. (1987). The household structure of the elderly population in Britain. *Ageing and Society*, 7(5): 37–56.

Dallos, R. and McLaughlin, E. (Eds) (1993). *Social Problems and the Family*, London: Sage.

Daniel, J.H., Newberger, E.H., Reed, R.B. and Kotelchuck, M. (1978). Child abuse screening. *Child Abuse and Neglect*, 2: 247–259.

Dare, C. (1986). Psychoanalytic marital therapy. In N. Jacobson and A. Gurman (Eds), *Clinical Handbook of Marital Therapy*. London: Guilford Press, pp. 13–28.

Daro, D. (1989). When should prevention education begin? *Journal of Interpersonal Violence*, 4: 257–260.

Daro, D. (1991). Prevention programs. In C. Hollin and K. Howells (Eds), *Clinical Approaches to Sex Offenders and their Victims*. London: Wiley, pp. 285–306.

Davenport, C.F., Browne, K.D. and Palmer, R. (1994). Opinions on the traumatizing effects of child sexual abuse: evidence for consensus. *Child Abuse and Neglect*, 18(9): 725–738.

Davis, L.V. and Carlson, B.E. (1987). Observation of spouse abuse: what happens to the children? *Journal of Interpersonal Violence*, 2(3): 278–291.

Day, A., Maddicks, R. and McMahon, D. (1993). Brief psychotherapy in Two-plus-One sessions with a young offender population. *Behavioural and Cognitive Psychotherapy*, 21: 357–369.

Day, D.E. and Roberts, M.W. (1983). An analysis of the physical punishment component of a parent training program. *Journal of Abnormal Child Psychology*, 11: 141–152.

Deal, J.E. and Wampler, J.E. (1986). Dating violence: the primacy of previous experience. *Journal of Social and Personal Relationships*, 3: 457–471.

Decalmer, P. and Glendenning, F. (1993). *Mistreatment of Elderly People*. London: Sage.

De Long, A.R. (1989). Sexual interactions among siblings and cousins: experimentation or exploitation? *Child Abuse and Neglect*, 13(2): 271–279.

DeLozier, P. (1982). Attachment theory and child abuse. In C.M. Parkes and J. Stevenson-Hinde (Eds), *The Place of Attachment in Human Behaviour*. London: Tavistock.

DeLuca, R.V., Boyes, D.A., Grayston, A.D. and Romano, E. (1995). Sexual abuse: effects of group therapy on pre-adolescent girls. *Child Abuse Review*, 4(4), October.

DeMarris, A. (1987). The efficacy of a spouse abuse model in accounting for courtship violence. *Journal of Family Issues*, 8(3): 291–305.

DeMarris, A. (1992). Male versus female initiation of aggression: the case of courtship violence. In E.C. Viano (Ed.), *Intimate Violence: Interdisciplinary Perspectives*. Washington, DC: Taylor & Francis, pp. 111–120.

Dembo, R., Bertke, M., La Voie, L., Borders, S., Washburn, M. and Schneidler, J. (1987). Physical abuse, sexual victimisation and illicit drug use: a structural analysis among high risk adolescents. *Journal of Adolescence*, 10: 13–33.

Department of Health and Social Security (1986). *Working Together*. London: HMSO.

Department of Health (1995a). *Children and young persons on Child Protection Registers—Year Ending 31 March 1995, England*, Personal Social Services Local Authority Statistics, London: HMSO (December 1995).

Department of Health (1995b). *Child Protection: Messages from Research*. London: HMSO.

Departments of Health, Education and Science, Home Office and Welsh Office (1991). *Working together under the Children Act 1989*. London: HMSO.

Department of Health and Social Security (1981). *Growing Older*. London: HMSO.

Department of Social Security (1993). *Households Below Average Income. A Statistical Analysis 1979–1990/91*. London: HMSO.

Deschner, J.P. and McNeil, J.S. (1986). Results of anger control training for battering couples. *Journal of Family Violence*, 1(2): 111–120.

Dicks, H. (1967). *Marital Tensions*. London: Routledge & Kegan Paul.

Dietrich, K.N., Starr, R.H. and Weisfield, G.E. (1983). Infant maltreatment: caretaker–infant interaction and developmental consequences at different levels of parentry failure. *Paediatrics*, 72: 532–540.

Dietz, C.A. and Craft, J.L. (1980). Family dynamics of incest: a new perspective. *Social Casework*, **61**: 602–609.

Dobash, R.E. and Dobash, R.P. (1979). *Violence against Wives: A Case Against Patriarchy*. London: Open Books.

Dobash, R.E. and Dobash, R.P. (1987). Violence towards wives. In J. Orford (Ed.), *Coping with Disorders in the Family*, Surrey: Guilford Press, pp. 169–193.

Dobash, R.E., Dobash, R.P., Cavanagh, K. and Wilson, M. (1978). Wifebeating: the victims speak. *Victimology*, **2**(3/4): 608–622.

Dobash, R.E., Dobash, R.P. and Cavanagh, K. (1985). The contact between battered women and social and medical agencies. In J. Pahl (Ed.), *Private Violence and Public Policy*. London: Routledge & Kegan Paul.

Dobash, R.P. and Dobash, R.E. (1996) *Research Evaluation of Programmes for Violent Men*. Edinburgh: HMSO.

Dodge, K.A. and Frame, C.L. (1982). Social cognitive biases and deficits in aggressive boys. *Child Development*, **53**: 620–635.

Dodge, K.A., Pettit, G.S., McClaskey, C.L. and Brown, M.M. (1986). Social competence in children. *Monographs of the Society for Research in Child Development*, **51**(2): 1–85.

Dollard, J., Doob, L.W., Miller, N.E., Mowrer, O.H. and Sears, R.R. (1939). *Frustration and Aggression*, New Haven: Yale University Press.

Douglas, R. (1983). Domestic neglect and abuse of the elderly: implications for research and service. *Family Relations*, **32** (July): 395–402.

Dryfoos, J. (1990). *Adolescents at Risk*. New York: Oxford University Press.

Duck, S.W. (1986). *Human Relationships: An Introduction to Social Psychology*. Beverly Hills, CA: Sage.

Dunn, J. (1984). *Sisters and Brothers*. London: Fontana.

Dunn, J. (1988). *The Beginnings of Social Understanding*. Cambridge, MA: Harvard University Press.

Dunn, J. (1993). *Young Children's Close Relationships: Beyond Attachment*. Newbury Park, CA: Sage.

Dunn, J. and Kendrick, C. (1982). *Siblings*. Oxford: Blackwell.

Durfee, M. and Tilton-Durfee, D. (1995). Multiagency child death review teams: experience in the United States. *Child Abuse Review*, **4**(5): 377–381.

Dutton, D.G. (1987). The criminal justice response to wife assault. *Law and Human Behaviour*, **11**(3): 189–206.

Dutton, D.G. (1988). *The Domestic Assault of Women: Psychological and Criminal Justice Perspectives*. Boston: Allyn & Bacon.

D'Zurilla, T. and Goldfried, M. (1971). Problem solving and behavior modification. *Journal of Abnormal Psychology*, **8**: 107–126.

Eastman, M. (1984). *Old Age Abuse*. Age Concern, England.

Eastman, M. (1989). Studying old age abuse. In J. Archer and K. Browne, (Eds), *Human Aggression: Naturalistic Approaches*. London: Routledge, pp. 217–229.

Eastman, M. (Ed) (1994). *Old Age Abuse: A New Perspective*. (Age Concern—2nd edn). London: Chapman & Hall.

Edinberg, M. (1986). Developing and integrating family orientated approaches in care of the elderly. In K. Pillemer and R. Wolf (Eds), *Elder Abuse: Conflict in the Family*. Dover: Auburn House, pp. 267–283.

Edleson, J.L. (1984). Working with men who batter. *Social Work*, **29**(3): 237–242.

Edleson, J.L., Eisikovits, Z. and Guttman, E. (1985). Men who batter women. *Journal of Family Issues*, **6**(2): 229–247.

Edleson, J.L. and Tolman, R.M. (1992). *Intervention for Men Who Batter: An Ecological Approach*. Newbury Park, CA: Sage.

Edmunds, G. and Kendrick, D.C. (1980). *The Measurement of Human Aggressiveness*, Chichester: Ellis Horwood (Wiley).

Edwards, S.S.M. (1989). *Policing 'Domestic' Violence: Women, the Law and the State*. London: Sage.

Egeland, B. (1988). Breaking the cycle of abuse implications for predication and intervention. In K.D. Browne, C. Davies and P. Stratton (Eds), *Early Prediction and Prevention of Child Abuse*. Chichester: Wiley; pp. 87–102.

Egeland, B. and Sroufe, L.A. (1981). Attachment and early maltreatment. *Child Development*, **52**: 44–52.

Egeland, B., Jacobvitz, D. and Papatola, K. (1987). Intergenerational Continuity of Abuse. In R. Gelles and J. Lancaster (Eds), *Child Abuse and Neglect: Biosocial Dimensions*, New York: Hawthorne, pp. 255–276.

Egeland, B., Jacobvitz, D. and Sroufe, A. (1988). Breaking the cycle of abuse. *Child Development*, **59**: 1080–1088.

Egan, G. (1975). *The Skilled Helper: A Model for Systematic Helping and Interpersonal Relating.* Monterey, CA: Brooks Cole.

Elander, J. and Rutter, M. (1996). An update on the status of the Rutter parents' and teachers' scales. *Child Psychology and Psychiatry Review,* 1: 31–35.

Elliott, M., Browne, K.D. and Kilcoyne, J. (1995). Child sexual abuse: what offenders tell us. *Child Abuse and Neglect,* 19(5): 579–594.

Ellis, P.L. (1982). Empathy: a factor in antisocial behaviour. *Journal of Abnormal Child Psychology,* 2: 123–133.

Elmer, E. and Gregg, G. (1967). Developmental characteristics of abused children. *Pediatrics,* 40: 596–602.

EPOCH—Ending Physical Punishment of Children in the Home (1990). Hitting people is wrong and children are people too. *Campaign Literature.* London: Radda Barnen Handbooks.

Epps, K. and Swaffer, T. (1997). Adolescent fire-setters. *Journal of Forensic Psychiatry* (in revision).

Erikson, E.H. (1965). *Childhood and Society* (revised edn). Harmondsworth: Penguin.

Evason, E. (1982). *Battered Women Who Kill: Psychological Self-Defense as Legal Justification.* Lexington, MA: Heath.

Ewing, C.P. (1987). *Battered Women Who Kill: Psychological Self-Defense as Legal Justification.* Lexington, MA: Lexington Books.

Eysenck, H.J. (1964). *Crime and Personality,* London: Penguin.

Fagen, J.A., Stewart, D.K. and Hansen, K.V. (1983). Violent men or violent husbands? In D. Finkelhor, R. Gelles, M. Straus and G. Hotaling (Eds), *The Dark Side of the Family: Current Family Violence Research.* Beverly Hills, CA: Sage, pp. 49–67.

Faller, K.C. (1989). Why sexual abuse? An exploration of the inter-generational hypothesis. *Child Abuse and Neglect,* 13: 543–548.

Falshaw, L., Browne, K.D. and Hollin, C.R. (1996). Victim to offender: a review. *Aggression and Violent Behaviour,* 1: 389–404.

Faragher, T. (1985). The police response to violence against women in the home. In J. Pahl (Ed.), *Private Violence and Public Policy: The Needs of Battered Women and the Response of the Public Services.* London: Routledge & Kegan Paul.

Farber, E.D., McCoard, W.D., Kinast, C. and Baum-Faulkner, D. (1984). Violence in families of adolescent runaways. *Child Abuse and Neglect,* 8: 295–299.

Farrington, D.P. (1995). The development of offending and anti-social behaviour from childhood: key findings from the Cambridge Study in delinquent development. *Journal of Child Psychology and Psychiatry*, **360**(6): 929–964.

Faulk, M. (1974). Men who assault their wives. *Medicine, Science and Law*, **14**: 180–183.

Feindler, E.L. and Ecton, R.B. (1986). *Adolescent Anger Control: Cognitive Behavioural Techniques*. New York: Pergamon.

FBI (1991). *Crime Statistics 1990*. Washington, DC: Federal Bureau of Investigation.

Feinmann, J. (1988). Elderly people: abused and forgotten. *Health Service Journal*, 22nd September: 1085.

Ferguson, D. and Beck, C. (1983). Half tool for assessment of elder abuse. *Geriatric Nurse* (Sept.–Oct.): 301–304.

Ferrara, M.L. (1992). *Group Counselling with Juvenile Delinquents*. London, New Delhi: Sage.

Ferreira, A. (1963). Family myth and homeostasis. *Archives of General Psychiatry*, **96**: 451–463.

Feshbach, S. (1964). The function of aggression and the regulation of the aggressive drive. *Psychological Review*, **71**: 257–272.

Feshbach, S. (1980). Child abuse and the dynamics of human aggression and violence. In G. Gerbner, C. Ross and E. Zigler (Eds), *Child Abuse: An Agenda for Action*. New York: Oxford University Press.

Field, D. (1992). Elderly people in British society. *Sociology Review*, **1**(4): 16–20.

Filsinger, E. (1983). *Marriage and Family Assessment: A Sourcebook for Family Therapy*. Beverly Hills, CA: Sage.

Fincham, F.D. and Bradbury, T.N. (1988). The impact of attributions in marriage: empirical and conceptual formulations. *British Journal of Clinical Psychology*, **27**: 77–90.

Finkelhor, D. (1980a). Sex among siblings: a survey on prevalence, variety and effects. *Archives of Sexual Behaviour*, **9**(3): 171–194.

Finkelhor, D. (1980b). Risk factors in the sexual victimization of children. *Child Abuse and Neglect*, **4**: 265–273.

Finkelhor, D. (1983). Common features of family abuse (Chapter 1). In D. Finkelhor, R. Gelles, G. Hotaling and M. Straus (Eds), *The Dark Side of Families: Current Family Violence Research*. Beverley Hills; CA: Sage, pp. 17–28.

Finkelhor, D. (1984). *Child Sexual Abuse: New Theory and Research.* New York: The Free Press.

Finkelhor, D. (1986). *A Source Book on Child Sexual Abuse.* Beverly Hills, CA: Sage.

Finkelhor, D. (1994). The international epidemiology of child sexual abuse. *Child Abuse and Neglect,* **18**: 409–417.

Finkelhor, D. and Baron, L. (1986). Risk factors for child sexual abuse. *Journal of Interpersonal Violence,* **1**(1): 43–71.

Finkelhor, D. and Yllö, K. (1982). Forced sex in marriage: a preliminary report. *Crime and Delinquency,* **28**: 459–478.

Finkelhor, D. and Yllö, K. (1985). *License to Rape: Sexual Abuse of Wives.* New York: Holt, Rinehart & Winston.

Finkelhor, D., Gelles, R.J., Hotaling, G.T. and Straus, M.A. (Eds) (1983). *The Dark Side of Families.* Beverly Hills, CA: Sage.

Finn, J. (1985). The stresses and coping behaviours of battered women. *Social Casework,* **66**: 341–349.

Finn, J. (1986). The relationship between sex role attitudes and attitudes supporting marital violence. *Sex Roles,* **14**(5/6): 235–244.

Flavigny, M.H. (1988). Violence in adolescents: organisation expressed by psychopathic means. In A.H. Esman (Ed.), *International Annals of Adolescent Psychiatry,* Vol. 1. Chicago: University Press.

Floyd, F.J. and Markman, H.J. (1984). An economical observational measure of couple communication skill. *Journal of Consulting and Clinical Psychology,* **52**: 97–103.

Floyd, F.J., O'Farrell, T.J. and Goldberg, M. (1987). Comparison of marital observational measure: the marital interaction coding system and the communication skills test. *Journal of Consulting and Clinical Psychology,* **55**(3): 423–429.

Forehand, R. and McMahon, R. (1981). *Helping the Noncompliant Child.* New York: Guilford.

Follingstad, D.R., Rutledge, L.L., McNeill-Harkins, K. and Polek, D.S. (1992). Factors Related to Physical Violence in Dating Relationships. In E.C. Viano (Ed.), *Intimate Violence: Interdisciplinary Perspectives.* Washington, DC: Taylor & Francis, pp. 121–138.

Freud, A. (1958). *Adolescence: Psychoanalytic Study of the Child.* New York: International University Press.

Freud, A. (1981). A psychoanalyst's view of sexual abuse by parents. In P. Beezley, P.B. Mrazek and C.H. Kempe (Eds), *Sexually Abused Children and their Families,* Oxford: Pergamon.

Freud, S. (1926). Inhibitions, symptoms and anxiety. In S. Freud (1956), *Standard Edition*, **20**: 87–172, London: Hogarth.

Freud, S. (1940). An outline of psychoanalysis. In J. Strachey (Ed. and Trans.), *The Standard Edition of the Complete Psychological Works of Sigmund Freud*, **23**. London: Hogarth.

Freud, S. (1949). An Outline of Psychoanalysis. *International Journal of Psychoanalysis*, **21**, 27–84. New York: Norton.

Freud, S. (1993/1950). Why War? In *Collected Works*, Vol. 16. London: Imago.

Friedrich, W.N. and Boroskin, J.A. (1976). The role of the child in abuse: a review of the literature. *American Journal of Orthopsychiatry*, **46**(4): 580–590.

Frodi, A.M. and Lamb, M.E. (1980). Child abusers' responses to infant smiles and cries. *Child Development*, **51**: 238–241.

Frude, N. (1980). Child abuse as aggression. In N. Frude (Ed.), *Psychological Approaches to Child Abuse*. London: Batsford, pp. 136–150.

Frude, N. (1989). The physical abuse of children (Chapter 7). In K. Howells and C. Hollin (Eds), *Clinical Approaches to Violence*. Chichester: Wiley, pp. 155–181.

Frude, N. (1991). *Understanding Family Problems: A Psychological Approach*. Chichester: Wiley.

Frude, N. (1994). Marital violence: an interactional perspective'. In J. Archer (Ed.), *Male Violence*. London: Routledge, pp. 153–169.

Fryer, G.E. and Miyoshi, T.J. (1994). A survival analysis of the revictimization of children: the case of Colorado. *Child Abuse and Neglect*, **18**(12): 1063–1071.

Fulmer, T. and Cahill, V. (1984). Assessing elder abuse. *Journal of Gerontological Nursing*, **10**(12): 16–20.

Gaensbauer, T.J. (1982). Regulations of emotional expression in infants from two contrasting caretaking environments. *Journal of American Academy of Child Psychiatry*, **21**: 163–171.

Galbraith, M.W. and Davison, D.C. (1985). Stress and elderly abuse. *Focus on Learning*, **11**(1): 87–92.

Galdston, R. (1965). Observations of children who have been physically abused by their parents. *American Journal of Psychiatry*, **122**(4): 440–443.

Garbarino, J. and Gilliam, G. (1980). *Understanding Abusive Families*, Lexington, MA: Lexington Books.

Gayford, J.J. (1975). Wife battering: a preliminary survey of 100 cases. *British Medical Journal*, **25**(1): 94–97.

Gayford, J.J. (1976). Ten types of battered wives. *The Welfare Officer*, **25**: 5–9.

Geller, J.A. (1992). *Breaking Destructive Patterns: Multiple Strategies for Treating Partner Abuse*. New York: The Free Press.

Gelles, R.J. (1973). Child abuse as psychopathology: a sociological critique and reformulation. *American Journal of Orthopsychiatry*, **43**: 611–621.

Gelles, R.J. (1981). The myth of the battered husband. In R. Walsh and O. Procs (Eds), *Marriage and Family*, Guildford, Surrey: Dustkin, pp. 81–82.

Gelles, R.J. (1983). An exchange/control theory. In D. Finkelhor, R. Gelles, G. Hotaling and M. Straus (Eds), *The Dark Side of Families: Current Family Violence Research*. Beverley Hills; CA: Sage, pp. 151–165.

Gelles, R.J. (1987a). *The Violent Home* (2nd edn). Beverly Hills, CA: Sage.

Gelles, R.J. (1987b). *Family Violence* (2nd edn). Beverly Hills, CA: Sage (Library of Social Research No. 84).

Gelles, R.J. (1993). Family violence. In R.L. Hampton, T.P. Gullotta, G.R. Adams, E.H. Potter and R.P. Weissberg (Eds), *Family Violence: Prevention and Treatment*. Newbury Park, CA: Sage, pp. 1–25.

Gelles, R.J. (1994a). Through a sociological lens: social structure and family violence. In R.J. Gelles and D.R. Loseke (Eds), *Current Controversies in Family Violence*. Newbury Park, CA: Sage, pp. 31–46.

Gelles, R.J. (1994b). Alcohol and other drugs are associated with violence—They are not its cause. In R.J. Gelles and D.R. Loseke (Eds), *Current Controversies on Family Violence*. Newbury Park, CA: Sage, pp. 182–196.

Gelles, R.J. and Straus, M.A. (1988). *Intimate Violence*. New York: Simon & Schuster.

Gelles, R.J. and Cornell, C.P. (1990). *Intimate Violence in Families* (2nd edn). Beverly Hills, CA: Sage.

Gelles, R.J. and Loseke, D.R. (Eds) (1994). *Current Controversies on Family Violence*. Beverly Hills; CA: Sage.

George, C. and Main, M. (1979). Social interactions of young abused children: approach, avoidance and aggression. *Child Development*, **50**: 306–318.

Gerson, L.W. (1978). Alcohol-related acts of violence. *Journal of Studies on Alcohol*, **39**: 1294–1296.

Getzel, G.S. (Ed.) (1988). *Violence: Prevention and Treatment in Groups*. London: Haworth.

Gibbens, T.C.W. (1978). Sibling and parent–child incest offenders: a long term follow-up. *British Journal of Criminology*, **18**(1): 40–52.

Gibbons, J., Callagher, B., Bell, C. and Gordon, D. (1995). *Development After Physcial Abuse in Early Childhood: A Follow-Up Study of Children on Protection Registers*. London: HMSO.

Gil, D. (1970). *Violence Against Children*. Cambridge, MA: Harvard University Press.

Gil, D. (1978). Societal violence in families. In J.M. Eekelaar and S.N. Katz (Eds), *Family Violence*. Toronto: Butterworths, pp. 14–33.

Gilbert, P. (1994). Male violence: towards an integration. In J. Archer. (Ed.), *Male Violence*. London: Routledge; pp. 352–389.

Giles-Sims, J. (1983). *Wife-beating: A Systems Theory Approach*. New York: Guildford.

Giles-Sims, J. (1985). A longitudinal study of battered children and battered wives. *Journal of Applied Family and Child Studies*, **34**(2): 205–210.

Giordano, N. and Giordano, J. (1984). Elder abuse: a review of the literature. *Social Work*, **29**(3): 232–236.

Glick, B. and Goldstein, A.P. (1987). Aggression replacement training. *Journal of Counselling and Development*, **65**: 356–367.

Goddard, C. and Hiller, P. (1993). Child sexual abuse: assault in a violent context. *Australian Journal of Social Issues*, **28**(1): 20–33.

Goldstein, A.P. and Keller, H. (1987). *Aggressive Behaviour: Assessment and Intervention*. New York: Pergamon.

Goldstein, D. (1983). Spouse abuse. In *Prevention and Control of Aggression: Principles, Practices and Research*. The Centre for Research on Aggression (Eds), Syracuse University. New York: Pergamon, pp. 37–65.

Goldstein, D. and Rosenbaum, A. (1985). An evaluation of the self esteem of maritally violent men: family relations. *Journal of Applied and Family and Child Studies*, **34**(3): 425–428.

Goldstein, J.H. (1986). *Aggression and Crimes of Violence* (2nd edn). Oxford: Oxford University Press.

Gondolf, E.W. (1987). Evaluating programs for men who batter: problems and prospects. *Journal of Family Violence*, **2**(1): 95–108.

Gondolf, E.W. (1993). Treating the batterer. In M. Hansen and M. Harway (Eds), *Battering and Family Therapy*, Beverly Hills, CA: Sage, pp. 105–118.

Goode, W. (1971). Force and violence in the family. *Journal of Marriage and the Family*, **33**: 624–636.

Gough, D. (1994). *Child Abuse Interventions*. London: HMSO.

Grafstrom, M., Nordberg, A. and Wimblad, B. (1992). Abuse is in the eye of the beholder. *Scandinavian Journal of Social Medicine*, **21**(4): 247–255.

Gray, M. and Wilcock, G. (1981). *Our Elders*. Oxford: Oxford University Press.

Gray, J.O., Cutler, C.A., Dean, J. and Kempe, C.H. (1977). Prediction and prevention of child abuse. *Child Abuse and Neglect*, **1**: 45–58.

Green, A.H. (1984). Child abuse by siblings. *Child Abuse and Neglect*, **8**(3): 311–317.

Greene, N.B. and Esselsteyn, T.C. (1972). The beyond control girl. *Juvenile Justice*, **23**: 13–19.

Greengross, S. (1986). *The Law and Vulnerable Elderly People*. Age Concern, England.

Grey, E. (1988). The link between child abuse and juvenile delinquency: What we know and recommendations for policy and research. In G.T. Hotaling, D. Finkelhor, J.T. Kirkpatrick and M. Straus (Eds), *Family Abuse and its Consequences: New Directions in Research*. Beverly Hills; CA: Sage.

Griffiths, R. (1988). *Community Care: Agenda for Action*, London: HMSO.

Groth, A.N. (1979). *Men Who Rape: The Psychology of the Offender*. New York: Plenum.

Groth, A.N. and Burgess, A. (1979). Sexual trauma in the life histories of rapists and child molesters. *Victimology*, **1**(1): 10–16.

Groth, A.N. and Burgess, A. (1980). Male rape: offenders and victims. *American Journal of Psychiatry*, **137**(7): 807–810.

Groth, A.N., Longo, R. and McFadin, J. (1982). Undetected recidivism among rapists and child molesters. *Crime and Delinquency*, **128**: 450–458.

Grych, J.H. and Fincham, F.D. (1990). Marital conflict and children's adjustment: a cognitive-contextual framework. *Psychological Bulletin*, **108**(2): 267–290.

Guerra, N.G. and Slaby, R.G. (1989). Evaluative factors in social problem solving by aggressive boys. *Journal of Abnormal Child Psychology*, **17**: 277–289.

Gully, K.J. and Dengerink, H.A. (1983). The dyadic interaction of persons with violent and non-violent histories. *Aggressive Behaviour*, 9(1): 13–20.

Gurman, A.S. and Kniskern, D.P. (1978). Research on marital and family therapy: progress, perspective and prospect. In S.L. Garfield and A.E. Bergin (Eds), *Handbook of Psychology and Behavior Change* (2nd edn). Chichester: Wiley.

Gurman, A.S., Kniskern, D.P. and Pinsoff, W.M. (1986). Research on the process and outcome of marital and family therapy. In S.L. Garfield and A.E. Bergin (Eds), *Handbook of Psychotherapy and Behavior Change* (2nd edn). Chichester: Wiley.

Hall, R.E. (1985). *Ask Any Woman* (A London enquiry into rape and sexual assault). London: Falling Wall Press.

Hall, D.N.B. (1995). *Health for All Children* (3rd edn). London: HMSO.

Hall, R. and Ryan, L. (1984). Therapy with men who are violent to their spouses. *Australian Journal of Family Therapy*, 4: 281–282.

Hallett, C. (1988). Research in child abuse: some observations on the knowledge base. *Journal of Reproductive and Infant Psychology*, 6(3): 119–124.

Hallett, C. and Birchall, E. (1992). *Coordination and Child Protection*, London: HMSO.

Hamilton, C. and Browne, K.D. (1997). The repeat victimisation of children: should the concept be revised? *Aggression and Violent Behaviour*, 2 (in press).

Hampton, R.L., Gullotta, T.P., Adams, G.R., Potter, E.H. and Weissberg, R. (Eds) (1993). *Family Violence: Prevention and Treatment*. Beverly Hills; CA: Sage.

Hanks, S.E. and Rosenbaum, C.P. (1978). Battered women: study of women who live with violent, alcohol-abusing men. *American Journal of Orthopsychiatry*, 47: 291–306.

Hanmer, J. (1978). Violence and the social control of women. In G. Littlejohn (Ed.), *Power and State*. London: Croom Helm.

Hanmer, J. (1989). Women and policing in Britain. In J. Hanmer, J. Radford and E.A. Stanko (Eds), *Women, Policing and Male Violence: International Perspectives*. London: Routledge.

Hanmer, J. and Stanko, E.A. (1985). Stripping away the rhetoric of protection: violence to women, law and the state in Britain and the USA. *International Journal of the Sociology of Law*, 13: 357–374.

Hanneke, C.R. and Shields, N.A. (1985). Marital rape: implications for the helping professions. *Social Casework*, **66** (October).

Hansen, M. and Goldenberg, I. (1993). Conjoint therapy with violent couples: some valid considerations. In M. Hansen and M. Harway (Eds), *Battering and Family Therapy*. Beverly Hills, CA: Sage, pp. 82–92.

Harbin, H. and Madden, D. (1979). Battered parents: a new syndrome. *American Journal of Psychiatry*, **136**: 1288–1291.

Hardiker, P., Exton, K. and Barker, M. (1989). (Personal communication).

Hart, B. Stuehling, J., Reese, M. and Stubbing, E. (1990). *Confronting Domestic Violence: Effective Police Responses*. Reading, Pennsylvania: Pennsylvania Coalition Against Domestic Violence. Cited in Morley and Mullender (1994).

Hart, S.N., Brassard, M.R. and Germain, R.B. (1987). Psychological maltreatment in education and schooling. In M. Brassard, R. Germain and S. Hart (Eds), *Psychological Maltreatment of Children and Youth*. New York: Pergamon, pp. 217–242.

Hart, S.N., Germain, R.B. and Brassard, M.R. (1987). The Challenge: To better understanding and combat psychological maltreatment of children and youth. In M.R. Brassard, R. Germain and S.N. Hart (Eds). *Psychological Maltreatment of Children and Youth*. New York: Pergamon, pp. 3–24.

Hartup, W.W. (1974). Aggression in childhood: developmental perspectives. *American Psychologist*, **29**: 336–341.

Haviland, S. and O'Brien, J. (1989). Physical abuse and neglect of the elderly: assessment and intervention. *Orthopaedic Nursing*, 8(4): 11–18.

Havighurst, R.J. (1973). History of developmental psychology: socialization and personality through the lifespan. In P.B. Baltes and K.W. Schaie (Eds), *Life-span Developmental Psychology*. New York: Academic Press.

Hazelrigg, M.D., Cooper, H.M. and Bordun, C.M. (1987). Evaluating the effectiveness of family therapies: an integrative review and analysis. *Psychological Bulletin*, **101**: 428–442.

Health Visitors' Association (1994). *A Cause for Concern*. London: HMSO.

Heide, K.M. (1995). *Why Kids Kill Parents: Child Abuse and Adolescent Homicide*. Beverley Hills; CA: Sage.

Heine, R.W. and Trosman, H. (1960). Initial expectations of the doctor–patient interaction as a factor in continuance in psychotherapy. *Psychiatry*, **20**: 275–278.

Helton, A. (1986). The pregnant battered female. *Response to the Victimisation of Women and Children*, **(1)**: 22–23.

Henderson, M. and Hollin, C.R. (1983). A critical review of social skills training with young offenders. *Criminal Justice and Behaviour*, **10**: 316–341.

Hendricks-Matthews, M. (1982). The battered woman: Is she ready for help? *Social Casework*, **63**: 131–137.

Henry, B., Moffitt, T., Robins, L., Earls, F. and Silva, P. (1993). Early family predictors of child and adolescent antisocial behaviour: Who are the mothers of delinquents? *Criminal Behaviour and Mental Health*, **3**: 97–118.

Henton, J.M., Cate, R., Koval, J., Lloyd, S. and Christopher, S. (1983). Romance and violence in dating relationships. *Journal of Family Issues*, **4**: 467–482.

Henwood, M. and Wicks, M. (1984). *The Forgotten Army: Family Care and Elderly People*. London: Family Policy Studies Centre.

Herbert, M. (1974). *Emotional Problems of Development in Children*. London: Academic Press.

Herbert, M. (1986). Social skills training with children. In C.R. Hollin and P. Trower (Eds), *Handbook of Social Skills Training*, Vol. 1. Oxford: Pergamon.

Herbert, M. (1987a). *Conduct Disorders of Childhood and Adolescence*. Chichester: Wiley.

Herbert, M. (1987b). *Behavioural Treatment of Children with Problems: A Practice Manual*. London: Academic Press.

Herbert, M. (1989). Aggressive and violent children. In K. Howells and C.R. Hollin (Eds), *Clinical Approaches to Violence*. Chichester: Wiley.

Herbert, M. (1991). *Clinical Child Psychology: Social Learning, Development and Behaviour*. Chichester: Wiley.

Herbert, M. (1992). *Child Care and their Family: Resource Pack*. Windsor: National Foundation of Educational Research.

Herbert, M. (1993). Foreword in V. Varma (Ed.), *How and Why Children Hate*. London: Kingsley.

Herbert, M. (1994). Behavioural methods. In M. Rutter, E. Taylor and L. Herson (Eds), *Child and Adolescent Psychiatry* (3rd edn). Oxford: Blackwell.

Herbert, M. (1995). A collaborative model of training for parents of children with disruptive behaviour disorders. *British Journal of Clinical Psychology*, **34**: 325–342.

Herbert, M. and Iwaniec, D. (1981). Behavioural psychotherapy in natural home settings: an empirical study applied to conduct disordered and incontinent children. *Behavioural Psychotherapy*, **9**: 55–76.

Herbert, M. and Wookey, J. (1997). *Child-Wise Parenting Manual*, Exeter: Impact Publications.

Herrenkohl, E.C., Herrenkohl, R.C. and Toedter, L.J. (1983). Perspectives on the intergenerational transmission of abuse. In D. Finkelhor, R.J. Gelles, G.T. Hotaling and M.A. Straus (Eds), *The Dark Side of Families: Current Family Violence Research*. Beverly Hills, CA: Sage.

Herrenkohl, R., Herrenkohl, C. Egolf, B. and Wu, P. (1991). The developmental consequences of child abuse: The Lehigh longitudinal study. In R. Starr and D. Wolfe (Eds), *The Effects of Child Abuse and Neglect: Issues and Research*. New York: Guilford, pp. 57–81.

Hill, C.E. (1989). *Therapist Techniques and Client Outcomes*. London: Sage.

Hilton, N.Z. (Ed.) (1993). *Legal Responses to Wife Assault: Current Trends and Evaluation*. Newbury Park, CA: Sage.

Hinde, R.A. (1979). *Towards Understanding Relationships*. London: Academic Press.

Hinde, R.A. (1982). Ethology and child development. In P.H. Mussen (Ed.), *Handbook of Child Psychology*, Vol. 2. New York: Wiley, pp. 27–93.

Hobbs, N. (1982). *The Troubled and the Troubling Child*. San Francisco: Jossey-Bass.

Hocking, E. (1994). Caring for carers: understanding the process that leads to abuse. In M. Eastman (Ed.), *Old Age Abuse: A New Perspective* (2nd edn). London: Chapman & Hall, pp. 51–66.

Hodge, J.E. (1992). Addiction to violence: a new model of psychopathy. *Criminal Behaviour and Mental Health*, **2**: 212–213.

Hoffman, M.L. (1970). Moral development. In P.H. Mussen (Ed.), *Carmichael's Manual of Child Psychology*. Chichester: Wiley.

Hollin, C.R. (1992). *Criminal Behaviour: A Psychological Approach to Explanation and Prevention*. London: Falmer Press.

Hollin, C.R. (1993). Contempory psychological research into violence: an overview. In P.J. Taylor (Ed.), *Violence in Society*.
London: Royal College of Physicians, pp. 55–68.

Hollin, C.R. (1994a). Designing effective rehabilitation programmes for young offenders. *Psychology, Crime & Law*, **1**(3):
193–199.

Hollin, C.R. (1994b). Substance abuse and offending. *Current
Opinion in Psychiatry*, **7**: 462–465.

Hollin, C.R. and Howells, K. (1989). An introduction to concepts, models and techniques. In K. Howells and C. Hollin
(Eds), *Clinical Approaches to Violence*. Chichester: Wiley, pp.
3–24.

Hollin, C.R. and Trower, P.T. (Eds) (1986). *Handbook of Social Skills
Training*, Vols I and II. Oxford: Pergamon.

Hollin, C.R., Wilkie, J. and Herbert, M. (1987). Behavioural social
work: training and application. *Practice*, **1**: 297–304.

Holmes, J. (1993). *John Bowlby and Attachment Theory*. London:
Routledge.

Holmes, J. (1994). Attachment theory—a secure theoretical base
for counselling. *Psychodynamic Counselling*, **1**(1): 65–78.

Holtzworth-Munroe, A. and Jacobson, N.S. (1985). Causal attributions of married couples: when do they search for causes?
What do they conclude when they do? *Journal of Personality
and Social Psychology*, **48**: 1398–1412.

Home Office (1992). *Criminal Statistics: England and Wales 1990*.
London: HMSO.

Homer, A.C. and Gilleard, C. (1990). Abuse of elderly people by
their carers. *British Medical Journal*, **301**: 1359–1362.

Hooyman, N.R. (1983). Abuse and neglect: community interventions. In J.I. Kosberg (Ed.), *Abuse and Maltreatment of the Elderly*.
Boston: Wright.

Hopson, B. and Scully, M. (1980). *Lifeskill Teaching: Education for
Self-Empowerment*. New York: McGraw-Hill.

Horley, S. (1986). Wife battering: police must act. *Social Work
Today*, **17**(39): 22.

Horowitz, M.J. (1981). Self-righteous rage and the attribution of
blame. *Archives of General Psychiatry*, **38**: 1233–1238.

Horowitz, A. and Shindelman, L. (1983). Reciprocity and affection: past influences on current care-giving. *Journal of
Gerontological Social Work*, **5**(3): 5–20.

House of Commons Home Affairs Committee (1993a). *Domestic Violence*, Vol. I. Report together with the Proceedings of the Committee. London: HMSO.

House of Commons Home Affairs Committee (1993b). *Domestic Violence*, Vol. II. Memoranda of Evidence, Minutes of Evidence and Appendices. London: HMSO.

Howells, K. (1986). Social skills training and criminal and anti-social behaviour in adults. In C.R. Hollin and P. Trower (Eds), *Handbook of Social Skill Training*, Vol. 1: *Application Across the Life Span*. Oxford: Pergamon.

Howells, K. (1989). Anger management methods in relation to the prevention of violent behaviour (Chapter 7). In J. Archer and K. Browne (Eds), *Human Aggression: Naturalistic Approaches*. London: Routledge, pp. 153–181.

Howitt, D. (1992). *Child Abuse Errors: When Good Intentions Go Wrong*. Hemel Hempstead: Harvester Wheatsheaf.

Hudson, M. (1986). Elder mistreatment: current research. In K. Pillemer and R. Wolf (Eds), op. cit., pp. 125–166.

Hudson, M. and Blane, M. (1985). The importance of non-verbal behaviour in giving instructions for children. *Child and Family Behaviour Therapy*, **7**: 1–10.

Hudson, M. and Johnson, T. (1986). Elder abuse and neglect: a review of the literature. *Annual Review of Gerontology and Geriatrics*, **6**: 81–134.

Hudson, W. and McIntosh, S. (1981). The assessment of spouse abuse: two quantifiable dimensions. *Journal of Marriage and Family*, **42**: 873–885.

Huesmann, L.R. and Eron, L.D. (1986). *Television and the Aggressive Child: A Cross-national Comparison*, Hillsdale, NJ: Lawrence Erlbaum.

Hughes, M. (1988). Psychological and behavioural correlates of family violence in child witnesses and victims. *American Journal of Orthopsychiatry*, **58**(1): 77–90.

Hughes, H.M. and Barad, J. (1983). Psychology functioning of children in a battered women's shelter: a preliminary investigation. *American Journal of Orthopsychiatry*, **53**(3): 525–531.

Hunter, R.S. and Kilstrom, N. (1979). Breaking the cycle in abusive families. *American Journal of Psychiatry*, **136**: 1320–1322.

Huston, A.C., Donnerstein, E., Fairchild, H., Freshbach, N.D., Katz, P.A., Murray, J.P., Rubenstein, E.A., Wilcox, B.L. and

Zuckerman, D. (1992). *Big World, Small Screen: The Role of Television in American Society*. Lincoln: University of Nebraska Press.

Hyman, C.A. (1977). A report on the psychological test results of battering parents. *British Journal of Social and Clinical Psychology*, **16**: 221–224.

Hyman, C.A. (1978). Non-accidental injury. (A report to the Surrey County Area Review Committee on Child Abuse). *Health Visitor*, **51**: 168–174.

Hyman, C.A. and Mitchell, R. (1975). A psychological study of child battering. *Health Visitor*, **48**: 294–296.

Hyman, C.A., Parr, R. and Browne, K.D. (1979). An observation study of mother–infant interaction in abusing families. *Child Abuse and Neglect*, **3**: 241–246.

Iwaniec, D. (1995). *Emotional Abuse and Neglect*. Chichester: Wiley.

Iwaniec, D., Herbert, M. and McNeish, S. (1985a). Social work with failure-to-thrive children and their families. Part I: Psychosocial factors. *British Journal of Social Work*, **15**(3): 243–259.

Iwaniec, D., Herbert, M. and McNeish, S. (1985b). Social work with failure-to-thrive children and their families. Part II: Behavioural casework. *British Journal of Social Work*, **15**(4): 375–89.

Iwaniec, D., Herbert, M. and Sluckin, A. (1988). Helping emotionally abused children who fail to thrive. In K.D. Browne, C. Davies and P. Stratton (Eds), *Early Prediction and Prevention of Child Abuse*. Chichester: Wiley, pp. 229–244.

Jacobs, M. (1985). *The Presenting Past*. Milton Keynes: Open University Press.

Jacob, T. (1987). *Family Interaction and Psychopathology: Theories, Method and Findings*. New York: Plenum.

Jacobson N.S. and Gurman, A.S. (1986). *Clinical Handbook of Marital Therapy*. London: Guilford Press.

Jacobson, N.S. and Holtzworth-Munroe, A. (1986). Marital therapy: a social learning cognitive perspective. In N.S. Jacobson and A.S. Gurman (Eds), *Clinical Handbook of Marital Therapy*. London: Guilford Press.

Jaffe, P.G., Wolfe, D.A., Telford, A. and Austin, G. (1986a). The impact of police charges in incidents of wife abuse. *Journal of Family Violence*, **1**(1): 37–49.

Jaffe, P.G., Wolfe, D.A., Wilson, S. and Zak, L. (1986b). Similarities in behaviour and social maladjustment among child victims and witnesses to family violence. *American Journal of Orthopsychiatry*, **56**: 142–146.

Jaffe, P.G., Wolfe, D.A. and Wilson, S.K. (1990). *Children of Battered Women*, Beverly Hills, CA: Sage, 132pp.

James, A.L. and Wilson, K. (1986). *Couples, Conflict and Change*. London: Tavistock.

Janus, M., McCormack, A., Burgess, A.W. and Hartman, C. (1987). *Adolescent Runaways: Causes and Consequences*. Lexington, MA: Lexington, Books.

Jason, J., Williams, S., Burton, A. and Rochat, R. (1982). Epidemiologic differences between sexual and physical child abuse. *Journal of the American Medical Association*, **247**: 3344–3348.

Jehu, D. (1988). *Beyond Sexual Abuse: Therapy with Women who were Childhood Victims*. Chichester: Wiley.

Johnson, R.L. and Shrier, D. (1987). Past sexual victimisation by females of male patients in an adolescent medicine clinic population. *American Journal of Psychiatry*, **144**: 650–652.

Johnson, S. and Lobitz, G. (1974). Parental manipulation of child behaviour in home observation. *Journal of Applied Behaviour Analysis*, **7**: 23–31.

Johnson, S.M. and Greenberg, L.S. (1985). Differential effects of experimental and problem-solving interventions in resolving marital conflict. *Journal of Consulting and Clinical Psychology*, **53**: 175–184.

Johnson, T. (1986). Critical issues in the definition of elder mistreatment. In K. Pillemer and R. Wolf (Eds), op. cit., pp. 167–196.

Johnson, T. (1988). Child perpetrators—children who molest other children: preliminary findings. *Child Abuse and Neglect*. **12**(2): 219–229.

Johnson, T. (1989). Female child perpetrators: children who molest other children. *Child Abuse and Neglect*, **13**(4): 571–585.

Jones, T., MacLean, B. and Young, J. (1986). *The Islington Crime Survey: Crime, Victimization and Policing in Inner-city London*. Aldershot, Hants: Gower.

Jouriles, E.N., Murphy, C.M. and O'Leary, K.D. (1989). Interspousal aggression, marital discord, and child problems. *Journal of Consulting and Clinical Psychology*, **57**: 453–455.

Jukes, A. (1993). *Why Men Hate Women*. London: Free Assoc. Books.

Kadushin, A. and Martin, J. (1981). *Child Abuse: An Interactional Event*. New York: Columbia University Press.

Kalmuss, D. (1984). The intergenerational transmission of marital aggression. *Journal of Marriage and the Family*, **46**: 11–19.

Kaplan, R.M. (1984). The measurement of human aggression. In R.M. Kaplan, V.J. Konecni and R.W. Novaco (Eds), *Aggression in Children and Youth*, The Hague: Nijhoff.

Kaul, T.J. and Bednar, R.L. (1986). Experimental group research: results, questions and suggestions. In S.L. Garfield and A.E. Bergin (Eds), *Handbook of Psychotherapy and Behavior Change* (3rd edn). Chichester: Wiley.

Kazdin, A.E., Enveldf-Dawson, K., French, N.H. and Unis, A.S. (1987). Problem solving skills training and relationship therapy in the treatment of anti-social child behaviour. *Journal of Consulting and Clinical Psychology*, **55**: 76–88.

Kelly, L. (1988). *Surviving Sexual Violence*. Cambridge: Polity Press.

Kempe, T.S. and Kempe, C.H. (1978). *Child Abuse*. London: Fontana/Open Books.

Kidscape (1985). *How Safe are our Children?* (revised 1993). A Kidscape special report. Available from Kidscape, 152 Buckingham Palace Road, London SW1W 9TR.

Kilpatrick, A.C. (1992). *Long-range Effects of Child and Adolescent Sexual Experiences: Myths, Mores and Menaces*. Hillsdale, NJ: Lawrence Erlbaum.

Kingston, P. and Penhale, B. (Eds) (1995). *Family Violence and the Caring Professions*, London: Macmillan.

Kirsta, A. (1994). *Deadlier than the Male*. London: Harper-Collins.

Kirkwood, C. (1993). *Leaving Abusive Partners*. London: Sage.

Klein, M. (1957). *Envy and Gratitude*, London: Tavistock.

Knutson, J.F. and Selner, M.B. (1994). Punitive childhood experiences reported by young adults over a ten year period. *Child Abuse and Neglect*, **18**(2): 155–166.

Kolvin, I., Miller, F.J., Fleeting, M. and Kolvin, P.A. (1988). Social and parenting factors affecting criminal offence rates: findings from the Newcastle Thousand Family Study (1947–1980). *British Journal of Psychiatry*, **152**: 80–90.

Konecni, V.J. (1975). The mediation of aggressive behaviour: arousal level versus anger and cognitive labelling. *Journal of Personality and Social Psychology*, **32**: 706–712.

Kosberg, J. (1983). The special vulnerability of elderly parents. In Kosberg, J. (Ed.), *Abuse and Maltreatment of the Elderly*. Littleton: Wright. pp. 263–275.

Kosberg, J. (1988). Preventing elder abuse: identification of high risk factors prior to placement decision. *Gerontologist*, **28**(1): 43–50.

Koski, P.R. (1987). Family violence and nonfamily deviance: taking stock of the literature. *Marriage and Family Review*, **12**: 23–46.

Koss, M.P. and Cook, S.L. (1994). Facing the facts: date and acquaintance rape are significant problems for women. In R.H. Gelles and D.R. Loseke (Eds), *Current Controversies on Family Violence*. Newbury Park, CA: Sage, pp. 104–119.

Kratcoski, P.C. (1984). Perspectives on intrafamily violence. *Human Relations*, **37**: 443–453.

Krugman, R.D. (1986). The relationship between unemployment and physical abuse of children. *Child Abuse and Neglect*, **10**(3): 415–418.

Kruttschnitt, C., Ward, D. and Sheble, M.A. (1987). Abuse resistant youth: some factors that may inhibit violent criminal behaviour. *Social Forces*, **66**: 501–519.

La Fontaine, J.S. (1993). Defining organised sexual abuse. In K.D. Browne and M.A. Lynch (Eds), Special Issue on Organised Abuse. *Child Abuse Review*, **2**(4): 223–231.

Landau, H.R., Salus, M.K., Striffarm, T. and Kalb, N.L. (1980). *Child Protection: The Role of the Courts*, Washington, DC: US Government Printing Office (cited in Hart, Gemain and Brassard, 1987).

Lane, D.A. (1989). Violent histories: bullying and criminality. In D.P. Tattum and D.A. Lane (Eds), *Bullying in Schools*. Stoke-on-Trent: Trentham Books, pp. 95–105.

Lane, D.A. and Tattum, D.P. (1989). *Supporting the Child in School*. Milton Keynes: OUP.

Lappin, J. and Covelman, C. (1985). Adolescent runaways: a structural family therapy perspective. In M. Mirkin and S. Koman (Eds), *Handbook of Adolescents and Family Therapy*. New York: Gardner.

Larson, K.A. (1988). A research review and alternative hypothesis explaining the link between learning disability and delinquency. *Journal of Learning Disabilities*, **21**: 357–366.

Lau, C. and Kosberg, J. (1979). Abuse of the elderly by informal care providers. *Ageing*, **299**: 10–15.

Laviola, M. (1989). Effects of older brother–younger sister incest: a review of four cases. *Journal of Family Violence*, 4(3): 259–274.

Law Society (1987). *Splitting Up*. London: The Law Society.

Lazarus, A.A. (1968). Behaviour therapy in groups. In G.M. Gazda (Ed.), *Basic Approaches to Group Psychotherapy and Counselling*. Springfield: Thomas.

Lee, S.G. and Herbert, M. (1970). *Freud and Psychology*. Harmondsworth: Penguin.

•Leighton, B. (1989). *Spousal Abuse in Metropolitan Toronto: Research Report on the Response of the Criminal Justice System* (Report No. 1989–02). Ottawa: Solicitor General of Canada.

Leventhal, J. (1988). Can child maltreatment be predicted during the perinatal period: evidence from longitudinal cohort studies. *Journal of Reproductive and Infant Psychology*, 6(3): 139–162.

Levine, E.M. (1986). Sociocultural causes of family violence: a theoretical comment. *Journal of Family Violence*, 1(1): 3–12.

Levine, E.M. and Kanin, E.J. (1987). Sexual violence among dates and acquaintance: trends and their implications for marriage and family. *Journal of Family Violence*, 2(1): 55–65.

Levine, M.B. (1975). Interparental violence and its effects on the children: a study of families in general practice. *Medical Science and Law*, **15**: 172–176.

Levinson, D. (1985). On wife-beating and intervention. *Current Anthropology*, 26(5): 665–666.

Levinson, D. (1989). *Family Violence in Cross-Cultural Perspective*. Beverly Hills, CA: Sage.

Levy, B. (Ed.) (1991). *Dating Violence: Young Women in Danger*. New York: Seal Press.

Levy, B. and Lobel, K. (1991). Lesbian teens in abusive relationships. In B. Levy (Ed.), *Dating Violence: Young Women in Danger*. Seattle, WA: Seal Press, pp. 203–208

Lewis, B.Y. (1987). Psychosocial factors related to wife abuse. *Journal of Family Violence*, 2(1): 1–10.

Lewis, M. and Schaeffer, S. (1981). Peer behaviour and mother–infant interaction in maltreated children. In M. Lewis and L.A. Rosenblum (Eds), *The Uncommon Child*. New York: Plenum.

Lewis, J. and Meredith, B. (1988). Daughters caring for mothers: the experience of caring and its implications for professional helpers. *Ageing and Society*, **8**(1): 1–21.

Lewis, D.D., Mallouh, C. and Webb, V. (1989). Child abuse, delinquency and violent criminality. In D. Cicchetti and V. Carlson (Eds), *Child Maltreatment*. New York: Cambridge University Press, pp. 707–721.

Lieberman, M.A., Yalom, J.D. and Miles, M.D. (1973). *Encounter Groups: First Facts*. New York: Basic Books.

Lincolnshire Area Child Protection Committee (1990). *'Being a Parent': Poster and Leaflet Publicity Campaign*. Lincoln: ACPC.

Livingstone, L.R. (1986). Children's violence to single mothers. *Journal of Sociology and Social Welfare*, **13**: 920–933.

Lloyd, S. (1995). Social Work and domestic violence. In P. Kingston and B. Penhale (Eds), *Family Violence and the Caring Professions*. Malaysia: Macmillan, pp. 149–180.

Lloyd, S., Farrell, G. and Pease, K. (1994). *Preventing Repeated Domestic Violence: A Demonstration Project on Merseyside*. Crime Prevention Unit Series Paper No. 49. London: Home Office Police Research Group.

Loeber, R. and Dishion, T.J. (1983). Early prediction of male adolescent delinquency: a review. *Psychological Bulletin*, **94**: 68–99.

Loeber, R. and Dishion, T.J. (1984). Boys who fight at home and school: family conditions influencing cross-setting consistency. *Journal of Consulting and Clinical Psychology*, **52**: 759–768.

London, J. (1978). Images of violence against women. *Victimology*, **2**: 510–524.

Long, D. (1987). Working with men who batter. In M. Scher, M. Stevens, G. Good and G.A. Eichenfield (Eds), *Handbook of Counselling and Psychotherapy with Men*. Newbury Park, CA: Sage, pp. 305–320.

Lorenz, K. (1965). *Evolution and the Modification of Behaviour*. Chicago: University of Chicago Press.

Lorenz, K. (1966). *On Aggression*. New York: Harcourt, Brace & World.

Luborsky, L., McLellon, A., Woody, G., O'Bren, C. and Auerbach, A. (1985). Therapist success and its determinants. *Archives of General Psychiatry*, **42**: 602–611.

Luckenbill, D.F. (1977). Criminal homicide as a situated transaction. *Social Problems*, **25**: 176–186.

Lynch, M.A. (1975). Ill health and child abuse. *Lancet* II: 317–319.

Lynch, M., Roberts, J. and Gordon, J. (1976). Early warning of child abuse. *Developmental Medicine and Child Neurology*, **19**: 373–387.

Lynch, M. and Roberts, J. (1977). Predicting child abuse. *Child Abuse and Neglect*, **1**: 491–492.

Lynch, M. and Roberts, J. (1982). *Consequences of Child Abuse.* London: Academic Press.

Lynam, D., Moffitt, T. and Stouthamer-Loeber, M. (1993). Explaining the relation between IQ and delinquency: class, race, test motivation, school failure or self control? *Journal of Abnormal Psychology*, **102**: 187–196.

Maccoby, E.E. (1980). *Social Development: Psychology Growth and the Parent–Child Relationship.* New York: Harcourt Brace Jovanovich.

MacLeod, L. (1989). Wife battering and the web of hope: progress, dilemmas and visions of prevention. Discussion paper for *Working Together: 1989 National Forum on Family Violence.* Ottowa, Ontario: the National Clearinghouse on Family Violence (cited in Morley and Mullender, 1994).

Magura, M. (1981). Are services to protect children effective? *Children and Youth Services Review*, **3**: 193.

Mahler, M. (1975). *The Psychological Birth of the Human Infant.* London: Hutchinsons

Main, M. and George, C. (1985). Responses of abused and disadvantaged toddlers to distress in agemates: a study in a day-care setting. *Developmental Psychology*, **21**: 407–412.

Makepeace, J.M. (1981). Courtship violence among college students. *Family Relations*, **30**(1): 97–102.

Makepeace, J.M. (1983). Life events-stress and courtship violence. *Family Relations*, **32**(1): 101–109.

Malan, D.H. (1979). *Individual Psychotherapy and the Science of Psychodynamics.* London: Butterworths.

Manthei, R.H. and Matthews, D.A. (1989). Helping the reluctant client to engage in counselling. In W. Dryden (Ed.), *Key Issues for Counselling in Action.* London: Sage, pp. 37–44.

Margolin, L. (1990). Child abuse by adolescents caregivers. *Child Abuse and Neglect*, **14**(3): 365–373.

Margolin, G. and Burman, B. (1993). Wife abuse versus marital violence: different terminologies, explanations, and solutions. *Clinical Psychology Review*, **13**(1): 59–74.

Mark, V.H. and Ervin, F.R. (1970). *Violence and the Brain*. New York: Harper & Row.

Marshall, L. and Rose, P. (1988). Family of origin violence and courtship abuse. *Journal of Counselling and Development*, **66**: 414–418.

Martin, D. (1976). *Battered Wives*. New York: Pocket Books.

Martin, H.P. and Rodeheffer, M. (1976). Learning and intelligence. In H.P. Martin (Ed.), *The Abused Child: A Multidisciplinary Approach to Developmental Issues and Treatment*. Cambridge, MA: Ballinger.

Martin, H. and Beezley, P. (1977). Behavioural observations of abused children. *Developmental Medicine and Child Neurology*, **19**: 373–387.

Mawson, C. (1994). Conforming anxiety in work with damaged children. In A. Obholzer and V.Z. Roberts (Eds), *The Unconscious at Work*. London: Routledge.

Mayhew, P., Maung, N.A. and Mirrless-Black, C. (1993). *The 1992 British Crime Survey*. A Home Office Research and Planning Unit Report. London: HMSO.

McCandless, B. (1969). *Children: Behavior and Development*. New York: Holt, Rinehart & Winston.

McCann, I.L., Sakheim, D.K. and Abrahamson, D.J. (1988). Trauma and victimisation: a model of psychological adaptation. *The Counselling Psychologist*, **16**(4): 531–594.

McClintock, F.H. (1978). Criminological aspects of family violence. In J.P. Martin (Ed.), *Violence in the Family*. Chichester: Wiley.

McCord, J. (1988). Parental aggressiveness and physical punishment in long-term perspective (Chapter 5). In G. Hotaling, D. Finkelhor, J. Kirkpatrick and M. Straus (Eds), *Family Abuse and its Consequences: New Directions in Research*. Beverly Hills, CA: Sage, pp. 91–98.

McCord, J. (1990). Long-term perspectives on parental absence. In L. Robins and M. Rutter (Eds), *Straight and Deviant Pathways from Childhood to Adulthood*. Cambridge: University Press, pp. 116–134.

McCormack, A., Janus, M. and Burgess, A.W. (1986). Runaway youths and sexual victimisation: gender differences in an adolescent runaway population. *Child Abuse and Neglect*, **10**: 387–395.

McCreadie, C. (1994). Introduction: the issues, practice and policy. In M. Eastman (Ed.), *Old Age Abuse: A New Perspective*. London: Chapman & Hall, pp. 3–22.

McCuan et al. (1986). In K.A. Pillemer and R.S. Wolf (Eds), *Elder Abuse, Conflict in the Family*, Dover, MA: Auben House.

McCubbin, H.I and Patterson, J.M. (1983). Stress: the family inventory of life events and change. In E. Filsinger (Ed.), *Marriage and Family Assessment*. Beverly Hills, CA: Sage, pp. 275–298.

McFarlane, J. (1991). Violence during teen pregnancy: health consequences for mother and child. In B. Levy (Ed.), *Dating Violence: Young Women in Danger*. Seattle, WA: Seal Press, pp. 136–141.

McIndoe, R. (1989). A pilot study of child compliance to rules. Unpublished dissertation, Phillip Institute of Technology, Melbourne, Australia.

McLeer, S.V. and Anwar, R. (1989). A study of battered women presenting in an emergency department. *American Journal of Public Health*, **79**: 65–66.

Meadow, R. (1982). Munchausen syndrome by proxy. *Arch. Dis. Child*. **57**: 92–98.

Megargee, E.I. (1982). Psychological determinants and correlates of criminal violence. In M.E. Wolfgang and N.A. Weiner (Eds), *Criminal Violence*. Beverly Hills, CA: Sage.

Meichenbaum, D. (1985). *Stress Inoculation Training*. Oxford: Pergamon.

Meichenbaum, D.H. and Goodman, J. (1971). Training impulsive children to talk to themselves: a means of developing self-control. *Journal of Abnormal Psychology*, **77**: 115–126.

Melville, J. (1987). Helping victims survive. *New Society*, **82**(1297): 18–19.

Merrick, J. and Michelsen, N. (1985). Child at risk: child abuse in Denmark. *International Journal of Rehabilitation Research*, **8**(2): 181–188.

Meth, R.L. and Pasick, R. (1990). *Men in Therapy: The Challenge of Change*. London: Guilford Press.

Miller, D., Miller, D., Hoffman, F. and Duggan, R. (1980). *Runaways—Illegal aliens in their own land: Implications for service*, New York: Praeger.

Milner, J.S. (1986). *The Child Abuse Potential Inventory Manual* (2nd edn). De Kalb, IL: Psytec.

Milner, J.S. and Gold, R.G. (1986). Screening spouse abusers for child abuse potential. *Journal of Clinical Psychology*, **42**(1): 169–172.

Mindel, C. and Wright, R. (1982). Satisfaction in multigenerational households. *Journal of Gerontology*, **37**: 483–489.

Minuchin, S. and Fishman, H.C. (1981). *Family Therapy Techniques*. Cambridge, MA: Harvard University Press.

Mooney, J. (1993). *The Hidden Figure: Domestic Violence in North London*. The findings of a survey conducted on domestic violence in the North London Borough of Islington. Islington Council (cited in Morley and Mullender, 1994).

Moore, D.M. (1979). An overview of the problem. In D.M. Moore (Ed.), *Battered Women*. Beverly Hills, CA: Sage, pp. 7–32.

Mones, P. (1993). When the innocent strike back: abused children who kill their parents. *Journal of Interpersonal Violence*, 8(2): 297.

Morley, R. and Mullender, A. (1994). Preventing Domestic Violence to Women. *Police Research Group—Crime Prevention Unit Series: Paper 48*. London: Home Office Police Department.

Morgan, P. (1975). *Child Care: Sense and Fable*. London: Templesmith.

Morris, H.H., Escoll, P.J. and Wexler, R. (1956). Aggressive behaviour disorders of childhood: a follow-up study. *American Journal of Psychiatry*, **112**: 991–997.

Mowrer, O.H. (1960). *Learning Theory and Behavior*. New York: Wiley.

Mueller, E. and Silverman, N. (1989). Peer relations in maltreated children. In D. Cicchetti and V. Carlson (Eds), *Child Maltreatment: Theory and Research on the Causes and Consequences of Child Abuse and Neglect*. Cambridge University Press, pp. 529–578.

Mufson, S. and Kranz, R. (1993). *Straight Talk about Date Rape*. New York: Facts on File.

Murgatroyd, S. and Woolfe, R. (1985). *Helping Families in Distress: An Introduction to Family Focussed Helping*. London: Harper & Row.

Murphy, J.E. (1988). Date abuse and forced intercourse among college students. In G.T. Hotaling, D. Finkelhor, J.T. Kirkpatrick and M. Straus (Eds), *Family Abuse and its Consequences: New Directions in Research*. Beverly Hills, CA: Sage, pp. 285–296.

National Committee for Prevention of Child Abuse (1988–1992). Child Abuse Advertising Campaign. Box 2866E: Chicago, Illinois 60690.

National Committee for Prevention of Child Abuse (1993). *Child Abuse Prevention: Everyone has a Role to Play.* Chicago: NCPCA.

National Society for the Prevention of Cruelty to Children (1985). Child abuse deaths. *Information Briefing No. 5.* London: NSPCC.

Newberger, E.H., Barkan, S., Lieberman, E., McCormick, M., Yllö, K., Gary, L. and Schechter, S. (1992). Abuse of pregnant women and adverse birth outcome: current knowledge and implications for practice. *The Journal of the American Medical Association,* **267**(17).

Newman, C. (1989). *Young Runaways: Findings from Britain's First Safe House.* London: The Children's Society.

Newson, E. (1994a). Video violence and the protection of children. *The Psychologist: Bulletin of the British Psycholgical Association,* **7**(6): 272–274.

Newson, E. (1994b). Aide-memoire on Video Violence: Direct Causal Links. *Memorandum 17: In the Home Affairs Committee Fourth Report: Video Violence and Young Offenders.* Westminster: House of Commons.

Ney, P.G., Fung, T. and Wickett, A.R. (1994). The worst combinations of child abuse and neglect. *Child Abuse and Neglect,* **18**(9): 705–714.

Norris, A. (1986). *Reminiscence with Elderly People.* Oxon: Winslow Press.

Novaco, R.W. (1975). *Anger Control: The Development and Evaluation of an Experimental Treatment,* Lexington MA: Heath.

Novaco, R.W. (1976). The functions and regulation of the arousal of anger. *American Journal of Psychiatry,* **133**: 1124–1128.

Novaco, R.W. (1978). Anger and coping with stress. In J.P. Forey et al. (Eds), *Cognitive Behaviour Therapy.* New York: Plenum.

Novaco, R.W. (1985). Anger and its therapeutic regulation. In M.A. Chesney and R.H. Rosenman (Eds), *Anger and Hostility in Cardiovascular and Behavioural Disorders.* New York: Hemisphere.

Nye, F. (1980). A theoretical perspective on running away. *Journal of Family Issues,* **1**(2): 147–151.

O'Brien, J. (1971). Violence in divorce-prone families. *Journal of Marriage and the Family,* **33**: 692–698.

O'Connell Higgins, G. (1994). *Resilient Adults: Overcoming a Cruel Past*. New York: Jossey-Bass.

O'Keefe, N.K., Brockopp, K. and Chew, E. (1986). Teen dating violence. *Social Work*, **31**(6): 465–468.

O'Leary, K.D. (1993). Through a psychological lens: personality traits, personality disorders and levels of violence. In R.J. Gelles and D.R. Loseke (Eds), *Current Controversies on Family Violence*. Newbury Park, CA: Sage, pp. 7–30.

O'Leary, K.D., Fincham, F.D. and Turkewitz, H. (1983). Assessment of positive feelings toward spouse. *Journal of Consulting and Clinical Psychology*, **15**: 949–951.

O'Malley, T., O'Malley, H., Everitt, T. and Jason, D. (1984). Categories of family-mediated abuse and neglect of elderly persons. *Journal of the American Geriatrics Society*, **32**(5): 362–369.

Ogg, J. and Bennett, G. (1992). Elder abuse in Britain. *British Medical Journal*, 24 October: 998–999.

Olds, D.L. and Henderson, C.R. (1989). The prevention of maltreatment. In D. Cicchetti and V. Carlson (Eds), *Child Maltreatment: Theory and Research on the Causes and Consequences of Child Abuse and Neglect*. Cambridge University Press, pp. 722–763.

Olds, D.L., Henderson, C.R. and Kitzman, H. (1994). Does prenatal and infancy nurse home visitation have enduring effects on the qualities of parental care giving and child health at 25 to 50 months of life? *Pediatrics*, **93**(1): 89–98.

Olds, D., Henderson, C., Chamberlin, R. and Tatelbaum, R. (1986) Preventing child abuse and neglect: randomized trial of nurse home visiting. *Pediatrics*, **78**: 65–78.

Olds, D.L., Henderson, C.R., Tatelbaum, R. and Chamberlin, R. (1988). Improving the life-course development of socially disadvantaged mothers: a randomized trial of nurse home visitation. *American Journal of Public Health*, **78**(ii): 1436–1445.

Olds, D.L., Henderson, C.R., Phelps, C., Kitzman, H. and Hanks, C. (1993). Effect of prenatal and infancy nurse home visitation on Government spending. *Medical Care*, **31**(2): 155–174.

Ollendick, T.H. and Henson, M. (1979). Social skills training for juvenile delinquents. *Behaviour, Research and Therapy*, **17**: 547–554.

Ollendick, T.H. and Cerny, J.A. (1981). *Clinical Behaviour Therapy with Children*. New York: Plenum.

Olweus, D. (1979). Stability of aggressive reaction patterns in males: a review. *Psychological Bulletin*, **86**: 852–875.

Olweus, D. (1984). Development of stable aggressive reaction patterns in males. In R.J. and D.C. Blanchard (Eds), *Advances in the Study of Aggression*, Vol. 1. New York: Academic Press.

Olweus, D. (1989). Bully/victim problems among schoolchildren: basic facts and effects of a school based intervention program. In K. Rubin and D. Pepler (Eds), *The Development and Treatment of Childhood Aggression*. Hillsdale, NJ: Lawrence Erlbaum.

Oppenheim, C. (1993). *Poverty: the Facts*. London: Child Poverty Action Group.

Orkow, B. (1985). Implementation of a family stress checklist. *Child Abuse and Neglect*, **9**: 405–410.

Pagelow, M.D. (1981). *Woman Battering: Victims and their Experiences*. Beverly Hills, CA: Sage.

Pagelow, M.D. (1984). *Family Violence*. New York: Praeger.

Pahl, J. (1978). *A Refuge for Battered Women*. London: HMSO.

Pahl, J. (1985). Violent husbands and abused wives: a longitudinal study. In J. Pahl (Ed.), *Private Violence and Public Policy: The Needs of Battered Women and the Responses of the Public Services*. London: Routledge & Kegan Paul, pp. 23–94.

Pahl, J. (1995). Health professionals and violence against women. In P. Kingston and B. Penale (Eds), *Family Violence and the Caring Professions*. Malaysia: Macmillan, pp. 127–148.

Painter, K. (1991). *Wife Rape, Marriage and the Law*. Survey Report: Key Finding and Recommendations. Faculty of Economic and Social Studies University of Manchester, Department of Social Policy and Social Work (cited in Morley and Mullender, 1994).

Papadopoulos, A. (1990). *Counselling Carers*. Oxon: Winslow Press.

Parentline (1990). Organisation for parents under stress. *Annual Report*. Thundersley, Essex: OPUS.

Parentline (1994). Organisation for parents under stress. *Annual Report*, Thundersley, Essex: OPUS.

Parrot, A. (1988). *Coping with Date Rate and Acquaintance Rape*. New York: The Rosen Publishing Group.

Parrot, A. and Bechhofer, B. (1991). *Acquaintance Rape: The Hidden Crime*. New York:

Parton, N. (1985). *The Politics of Child Abuse*. London: Macmillan.

Patterson, G.R. (1965). Responsiveness to social stimuli. In L. Krasner and L.P. Ullmann (Eds), Research in behaviour modification. New York: Holt, Rinehart & Winston.

Patterson, G.R. (1976). The aggressive child: victim and architect of a coercive system. In L.A. Hamerlynck, L.C. Handy and E.H. Marsh (Eds), *Behaviour Modification and Families*. New York: Brunner/Mazel.

Patterson, G.R. (1982). *Coercive Family Process*, Eugene, OR: Castalia, 368pp.

Patterson, G.R. (1986). Maternal rejection. Determinant or product for deviant child behaviour. In W.W. Hartup and Z. Rubin (Eds), *Relationships and Development*. Hillsdale, NJ: LEA Inc.

Patterson, G.R. and Fleischman, M.J. (1979). Maintenance of treatment effects: some considerations concerning family systems and follow up date. *Behavior Therapy*, **10**: 168–185.

Patterson, G.R., Chamberlain, P. and Reid, J.B. (1982). A comparative evaluation of a parent training program. *Behavior Therapy*, **13**: 638–650.

Patterson, G.R., DeBaryshe, B.D. and Ramsey, E. (1989). A developmental perspective on antisocial behaviour. *American Psychologist*, **44**(2): 329–335.

Patterson, G.R., Reid, J.B., Joness, J.J. and Conger, R.E. (1975). *A Social Learning Approach to Family Interventions*, Vol. 1: *Families with Aggressive Children*. Eugene, OR: Castalia.

Paulson, M.J., Coombs, R.H. and Landsvert, J. (1990). Youths who physically assault their parents. *Journal of Family Violence*, **5**(2): 121–133.

Pearce, J.W. and Pezzot-Pearce, T.D. (1994). Attachment theory and its implications for psychotherapy with maltreated children. *Child Abuse and Neglect*, **18**(5): 425–438.

Pease, K., Sampson, A., Croft, L., Phillips, C. and Farrell, G. (1991). Strategy for the Manchester University Violent Crime Prevention Project. August (cited in Morley and Mullender, 1994).

Pedrick-Cornell, C. and Gelles, R. (1982). Elderly abuse: the status of current knowledge. *Family Relations*, **31**: 457–465.

Peek, C., Fisher, J.L. and Kidwell, J.S. (1985). Teenage violence towards parents: a neglected dimension of family violence. *Journal of Marriage and the Family*, **47**(4): 1051–1058.

Pepper, C. and Oaker, M. (1981). Elder abuse: an examination of a hidden problem. *US House of Representatives Select Committee on Ageing*. Washington, DC: US Govt. Printing Office.

Pernanen, K. (1991). *Alcohol in Human Violence*. London: Guilford Press.

Persky, H., Smith, K.D. and Basu, G.K. (1971). Relation of psychological measures of aggression and hostility to testosterone production in man. *Psychosomatic Medicine*, **33**: 265–277.

Peters, S.D. (1988). Child sexual abuse and later psychological problems. In G. Wyatt and G. Powell (Eds), *Lasting Effects of Child Sexual Abuse*. Beverly Hills, CA: Sage, pp. 101–118.

Phillips, L. (1983). Abuse and neglect of the frail elderly at home: an exploration of the theoretical relationships. *Journal of Advanced Nursing*, **9**: 379–392.

Phillips, L. (1986). Theoretical explanations of elder abuse: competing hypothesis and Unresolved Issues. In K. Pillemer and R. Wolf. (Eds), op. cit., pp. 197–218.

Pierce, L.H. and Pierce, R.L. (1987). Incestuous victimization by juvenile sex offenders. *Journal of Family Violence*, **2**: 351–364.

Pierce, R. and Trotta, R. (1986). Abused parents: a hidden family problem. *Journal of Family Violence*, **1**(1).

Pilkington, B. and Kremer, J. (1995a). A review of the epidemiological research on child sexual abuse: community and college student samples. *Child Abuse Review*, **4**(2): 84–98.

Pilkington, B. and Kremer, J. (1995b). A review of the epidemiological research on child sexual abuse: clinical samples. *Child Abuse Review*, **4**(3).

Pillemer, K. (1986). Risk factors in elder abuse: results from a case-control study. In K. Pillemer and R. Wolf (Eds), *Elder Abuse: Conflict in the Family*. Dover: Auburn House, pp. 239–263.

Pillemer, K. and Finkelhor, D. (1988). The prevalence of elder abuse: a random sample survey. *Gerontologist*, **28**(1): 51–57.

Pillemer, K. and Suitor, J. (1988). Elder abuse. In V. Van Hasselt, R. Morrison and M. Herson (Eds), *Handbook of Family Violence*. New York: Plenum, pp. 247–271.

Pillemer, K. and Suitor, J. (1992). Violence and violent feelings: what causes them among family caregivers? *Journal of Gerontology: Social Sciences*, **47**(4): S165–S172.

Pillemer, K. and Wolf, R. (Eds) (1986). *Elder Abuse: Conflict in the Family*. Dover: Auburn House.

Piper, W.E., Derbane, E.G., Bienvenu, J.P. and Garant, J. (1984). A comparative study of four forms of psychotherapy. *Journal of Consulting and Clinical Psychology*, **52**: 268–279.

Pirog-Good, M.A. (1992). Sexual abuse in dating relationships. In E.C. Viano (Ed.), *Intimate Violence: Interdisciplinary Perspectives*. Washington, DC: Taylor & Francis, pp. 101–109.

Pithers, W.D., Kashima, K.M., Cumming, G.F. and Beal, L.F. (1988). Relapse prevention: a method of enhancing maintenance of change in sex offenders. In A.C. Salter (Ed.), *Treating Child Sex Offenders and Victims: A Practical Guide*. Beverly Hills, CA: Sage.

Pizzey, E. (1974). *Scream Quietly or the Neighbours will Hear*. Harmondsworth: Penguin.

Pizzey, E. and Shapiro, J. (1982). *Prone to Violence*. London: Hamlyn.

Platt, J.J., Pout, M.F. and Metzger, D.S. (1986). Interpersonal cognitive problem-solving therapy (ICPS). In W. Dryden and W. Golden (Eds), *Cognitive-Behavioural Approaches to Psychotherapy*. London, Harper & Row.

Pleck, E., Pleck, J., Crossman, M. and Bart, P. (1978). The battered data syndrome: a comment on Steinmetz's article. *Victimology*, **2**(3/4): 680–683.

Potter-Effron, R.T. and Potter-Effron, P.S. (Eds), (1990). *Aggression, Family Violence and Chemical Dependency*. New York: Haworth.

Pound, A. and Mills, M. (1985). A pilot evaluation of NEWPIN: a home visiting and befriending scheme in South London. *ACPP Newsletter*, **7**: 13–15.

Powers, R.J. (1986). Aggression and violence in the family. In A. Campbell and J. Gibbs (Eds), *Violent Transactions*. Oxford: Blackwell, pp. 225–248.

Powills, S. (1988). Elder abuse: what role do hospitals play. *Hospitals*, **62** (7): 84–88.

Pratt, C., Koval, J. and Lloyd, S. (1983). Service workers responses to abuse of the elderly. *Social Casework* (March): 142–153.

Prior, V., Lynch, M.A. and Glaser, D. (1994). *Messages from Children: NCH Action for Children*. London.

Pritchard, J. (1995). *The Abuse of Elderly People: A Handbook for Professionals*. (2nd edn). London: Kingsley.

Purdy, F. and Nickle, N. (1981). Practice principles for working with groups of men who batter. *Social Work with Groups*, **4**: 111–122.

Quay, H.C. (1986). Conduct disorders. In H.C. Quay and J.S. Werry, (Eds), *Psychopathology Disorders of Childhood* (3rd edn). New York: Wiley.

Quay, H.C. and Peterson, D.R. (1983). Manual for the Revised Behavioral Problem Checklist (unpublished manuscript).

Quinn, M. and Tomita, S. (1986). *Elder Abuse and Neglect: Causes, Diagnosis and Intervention Strategies*, New York: Springer.

Rada, R.T., Laws, D.R. and Kellner, R. (1976). Plasma testosterone levels in the rapist. *Psychosomatic Medicine*, **38**: 257–268.

Rathbone-McCuan, E. (1980) Elderly victims of family violence and neglect. *Social Casework*, **61**(5): 296–304.

Rathbone-McCuan, E. and Voyles, B. (1982). Case detection of abused elderly parents. *American Journal of Psychiatry*, **139**(2): 189–192.

Ratigan, B. (1989). Counselling in Groups. In W. Dryden, D. Charles-Edwards and R. Wolfe, *Handbook of Counselling in Britain*. London: Routledge, pp. 90–106.

Reay, A. (1996). Personal communication.

Rees, G. (1993). *Hidden Truths: Young People's Experience of Running Away*. London: The Children's Society.

Reichman, R. (1989). *The stranger in Your Bed: How to Break Down the Barriers in Your Relationship and Achieve True Intimacy*. Chichester: Wiley.

Reid, J.B. (Ed.) (1978). *A Social Learning Approach to Family Intervention*, Vol II: *Observation in Home Settings*, Eugene, OR: Castalia.

Reid, J.B., Taplin, P. and Loeber, R. (1981). A social interactional approach to the treatment of abusive families. In R. Stewart (Ed.), *Violent Behavior: Social Learning Approaches to Prediction, Management and Treatment*. New York: Brunner/Mazel.

Renvoize, J. (1978). *A Web of Violence: A Study of Family Violence*. London: Routledge & Kegan Paul.

Renzetti, C.M. (1992). *Violent Betrayal: Partner Abuse in Lesbian Relationships*. London: Sage.

Retzinger, S.M. (1991). *Violent Emotions: Shame and Rage in Marital Quarrels*. Beverley Hills, CA: Sage.

Reynolds, M.M. (1982). Negativism of preschool children: an observational and experimental study. *Contributions to Education. No. 228*. New York: Bureau of Publications, Teachers College, Columbia University.

Richman, N., Stevenson, S. and Graham, P.J. (1982). *Pre-School to School: A Behavioural Study*. London: Academic Press.

Roberts, A.R. (1982). Adolescent runaways in suburbia: a new typology. *Adolescence*, **17**: 387–396.

Roberts, A.R. (1987). Psychosocial characteristics of batterers: a study of 234 men charged with domestic violence offenders. *Journal of Family Violence*, **2**(1): 81–94.

Roberts, J. (1993). Abused children and foster care: the need for specialist resources. *Child Abuse Review*, **2**(1): 3–14.

Roberts, M.V., Hatzenbuehler, L.C. and Bean, A.W. (1981). The effects of differential attention and time-out on child noncompliance. *Behaviour Therapy*, **12**: 93–99.

Robinson, E.A., Eyberg, S.M. and Ross, A.W. (1980). The standardization of child conduct problem behaviors. *Journal of Clinical Child Psychology*, **9**: 22–28.

Rogers, C.M. and Terry, T. (1984). Clinical intervention with boy victims of sexual abuse. In I.R. Stuart and J.G. Greer (Eds), *Victims of Sexual Aggression: Men, Women and Children*. New York: Van Nostrand Reinhold, pp. 91–103.

Rogers, C.R. (1951). *Client Centred Therapy*. Dallas: Houghton Mifflin.

Rogers, C.R. (1973). *Becoming Partners: Marriage and its Alternatives*. London: Constable.

Rohner, R.P. (1986). *The Warmth Dimension: Foundations of Parental Acceptance-Rejection Theory*. Beverly Hill, CA: Sage.

Rose, S.D. (1986). Group methods. In F.H. Kanfer and A.P. Goldstein (Eds), *Helping People Change* (3rd edn). Oxford: Pergamon.

Roscoe, B. and Benaske, N. (1985). Courtship violence experienced by abused wives: similarities in pattern of abuse. *Journal of Applied Family Child Studies*, **34**(3): 419–424.

Rosenbaum, A. and Maiuro, R.D. (1990). Perpetrators of spouse abuse. In R.T. Ammerman and M. Hersen (Eds), *Treatment of Family Violence*. New York: Wiley, pp. 280–309.

Rosenbaum, A. and O'Leary, K.D. (1981). Marital violence: characteristics of abusive couple. *Journal of Consulting and Clinical Psychology*, **49**: 63–71.

Rosenbaum, A. and O'Leary, K.D. (1986). The treatment of marital violence. In N. Jacobson and A. Gurman (Eds), *Clinical Handbook of Marital Therapy*. New York: Guilford.

Rosenberg, S. (1987). Children of battered women: the effects of witnessing violence on their social problem-solving abilities. *Behaviour Therapist*, **10**: 85–89.

Rosenberg, S. and Repucci, N.D. (1983). Abusive mothers: perceptions of their own and their children's behaviour. *Journal of Consulting and Clinical Psychology*, **51**(5): 674–682.

Rouse, L.P. (1988). Conflict tactics used by men in marital disputes. In G.T. Hotaling, D. Finkelhor, J.T. Kirkpatrick and M. Straus (Eds), *Family Abuse and its Consequences: New Directions in Research*. Beverly Hills, CA: Sage, pp. 176–191.

Rowe, J., Cain, H., Hundleby, M. and Keane, A. (1984). *Long-Term Foster Care*, London: Batsford.

Roy, M. (1977). A survey of 150 cases. In M. Roy (Ed.), *Battered Women: A Psychosociological Study of Domestic Violence*. New York: Van Nostrand Reinhold, pp. 45–69.

Roy, M. (1982a). *The Abusive Partner*. New York: Van Nostrand Reinhold.

Roy, M. (1982b). Four thousand partners in violence: a trend analysis. In M. Roy (Ed.), *The Abusive Partner: An Analysis of Domestic Battering*. New York: Van Nostrand Reinhold.

Russell, D.E.H. (1982). *Rape in Marriage*, New York: Macmillan.

Russell, D.E.H. (1990). *Rape in Marriage* (rev. edn). Bloomington: Indiana University Press.

Russell, D.E.H. (1991). Wife rape. In A. Parrot and L. Bechhofer (Eds), *Acquaintance Rape: The Hidden Crime*. New York: Wiley, pp. 129–139.

Rutter, M. (1967). A children's behaviour questionnaire for completion by teachers: preliminary findings. *Journal of Child Psychology and Psychiatry*, **8**: 1–11.

Rutter, M. (1981). *Maternal Deprivation Reassessed* (2nd edn). Harmondsworth: Penguin.

Rutter, M. (1985). Aggression and the family. *Acta Paedopsychiatrica*, **6**: 11–25.

Rutter, M. and Giller, H. (1983). *Juvenile Delinquency: Trends and Perspectives*. Harmondsworth: Penguin.

Salend, E., Kane, R., Satz, M. and Pynoor, J. (1984). Elder abuse reporting: limitations of statutes. *Gerontologist*, **24**(1): 61–69.

Sanders, A. (1988). Personal violence and public order: the prosecution of 'domestic' violence in England and Wales. *International Journal of the Sociology of Law*, **16**: 359–382.

Sanderson, C. (1995). *Counselling Adult Survivors of Child Sexual Abuse* (2nd edn). London: Kingsley.

Saunders, D.G. (1986). When battered women use violence: husband abuse or self-defense? *Violence and Victims*, 1(1): 47–60.

Saunders, D.G. (1995). Prediction of wife assault. In J.C. Campbell (Ed.), *Assessing Dangerousness: Violence by Sexual Offenders, Batterers and Child Abusers*. Newbury Park, CA: Sage, pp. 68–95.

Schaffer, H.R. (1990). *Making Decisions about Children: Psychological Questions and Answers*. Oxford: Blackwell.

Scharff, D.E. and Scharff, J.S. (1987). *Object Relations Family Therapy*. New York: Aronson.

Scharff, D.E. and Scharff, J.S. (1991). *Object Relations Couple Therapy*. New York: Aronson.

Schneider, M. (1973). Turtle technique in the classroom. *Exceptional Children*, 42: 201.

Schneider-Rosen, K., Braunwald, K.G., Carlson, V. and Cicchetti, D. (1985). Current perspectives in attachment: illustrations from the study of maltreated infants. In I. Bretherton and R. Waters (Eds), *Growing Points in Attachment Theory and Research*. Monographs of the Society for Research in Child Development (No. 209).

Schroder, T. (1989). Couples in counselling. In W. Dryden, D. Charles-Edwards and R. Wolfe, *Handbook of Counselling in Britain*. London: Routledge, pp. 58–72.

Schultz, L.G. (1960). The wife assaulter. *Journal of Social Therapy*, 6: 103–112.

Scott, M.J. and Stradling, S.G. (1987). Evaluation of a group programme for parents of problem children. *Behavioural Psychotherapy*, 15: 224–239.

Scudder, R.G., Blount, W.R., Heide, K.M. and Silverman, I.J. (1993). Important links between child abuse, neglect and delinquency. *International Journal of Offender Therapy and Comparative Criminology*, 37: 315–323.

Search, G. (1988). *The Last Taboo: Sexual Abuse of Children*. Harmondsworth: Penguin.

Sears, R., Maccoby, E.E. and Levin, H. (1957). *Patterns of Child Rearing*. Illinois: Row Peterson.

Seghorn, T.K., Prentky, R.A. and Boucher, R.J. (1987). Childhood sexual abuse in the lives of sexually aggressive offenders.

Journal of the American Academy of Child and Adolescent Psychiatry, **26**: 262–267.

Sengstock, M. and Barrett, J. (1986). Elderly victims of family abuse, neglect and maltreatment. Can legal assistance help? *Journal of Gerontological Social Work*, **9**(3): 43–60.

Sherman, L.W. (1992). The influence of criminology on criminal law: evaluating arrests for misdemeanour domestic violence. *The Journal of Law and Criminology*, **83**(1): 1–45.

Sherman, L.W. and Berk, R.A. (1984). The specific deterrent effects of arrest for domestic assault. *American Sociological Review*, **49**: 261–272.

Shure, M.B. (1981). Social competence as a problem solving skill. In S.S. Wine and M.D. Smye (Eds), *Social Competence*. New York: Guildford.

Siann, G. (1985). *Accounting for Aggression: Perspectives on Aggression and Violence*, London: Allen & Unwin.

Sigler, R.T. (1989). *Domestic Violence in Context: An Assessment of Community Attributes*. Toronto: Lexington Books.

Silver, L.R., Dublin, C.C. and Lourie, R.S. (1969). Does violence breed violence? Contributions from a study of the child abuse syndrome. *American Journal of Psychiatry*, **126**: 152–155.

Sinclair, D. (1985). *Understanding Wife Assault: A Training Manual for Counsellors and Advocates*. Toronto: Ontario Government Books (cited in Jaffe et al., 1990).

Sines, J.O. (1987). Influence of home and family environment on childhood dysfunction. In B.B. Lahey and A.E. Kazdin (Eds), *Advances in Clinical Child Psychology*. New York: Plenum.

Skynner, A.C.R. (1987). *Explorations with Families*. London: Methuen.

Skynner, A.C.R. (1976). *One Flesh: Separate Persons*. London: Constable.

Smith, G.C., Smith, M.F. and Toseland, R.W. (1991). Problems identified by family caregivers in counselling. *The Gerontologist*, **31**(1): 15–22.

Smith, G.D. and Egger, M. (1993). Socioeconomic differentials in wealth and health. *British Medical Journal*, **307**: 1085–1087 (30 Oct. 1993).

Smith, L. (1989). *Domestic Violence: An Overview of the Literature*. Home Office Research Study No. 107. London: HMSO.

Smith, M., Bee, P., Heverin, A. and Nobes, G. (1995). *Parental Control within the Family: The Nature and Extent of Parental Violence to Children.* London: Thomas Coram Research Unit (cited in Department of Health, 1995b).

Smith, N.J. and Ardern, M.H. (1989). 'More in sickness than in health': a case study of Munchausen by proxy in the elderly. *Journal of Family Therapy,* **11**(4): 321–334.

Smith, P.K. (1990). The silent nightmare: bullying and victimization in school peer groups. Paper read to British Psychological Society London Conference.

Smith, P.K. and Boulton, M.J. (1996). Rough-and-tumble play, aggression and dominance: perception and behaviour in children's encounters. *Human Development* (in press).

Smith, S. (1975). *The Battered Child Syndrome.* London: Butterworths.

Smith, S., Baker, D., Buchan, A. and Bodiwala, G. (1992). Adult domestic violence. *Health Trends,* **24**(3): 97–99.

Snyder, D.K. and Wills, R.M. (1989). Behavioral versus insight-oriented marital therapy: effects on individual and inter-spousal functioning. *Journal of Consulting and Clinical Psychology,* **57**: 39–46.

Snyder, D.K., Wills, R.M. and Grady-Fletcher, A. (1991). Long-term effectiveness of behavioural versus insight-oriented marital therapy: a 4 year follow up study. *Journal of Consulting and Clinical Psychology,* **59**: 138–141.

Social Services Inspectorate (1990). *Child Protection in London: Aspects of Management Arrangements in Social Service Departments.* London: DHSS, Sept. 1990.

Sonkin, D., Martin, D. and Walker, L. (1985). *The Male Batterer: A Treatment Approach.* New York: Springer.

Spielberger, C.D., Jacobs, G.A., Russell, S. and Crane, R.S. (1983). Assessment of anger: the state-trait anger scale. In J. Butcher and C.D. Spielberger (eds). *Advances in Personality Assessment,* Vol. 2. Hillsdale, NJ: Lawrence Erlbaum; pp. 159–187.

Spivak, G., Platt, J.J. and Shure, M.B. (1976). *The Problem Solving Approach to Adjustment.* San Francisco, CA: Jossey-Bass.

Spival, G., Marus, J. and Swift, M. (1986). Early classroom behaviours and later misconduct. *Developmental Psychology,* **22**: 124–131.

Stanko, E.A. (1985). *Intimate Intrusions: Women's Experience of Male Violence.* London: Routledge & Kegan Paul.

Stanko, E.A. (1989). Missing the mark? Policing battering. In J. Hanmer, J. Radford and E.A. Stanko (Eds), *Women, Policing, and Male Violence: International Perspectives*. London: Routledge.

Star, B. (1980). Patterns of family violence. *Social Casework*, **61**: 339–346.

Stark, R. and McEvoy, J. (1970). Middle class violence. *Psychology Today*, **4**: 52–65.

Starr. R.H. (1982). *Child Abuse and Prediction Policy Implications*. Cambridge, MA: Ballinger.

Starr, R.H. (1988). Pre and perinatal risk and physical abuse. *Journal of Reproductive and Infant Psychology*, **6**(3): 125–138.

Staub, E. (1975). *The Development of Prosocial Behavior in Children*, Morrison, NJ: General Learning Press.

Steele, B.F. and Pollock, C.B. (1968). A psychiatric study of parents who abuse infants and small children. In R.E. Helfer and C.H. Kempe (Eds), *The Battered Child*. University of Chicago Press, pp. 103–147.

Steele, B.F. and Alexander, H. (1981). Long-term effects of sexual abuse in childhood. In P.B. Mrazek and C.H. Kempe (Eds), *Sexually Abused Children and their Families*. New York: Pergamon.

Stein, A. and Lewis, D.O. (1992). Discovering physical abuse: insights from a follow-up study of delinquents. *Child Abuse and Neglect*, **16**: 523–531.

Stein, M., Rees, G. and Frost, N. (1994). *Running the Risk: Young People on the Streets of Britain Today*. London: The Children's Society.

Steinfield, G.J. (1986). Spouse abuse: clinical implications of research on the control of aggression. *Family Violence*, **1**(2): 197–208.

Steinglass, P. (1987). *The Alcoholic Family: Drinking Problems in a Family Context*. London: Hutchinson.

Steinmetz, S.K. (1977a). *The Cycle of Violence: Assertive, Aggressive and Abusive Family Interaction*. New York: Praeger.

Steinmetz, S.K. (1977b). The battered husband syndrome. *Victimology*, **2**(3/4): 499–509.

Steinmetz, S.K. (1978). Battered parents. *Society*, **15**(5): 54–55.

Steinmetz, S.K. (1983). Dependency stress and violence between middle-aged caregivers and their elderly relatives. In J.I. Kobert (Ed.), *Abuse and Maltreatment of the Elderly*. Boston: Wright.

Steinmetz, S.K. (1988). *Duty Bound: Elder Abuse and Family Care.* New York: Sage.

Steinmetz, S.K. and Straus, M.A. (Eds) (1974). *Violence in the Family.* New York: Harper & Row.

Stevenson, J., Bailey, V. & Simpson, J. (1988) Feasible intervention in families with parenting difficulties: a primary preventive perspective on child abuse. In *Early Prediction and Prevention of Child Abuse* (Browne K.D., Davies C. & Stratton P. eds). John Wiley, Chichester, pp. 121–138.

Stevenson, O. (1989). *Age and Vulnerability: A Guide to Better Care.* Age Concern, London.

Stiffman, A.R. (1989). Physical and sexual abuse in runaway youths. *Child Abuse and Neglect,* **13**: 417–426.

Stokes, J. (1994). Institutional chaos and personal stress. In A. Obholzer and V.Z. Roberts (Eds), *The Unconscious at Work.* London: Routledge.

Stordeur, R.A. and Stille, R. (1989). *Ending men's violence against their partners,* Newbury Park, CA: Sage.

Stout, K.D. (1989). 'Intimate femicide': effect of legislation and social services. *Affilia,* **4**(2), Summer: 21–30.

Strang, H. (1992). *Homicides in Australia 1991–92.* Canberra: Australian Institute of Criminology.

Stratton, P. and Swaffer, A. (1988). Maternal causal beliefs for abused and handicapped children. *Journal of Reproductive and Infant Psychology,* **6**: 201–216.

Straus, M.A. (1979). Measuring intrafamily conflict and violence: the conflict tactics scales. *Journal of Marriage and the Family,* **41**: 75–86.

Straus, M.A. (1980). A sociological perspective on causes of family violence. In R. Green (Ed.), *Violence and the Family.* New York: Bould & Westview, pp. 7–13.

Straus, M.A. (1990). Social stress and marital violence in a national sample of American families. In M.A. Straus and R.J. Gelles (Eds), *Physical Violence in American Families.* New Brunswick, NJ: Transaction Publishers.

Strauss, M.A. (1993). Physical assaults by wives: a major social problem. In R.J. Gelles and D.R. Loseke (Eds), *Current Controversies on Family Violence.* Beverly Hills, CA: Sage, pp. 67–87.

Straus, M.A. (1994). *Violence in the Lives of Adolescents.* New York: Norton.

Straus, M.A. and Gelles, R.J. (1986). Societal change and family violence from 1975 to 1985 as revealed by two national surveys. *Journal of Marriage and the Family*, **48**: 465–479.

Straus, M. and Gelles, R.J. (1988). How violent are American families? Estimates from the National Family Violence Resurvey and other studies (Chapter 1). In G. Hotaling, D. Finkelhor, J. Kirkpatrick and M. Straus (Eds), *Family Abuse and its Consequences: New Directions in Research*. Beverly Hills, CA: Sage, pp. 14–37.

Straus, M.A., Gelles, R.J. and Steinmetz, S.K. (1980). *Behind Closed Doors: Violence in the American Family*, New York: Anchor Press.

Straus, M.A., Gelles, R.J. and Steinmetz, S.K. (1988). *Behind Closed Doors: Violence in the American Family* (rev. edn). Newbury Park, CA: Sage.

Sugarman, D.B. and Hotaling, G.T. (1989). Dating violence: prevalence, context and risk markers. In M.A. Pirog-Good and J.E. Stets (Eds), *Violence in Dating Relationships: Emerging Issues*. New York: Praeger, pp. 3–32.

Sugarman, D.B. and Hotaling, G.T. (1991). Dating violence: a review of contextual and risk factors. In B. Levy (Ed.), *Dating Violence: Young Women in Danger*. Seattle, WA: Seal Press, pp. 100–118.

Summit, R.C. (1983). The child sexual accommodation syndrome. *Child Abuse and Neglect*, **7**: 177–193.

Sutton, C. (1988). Behavioural parent training: a comparison of strategies for teaching parents to manage their difficult young children. Unpublished PhD thesis, University of Leicester.

Swensen, C.H. (1972). Commitment and the personality of the successful therapist. *Psychological Bulletin*, **77**: 400–404.

Szur, R. (1987). Emotional abuse and neglect. In P. Maher (Ed.), *Child Abuse the Educational Perspective*. Oxford: Blackwell, pp. 104–126.

Takii, Y. (1992). Sexual abuse and juvenile delinquency. *Child Abuse Review*, **1**(1): 43–48.

Taler, G. and Ansello, E. (1985). Elder abuse. *American Family Physician*, **32**(2): 107–114.

Thobaben, M. and Anderson, L. (1985). Reporting elder abuse: it's the law. *American Journal of Nursing*, **85**(4): 371–374.

Tobin, D.L., Holroyd, K.A., Reynolds, R.V. and Wigal, J.K. (1989). The hierarchical factor structure of the coping strategies inventory. *Cognitive Therapy and Research*, **13**(4): 343–361.

Toch, H. (1969). *Violent Men*. Chicago: Aldine.

Tooley, K.M. (1977). The young child as victim of sibling attack. *Journal of Social Casework*, **58**: 25–28.

Trickett, P.K. and Kuczynski, (1986). Children's misbehaviours and parental discipline strategies in abusive and non-abusive families. *Developmental Psychology*, **22**: 115–123.

Truax, C.B. and Carkhuff, R.R. (1967). *Toward Effective Counselling and Psychotherapy*. Chicago: Ardine.

Truesdell, D., McNeil, J. and Deschner, J. (1986). Incidence of wife abuse in incestuous families. *Social Work*, **31**(2): 138–140.

Truninger, E. (1971). Marital violence: the legal solutions. *Hasting Law Review*, 259–276.

Ursano, R.J. and Hales, R.E. (1986). A review of brief individual psychotherapies. *American Journal of Psychiatry*, **143**: 1507–1517.

US Congress Select Committe on Ageing (1981). US House of Representatives. *Elder Abuse: An Examination of a Hidden Problem*. Washington, DC.: Committee Publication No. 97, p. 270, US Printing Office.

Valentine, D. and Cash, T. (1986). A definitional discussion of elder maltreatment. *Journal of Gerontological Social Work*, **9**(3): 17–18.

Van der Eyken, W. (1982). *Home Start. A Four Year Evaluation*. Leicester: Home Start Consultancy.

Van Hasselt, V.B., Morrison, R.L. and Bellack, A.S. (1985). Alcohol use in wife abusers and their spouses. *Addictive Behaviours*, **10**: 127–135.

Van Hasselt, V.B., Morrison, R.L., Bellack, A.S. and Hersen, M. (1987). *Handbook of Family Violence*. New York: Plenum.

Vaselle-Augenstein, R. and Ehrlich, A. (1992). Male batterers: evidence for psychopathology. In E.C. Viano (Ed.), *Intimate Violence: Interdisciplinary Perspectives*. Washington, DC: Taylor & Francis, pp. 139–156.

Viano, E.C. (Ed.) (1992). *Intimate Violence: Interdisciplinary Perspectives*, Bristol: Taylor & Francis.

Victim Support (1992). *Domestic Violence: Report of a National Inter-Agency Working Party on Domestic Violence*. London: Victim Support.

Wahler, R.G. (1976). Deviant child behaviour within the family, development speculations and behaviour change strategies. In H. Leitenberg (Ed.), *Handbook of Behaviour Modification and Behaviour Therapy*. Englewood Cliffs, NJ: Prentice Hall.

Wahler, R.G. and Dumas, J. (1985). Maintenance factors in coercive mother–child interactions: the compliance and predictability hypothesis. *Journal of Applied Behavior Analysis*, **19**: 13–22.

Walker, L.E. (1979). *The Battered Women*. New York: Harper & Row.

Walker, L.E. (1984). *The Battered Woman Syndrome*. New York: Springer.

Walker, L.E. (1993). The battered woman syndrome is a psychological consequence of abuse. In R.J. Gelles and D.R. Loseke (Eds), *Current Controversies on Family Violence*. Newbury Park, CA: Sage, pp. 133–153.

Walker, L.E. and Browne, A. (1985). Gender and victimization by intimates. *Journal of Personality*, **53**: 179–195.

Walker, M. (1990). *Women in Therapy and Counselling*. Buckingham: Open University Press.

Walsh, B.W. and Rosen, P.M. (1988). *Self-mutilation: Theory, Research and Treatment*. New York: Guilford.

Walters, G.D. and White, T.W. (1990). Therapeutic interventions with the life style criminal. *Journal of Offender Counselling Services and Rehabilitation*, **14**: 159–169.

Ware, J.R. and Browne, K.D. (1996). *Research into Practice C.A.R.E. (Child Assessment Rating and Evaluation)*. Proceedings of the 11th International Congress on Child Abuse and Neglect, University College Dublin, August 1996. Chicago: International Society for the Prevention of Child Abuse and Neglect.

Wasserman, G.A., Green, A. and Allen, R. (1983). Going beyond abuse: maladaptive patterns of interaction in abusing mother–infant pairs. *Journal of American Academy of Child Psychiatry*, **22**(3): 245–252.

Watkins, B. and Bentovim, A. (1992). The sexual abuse of male children and adolescents: a review of current research. *Journal of Child Psychology and Psychiatry*, **33**(1): 197–248.

Webster-Stratton, C. (1982). Long term effects of a videotape modeling parent education program: comparison of immediate and one year follow-up results. *Behavior Therapy*, **13**: 702–714.

Webster-Stratton, C. (1984). Comparing two parent training models for conduct disordered children. *Journal of Consulting and Clinical Psychology*, **52**: 666–678.

Webster-Stratton, C. (1988). *Parents and Children Videotape Series. Basic and Advanced Programs 1 to 7*. 1411 8th Avenue West, Seattle, WA 98119.

Webster-Stratton, C. and Herbert, M. (1993). What really happens in parent training? *Behavior Modification*, **17**: 407–456.

Webster-Stratton, C. and Herbert, M. (1994). *Troubled Families— Problem Children: Working with Parents—A Collaborative Process*. Chichester: Wiley.

Weiss, R.L., Hops, H. and Patterson, G.R. (1973). A framework for conceptualizing marital conflicts: a technology for altering it, some data for evaluating it. In L.A. Hamerlynck, L.C. Handy and E.L. Mash (Eds), *Behavior Change: Methodology, Concepts, and Practice*. Champaign, IL: Research Press, pp. 309–342.

Weiss, R.L. and Summers, K.H. (1983). Marital interaction coding system, III. In E. Filsinger, (Ed.), *Marriage and Family Assessment: A Sourcebook for Family Therapy*. Beverly Hills, CA: Sage, pp. 85–116.

Weissberg, M. (1983). *Dangerous Secrets: Maladaptive Responses to Stress*. New York: Norton.

Weitzman, J. and Dreen, K. (1982). Wife beating: a view of the marital dyad. *Social Casework*, **63**: 259–265.

Welldon, E.V. (1994). Forensic psychotherapy. In P. Clarkson and M. Pokorny (Eds), *The Handbook of Psychotherapy*. London: Routledge, pp. 470–493.

West, D.J. and Farrington, D.P. (1973). *Who Becomes Delinquent?* London: Heinemann.

Wharton, C.S. (1987). Establishing shelters for battered women: local manifestations of a social movement. *Qualitative Sociology*. **10**(2): 146–163.

Whipple, V. (1985). The use of reality therapy with battered women in domestic violence shelters. *Journal of Reality Therapy*, **5**: 22–27.

White, J.L. (1989). *The Troubled Adolescent*. New York: Pergamon.

White, R. (1991). Examining the threshold criteria. In M. Adcock, R. White and A. Hollows (Eds), *Significant Harm*. Croydon: Significant Publications, pp. 3–10.

Widom, C.S. (1989a). The intergenerational transmission of violence. In N.A. Weiner and M.E. Wolfgang (Eds), *Pathways to Criminal Violence*. Beverly Hills, CA: Sage, pp. 137–201.

Widom, C.S. (1989b). The cycle of violence. *Science*, **244**: 160–166.

Widom, C.S. (1989c). Does violence beget violence? A critical examination of the literature. *Psychological Bulletin*, **106**: 3–28.

Widom, C.S. (1991). Avoidance of criminality in abused and neglected children. *Psychiatry*, **54**: 162–174.

Widom, C.S. and Ames, M.A. (1994). Criminal consequences of childhood sexual victimization. *Child Abuse and Neglect*, **18**(4): 303–318.

Wiehe, V.R. (1987). Empathy and locus of control in child abusers. *Journal of Social Service Research*, **9**(2/3): 17–30.

Wile, D.B. (1988). *After the Honeymoon: How Conflict Can Improve Your Relationships*. Chichester: Wiley.

Wile, D.B. (1993). *Couples Therapy: A Nontraditional Approach*. Chichester: Wiley.

Willis, D.J., Holden, E.W. and Rosenberg, M. (1992). *Prevention of child maltreatment*, New York: Wiley.

Wilson, W. and Durrenberger, R. (1982). Comparison of rape and attempted rape victims. *Psychological Reports*, **50**: 198.

Wilson, K., Jaffe, P. and Wolfe, D. (1989). Children exposed to wife abuse: an intervention model. *Social Casework*, **70**: 180–184.

Winnicott, D.W. (1950). The deprived child and how he can be compensated for loss of family life. In C. Winnicott, R. Shepherd and M. Davis (Eds) (1984), *Deprivation and Delinquency: Selected Papers*. London: Tavistock.

Winnicott, D.W. (1956). The anti-social tendency. In C. Winnicott, R. Shepherd and M. Davis (Eds) (1984), *Deprivation and Delinquency: Selected Papers*. London: Tavistock.

Winnicott, D.W. (1963). Struggling through the doldrums. In C. Winnicott, R. Shepherd and M. Davis (Eds) (1984), *Deprivation and Delinquency: Selected Papers*. London: Tavistock.

Winnicott, D.W. (1964). *The Child, the Family and the Outside World*, Harmondsworth: Penguin.

Wolf, R. (1986). Major findings from three model projects on elderly abuse. In K. Pillemer and R. Wolf (Eds), *Elder Abuse: Conflict in the Family*. Dover: Auburn House, pp. 218–234.

Wolf, R. (1988). Elder abuse: ten years later. *Journal of the American Geriatrics Society*, **36**(8): 758–762.

Wolfe, A. (1949). The psychoanalysis of group. *Americal Journal of Psychotherapy*, **3**: 16–50.

Wolfe, D.A. (1985). Child-abuse parents. An empirical review and analysis. *Psychological Bulletin*, **97**: 461–482.

Wolfe, D.A. (1987). *Child Abuse: Implications for Child Development and Psychopathology*. Beverly Hills, CA: Sage.

Wolfe, D.A. (1991). *Preventing Physical and Emotional Abuse of Children*. New York: Guilford.

Wolfe, D.A. (1993). Child abuse prevention: blending research and practice. *Child Abuse Review*, **2**: 153–165.

Wolfe, D.A., Fairbank, J.A., Kelly, J.A. and Bradlyn, A.S. (1983). Child abusive parents' physiological responses to stressful and nonstressful behaviour in children. *Behavioural Assessment*, **5**: 363–371.

Wolfgang, M. and Farracuti, (1982). *The Subculture of Violence* (2nd edn). London: Tavistock.

Wolpe, J. (1973). *The Practice of Behaviour Therapy*. Oxford: Pergamon.

Wood-Schuman, S. and Cone, J. (1986). Differences in abusive, at risk for abuse and control mothers' descriptions of normal child behaviour. *Child Abuse and Neglect*, **10**: 397–405.

Wright, D.S. (1971). *The Psychology of Moral Behaviour*. Harmondsworth: Penguin.

Wyatt, G.E. and Peters, S.D. (1986). Issues in the definition of child sexual abuse in prevalence research. *Child Abuse and Neglect*, **9**: 507–519 (cited in D. Jehu, 1989).

Yalom, I.D. (1975). *The Theory and Practice of Group Psychotherapy*. (2nd edn). New York: Basic Books.

Ylló, K.A. (1993). Through a feminist lens: gender, power and violence. In R.J. Gelles and D.R. Loseke (Eds), *Current Controversies on Family Violence*. Newbury Park, CA: Sage, pp. 47–62.

Ylló, K.A. and Bograd, M. (Eds) (1988). *Feminist Perspectives on Wife Abuse*. Beverly Hills, CA: Sage.

Young, R.L., Codfrey, W., Mathews, B. and Adams, G.R. (1983). Runaways: a review of negative consequences. *Family Relations*, **32**: 275–281.

Zarit, S., Reever, K. and Bach-Peterson, J. (1980). Relatives of the impaired elderly: correlates of feelings of burden. *Gerontologist*, **20**: 649–655.

Zdorkowski, R. and Galbraith, M. (1985). An inductive approach to the investigation of elder abuse. *Ageing and Society*, **5**(4): 413–429.

Zeilberger, J., Sampen, S. and Sloane, H. (1968). Modification of a child's problem behaviour in the home with the mother as therapist. *Journal of Applied Behavior Analysis*, **1**: 47–53.

Zimmerman, L.S. (1988). Attorney General's Family Violence Task Force. *Violence Against Elders*. Pennsylvania, USA.

AUTHOR INDEX

SUBJECT INDEX

Note: Page numbers in *italic* refer to figures and/or tables

Index compiled by Caroline Sheard